GLORY-HUNTER

"The Boy General with the Golden Locks"
Custer in his self-designed uniform, from a photograph by Brady taken
in 1863

GLORY-HUNTER

A LIFE OF
GENERAL CUSTER

BY FREDERIC F. VAN DE WATER

Introduction by Paul Andrew Hutton

University of Nebraska Press
Lincoln and London

First Bison Book printing: 1988
Most recent printing indicated by the first digit below:
1   2   3   4   5   6   7   8   9   10

Library of Congress Cataloging-in-Publication Data
Van de Water, Frederic Franklyn, 1890–1968.
   Glory-hunter: a life of General Custer.
   Reprint. Originally published: 1st ed. Indianapolis:
Bobbs-Merrill Co., c1934.
   Bibliography: p.
   Includes index.
   1. Custer, George Armstrong, 1839–1876.   2. Generals
—United States—Biography.   3. United States. Army—
Biography.   I. Title.
E467.1.C99V3 1988   973.8′2′0924   87-35772
ISBN 0-8032-6907-X (pbk.)

Reprinted by arrangement with Frederic F. Van de Water, Jr.

ACKNOWLEDGMENT

THE list of those to whom the author is grateful for counsel or more material aid is too long for complete inclusion here.

E. A. Brininstool, historian, has displayed a more than friendly interest and generosity throughout this book's creation, giving freely of his wide knowledge and permitting inspection of otherwise unprocurable documents in his possession.

The author is no less grateful to Colonel T. M. Coughlan, United States Army (retired), for much valuable aid which has included permission to examine his still unpublished life of Colonel Charles A. Varnum.

Special thanks also are due Dr. Philip G. Cole whose monumental collection of frontier memorabilia, particularly the letters of Frederick W. Benteen, has been at this book's service. The volume also owes much to the following:

C. H. Asbury, one-time agent on the Crow Reservation.

Miss Stella Drumm, librarian, Missouri Historical Society.

W. A. Falconer, historian of the West.

Major R. E. Eichelberger, United States Army, Adjutant, United States Military Academy.

Dwight Franklin, artist and historian.

Colonel W. A. Graham, United States Army, author of *The Story of the Little Big Horn.*

Theodore W. Goldin, survivor of the Little Bighorn battle.

General E. A. Garlington, United States Army (retired).

Frank B. Linderman, pioneer and author.

H. B. McConnell, editor of the Cadiz, Ohio, *Republican.*

Dr. C. C. O'Harra, president of the South Dakota School of Mines.

Major A. B. Ostrander, soldier and historian.

The late General Hugh L. Scott.

ACKNOWLEDGMENT

L. M. Spaulding of Buffalo, New York.

Colonel Charles A. Varnum, United States Army (retired).

Sylvester L. Vigilante, New York Public Library.

Captain Donald A. Young, United States Army, Adjutant, 7th Cavalry.

Without the kindly patience of all these, vital portions of this book could never have been written by their grateful debtor.

FREDERIC F. VAN DE WATER.

CONTENTS

INTRODUCTION   11

PART ONE: SOLDIER

I   BEGINNINGS   17

II   INSURGENT   26

III   SUBORDINATE   35

IV   GENERAL   45

V   FULFILMENT   53

VI   SHERIDAN   63

VII   SHENANDOAH   72

VIII   FIRE AND ROPE   80

IX   FIVE FORKS   89

X   VIEW HALLOO   100

XI   CLIMAX   108

XII   AFTERMATH   116

XIII   MUTINY   127

PART TWO: INDIAN FIGHTER

I   INTERLUDE   139

II   RED BACKGROUND   147

III   HANCOCK MARCHES   158

CONTENTS—*Continued*

CHAPTER		PAGE
IV	COURT MARTIAL	168
V	REINSTATEMENT	178
VI	WASHITA	187
VII	INQUEST	197
VIII	PURSUIT	209
IX	PORTRAIT OF A HERO	220

PART THREE: HERO

I	PROLOGUE	233
II	YELLOWSTONE	241
III	THE LEASHED LION	250
IV	EXPLORATION	258
V	COURSE OF EMPIRE	267
VI	WHOM GODS DESTROY	275
VII	STRUGGLE	287
VIII	SOLDIERS' FAREWELL	296
IX	HIDE-AND-SEEK	306
X	LAST PARADE	316
XI	PRELUDE TO SLAUGHTER	325
XII	CRESCENDO	336
XIII	DIES IRAE	347

CONTENTS—*Concluded*

CHAPTER		PAGE
XIV	POST MORTEM	356
	BIBLIOGRAPHY	373
	INDEX	379

ILLUSTRATIONS

FACING
PAGE

"The Boy General with the Golden Locks"........... *Frontispiece*

"Father," he confided, "you and me can whip all the Whigs in Ohio."   22

George Armstrong and Elizabeth Bacon Custer....................   46

General Pleasonton and His Youngest Brigadier..................   56

Captain and Brevet Brigadier General Frederick W. Benteen........   152

"In years long numbered with the past," he wrote, "my every thought
   was ambitious—not to be wealthy, not to be learned, but to be
   great . . . to future generations."...........................   162

Plainsman—Custer in Frontier Garb.............................   190

General and Mrs. Custer in His Study..........................   224

Officers of the Black Hills Expedition..........................   260

"The Custer Clan"...   298

Map of the 1876 Campaign Against the Sioux....................   308

"Now, Custer!" calls Gibbon in jest or out of his knowledge of the
   man. "Don't be greedy! Wait for us!" "No," the buckskin-clad
   horseman calls back cryptically, "I won't."....................   322

Map of the Little Bighorn Battlefield............................   332

Custer's Last Stand..   350

Major Marcus A. Reno..   358

INTRODUCTION
BY PAUL ANDREW HUTTON

"Frederic F. Van de Water has written the Custer book to end all Custer books," declared the reviewer for *Books* on November 18, 1934, in announcing the publication of *Glory-Hunter: A Life of General Custer.* R. L. Duffus, in the *New York Times,* could not have agreed more, declaring *Glory-Hunter* to be the definitive work on the subject, a sentiment echoed by W. R. Benét in the *Saturday Review of Literature.* Thoughts that Van de Water's book might bring an end to the Custer controversy, and the steady stream of Custer books, were certainly premature, but the reviewers were absolutely correct in their recognition of the book as an important and influential work. Few books have had so immediate and dramatic an impact as Van de Water's biography did on historical interpretation and the popular mind.

For fifty-eight years George Armstrong Custer had occupied a prominent place in the pantheon of American heroes. Books had helped to put him there, for his fatal encounter on the Little Big Horn provided marvelous romantic grist for the publishing mills. A hack writer possessed of some talent and a most vivid imagination had a Custer biography finished before that fateful centennial year ended. Frederick Whittaker's *A Complete Life of General George A. Custer* (1876) presented a hero of epic proportions—"one of the few really great men that America has produced," and a soldier with "no spot on his armor." Popular histories of the frontier, such as those by William F. Cody, D. M. Kelsey, J. W. Buel, John Beadle, and W. L. Holloway, adhered closely to the "facts" as presented by Whittaker. The general's widow, Elizabeth B. Custer, added three worshipful books of her own that proved quite popular: *Boots and Saddles* (1885), *Tenting on the Plains* (1887), and *Following the Guidon* (1890).

Custer's critics in the military establishment, and there were many, held their tongues concerning him so long as his widow lived. But she outlived them all, not dying until 1933. She carefully guarded her hero's flame, nourishing his growing legend and disarming his critics. As America moved into the twentieth century she could take solace in a steady stream of paintings, poems, children's books, novels, and films that presented her "Autie" as a symbol of martial glory and triumphant martyrdom. The first two twentieth-century biographies, Frederick S. Dellenbaugh's *George Armstrong Custer* (1926) and Frazier Hunt's *Custer: The Last of the Cavaliers* (1928), were wildly hagiographic.

Then came *Glory-Hunter*. Van de Water was well known in eastern circles as editor, critic, poet, and novelist, but had never attempted a biography. He had no intention of writing a history when he began researching the enigmatic George A. Custer, but, rather, was gathering background materials for his ambitious novel of the Indian wars, *Thunder Shield* (1933). That novel told the story of a white man adopted by the Cheyennes who rides to his death beside Crazy Horse at Little Big Horn. Writing the novel hooked the author on Custer and he threw himself into the task of explaining the man's fascinating contradictions by attempting a biography.

In this task he would be heavily influenced by the work of Sigmund Freud as well as by the so-called debunking spirit of the biographical writing of the 1920s, best exemplified by Lytton Strachey's *Eminent Victorians* (1918). When he finished *Glory-Hunter*, Van de Water had written a compelling portrait of a man consumed with ambition, driven by demons of his own making, and finally destroyed by his own hubris. Van de Water was clearly selective in his use of source materials—but all writers must be—as he crafted his compelling narrative to portray truthfully a brutal and strict commander who was dangerously insubordinate; a soldier distrusted by many of his own officers and men and yet worshipped by others; a man of little military talent whose victories were often the result of incredible good fortune, the action of more cautious subordinates, or overwhelming odds in his favor. Finally, ineptitude, arrogance, and his headlong pursuit of glory conspired to destroy Van de Water's Custer at the Little Big Horn. Here, at last, was a biography that dismantled the marble hero of the past and created instead an understandable, believable human being.

Other writers quickly followed Van de Water's lead, so that within a few years the glory-hunter interpretation became the standard portrayal of Custer. It appeared in novels such as Harry Sinclair Drago's *Montana Road* (1935), Ernest Haycox's *Bugles in the Afternoon* (1944), Will Henry's *No Survivors* (1950), Clay Fisher's *Yellow Hair* (1953), Frank Gruber's *Bugles West* (1954), Thomas Berger's *Little Big Man* (1964), and Lewis B. Patten's *The Red Sabbath* (1968). Postwar Hollywood also followed Van de Water's interpretation in films such as *Fort Apache* (1948), *Sitting Bull* (1954), *Tonka* (1958), *The Great Sioux Massacre* (1965), *Custer of the West* (1968), and *Little Big Man* (1970). Every historian of the Indian wars since 1934 had to acknowledge *Glory-Hunter,* and most have followed its themes closely. This indebtedness is especially evident in Charles G. Brill's *Conquest of the Southern Plains* (1938), David H. Miller's *Custer's Fall* (1957), Mari Sandoz's *The Battle of the Little Big Horn* (1966), Dee Brown's *Bury My Heart at Wounded Knee* (1971), Stephen E. Ambrose's *Crazy Horse and Custer* (1975), Stan Hoig's *The Battle of the Washita* (1976), and Evan S. Connell's *Son of the Morning Star* (1984). Van de Water's biography is, without a doubt, the most influential book ever written on Custer.

The author of *Glory-Hunter* was born in Pompton, New Jersey, on September 30, 1890, and graduated from Columbia University in 1914. He honed his writing skills as a reporter on the *New York American* and *New York Tribune* before joining the *Ladies Home Journal* as a staff writer in 1923. From 1928 to 1932 he served as book critic for the *New York Evening Post.* By that time he had already won acclaim as a critic, essayist, and novelist. His detective stories were his best known, but he wrote on a wide variety of subjects. After his move to Vermont in the late thirties Van de Water became something of a professional booster for that state. Among his notable works on Vermont were *We're Still in the Country* (1938), *The Reluctant Republic: Vermont 1724–1791* (1941), and *In Defense of Worms, and Other Angling Heresies* (1949). In all, Van de Water published over twenty books of fiction, history, and travel before he died at Brattleboro, Vermont, on September 16, 1968.

In his long career as a free-lance writer after the publication of *Glory-Hunter,* Van de Water never returned to the Custer story. Perhaps the strident tone of Custer's defenders, both at the time of the book's publication and since, led him to shy away from the subject. The tone of the bitter attacks on Van de Water was set by General Hugh S. "Iron Pants" Johnson of New Deal fame, in his December 29, 1934, review of *Glory-*

Hunter in *Today Magazine*. "As history this book is just adverse advocacy," Johnson thundered. "As biography, it is merely muckraking. As military criticism, it sounds like the musings of a daisy-crunching doughboy." According to the general, Van de Water had done "that which even an acorn-eating Digger Indian would scorn to consider—scalp an heroic warrior found dead on the field of honor."

The passage of time since 1934 has not stilled the Custer controversy, or abated the public's enduring fascination with that fateful warrior. Nor have the publication of additional Custer biographies—Jay Monaghan's *Custer* (1959) and D. A. Kinsley's *Favor the Bold* (1968)—come close to ending the debate or seriously challenging the preeminence of Van de Water's book. The forthcoming publication of Robert M. Utley's *Cavalier in Buckskin* will undoubtedly supplant *Glory-Hunter* as the best life of Custer, but it will not negate the book's influence or its status as a fine biography still worth reading.

Van de Water was not surprised by the controversy swirling about his book. In 1932 he wrote to Custer partisan William J. Ghent that he was "learning the strange, truculence-inspiring fascination that Custer and his career still exert on the minds of men. After sixty years, men still are his violent defenders or equally ardent detractors."

Van de Water came to understand this strange power that Custer, even though long dead, still held over people. He was also caught up in Custer's enigmatic spell. Perhaps by writing *Glory-Hunter* he freed himself from the general's ghost. Nevertheless, he wrote his biography in order to comprehend the truth about Custer, not out of any desire to destroy a glorious reputation. And he was successful, at least in portraying the essence of the man—and no biographer can hope for more. As he explained to Ghent in 1932: "If I side with Brininstool and Wheeler—and incidentally General Charles King as well as a respectable number of others—instead of you, General Godfrey and a probably more numerous band of like believers, it is not for lack of study or, let me suggest, because of any conscious defection from the pursuit of truth."

PART ONE
SOLDIER

GLORY-HUNTER

PART ONE: SOLDIER

CHAPTER ONE

BEGINNINGS

HE FOLLOWED Glory all his days. He was her life-long devotee. She gave him favor withheld from most men, and denied herself when his need of her was sorest.

When, desperately pursuing, he died on the heights above the Little Bighorn, Glory, the perverse, relented and gave eternal brilliance to the name of George Armstrong Custer, Lieutenant-Colonel, 7th United States Cavalry, Brevet Major-General, United States Army, the "Boy General with the Golden Locks," "the Murat of the American Army," the good sword, the hero, the martyr.

His memory has been clothed in glamour by the mystery of his death. He rode away at the head of five troops into the bare brown hills, and dust, smoking up beneath the hoofs of weary horses, hid him. Men found his stripped body at the apex of a corpse-littered angle of rout. No one will ever completely know his purpose or learn the instant and manner of his end.

Wherefore he is immortal, by his enigmatic death, by the no less vivid inconsistencies of his immoderate life. His body lies at the United States Military Academy where his brief and furious career began. There is no such rest for those who follow the singular course that body took through life. Angry controversy beclouds his every step. It is as though the unbridled spirit of him still were clearly discernible to mortal eyes.

17

In the flesh, he was greatly loved and hated. So he remains, almost sixty years since he fell, twice pierced by bullets of the Sioux. Few still endure who saw him in the flesh, but over his memory, his deeds, his character and particularly his death, Custer-phobe and Custerphile strive with the heat of the man's actual intimates. No winds of partizanship disturb the ashes of other warriors of his day. Merritt, Kilpatrick, Devin, MacKenzie, Crook, captains of Union horse and Indian fighters alike, have the peace that is obscurity's twilight. Men keep the fame of Custer burnished while that of equal or better soldiers grows dim.

While he lived, few saw him accurately. Contemporaries accorded him the unreliable tributes of infatuated praise or vindictive condemnation. He was a person whom it was impossible to regard with balance. His death did not placate, though it hushed, his enemies. The years that elapsed before their own ends never diminished the clear loyalty of his adherents.

Major and Brevet Brigadier-General Frederick W. Benteen, most valiant and able of his troop captains, hated him profoundly. General E. S. Godfrey, who served as lieutenant under Custer, devoted much of his life to his hero's defense. The last of his officers, Colonel Charles A. Varnum, still protects the memory of his old chieftain. Later men, who never saw that golden head gleam in the murk of battle, speak and write of him with odd personal heat.

Death submerges heroes, hiding actual dimensions and qualities from inquiring eyes. The flood covers men and all that remains visible are islands that were peaks of their careers. Many of these vestiges, as the years pass, slip lower or disappear. From the scattered and incongruous archipelago that still endures, one must try to surmise the outline and substance of vanished actuality. Few have left to the biographer more wholly divergent islets of fact than the Glory-Hunter. He seems in his brief time to have been many men.

He followed Glory to his doom. Thereafter, woman-like, she followed him. The paradox is consonant with the career of George Armstrong Custer. He himself was paradox; the word made flesh.

Few men have been more vehemently positive in character. None has thwarted generalization with more baffling contradictions.

He was a popular hero who was scorned by many in his own profession.

He was the idol of a few subordinates and distrusted by others.

He was a tenderly devoted son and husband and a brutal commander.

He was gentle with his dogs and horses, yet blind to suffering he inflicted on men.

He was a dangerously insubordinate officer; he had been a most slovenly cadet and subaltern, but he enforced discipline on his own troops implacably.

He has been praised as a knightly and gallant foe; he had been decried as butcher and lyncher.

He was renowned for his flaming valor in battle, yet his record is marred by one stain, that is the blood of Major Joel H. Elliot and nineteen men, killed by what was, at best, the incredible callousness of George Armstrong Custer.

He is best remembered as the foremost Indian fighter of his day but his only positive victory in battle against the red men was massacre rather than conflict, and his chief surviving fame as a soldier is based upon a defeat as complete as ever United States regulars sustained.

These and lesser inconsistencies defy plausible solution unless the biographer abandon any attempt to harmonize discordant facts and admit that the man was demented. Custer was not crazy, though some contemporaries thought him so. He was the life-long infatuate of renown. Through the strange contradictions of his character, that one trait runs constant. He loved fame with insatiable ardor. His pursuit of renown was medieval and adolescent. All his life, he rode after Glory.

Precocious, valiant and fortunate, he followed her through the Civil War and Glory smiled upon him. She accorded him favor denied to older, more experienced soldiers, raising him at the age of twenty-five to the rank of major-general of volunteers, showering him with praise, adorning him with honors, and sardonically contriving his later doom.

Swashbuckler, hard rider, headlong fighter, with uncropped golden hair and a self-contrived uniform of velveteen and gilt, George Armstrong Custer, commander of the Michigan Brigade and later of a division in Sheridan's cavalry, was a shining mark for death who ignored him. Death had ordained a later tryst and the need of glory was to lead Custer thither.

He drank deep of fame during the last years of the Civil War, and became its devotee. Nothing less was sweet in his throat and as years passed and the opportunity for slaking thirst dwindled, Custer displayed in the violence and unscrupulousness of his search the aberration of the deprived addict.

The source of his craving for renown is, of itself, mystery and contradiction. The baby who was born in New Rumley, Harrison County, Ohio, December 5, 1839, did not come of an ambitious or warrior strain. His father was Emmanuel, a stalwart, Maryland-born blacksmith and a widower. His mother was Maria Ward Fitzpatrick, formerly of Pennsylvania and a widow.

George Armstrong was the oldest child of their union. His parents were plain folk who thought little of lineage or else found little that was noteworthy therein to extoll. The tale that the original Custer in America had been one Kuester, officer of Hessian mercenaries under Burgoyne, is the earliest of the host of Custer legends.

The only soldier actually discernible in the ancestry of George Armstrong was his great-grandfather, Emmanuel, born in Allegheny County, Maryland, 1754, and one time sergeant in the 8th Company, 10th Philadelphia County Militia. The first Emmanuel lived a hundred years, and may have been the source of his most famous descendant's phenomenal vitality.

Whatever the nationality of the Custer clan—German, English, Dutch—they were a sound and wholesome folk, originally of some position in the New World, for the centenarian Emmanuel's father, Paul, married Sara Martha Ball, cousin to the mother of George Washington.

Thereafter, it appears that the line lay fallow, gathering energy for its most remarkable creation. Sergeant Emmanuel's son was John, and John's son, the second Emmanuel, was born in Cryssoptown, Maryland, 1806. He learned the blacksmith's trade and in early manhood moved to the hamlet of New Rumley, scarcely larger now than then, in Ohio. The township had been platted in 1813 by Jacob Custer, a kinsman.

Emmanuel, father of George Armstrong, prospered. At twenty-two he married Matilda Viers. Three children were born of that union. Their mother died in 1834.

A year later, Israel R. Fitzpatrick died, leaving Maria Ward, his widow, and three children, one a daughter, Lydia A., who was to become half-sister and second mother to George Armstrong Custer.

Emmanuel Custer and Maria Ward Fitzpatrick were married April 14, 1837. To the six children of their combined households, five more were to be added—George Armstrong, 1839, Nevin J., 1843, Thomas W., 1845, Boston, 1848, and Margaret Emma, 1852.

Nevin was not surcharged with the restless energy that bedeviled his brothers. He became a farmer and lived in peace. George Armstrong and Thomas, Boston, and the husband of Margaret Emma, died together on a clouded and sultry Sabbath beside the Little Bighorn.

The children of Emmanuel and Maria were reared in the rough plenty and God-fearing rectitude of a mid-nineteenth-century household, where the rod logically demonstrated parental affection, and independence and respect were taught together. It must have been a riotous family. The Custers had a perverse love for practical jokes in which their father joined. Emmanuel and his wife were remarkable in that they seemed able to ignore all lines of demarcation that the varied parentage of their brood might have drawn. In later years, George Armstrong Custer never could recall which were only his half relatives. Next to his mother, his half-sister Lydia Fitzpatrick was most dear to him.

The family was a cooperative unit, to which each child as he grew able, contributed his share of labor—chores, gardening and

later, ax work and plowing. It may have been only the transform-
ing light of later tragedy that made the first-born of Emmanuel
and Maria Custer appear in retrospect the brightest, most vigorous
and most unruly of their charges.

"Autie" as his family called him was a tow-headed, ruddy child
whom the exhilaration of immense vitality forever thrust toward
precociousness and, whatever the faults of his training, it at least
filled him with a lifelong, passionate fondness for his parents.

In the light of tragedy, still thirty-odd years distant, incidents
of his babyhood cast significant shadows. Happenings of his in-
fancy later seemed to have offered half-veiled prophecy.

From his earliest years, arms and uniforms thrilled the boy.
War with Mexico was in the air and the men of the hamlet organized a militia company under the not too modest title of "The New
Rumley Invincibles." Emmanuel Custer drilled with them and his
little son wore a miniature replica of their uniform. The child,
while words still were difficult, startled his father one day by lifting an arm in imitation of an older half-brother who had been
practising a "speaking piece" for school and declaiming:

"My voice is for war!"

It always was. It was to be lifted in wild shrill whooping in the
forefront of a hundred cavalry charges.

Emmanuel took the four-year-old Autie to the doctor to have an
aching tooth pulled. The child bore the agony with only the
minimum of tears and seemed to find compensation in his father's
subsequent praise. Even then applause was a panacea for all ills.
The Custers were staunch Jacksonian Democrats but they were
outnumbered in New Rumley. The little boy gave a bloody grin
as he and his parent left the doctor's.

"Father," he confided, "you and me can whip all the Whigs in
Ohio."

It was a variation of this belief that killed him.

The intense high spirits that many contemporaries later were to
damn as play-acting pose dominated him even then. His child's

"Father," he confided, "you and me can whip all the Whigs in Ohio."

world was filled with challenges that he would not ignore. Jealously guarded orchards were provocations to raids. Horses who were dangerous for short legs to bestride must be ridden. Autie Custer was one of the major afflictions of the New Rumley district school's master. The boy's intelligence was quick but his marks were uniformly bad, and he was the provocative agent of many scholastic upheavals. In swimming and boating alone he was unwilling to take the lead. He had an odd fear of water.

Raucous and rowdy and defiant though he was, stern reproof instantly could bring him to tears and abject contrition. Then and later, he respected the harsher voice and the heavier hand than his.

He had the plain recreations and the heavy tasks of a country lad in his era. There was stock to feed and gardens to tend. Emmanuel gave each of his sons a piglet to raise, and all the rest of his days George Armstrong Custer cherished an interest in swine. He rode almost as soon as he could walk. He learned to swing an ax with skill and to follow the plow and the hearty life of his boyhood hardened his big-boned frame and gave him an endurance and a strength that later were to be the marvel of his comrades.

In 1849, his dear half-sister, Lydia, married David Reed of Monroe, Michigan. Through her, circumstance first laid a directing hand on George Armstrong Custer. Lydia begged that the boy might accompany her and her husband to a land that only recently was frontier. For two years, Autie dwelt with his second mother in the town on the shore of Lake Michigan. There he attended Stebbins Academy and was chiefly remembered for the skill with which he read *Charles O'Malley* and other romances of conflict, undetected, behind the concealment of his open geography.

While he was absent, his family moved out of the New Rumley village to a farm on the township's edge. In 1851, the lad rejoined his parents and for two years thereafter, his time was divided between farm work and attending a school founded by A. B. Creal, who had frequent cause to regret it during George Armstrong's sojourn. The seven-year-old Tom Custer bestowed upon his older brother the beginnings of that worship which was to endure until they died together. The gangling thirteen-year-old and his chubby junior were chronically in trouble. In 1854, George was sent back to his half-sister again.

This time he was entered in Boyd's Seminary at Monroe. No school seems to have been overwilling to harbor him long. His record was more distinguished for insurgency than brilliance. While on this visit to Monroe he had an encounter which both participants remembered all their lives.

The boy was returning from school, book laden. As he passed the mansion of the wealthy Daniel S. Bacon, one of Monroe's first settlers, territorial legislator, Judge of Probate and President of the Monroe Bank, a child was swinging on the garden gate. Her dark eyes, greatly daring, stared at the awkward, disheveled figure.

"Hello," small Elizabeth Bacon stammered. "Hello, you Custer boy," and overcome by shyness fled. It was their first meeting. Ten years later, he married her.

At fifteen, the Custer boy returned to his own home. He seems to have been a difficult problem which the family passed back and forth in hope of solution. By now enough education had stuck to qualify him to teach school.

He served as master, briefly, in the Beech Point School at New Athens, Ohio, and the Harrison County subscription school. Between times he attended the McNeely Normal School at Hopedale.

The boy was tall and prodigiously strong for his age. His pale hair had darkened into pure golden hue. His voice cherished new and disconcerting notes that presaged the shrill penetration of its maturity.

Girls were no longer afflictions to be endured. He flung himself with the zest that never left him till life departed, into the simple, vigorous social events of the countryside. There were dances to which he rode with his partner on a pillion behind him. The town hall at Conotton was the social center of the neighborhood. There, young Custer pranced through the square dances of the period and the more novel schottische and polka, or added the voice of his accordion to the squealing fiddles. In the winter, there were straw rides and once Joe Dickerson connived with Custer in driving the sled up a snow bank and capsizing it to hear the girls scream. There were picnics and parties and spelling-bees.

At one of these last, Custer was irked by the antics of a boyhood enemy who crept up outside a window and made opprobious faces and gestures through the pane. The victim endured the affront only briefly. Derision or belittlement always smarted on his tender ego. He rushed to the window and drove his fist through the pane at his enemy's face. The thought of a possibly mutilated hand did not deter him. Then or later, with a foe in sight, he rarely paused to consider cost.

The catlike leap of the furious stripling; the tinkling crash that imposed awed silence; the wide-eyed regard of Custer's fellow youngsters—these were an enigmatically uttered prophecy.

Chapter Two

INSURGENT

DEATH made him immortal. It is only by the cryptic tragedy of his end that most men remember George Armstrong Custer ever lived. History and controversy concern themselves chiefly with the last few weeks of his existence. Beyond the circle of that intense illumination much of the man's story lies in shadow and not a little is completely dark. There are gaps in the record that now may never be filled, since those who might have bridged them held their peace during the lifetime of his widow, who outlived them all.

The youth of Custer lies far beyond that spotlight radiance. Out of the consequent obscurity no one may draw the exact reason why the shrill and restless normal-school student, the raw-boned embryo school-teacher, turned from that career toward the army. The most plausible reason is the boy's innate love of romance and activity. The small military establishment of the 1850's was not replete with either, but subterranean tremblings in the nation presaged eruption. They may have shaken and inspired George Custer.

Whatever the source of his ambition, he pursued it beyond what his staunchly Democratic family considered propriety. Representative John A. Bingham, whose congressional district included New Rumley, was a Republican, and therefore an enemy. Emmanuel Custer refused to appeal on his son's behalf to a political foe but the boy ignored partizan frontiers. On May 27, 1856, he wrote to Bingham from normal school, asking for an appointment to West Point and describing himself as "above the medium height and of remarkably strong constitution and vigorous frame."

Bingham replied that the appointment for that district had been awarded. This refusal plus paternal indignation and maternal dis-

26

may did not discourage the aspirant. He scandalized his family by graver political apostasy. In the parade held for Fremont, Republican presidential candidate, at Cadiz that year George Armstrong Custer rode, disguised as a Border Ruffian, and afterward completed his heresy by shaking hands with Bingham, and making a personal appeal for aid.

It may have been the headlong ardor of the boy, which later fascinated many men; it may have been Bingham's hope of winning converts to his party that gave Custer his appointment. The politician assured him that it would be forthcoming and in the spring of 1857, the document arrived. It was signed by the then Secretary of War, Jefferson Davis. On June third, George Armstrong Custer registered at the United States Military Academy.

"My career as a cadet," he wrote years later, "had but little to recommend it to the study of those who came after me, unless as an example to be carefully avoided." It is probable that none of his classmates, certainly none of his superiors, had warrant to disagree with this self-judgment. Much that may have been significant in Custer's four years at West Point has slipped away, unchecked, into oblivion. His autobiography on which he was at work when he died, aged thirty-six, slides briefly and with dubious accuracy over that period. Classmates have supplied incidents. Legend that here begins to cloud the man's authentic outline furnishes more.

The most reliable though reticent account of Custer's career as a cadet is set down in fading ink on the brittle pages of the Academy records.

The lad was seventeen now. Farm work and the intense vigor that filled him already had given him more than the average man's stature. He was just under six feet in height, broad-shouldered and big-boned. He is said to have been the second strongest man in his class. His eyes were bright blue, his hair golden yellow and his complexion so innocent a pink and white that the cadets, to his horror, nicknamed him "Fanny."

Colonel Richard L. Delafield was superintendent at the Academy and Lieutenant-Colonel William J. Hardee, later a lieutenant-general, Confederate States Army, commandant of the corps. These were to become well if unfavorably acquainted with Cadet Custer in the years immediately to follow.

From June to August twenty-ninth, the incoming class was in summer camp where it learned the rudiments of drill. Thereafter it was quartered in the old North Barracks. Custer roomed with James P. Parker, of Missouri, and had as next-door neighbor Thomas Lafayette Rosser, of Texas, whom he later was to meet in battle. Later still he was to guard Rosser's surveyors who laid out the route of the Northern Pacific along the Yellowstone.

Men recalled him at West Point as a defiant insubordinate cadet, forever in trouble and as constantly on the verge of more. There is no hope of reconciling his resentment toward and disregard of authority with the feverish eagerness whereby he wheedled an appointment out of Bingham. Inconsistency and George Armstrong Custer were twins. He was never amenable to the dull routine of army discipline. The precisely ordered hours of the cadets' days were to him challenge and provocation. Out of his insurgence legends have stemmed. One of the most durable has insisted that he received no diploma at graduation and when later, radiant with honors, he revisited the Point and the document was offered him, he profanely refused it.

There seems to have been less truth here than in many similar myths. Nothing indicates that he did not get his diploma in due course. The parchment itself is among the mementoes left by his widow. Another legend concerning his graduation, which Custer himself sponsored, will be examined later.

The impartial voice of the Academy records portrays George Armstrong Custer as a slovenly soldier and a deplorable student. For the first twenty days of his sojourn at West Point whatever high resolutions he had brought with him appear to have endured. It is not until June twenty-third that the "skin book" in which demerits are listed first cites him. On that date he received two demerits for "not casting eyes to the front after being ordered to do so at parade" and another for being late at parade.

These were drops, heralding downpour. He was an indifferent, a tardy and a clumsy recruit who persistently was punished for slackness in drill, dirty equipment or disordered uniform. One hundred demerits in any six-months period supposedly caused the delinquent's expulsion from the academy. During his first half-year, Custer ran up one hundred and twenty-nine. This total was reduced to sixty-nine by some unidentified Samaritan.

In the subsequent six months, he had eighty-two demerits, four of these for "tobacco smoke in quarters," though in later years he touched neither tobacco nor liquor. He skated nearer the deadline in 1858 for he had ninety-eight demerits during the first half-year and ninety-four during the second.

Most of his offenses at drill disappear during 1859 and 1860. He has learned the exterior appearance of a soldier. Ineptitude is replaced by a general insurgence and slackness—talking, sitting down on sentry duty, visiting out of hours, room unswept, table-cloth dirty, person slovenly.

On March 18, 1860, he got seven demerits for "room grossly out of order, bed down and floor not swept" and also for "bread, butter, potatoes, plates, knives and forks in qrs." That left the wild colt with one hundred and twenty-nine marks against him, twenty-nine more than enough to insure his expulsion at the term's end. Through the intervention of some unidentified "S. B. H.," thirty of these were removed. Presumably S. B. H. managed to put the fear of God temporarily into Custer's heart, for from March nineteenth to June sixth when the half-year ended, no single demerit was set down against him. When authority was sufficiently severe and impressive, he could always be the model soldier.

The reform was not permanent. In the subsequent six months, he ran up ninety-five demerits, largely for neglect of his person or his studies.

His record was as spectacularly undistinguished in the classroom as elsewhere. He stood fifty-eighth in a class of sixty-five during his first year; fifty-sixth out of fifty-nine at the end of his second and fifty-seventh out of fifty-seven when the third concluded.

Despite the rhapsodies of biographers, despite Custer's own assurances to Bingham, few embryo soldiers ever have shown less qualification or ardor for the life they have chosen.

During his last year at West Point a greater affliction than he was disrupting the Academy. Immediately after the election of Lincoln and before their own state had seceded, two South Carolina cadets resigned from the corps and hurried home. As the seceding commonwealths left the Union, their sons departed from West Point. Custer, "walking an extra" for punishment one Saturday afternoon, saw from a distance the departure of his first two classmates, Cadets Kelley and Ball, who were borne away on the shoulders of cheering southerners. Thereafter, the corps dwindled rapidly.

The approaching crisis hurried into effect a change already planned in the academic system. Heretofore, it had taken five years to complete the course. This was now compressed into four, so that two classes were graduated in 1861; the first in April; the second, Custer's, in late June.

There were only thirty-four cadets who received diplomas that June and among them Custer stood thirty-fourth. He was, the records show, fifth from the bottom in "Cavalry Tactics & Outpost Duty," fourth from the foot in "Artillery Tactics, Army Ordnance & Administration" and "Drawing & Conduct," third from the bottom in "Infantry Tactics, Strategy & Grand Tactics" and at the foot of the class in "Electrics & Chemistry" and "General Merit."

He was assigned tentatively to one of the branches of the service where it was supposed least ability was demanded. His record bears the notation: "Recommended for Infantry, Dragoons, Mounted Rifles or Cavalry."

There was much haste and confusion during those last months at the Academy which had become, all at once, not a college for training in the theory of war but a supply source for officers in the forming Union armies. Colonel Delafield remained as superintendent but Hardee had been replaced as cadet commandant by Lieutenant-Colonel John F. Reynolds who was to die at Gettysburg. There was dire work ahead for the 1861 graduates but this does not seem to have impressed Cadet Custer. In the half-year ending June sixth, he had ninety-seven demerits, and he managed from June sixth to twenty-ninth to collect fifty-two more.

To the end of his course, he was a negligent and shabby soldier. On June tenth and thirteenth, he was late at parade. "June 19th, not shaved at gd. mtg. No buttons on collar at gd mtg." "June 25th; Tent out of police at ev'g insp." "June 26th: Tent out of order a.m."

The last of the multitudes of demerits which the chronic insurgent received from his alma mater were the outcome of an incident whose result Custer himself presents as fact and the records at West Point brand as fable. On June twenty-ninth, the corps was in summer camp where each cadet of the graduating class served in turn as officer of the guard. Custer, so serving, discovered at dusk a fight among the tents. He writes: "I pushed my way through the surrounding line of cadets, dashed back those who were interfering in the struggle and called out loudly: 'Stand back, boys; let's have a fair fight!' "

Lieutenant William B. Hazen, officer of the day and destined to interfere again, years after, in another enterprise of Custer's, intruded and broke up the quarrel. On the morrow, according to the culprit's relation, he was brought before Reynolds, the commandant, who ordered him held for a court martial while the rest of his class was graduated.

"I was ordered to my tent in arrest," Custer narrates, and then gives a circumstantial account of the court martial's proceeding. He names as Judge-Advocate Lieutenant, later Chief of Ordnance, Stephen Vincent Benet, grandfather of the poets, William Rose and Stephen Vincent. "The trial," Custer assures us, "was brief, scarcely occupying more time than did the primary difficulty."

Meanwhile, according to his story, his class had been graduated and had reported at once to Washington where influential members prevailed on authority to order the prisoner's release.

"This order practically rendered the action and proceeding of the court martial nugatory. What the proceeding of the court on this decision was, I have never learned." Nor to this day has any one else. Among the meticulously kept records of the Academy there is no mention of any such court ever having been held. Only a single entry on the pages dedicated to Custer has bearing upon this mythical or otherwise affair. It reads: "June 29th. Officer of the Gd. Gross neglect of duty not suppressing a quarrel in the immediate vicinity of gd tent he being present 8 & 9 PM." For this offense, the record shows that Custer was not court-martialed but received five demerits.

Major R. L. Eichelberger, the present adjutant at West Point, has looked for any possible confirmation of the picturesque account Custer gives of his exit from the Academy. "I have had the records very carefully searched in this regard and no record whatever concerning this matter has been found. It seems highly improbable that anything of the kind could have occurred without a record of some kind being kept of it. The offense, while serious enough to a certain extent, is one that would call for the routine punishment which records indicate was awarded rather than for a court martial."

So rests one of the earlier and minor mysteries concerning a mysteriously contradictory character and no man can tell whether the records or Custer's tale be false. Perhaps the headquarters clerk who gathered up the burden of worn folios to return them to their places uttered the most penetrating comment possible.

"You know," said he, "some birds like to make themselves sound tougher than they are."

There remains a hiatus that either the unrecorded court martial or some other hypothesis is required to bridge. Custer's class was graduated the last of June. Custer writes that he himself did not leave West Point until mid-July and hurried, an individual reenforcement, to the defense of Washington. Thither had gone besides his classmates, many instructors and even the battery of artillery usually employed at West Point for drill.

Second Lieutenant Custer, United States Army, tarried in New York long enough to buy himself field equipment—sword and pistol, sash, spurs and other accouterments—at the then famous military outfitting firm of Horstman's. He arrived in Washington July nineteenth.

The capital was packed with people and surcharged with emotion. Dust from Pennsylvania Avenue subdued the glitter of brand-new uniforms. Troops that had barely learned to keep step tramped its length in storms of cheers. Washington was swept with alternate convulsions of boastfulness and dread—fear lest the rebels, massing in Virginia, break the portly McDowell's multi-hued army and smash through the city's fragile defenses; confidence that the Union host of ill-drilled militia and a handful of regulars would crush the rebellion with one mighty stroke. The capital was ablaze with flags and vociferous with crowd hysteria. Through the dust and tumult a gaunt young man, his upper lip blurred with the beginning of a blond mustache, his deep-set blue eyes brilliant with excitement, made his way to the Ebbit House where Parker, his roommate, lodged.

Parker had been one of the more provident than conscientious who had remained at the Academy until he had been graduated and then had started home to join the Confederate army. He made Custer welcome. Later at the door of the hotel, the roommates told each other good-by. One journeyed southwest to help protect his native state, Missouri, from federals. The other strode toward the seething madhouse that had been the War Department to report for duty with the Union army.

It was two A. M. before Custer could fight his way through the milling horde of officers, aides and couriers and report to the Adjutant-General who for some reason, at this distance obscure, took the youngster to an inner chamber and introduced him to the generalissimo of the Union armies, the gigantic and dropsical Winfield Scott.

The old hero shifted attention from the map of northern Virginia over which he had been brooding and welcomed Custer kindly. The lad had been assigned to the 2nd United States Cavalry, now with McDowell at Centerville. Scott asked if Custer would prefer to report to his command or be detailed to drill recruits in Washington. No one in later years would have thought of asking the yellow-haired firebrand such a question. Scott nodded solemn agreement when Custer elected to take the field.

"A very commendable resolution, young man," said he, and bade the Lieutenant return the following evening with a horse, prepared to carry dispatches to McDowell.

Later that morning, Custer found to his dismay that horses were as scarce in Washington as Eskimos. The army had commandeered many. The rest had been taken by civilians who had ridden or driven out toward Bull Run to witness the battle that was to end the war and flavor a picnic. No livery-stable harbored a single nag and harried officers laughed at the youngster's request for a mount.

The good fortune that future envious rivals were to curse, now smiled for the first time upon the youngster. In time its benefactions were to grow so lavish that "Custer's luck" was to be an army byword and men were to attribute many of his triumphs solely to fortune's intercession. It awarded him now, not with victory in battle, but a horse.

Ranging Washington on his search, Custer encountered a soldier of the battery lately quartered at West Point. The man had been sent to Washington to bring back a horse that had been left behind. It was Wellington, an animal Custer often had ridden. By persuasion or bribery, the youngster obtained possession of him.

That night the young Lieutenant rode across the long bridge and over troop-choked highways, bearing dispatches to McDowell and fearful lest the war should be over before he reached the front.

CHAPTER THREE

SUBORDINATE

WAR, that would transform many, would only burnish the cocksure lad who guided his purloined horse, on that eve of battle, by smoldering camp-fires and men who slumbered in furrows beside stacked muskets; past darker confusion on a dark highway where weary amateur regiments groped forward.

Two years of campaigning would turn West Point's indifferent sloven into a soldier. It would not change his substance. Battle that reconstructed others, sobering and deepening their spirits, would only sharpen George Armstrong Custer. He would become a keen weapon, terrible to the enemy, difficult for a weak superior to wield, yet intrinsically he would remain the raucous and reckless youngster who had defied his parents to clasp the hand of a political foe and had been the Academy's chronic insurgent. His nature was bright and volatile, yet durable past the power even of war to alter.

There were to be months of aimless, haphazard service before he clearly saw his life's great purpose. Once that had been discerned, once he had looked with comprehension upon the bright face of Glory, existence thereafter was to be ordered by him for one simple purpose from which death alone could distract him.

Now, on the night of June twentieth, he rode like "Charles O'Malley, the Irish Dragoon" and other geography-shielded heroes of his boyhood, through a countryside vocal with the blunderings of an untempered army and it is probable that his heart sang.

It was two-thirty A. M. when Custer reached Centerville where the unhappy McDowell's headquarters was surrounded by the tents and carriages of congressmen and unofficial sightseers who had driven out to picnic on the morrow and witness the collapse

35

of the Confederacy. The Lieutenant delivered his dispatches to Major Wadsworth and declined the offer of a camp-bed. He was tasting for the first time the tingling wine of imminent conflict, and sleep was a distraction to be ignored. Slumber was rarely a necessity to him though he had the doglike ability, denied most human beings, to lie down and nap at any hour, anywhere.

Lieutenant Kingsbury of his class at the Academy and now on McDowell's staff, found breakfast for the new arrival and directed him to Major I. N. Palmer's squadron of the 2nd Cavalry. The command already was moving out through the night when Custer reached it, with G Troop, to which he had been assigned, in the advance. He reported to Lieutenant Drummond, troop commander, and rode on toward his first battle.

Custer's part in this conflict was little more than the visiting congressmen's. The handful of cavalry with the Union army was placed in support on the right flank. There it remained through that long series of accidents, delays and blunders that was Bull Run.

Once, it appeared that the cavalry were about to charge and in the excitement of the moment G Troop's Second Lieutenant rummaged vainly through what military knowledge he had brought away from West Point to determine whether he should charge with saber or with pistol drawn. He could not remember. He drew first one and then the other and was racked by uncertainty until the order to advance was countermanded. This was the only time he wielded weapon at Bull Run.

From his position behind the battle, he saw the Union attack swarm up toward the Henry House and fall back and come again. At four that afternoon, from a distance, he marked how Kirby Smith's freshly arrived Brigade flanked the Federal right and saw McDowell's line go to pieces. Brightly uniformed militia regiments, volunteers in blue fell back like laborers who would work no more that day. Palmer's Squadron remained at its station until Colonel Samuel P. Heintzelman added it to the impromptu command of regulars he was assembling to act as rear-guard in the retreat.

Confederate guns opened upon the host that was pouring across the Cub Run bridge. Shells blossomed above it and McDowell's army burst apart into a panic-smitten mob. Scarlet zouaves, gay "Garibaldi Guards" and the rest of the amateur host fought for passage over a causeway that grew choked by broken wagons and the overturned carriages of spectators. Men deserted their commands, plunged into the stream and fled up the far bank in a shell-harried, blind stampede.

Heintzelman's regulars kept their heads, withdrawing in good order before the strange torpidity of the Gray advance, and G Troop, 2nd Cavalry, which had got a new second lieutenant that morning was the last intact unit to ford Cub Run and leave the battle-field. The troop paused at Centerville but there was no hope of reforming the runaway army. The cavalry pushed on through a night of rain to Arlington and there, stretched flat in the down-pour, Lieutenant Custer who had not known slumber for forty-eight hours went to sleep under the dubious shelter of a tree.

The Confederate army might have taken Washington had it pressed forward. Instead, it halted and in the wide-spread reorganization of the Union forces that followed Bull Run, the 2nd Cavalry was attached to the New Jersey Brigade, commanded by a one-armed, hawk-faced soldier with an imperial beard and blistering temper. G Troop had three officers instead of the necessary two and the youngest of these, Lieutenant Custer, was transferred as aide to the staff of Brigadier-General Philip Kearny.

Here was a man who might have stepped out of one of the military romances a youngster had devoured. Kearny had served as a Chasseur d'Afrique in Algeria while studying French cavalry organization at the American government's behest. He had charged first into Mexico City at the head of his dragoons and had paid his left arm for that exploit. He had fought under Louis Napoleon at Solferino and had won the cross of the Legion of Honor.

A martinet and a thoroughly able soldier, utterly brave, restless and transfigured by the glamour of battles in far places, he must have been a demigod to a romantic young lieutenant, who, it is quite possible, chose Kearny for his own ideal of what a soldier should be. Custer's own later description of the General might serve also as a self portrait:

> "Of the many officers of high rank with whom I have served, Kearny was the strictest disciplinarian. . . . He constantly chafed under the restraint and inactivity of camp life and was never so contented and happy as when moving to the attack."*

If the young man made Kearny his model, his personal alteration proceeded as deliberately as the reconstruction of the army. The summer passed while the South insisted the Union would sue for peace and the North hailed McClellan as organizer of victory. During these months, Custer was party to only one military exploit, insignificant in purpose, ridiculous in outcome.

One Colonel Buck with three hundred cavalry was ordered to surround and capture a Confederate outpost near Centerville and Kearny's restless young aide won permission to accompany the expedition. This marched out valiantly by moonlight, but darkness and silence worked havoc with the nerves of unseasoned troopers. When they approached the house where the outpost was quartered and a sentry fired upon them, the entire valiant three hundred wheeled about and fled.

Even so inglorious an escapade was preferable to the monotony of a minor aide's part in building an army and the youngster whose mane of unshorn yellow hair lent him the aspect of a gaunt young lion fretted, as he would always fret, on the treadmill of routine. He devoted himself to those pursuits which have been the relaxation of youthful staff officers since the beginning of armies: swaggering in, staggering out.

When summer slid into autumn and the prospect of battle withdrew entirely, McClellan ordered that hereafter regular army officers must not serve on the staffs of volunteer generals. Custer was parted from his hero and returned to his regiment. He promptly

---

* Whittaker, Frederick; *A Complete Life of General George A. Custer,* New York, 1877,

applied for sick leave. Romance was hard to find amid the birth throes of the Army of the Potomac. It might be easier to discover in Monroe, Michigan, where second lieutenants of cavalry were far less plentiful. From October, 1861, to February, 1862, Custer dwelt with his half-sister, Lydia Reed, in Monroe. The "illness" that gained him his leave does not seem to have been of long duration. He was lionized at Monroe but even in that little town, mere lieutenants were not an inexhaustible sensation. If boredom followed him to Michigan, there was liquor there to dispel it.

In that era when men drank to excess, ladyhood always presumed that no reputable person ever got drunk. The second recorded meeting of Custer and the girl who was to be his wife took place one afternoon when Elizabeth Bacon saw her future spouse beating his way home through an imperceptible head-wind and making heavy weather. Until her death, she spoke of this encounter as "that terrible day."

She did not speak then but stood aghast and watched him reel away. Lydia, Custer's half-sister, was less reticent. When her denunciation ended, the contrite warrior, ever penitent before stern and justly outraged authority, signed the pledge of abstinence. In the fourteen remaining years of his life, there is no evidence that he ever violated it.

General George Stoneman had been appointed chief of cavalry in the Army of the Potomac. Under his reorganizing hand, the 1st and 2nd Dragoons and the 1st Mounted Rifles of the regular establishment became respectively the 1st, 2nd and 3rd Cavalry. The old 2nd Cavalry that Custer rejoined in February, 1862, was now the 5th.

On March ninth, Stoneman led the Union horse out along the Orangeburg & Alexandria Railway to drive the Confederates beyond the Rappahannock. It was an empty maneuver for Johnston already had retired thither and the only engagement on this march was a charge by Troop G, 5th Cavalry, led by a whooping yellow-haired youngster, captain and first lieutenant being absent, against a Confederate picket. This was the first cavalry charge Custer ever launched. Trooper John W. Bryant was wounded and was hailed by the press as the first casualty of the Army of the Potomac.

That invincible host now moved to the Peninsula to wage a foot-less campaign, based more on political than on military exigencies. Though he had fought the army's first action, Custer apparently was not yet highly regarded as a troop commander. He was detached from his regiment for service under Lieutenant Nicholas Bowen, chief engineer on the staff of General W. F. "Baldy" Smith. This service seems to have entailed a variety of official and self-imposed tasks.

He was observer in the captive balloon that hung above York-town and was one of the first to detect Johnston's evacuation of the village. He galloped here and there on errands for his superiors. He was temporarily with Hancock's Brigade at the Williamsburg fight and guided the 5th Wisconsin and the 6th Maine over the mill-pond dam for their flank assault on Longstreet. No one embroiled himself more industriously in the war and no one was heeded less. There was little in the appearance of the man, who later was to be the most spectacular of officers, to warrant a second glance.

He was still the sloven. He had ridden himself gaunt and there was Virginia mud in his long hair. It was plastered on his cavalry jacket and even adorned his disreputable hat. General Smith was indulgent or indifferent and Custer flitted, more spectator than participant, about the ponderous advance of the army. On May twenty-second, his luck showed him the favor his superiors had withheld.

Bridges had been destroyed over the Chickahominy and Blue and Gray faced each other across its brown flood. General Barnard, chief of engineers, rode out to find a ford and encountering a long-haired young disreputable, ordered him into the stream. Custer had not the appearance of one a wetting would harm.

The water was only armpit deep and the bottom was firm. Custer crossed to the farther shore and then, since no sentry had fired at him, added a clause of his own to Barnard's instructions. He crept into the brush and returning at last, floundered back through the river and in his rattling, excited voice proclaimed his discovery.

There was an outpost on the river bend, isolated, easy to capture. Luck at this moment ordered the approach of McClellan.

The little General whom subordinates loved and superiors disparaged sat his charger in the surrounding splendor of his staff and heard Barnard's report. Presently, McClellan summoned the dripping Custer and questioned him. Later, he remembered the youngster at their first encounter as "a slim, longhaired boy, carelessly dressed." Immersion in the Chickahominy offered plausible excuse for Custer's deplorable appearance. While he rattled eager responses to the General's queries, whimsical fortune smiled further upon him. The artless earnestness of the thin high-strung lad appealed to McClellan, who asked:

"Would you care to join my staff, sir? I can offer you the rank of captain."

Would he care! That inquiry kindled in Custer an abiding devotion, that would not burn quite so brightly toward any other leader. The Glory-Hunter, whom some were to brand a self-seeking unreliable, never wavered in that loyalty. Others were to shrug theirs off when the little General was cast aside. Custer remained faithful. He accorded similar affection to only one other man, the actor, Lawrence Barrett. To his death, he remained in speech and written word the worshiper of McClellan and thereby inherited much suspicion and not a few rebuffs. The last magazine article he wrote was a glorification of his old chief.

To the youngster McClellan showed an indulgent affection. He wrote in his memoirs:

"In those days Custer was simply a reckless, gallant boy, undeterred by fatigue, unconscious of fear; but his head was always clear in danger and he always brought me clear and intelligible reports of what he saw under the heaviest fire. I became much attached to him."*

The General's first indulgence followed the advice of his newest aide. If, as Captain Custer believed, the enemy post on the

---

* McClellan, General George B.: *McClellan's Own Story,* New York, 1866.

Chickahominy's far shore might be captured, Captain Custer could have a troop of cavalry and two companies of infantry with which to take it.

At dawn of the next day, Custer led his little host across the ford he had discovered and was shaken out of his dreams of glory by a nasal voice exclaiming: "Why 'tis Armstrong! How be ye, Armstrong?"

The infantry he led were Michigan men and one of the companies had been recruited largely in Monroe. It was a former playmate who so hailed him. They captured the outpost and a flag. Tidings of that little action, reaching Monroe, may have helped to mitigate Elizabeth Bacon's latest memory of the Custer boy.

McClellan favored his aide. He and later Sheridan were the only men who dared give the mettlesome colt loose rein. Custer served his chief through the inconclusive battles of that campaign, tearing headlong under fire on sundry missions, engaging in numerous minor adventures. Though temporarily a staff captain, he was promoted to first lieutenant, 5th Cavalry, July seventeenth.

At Malvern Hill, he and Captain Bowen, another staff member, were fired upon by a Confederate outpost. The officers and their orderlies charged the enemy and captured them. Since time pressed and they were too few to shepherd their prisoners into the Union lines, they let them go and contented themselves with reporting to McClellan with their arms full of captured weapons. On another foray, Custer won the sword he bore through the rest of the war.

The tale of that trophy is worth examination. It was set forth in a letter Custer wrote August 8, 1862, to his relatives, the Reeds, in Monroe. Colonel Averill and the 5th Cavalry with four guns moved out on a foray against a Confederate post in White Oak Swamp and Custer accompanied his old regiment. The enemy fled. The cavalry pursued and Custer chose as his quarry an officer "mounted on a splendid horse."

"And then," he confides, "followed the most exciting sport I ever engaged in." He yelled to the fugitive to surrender.

"He paid no attention and I fired, taking as good aim as was possible on horseback. If I struck him he gave no indication of it but pushed on. . . . I took deliberate aim at his body and fired. He sat for a minute in the saddle, reeled and fell to the ground. His horse ran on and mine also. . . .

"I was not able to see the officer after he fell from his horse but Lieutenant Byrnes told me he saw him after he fell and that he rose to his feet, turned around, threw up his hands and fell to the ground with a stream of blood gushing from his mouth. I had either shot him in the neck or body. In either case, the wound must have been fatal."*

This was probably the first man George Armstrong Custer ever killed. There is no trace of sentiment in the narrative by one who could be the most sentimental of men. He describes the unhappy Confederate's death throes with the zest of a fisherman detailing the struggle of a hooked trout.

It is more the myopia of the egotist than sadism which impels him to set forth so fully his victim's ensanguined end. What was Custer's, he cherished. He was a generous kinsman, a devoted son, a tender husband, a charming friend. Beyond the periphery of his own interests he could not see. "Woe to the conquered!" might be a savage maxim but he found it logical. His sympathy was limited by the radius of self.

He killed the man and spared the horse that must have been a far larger mark. But the horse was "splendid" and Custer wanted him. He got him and rode him much thereafter. He also took his victim's sword.

It was heavy with a long straight blade on which was etched: "*No me tires sin razon: no me envaines sin honora.*" (Draw me not without reason; sheathe me not without honor.) It became his favorite weapon.

The campaign that was to have ended the war was sagging toward its futile close. Troops already were being withdrawn from the Peninsula to meet Stonewall Jackson's threat against Washing-

---

* Whittaker's *Life.*

ton. Custer tarried in Williamsburg where a classmate, Lieutenant John W. Lee, Confederate States Army, who had been wounded, recovered on parole. Lee dwelt in the home of residents and on the verge of marrying the girl who had nursed him.

With McClellan's permission, Custer remained in Williamsburg for two weeks until the advancing Confederates drove him out. His letters—he also had the epistolatory loquacity of the egotist— tell of Lee's wedding, at which he appeared as best man in a new blue uniform and of the subsequent involved flirtation he had with the bride's fair cousin. The approach of the Gray army blighted that romance. Meanwhile he had been including in profuse letters to friends in Monroe presumptuously tender messages to the unappreciative Elizabeth Bacon, whom he had met twice, but never formally. He had more forethought in love than in war.

CHAPTER FOUR

GENERAL

FORTUNE that had smiled on Captain Custer of General McClellan's staff smote him and then offered compensation in November, 1862. His chief was removed from command of the Army of the Potomac and the young soldier met his future wife with due formality.

On November seventh, when McClellan was replaced by Burnside, none of the staff had raged more violently or adorned potent personages with more reckless defamation than Custer. McClellan magnanimously had hushed wild objurgations with kindly reproof. He had been bidden merely to await further orders and because the yellow-haired firebrand was dear to the General and possibly because so furious an adherent was an embarrassment, McClellan obtained leave for his favorite who went back to Monroe.

Social barriers there that had seemed impregnable to a humbly reared lad and that even a wild young lieutenant had not ventured to scale were easily surmounted by a veteran soldier who was still a staff captain pending the War Department's further action. Custer was able to penetrate even those safeguards that the vigilance of the widowed Judge Bacon had erected about his only child.

They met under the benison of formal introduction and to punish him for his messages and perhaps for the rankling memory of him drunken, the slender dark-eyed girl was as coldly hostile as so gentle a being could be and, because she was so many things that he was not—timid and kindly and soft-hearted and unselfish—she straightway loved him. Under the forbidding eyes of her father, Monroe's foremost patrician, Elizabeth Bacon fell in love with the swaggering, strident Custer boy. Thenceforth he was her idol. All his life she asked no greater glory than his presence and she dedicated fifty-six years of widowhood to glorification of his memory.

She was his in spirit from their first meeting. She would be his wholly as soon as her father consented. Judge Bacon looked upon Custer with more than the normal animus the widowed father of one daughter displays toward her suitor. He disliked his prospective son-in-law and he forestalled Custer's plea for paternal sanction by sending for him and bluntly bidding him cease his attentions. Meekly the young man obeyed.

His wooing had none of the heart-stirring drive of his conduct in war. If he had fought no more recklessly than he made love, history would not mention him. Bacon in the double rôle of the town's leading citizen and the father of his beloved was sternly impressive authority, in the presence of which Custer always was humble and compliant. So he became now. He did not argue with the portentous judge. He did not try to defend himself. He carried out Bacon's instructions to the letter.

Frederick Whittaker, Custer's earliest biographer, who wrote under the guidance of the General's widow, hints that Elizabeth Bacon was ready to elope with her suitor. If so, Custer gave her no opportunity. No other man on earth ever awed him more thoroughly than Judge Bacon.

This rebuff was followed by another. It may have been the hope of impressing the Judge that led Custer to apply to Governor Blair of Michigan for command of the 7th Michigan Cavalry, then organizing. Blair refused on the ground that the applicant was a McClellan adherent. In mid-January, Custer was summoned by his chief and spent most of the winter with him in work upon McClellan's final report on his command of the Army of the Potomac.

Judge Bacon had not specifically forbidden the staff Captain to write to his Elizabeth but, during this absence, Custer sent her no line—he, the chronic letter-writer—save second-hand messages by way of a friend. When he returned briefly in March to Monroe, he paid violent court to another girl. His strategy may have been

GEORGE ARMSTRONG AND ELIZABETH BACON CUSTER
From a photograph taken shortly after their marriage, 1864
(Copyright, Cosmopolitan Book Corporation)

better than it appears at this distance but Whittaker assures us that his conduct affronted and disgusted Bacon.

Thereafter, Custer returned to Washington, still on "nominal staff duty" and remained there, idle and restless, until in April he was ordered to join Troop M, 5th Cavalry, as first lieutenant. His temporary captain's rank had been taken away.

Heretofore, the Union horse had been the most neglected and inefficient arm of the service. It was Hooker who had asked caustically, "Whoever saw a dead cavalryman?" and Hooker was now in command of the Army of the Potomac. He had swept together the scattered and aimlessly employed cavalry units and had bidden General Stoneman organize them into three divisions under Generals Pleasonton, Gregg and Averill. Shortly thereafter the first of these succeeded Stoneman. Custer's duty as a company officer was brief, for Pleasonton, on May fifteenth, invited McClellan's former aide to join his own staff and the Lieutenant accepted gratefully. The active and varied existence of an aide offered respite to one whom the routine of company administration galled. He bought a dog and an extra horse and prepared once more to enjoy the war.

The adventure his spirit craved came quickly. On May twenty-first he was detailed with seventy-five men to move out for Hooker on a secret mission, the exact purpose of which no one now knows. Custer was ordered to get across country to the Rappahannock near Urbana, capture a certain sailboat bound downstream from Richmond, and bring in its passengers as prisoners. He never revealed the reason for this foray, if he knew it, and history ignores it, but it at least gave him the activity and excitement a thwarted spirit craved. The embellishments Custer added to Hooker's mission may have been obscurely a retort to Judge Bacon's brusk dismissal and Governor Blair's implicit disparagement.

A steamer took him and his men down the Potomac and up the Yocomico River. The party landed at eleven A. M. and rode cross-country to the Rappahannock's shore where it hid all night in the woods, Custer's first employment of his later favorite strategy. On the morrow, the sailboat appeared. Custer and ten men chased it in a skiff and captured its crew and passengers, among whom were two women, as well as a quantity of Confederate money. He then launched into improvisation.

He saw a house, so he captured that. In a hammock slung on the veranda a Confederate officer smoked and read *Hamlet*. He looked up inquiringly at the red, hard-breathing enemy who had so suddenly appeared.

"You're my prisoner, sir," Custer barked. The other sighed and closed his book.

"Yes," he remarked resignedly, "I suppose I am."

There were many horses in the stable. Custer took these and then, to crown his achievement, rowed with twenty men across to Urbana, drove in a Confederate picket and burned two schooners and a bridge. He avoided a retaliatory blow by marching swiftly back to the Potomac and rejoined the army with twelve prisoners— he had confiscated a carriage so that the women might ride—and thirty horses. He had had a fine time and Hooker's thanks was its climax.

He was displaying no such resource and ardor in his courtship. It still was limited to messages enclosed in a letter to a friend in Monroe and relayed to his Elizabeth, who did not find warmed-over passion particularly palatable. When Custer's friend warned his principal that the lady grew cold, her suitor took the disastrous tidings with a singular equanimity. His reply was philosophical and adolescent:

"That time may come, perhaps soon. When it does come, I hope it will find me the same soldier I now try to be as capable of meeting the reverses of life as I am of war. You, no doubt, know me as well, perhaps better than any person in Monroe except Lydia and yet you know little of my disposition. You, fearing that disappointment might render me unhappy, are doubtful whether it is better for me to cherish the remembrance of one who is now to me all that she ever will be. I would think the same, were I the adviser instead of the person advised. Do not fear for me."*

---

* Whittaker's *Life*.

These sentimentalities may have been composed for the eyes of Elizabeth Bacon. If she saw them, they scarcely would have advanced his cause. In love, Custer held that a good defense was the best attack.

Henceforth for many weeks, he had little time for amorous strategy. The apathy following Fredericksburg and Chancellorsville had departed from both armies. Lee had cast a cavalry screen before his host and behind it there was movement progressing that worried Hooker. On June ninth he made his first attempt to break through that barrier.

Pleasonton's cavalry crossed the Rappahannock and strove to discover whether Lee aimed at Maryland or Pennsylvania. The staff officer whose long golden hair was crowned now by a wide straw hat took part in a multitude of inconclusive skirmishes between the Union horse and Stuart's riders. He had thirst for action that footless little engagements could not slake.

He may have believed that he sought renown as a retort to Judge Bacon and Governor Blair. He still worshiped the small deities of rebuttal and self-justification. He had not yet looked upon Glory, that urgent goddess who was to direct his existence.

For fame, the reluctant, he substituted braggadocio and grew tiresome, not over his accomplishments but his intentions. His favorite prediction: "I'll be a general before this is over" became an enduring jest among fellow-members of Pleasonton's staff. On June 17, 1863, the Lieutenant showed that his warrior spirit was not all vocal.

The Union cavalry still strove to learn the intentions of Lee who, behind the rampart of the Blue Ridge, was moving north. Stuart's horse shielded the Confederate right. At Aldie, a portion of his command met Kilpatrick's Brigade of Gregg's Division.

Judson Kilpatrick had a hard mouth, pale eyes, gingery sidewhiskers and disposition, and a Covenanter love of battle that equaled the later zest for conflict of Custer who was attached that day to his command. The Union leader deployed his brigade across the path of the Confederate advance and drove in the Gray skirmishers with carbine fire. Stuart charged.

He came hard and fast. The impact of his yelling troopers tore the Union line apart. There was confusion and the beginning of panic among the clattering pistols and the hard-swung sabers but Kilpatrick and Colonel Calvin S. Doughty rallied the troops, flung Stuart back and led a counter-charge. Close behind them, with heavy sword gleaming and voice uplifted, rode a youngster whose bright curls blew out behind a disreputable straw hat.

Guns were empty and there was no time to load. The dust was filled with the rasp of blades and the grunting yelps of men who wielded them. Kilpatrick's horse went down; Doughty fell dead, and the brigade followed a transfigured staff lieutenant who rode like a centaur and swung his long straight sword like a blacksmith. The Gray cavalry gave way; the Blue halted at last, breathless and victorious, but Custer went on.

He plunged deep into the ranks of the retiring enemy. For an instant steel shone in the dust where horses plunged and men yelled. Then Custer, waving a red blade, emerged and came galloping, breathless but unhurt, back to the reforming Blue brigade. He had been surrounded but in the confusion had whirled about and escaped, cutting down the single man who barred his passage. Luck and his hat had preserved him.

"I made my way out safely," he wrote to Lydia, "all owing to my hat which is a large broadbrim, exactly like that worn by the rebels. Everyone tells me that I look more like a rebel than our own men."*

He had joined the first saber charge of the Cavalry Corps. He had led its final moments which had won a hundred prisoners and a flag.

Here intrudes one of the puzzling gaps in the record of George Armstrong Custer concerning which history is silent. The men who might have explained it all are dead.

On June twenty-seventh, Custer, returning to headquarters from some mission, was hailed as "General" by his fellow-aides—

---

* Whittaker's *Life*.

"Good evening, General." "Let me congratulate you, General."

He flung himself from his horse and faced his tormentors with his familiar boast. "Laugh all you please," he invited. "I'll be a general yet before this is over. Wait and see."

Lieutenant George W. Yates, who later was to die with him at the Little Bighorn, laid a hand on Custer's arm and led him to his tent. On the table lay a long official envelope. It was addressed to Brigadier-General George Armstrong Custer.

The boy—he then was only twenty-three—turned pale, groped for a chair and sat down. At length, he managed to open the envelope. In it was his commission as brigadier-general of volunteers and orders assigning him to command of the 2nd Brigade of the Third Division, "the Michigan Brigade."

Governor Blair, who rejected my appeal for command of the 7th Michigan Cavalry, look at me now! I lead that regiment and the 1st, 5th and 6th Michigan Cavalry besides. Elizabeth Bacon and your austere, hostile father—I am General as I said I should be! That Custer boy is a general at twenty-three, youngest in the army and the war is not over. A General!

There were tears in his eyes when men pressed into the tent and wrung the hand of him who, that morning, had ridden out a first lieutenant.

Captain, major, lieutenant-colonel, colonel—he had rocketed past all these grades. Kilpatrick had been moved up to command of the Third Division. Captain E. J. Farnsworth of the 8th Illinois Cavalry, another of Pleasonton's aides, and Wesley Merritt, a captain of regulars, also had been advanced to the rank of brigadier. The chieftain of the Cavalry Corps must have felt sore need for young blood in command. There is no other discernible reason for Custer's elevation. The minor affray at Aldie had been the only thing approaching battle dimensions in which he ever had led troops and there his leadership had been impromptu and distinguished, like many of his later exploits, more by flaming courage than forethought. Yet for one obscure cause or many, he was general of the Michigan Brigade which shortly discovered, as other troops learned later, how strait and thorny was the way of the command that followed Custer to fame.

On the evening of June twenty-ninth, the new General joined his brigade at Hanover, Pennsylvania, with his horses and his dog, and two bugler orderlies from the 5th Cavalry. By morning, the Michigan Brigade was thoroughly miserable.

There was an echo of the now dead Kearny's harsh infliction of discipline in Custer's first orders. There also was irony, that he himself never discerned, in this spectacle of an erstwhile unruly and defiant cadet so vehemently reproving others' slackness. He gripped his easy-going brigade by the collar and shook it into smartness, officers and troopers alike, clamping upon volunteers the strict ritual of West Point, silencing their mounting protest by his own brilliance in battle.

That soon was to be displayed, for Lee was deep in Pennsylvania now and Chambersburg had burned and Hooker had been removed and Meade was chief of the Army of the Potomac that ponderously raced to head off the gray fox. On the morning after Custer took command of his brigade, Pettigrew's Brigade of the Confederate army, foraying from Cashtown in search of shoes, were driven by Buford's advancing cavalry out of the town of Gettysburg.

Chapter Five

FULFILMENT

HE WAS a general now. George Armstrong Custer may have believed he had fulfilled his ambition. He was to learn at Gettysburg that his miraculous attainment of each soldier's dream was not enough. He had been a lieutenant and then, suddenly, he was a general at twenty-three. The incredible and splendid fact did not assuage; instead, it spurred a fundamental craving. On that hot yellow head, laurels achieved withered quickly and the evaporating joy of gaining them quickened lust for fresh adornment.

Custer had been lifted to what he believed would be the summit of his career. He discovered on that eminence only a further upward road. Fame, like the erstwhile stinging bliss of the liquor he had forsworn, briefly slaked and then refortified a craving that demanded ever more clamorously, fresh draughts of fame.

It was his fortune to be whetted and oriented by war; to live during his first and formative professional years an existence that was predicated on the winning of renown. His elevation had raised him now beyond such petty distractions as retort to a hostile judge or an unwilling governor. The road that he saw before him led toward Glory.

Within a week after he had assumed command of the Michigan Brigade, Custer had seen her clearly for the first time. At Gettysburg, he looked upon her perilous beauty. He tasted the rapture of her favor and became for life her dedicated suitor. The rest of his biography is the tale of his quest for her.

On the ridges about the little Pennsylvania town, the massing forces of Gray and Blue clashed and surged that hot July first and north and east of the battle, beyond the Union right, Farnsworth's and Custer's Brigades of Kilpatrick's Division held the road that ran through Hanover lest Stuart, loose somewhere to the north, drive down upon the Federal flank.

They heard on July second the protracted low thunder of battle that raged about Culps Hill, The Peach Orchard and Round Top. Only the sound of conflict disturbed the waiting squadrons until at four o'clock that afternoon, Wade Hampton's Division of Stuart's Corps trotted down the road from the north.

Cramped by long waiting, eager to recapture the harsh thrill of Aldie, determined to show his hostile command the temper of its young leader, Custer charged Hampton. It was not his place as a general to gallop screeching and waving his hat at the head of Troop A, 6th Michigan, down upon the Gray advance. It was scarcely the rôle of a wise commander to assail the Confederate host with so puny a force.

Custer did not wait to learn the strength of the advancing enemy and his wild charge came close to being his last. The volleys of Hampton's riders blew the troop to pieces. Captain Thompson and many more were killed. Custer's own horse was shot. A Confederate bore down upon the prostrate General, gun raised. Trooper Churchill of the 6th Michigan shot him dead and gave his commander a lift back to safety.

Thereafter, when the broken remnants of Troop A had returned, the horse artillery batteries of Pennington and Elder opened on Hampton and drove him back, an expedient that might have been as profitably employed without the reckless charge which accomplished little save to inform the Michigan Brigade their new commander at least was no coward.

That night, Kilpatrick withdrew Farnsworth's Brigade to guard the Union left. Gregg's Second Division was to relieve Custer on the morrow and his command was then to rejoin Kilpatrick. Before Gregg arrived, Custer's horse batteries had long-range argument with guns of Stuart who was massing down the Hanover Road for further attack. This was designed to strike the Union rear as Pickett assailed its front. When Gregg came up, the Confederate force before him was so large that he ordered Custer to keep his brigade on the field. The young General disobeyed his orders from Kilpatrick and remained.

Early that afternoon, the rattle of carbines close at hand distracted men from the uneven roar of the distant battle. Stuart's skirmishers crowned a ridge to the north. Behind them, appeared dismounted Gray regiments. Gregg's 1st New Jersey and 3rd Pennsylvania, on foot, held up the advance with carbine fire in which Custer's 5th Michigan joined, pumping their repeating Spencers so rapidly that their ammunition soon ran low.

A mounted charge by Fitzhugh Lee's 1st Virginia bent the Blue line inward until the Gray met the 7th Michigan, advancing in column of squadrons. There was violent fighting along a rail fence where revolvers flamed in enemies' faces. The 7th Michigan was thrust back by the Jeff Davis Legion and the 1st North Carolina Cavalry, thrown into battle by Stuart. Again the 1st Virginia charged, but its yelling approach faltered as the Union artillery opened and the carbine fire of the 3rd Pennsylvania caught it on the flank. It fell back upon the brigades of Hampton and Fitzhugh Lee. These came on in column of squadrons, sabers drawn, alignment beautiful, despite hammering by Union shells. Custer charged them at the head of the 7th Michigan.

From his ornate report of that day's fighting, it would appear that he and the 7th Michigan alone broke the Confederate assault. "I challenge," he boasts, "the annals of warfare to produce a more brilliant charge of cavalry." He does not mention that Gregg's 1st New Jersey also struck the Confederate front nor that Gregg's 3rd Pennsylvania took Hampton and Lee on the flank. Colonel John B. McIntosh, commanding Gregg's 1st Brigade, also joined the assault with the fragments of other scattered units.

Custer's not entirely solitary charge may or may not find its superior in history but it is certain no Union force since the war began had smashed more heavily into an advancing foe. Bareheaded and whooping, he led the 7th Michigan at a hard gallop square into the Confederate line. The crash of the impact sounded above the tumult of guns and voices. Sabers flailed in the mess of plunging horses and screaming men. The Gray advance broke.

Stuart's cavalry fled up-hill and over the ridge and a yellow-haired youngster with the rapture of battle still upon him, rode back, shouting and waving his sword, to a command that had revised still further its original opinion of its new general. The Michigan Brigade lost two hundred and fifty-seven men, killed, wounded and missing, in the battle of Gettysburg.

There was no rest for Custer, now that the field was won. He rejoined Kilpatrick and all July fourth followed Lee's retreat through the rain. All day the Union horse pressed forward on the littered trail of the Confederate withdrawal and when darkness fell, continued to follow it up a mountain road to Monterey Gap. Here in the rain-swept blackness a gun opened upon the 5th Michigan that rode in advance and a subsequent blast of musketry threw the regiment into panic.

Custer's voice, shrill and piercing as a trumpet when launched full force, rallied his confused men. The charge he led cleared the gap and the 1st West Virginia and the 1st Ohio, riding on down through a thunder-storm, struck Ewell's train and captured many wagons. Kilpatrick reached Ringgold, just across the Maryland line, at daybreak and there halted briefly. Custer got two hours' sleep stretched in the mud beneath the dripping eaves of a church.

He had had his vision. He had known the stinging ecstasy of battle, not as one who swung a saber at a superior's behest, but as that superior himself. He had led men into conflict. He had seen hundreds, obedient to his will, scatter a foe and their triumph was contribution to his. For the first time in his careless and erratic existence, he had fathomed the gleaming profundities of Glory. She offered sustenance for a spirit that had starved for fame. She proffered battle, which was bliss, and the respect of his fellow-leaders, which was tribute, and public praise whose flavor was novel and sweet.

Kilpatrick's Division joined Buford's on the morrow, and there followed days of inconclusive sparring with Stuart's cavalry while Lee's battered army limped south. Meade was less energetic than Lee had feared and the Union horse, unsupported, could not break through Stuart, though on July seventh, Buford, with Custer's

GENERAL PLEASONTON AND HIS YOUNGEST BRIGADIER—1863

Photo U. S. Signal Corps

Brigade joined to his division, overwhelmed a rear-guard at Falling Waters, taking sixteen hundred prisoners, three flags and two guns.

Thereafter the wary Lee and the apprehensive Meade faced each other across the Rappahannock, feinting, sidling, shifting, while both armies recuperated. In the camp of Custer's Michigan Brigade life became riveted to a routine of drill, strict enforcement of all regulations and more drill as the General pursued his intention to make his men the equal of any regulars in the service. It is difficult to turn volunteers into regulars and retain their affection. The most that Custer ever received from any command he led was its respect.

Under the indulgent eyes of Glory, he burgeoned amazingly. While insisting that his men be forced into the mold of regulars, he evolved for himself a most irregular uniform. Modesty was not one of his virtues. The profusely embellished semi-brigand costume he adopted could never be forgotten by a beholder. Trousers were of black velveteen with twin gold stripes down the seams. These were tucked into high boots. The jacket was black velveteen too, and either sleeve bore a complicated adornment of looping gilt braid. Beneath this garment, Custer wore a navy blue flannel shirt. Either tip of its wide collar bore an embroidered star and, between these, drooped the wide cravat of scarlet which became the badge of his brigade. There was a gilt cord about his hat and another star on the front of its crown. Any one encountering so profusely asterisked and brass-bound a being would not have identified the shabby officer of a few short weeks before.

He assumed other perquisites permissible to his rank. At Amosville, Virginia, in August, he adopted a runaway slave woman, Eliza, and elevated her to the rank of brigadier-general's cook. She served him throughout the war and later followed him and his wife to the frontier. He also plucked from the welter of waifs and masterless who followed the army, a youngster, Johnny Cisco, whom to all intents he adopted.

This is one of the acts of kindliness that crop up so strangely in a man whom many deemed harsh and wholly selfish. The lad had run away from home and was half starved when he came to Custer's tent. The General befriended him and Eliza fed him. Johnny became a juvenile orderly to his patron. The boy in a miniature uniform rode Custer's spare horse in the column and waited on table in camp. The General obtained an enlistment bounty for his charge and invested it for him. At the end of the war he placed Johnny in a school from which the lad ran away, to appear eighteen months later at Fort Riley where Custer then was quartered. Johnny wanted to enlist so that he might be near his idol. The General dissuaded him and got him a job as a Wells-Fargo messenger. He was killed by Indians during one of the plains uprisings.

With his squire and his official cook who accompanied his marches enthroned in a battered barouche; with the scarlet, gilt and black nuptial plumage that proclaimed his espousal to Glory, the Boy General of the Michigan Brigade was one of the major spectacles of the Army of the Potomac.

Despite his elevation and his mounting renown, he does not appear to have besieged Elizabeth Bacon the more ardently or confidently. She still heard from him only by messages relayed through that unidentified John Alden in Monroe, to whom Custer wrote, and through the increasing notice newspapers accorded the precocious and picturesque young officer. It was war's fortune, not his own initiative that brought him back to her. He was not one to turn from battle toward even the woman he loved.

On September thirteenth, Pleasonton crossed the Rappahannock and raided toward Culpeper Court House. In the advance on the town, Custer's Brigade was on the left of the line. His command was checked by a deep creek on its front and in attempting to find a ford, the brigade became involved in a swamp. Its leader, seeing a train about to pull out of the station and intent on capturing it, deserted his mired command and galloped into Culpeper with the brigade on his right. His horse was killed under him and he himself was wounded in the thigh by a piece of shell. There is no record of what Pleasonton or the gingery Kilpatrick said to the subordinate who had left his brigade to fend for itself in an attack.

Custer's wound—the only one he ever received until two Sioux bullets killed him—earned him twenty days' leave and he returned to Monroe.

Each successive visit since the war had begun had seen him in a more august rôle. The furor of greeting to the young General swept away even the compunctions of Judge Bacon who managed to forget his earlier dislike and even invited the famous warrior to his home. This belated cordiality and the worship Elizabeth accorded her gorgeously uniformed suitor did not abolish Custer's dread of the doughty Judge. When he left for the front again, he was as nearly betrothed as a gentleman of that day might be who had not yet proclaimed his intentions to his beloved's father.

The Boy General told his half-sister, Lydia Reed, that he was determined to confer with Bacon on a tender subject. He had frequent opportunities but each time his resolution failed. His last chance came at the railway station platform where Bacon appeared to bid Monroe's hero farewell. Custer, who could face steel and lead with glee, gulped commonplaces and resolved that it would be better to write a letter. The thought of provoking that awesome presence even at long range haunted him. He wrote to a friend in Monroe from Washington, October seventh:

"I have thought much of my intended letter to Libby's father. My mind had been alternating between hope and fear, hope that my letter will be well received; that now, when all else appears bright and encouraging no obstacle will be interposed to darken or cloud our happiness. And yet I cannot rid myself of the fear that I may suffer from some unfounded prejudice. Oh, I wish some guardian angel would tell me what course to pursue to ensure her happiness and mine. . . . Tell my little girl I am so lonely without her. Kiss her for me and tell her I have been real good since I left her."*

Somehow, he fortified his morale sufficiently to write to Judge Bacon. His return to his brigade may have improved his self-confidence. On October ninth, he informed his confidant that the

---

* Whittaker's *Life*.

fatal letter had been mailed and then proceeded to erect a psycho-
logical trench system into which he might retire in the event of
rejection. He wrote:

> "Whatever be the sentiments of the world at large, I feel
> that here, surrounded by my noble little band of heroes, I am
> loved and respected. Knowing my duty, all that is then requi-
> site to insure success is honesty of purpose and fixed intentions
> or, to express the same meaning in different language, I have
> only to adopt the well known motto: 'First be sure you're
> right, then go ahead.' To this simple rule, framed though it
> be in humble language, I can attribute more than to any other
> my success in life."*

His letters at times make it easier to understand why some of
his contemporaries found George Armstrong Custer insufferable.
The two defeats that he sustained in the subsequent ten days
may have been due in part to the torment of waiting for the
Judge's reply. On October twelfth, Stuart nearly trapped Custer's
entire Brigade at Brandy Station during an unsuccessful Union
cavalry raid toward James City. There were Confederate squadrons before and more in the rear but the Glory-Hunter charged at
the head of the 1st and 5th Michigan and managed to cut his way
through. A week later, it was "Custer's luck" that saved not only
his own command but Kilpatrick's entire Division.

That unit moved out against Stuart, October eighteenth, and
scouted toward Groveton. It camped at Gainsville and pushed
ahead on the morrow. Stuart fell back artfully before Kilpatrick's
advance and the Union General quickened his pace, ordering Custer to keep up with the other brigades.

The Boy General, who cherished small respect for his superior,
argued that his men and horses were unfed and must eat before
continuing the pursuit. Kilpatrick rushed off without him on
Stuart's heels and Custer's halt near Buckland half spoiled the trap
the Confederate General had set. Fitzhugh Lee, sweeping in from

---

* *Ibid.*

the right to take Kilpatrick in the rear, stumbled over Custer's Brigade.

The sudden brawl of gun-fire behind gave Kilpatrick time to turn. Thereafter he ran, with Stuart in pursuit, and Custer ran too. All the Gray cavalry saw of the Union force that day was a manifold twinkling of horse-shoes in the dust. It was worse than a retreat. It was a rout in which the entire Third Division train, including Custer's headquarters wagon and his personal baggage, was gobbled up by Stuart who when the breathless Blue troopers had taken refuge behind the I Corps lines withdrew and called the rout thereafter the "Buckland Races."

The Michigan Brigade lost one hundred and fifty prisoners, including Major Clarke of the 5th Michigan. Custer in his letters blamed the whole disaster on Kilpatrick. This was the inglorious end of his 1863 campaign.

The letter from Judge Bacon came at last. It contained neither dismissal nor blessing. It might be months, the Judge replied, before he could make up his mind concerning an engagement by his daughter but "meanwhile she is at full liberty to communicate with you."

Thus, the floodgates were opened for Custer's torrential correspondence. Now that his dreaded antagonist had weakened, he refused to permit him to make another stand. The spate of letters to his Libby and her father swept Bacon into consenting to an engagement late in November. They were married, February 8, 1864, in the Monroe Presbyterian Church. The bridegroom had had his golden curls shorne for the occasion and appeared, not in his bizarre personally designed costume, but in the full uniform of a brigadier-general. He was accompanied by his entire staff. Their honeymoon was eleven days long, spent partly in Washington and partly in the camp of Custer's Brigade. From this, the bride returned alone to the capital.

Kilpatrick was embarked on a fantastic raid. He purposed to ride around the Confederate army, capture Richmond, release all Union prisoners held there and return in triumph to the Army of the Potomac. Custer with three thousand cavalry and infantry support was called upon to feint before Stuart, pinning him down while Kilpatrick carried out the wild scheme. The Glory-Hunter accomplished his mission, but ill fortune and the bottomless Virginia mud thwarted Kilpatrick who finally led his mire-daubed force down the Peninsula to the lines of Butler's army. He had accomplished little beyond the ruination of three thousand of his own horses.

Custer returned from his almost bloodless diversion before Stuart and rejoined his wife in Washington. She meanwhile had savored for the first time the cup of loneliness she was to drain so often during their life together, and deem each draught a trivial price to pay for the incredible joy of subsequent reunion.

Chapter Six

SHERIDAN

Winter, that had brought relief to other Union arms, had been less kind to the Cavalry Corps. This was still the stepchild of the army. Generals borrowed regiments to act as their personal escorts. The bounty-jumping racket was at its height. Recruits were deserting by the hundreds, at their first turn on picket. A sixty-mile line of cavalry videttes surrounded the Army of the Potomac to keep its infantry sentries from decamping.

Artillery, infantry, engineers were comfortably quartered. Cavalry huts were erected outside the main camp and troopers grumbled at the endless duty as orderlies, escorts, patrols, scouts. No one resented the arduous monotony more than the commander of the Michigan Brigade, whom reporters had rechristened "the Boy General with the Golden Locks."

Custer learned early that friendship with newspapermen was profitable. Newspaper praise burnished his glory. Newspaper partizanship helped to kill him and a member of the craft died with him.

Routine forever galled the Boy General, but the aimless industry of the Cavalry Corps had been particularly hard to bear. Officers of the other arms won extended leaves. Custer rarely got to Washington, where his wife waited and learned the prayer she was to offer hereafter in many winters: the plea that spring, harbinger of a new campaign, might be late in coming. Custer and Kilpatrick kept boredom at bay by matching the best horse-flesh in the Third Division against racers from other commands, but weeks went by slowly. In the capital, the stalemate irked another man even more grievously.

Hooker and Meade had paid heavy blood rent in the last campaign to keep the ground their army had held in the preceding spring. Abraham Lincoln was looking again for a general, not among eastern leaders who seemed foredoomed to failure or only half-success, but in the victorious West.

On March 10, 1864, a shabby man with a cigar half buried in his beard climbed down from his horse before Meade's headquarters. The army gossiped mildly over the arrival of Lieutenant-General Grant. It had had so many organizers of victory. Grant, it was learned, was not to replace Meade. The Lieutenant-General was to command all forces of the Union but would remain for the present with the Army of the Potomac.

But if Meade were not displaced, other officers were. Pleasonton was removed from command of the Cavalry Corps and sent west. A Major-General Sheridan succeeded him. Grant, the army knew by repute, but this was an obscure commander of whom most men had never heard—a westerner, a divisional general of infantry. The troopers' chronic mutter of grievance swelled into apprehensive babble when on April fourth, the new chief of cavalry arrived at Corps Headquarters.

He was brusk; he was long-armed and short-legged; he was thick of body, bullet-headed, with hard black eyes that, in the heat of battle, took a strange ruddy glow. Among the gaily habited officers at headquarters he was dingy in a deplorable hat and a war-worn uniform. Beside the velveteen and gold-braided figure of Custer, Sheridan looked like an orderly. There was a recklessness of carriage and speech about the picturesque youngster that puckered the new commander's eyes with the beginnings of approval.

From Sheridan, Custer withheld the blind adolescent worship he had bestowed upon McClellan. In all things, the blunt cavalry leader was Custer's opposite. He awed his subordinate and woke in the younger man an abiding respect. In his *Memoirs,* Sheridan speaks of Custer only as he mentions other officers of the Cavalry Corps, but the insurgent boyishness of the youngster quickened enduring fondness in his heart.

It was Sheridan who gave Custer his division. It was Sheridan who overlooked insubordinations by Custer with unwonted charity. It was Sheridan who twice in later years when his protégé was in disgrace, interceded to mitigate punishment.

Others beside the Boy General were awed by this truculent stranger from the West, who knew what he wanted and minced no words in demanding it. Sheridan could, his subordinate learned shortly, erupt into the most amazing profanity when crossed. His first orders eliminated the chief complaint of his new command.

Hereafter, he announced, the corps would not ride herd on pickets who otherwise might desert. The corps would not engage in aimless and futile reconnoitering. The regiments of the corps that had been detached to heighten the pomp of generals would be immediately recalled.

When he had retrieved his entire command, Sheridan set about reorganization. Buford, commanding the First Division, had died of illness. General A. T. A. Torbert replaced him. Custer and his Michiganders were transferred from the Third Division to the First, where they were teamed with Devin's and Merritt's Brigades. Gregg retained the Second Division but Kilpatrick, whom troopers had nicknamed "Kill Cavalry," was transferred, like Pleasonton, to the West, and J. H. Wilson took command of the Third.

Designedly or by accident, Custer was placed under a sober and careful chief who was the antithesis of the volatile Kilpatrick. The unbridled spirit of the Boy General was curbed further by the sobriety of his fellow-brigadiers—Devin, whom Grant later valued next to Sheridan as a cavalry leader, and Merritt, canny, and careful.

On May 3, 1864, the Army of the Potomac, recruited to full strength, splendidly equipped, accompanied by an enormous train of wagons, moved out of winter quarters and once more turned its face to the south.

Four colossal Blue dragons, the II, V, VI and IX Corps, crawled ponderously behind a screen of cavalry to try to thrust their bulk between Lee and Richmond. They moved through a land of scrub-oak and pine—The Wilderness. Beyond was ground fair and open for maneuvering, but before they were clear of the forest, Lee attacked.

Battle was joined in the woods where dogwood flowered, a blundering brutal fight of mistaken orders and costly delays. The blazing guns kindled last year's leaves and set the forest afire about the screeching wounded. Lee struck and feinted and struck again at a foe who took his punishment and came on and took more. There was power in this stranger's blows that hurt his defter opponent. Henceforth, the Blue would stumble forward and Lee would give way before them.

There was no place for mounted men in that literal inferno among the budding trees. There was dismounted, inconclusive volleying about Tod's Tavern where the Third Division went in on foot against Stuart's dismounted troopers—and held its ground.

On May seventh, Torbert's Division with Gregg's in support beat off Stuart's attempt to reach the Union wagon train. Meade peevishly complained of the cavalry's inability to suppress Stuart, and Sheridan, hearing his ill-considered words, took violent offense. Meade vainly attempted to soothe the fiery warrior, but Sheridan cast his command into the older man's lap. Sheridan was through. Let Meade run the cavalry hereafter, since he knew so much about it. Sheridan could whip Stuart any day, anywhere. The Cavalry Corps commander stormed away with a final childish explosion of overwrought nerves and Meade, hardly more maturely, carried word of the quarrel to Grant.

"Says he can whip Stuart, eh?" Grant reflected aloud and puffed at his cigar. "Then we'll let him go out and do it."

Sheridan marched at six on the morning of May ninth. Ten thousand cavalry rode four abreast in a column thirteen miles long down the Telegraph Road from Fredericksburg to Richmond. Guidons whipped in the morning wind. Sheridan's red and white headquarters flag with its twin stars shone in the van. Pack-mules brayed; the guns of the horse artillery clanked along; forage wagons rumbled. Thudding hoof, squeaking leather and the clatter of metal blended in the throaty roar of cavalry on the march.

There were none of the violent bursts of speed that heretofore had characterized the Cavalry Corps raids, and also had dislocated the regiments and used up horses. The column went forward at the steady, mile-eating walk that was to characterize all Sheridan's movement hereafter. Foremost rode the Michigan Brigade and at its head a youngster whose face was hardly less radiant than the newly risen sun. Spectacle and movement and peril ahead lifted Custer's effervescent spirit.

The column moved so fast and so unexpectedly that it had been under way two hours and was well beyond Lee's right flank when Stuart assailed its rear but was beaten off. The Confederate cavalry then swung wide and hurried on to get before the Union advance. This, late in the afternoon reached Beaver Dam Station on the Virginia Central Railroad where a prospect, surpassingly fair, presented itself to the yellow-haired commander of the foremost brigade.

There, at the station, stood trains and locomotives, duplicates of the treasures Glory had shown him the year before at Brandy Station, only to withdraw, and there was no marsh to delay Custer now. Down a straight road with its yelling leader in front roared the Michigan Brigade. At the first sputter of gun-fire, the train guards fled. Horsemen plunged up the line to capture the locomotives, cheered on by three hundred and seventy-eight passengers in one train—Union prisoners who had been en route to Richmond. Rations and medical supplies for Lee's army were found in another string of cars. These were burned and the railway tracks torn up.

Part of Stuart's force had reached the head of Sheridan's column the following morning. It was not strong enough to check the Blue advance. The Gray cavalry made no determined stand until May eleventh at Yellow Tavern six miles from Richmond.

Long after, Sheridan remembered how handsomely in the final charge of that fray a golden-haired youngster led his brigade against a battery—walk, trot, then a headlong run that went up and over the guns, taking two of them and shattering the Gray's line.

Stuart's counter-charge hit Custer. There were a few hot minutes of yelling and shooting in the dust and a Union sergeant, reeling through the fight, fired a blind shot from his Colt, and after this brief instant, passed unnamed from history. The ball pierced the liver of J. E. B. Stuart. Custer's men, reforming and coming again, almost captured the ambulance in which the retiring enemy bore their great leader, dying, toward Richmond.

The Blue column rested at Yellow Tavern until midnight. Through the rain-swept darkness they could hear the clangor of alarm bells in Richmond. The threatened hive was swarming. When the corps moved out through utter darkness Sheridan had fulfilled his mission. He had drawn Lee's cavalry away from the Army of Northern Virginia. He had met and beaten Stuart. He sought now the road to Mechanicsville, so that he might swing to the north of Richmond and keeping the city on his right, go down the Peninsula as Kilpatrick had ridden to join Butler's army there.

Before Mechanicsville, the bridge across the Chickahominy had been partly destroyed and Wilson's Third Division at dawn opened fire on a Gray force on the farther bank. Dread hovered in the misty daybreak. Nervous officers told Sheridan that he was surrounded:

"Surrounded!" the little chief snorted to Lieutenant Charles Fitzhugh of the 4th Artillery who had brought his guns into action at the bridge. "I could capture Richmond if I wanted to, but I couldn't hold it. Surrounded by a lot of department clerks! Take it easy."

While Fitzhugh's guns banged away at the unsteady force on the farther bank, Sheridan, recalling perhaps that headlong, whooping charge upon the trains at Beaver Dam Station, ordered Custer forward and watched with grim satisfaction while the eager boy dismounted his men and led them, leaping from stringpiece to stringpiece, across the bridge.

Carbines hammered briefly on the far shore. The half-hearted Confederate force fled and while Merritt's troopers repaired the bridge, a newsboy from Richmond who had sneaked out through the lines found his papers gobbled up at twenty-five cents each by mire-daubed officers in blue.

Impeded only by mud and fatigue, the Cavalry Corps moved

down the Peninsula, rested briefly in Butler's lines, and on May twenty-fifth, rejoined the Army of the Potomac near Chesterfield Station.

The pucker of approval in the eyes of Sheridan deepened as he saw Custer ride at the head of his Michiganders. The boy's theatrical uniform was soiled with mire and a stubble of red beard blurred the outline of his face but otherwise he seemed as fresh and eager as when they had marched out, three weeks before. Here was one subordinate at least whom Sheridan had tested and felt that he knew. Here was no strategist; but a tireless body and a mind as hungry for war as a bent bow. Custer was a weapon that Sheridan knew how to use.

Only two days later, when the army was crossing the North Anna River, Sheridan thrust Custer into action again. Gregg's Second Division, moving ahead as a screen, was held up by a strong Confederate force at Hawes' Shop. He appealed for reenforcements and Custer was sent forward. At Gregg's order, he dismounted his brigade but he added what glamour he might to the shabby business of a charge on foot. His troopers went forward in column of platoons with their band playing them into action. They were the spearhead of the attack that broke and scattered Confederate resistance.

Custer's Brigade, with the rest of Torbert's command, held the line at Cold Harbor at the dawn of that day of savage slaughter, until relieved by the VI Corps. The shock of the battle did not stun Grant, or turn his stony mind from its battering purpose. With all his power, he had beaten against Lee's front. He sent Sheridan now to strike him from behind.

Torbert's First and Gregg's Second Division slipped around the Confederate left flank and, marching fast, went northwest for the vulnerable railway lines beyond Richmond. These Sheridan was to cut and, joining with a cavalry force under General Hunter that had been ordered to sweep down the Shenandoah Valley to Charlottesville, wreak what havoc he might in Lee's rear.

Trevilian Station, on the main line of the Virginia Central, was Sheridan's first objective and as the column moved through a land scorched by war, Wade Hampton and Fitzhugh Lee hurried in pursuit. They overtook the Blue on the morning of June eleventh near the town.

Sheridan sent Custer by a crossroad to burn Trevilian Station and thrust him thereby into a day of scrambled and bitter fighting, as impromptu and delirious as a barroom riot. Who was blameworthy, none to-day can tell.

Custer, emerging from a byway onto the Louisa Court House-Gordonsville Road, stepped directly on the tail of Hampton's column and before the Gray horsemen could wheel about and give battle, had charged and gathered in wagons, horses and three hundred and fifty men. Prisoners and booty were rushed to the rear and thereby straight into the welcoming arms of Fitzhugh Lee's command. Custer had moved out of the side-road into an empty space between Hampton's and Lee's marching columns and now found himself enclosed by them. Lee's first charge recovered the plunder taken by the Michiganders and also swept away Custer's train, caissons, headquarters wagon and, for good measure, Eliza herself, in the ruinous carriage she occupied on the march. She later escaped and rejoined her employer.

There was a panicky rattling of carbines on the Gordonsville Road and a frantic banging by Pennington's battery. The rebel yell soared as Lee burst through Custer's disorganized rear and captured a gun. Pennington, appearing before the frantic General, reported gravely:

"They've taken one of my pieces, sir, and I think they intend to keep it."

Custer's strident voice soared:

"Keep it! I'll be damned if they do."

The lash of his speech whipped into line some thirty men. At their head, he charged the Confederates who were dragging away the gun. A volley blew him back, but the raving leader in dust-blurred velveteen and gold organized another charge and recaptured the piece. He could not have held it, nor could his command have survived if Torbert and Gregg, pressing upon Hampton's left, had not distracted most of the force organizing to overwhelm the Michigan Brigade.

Even this diversion left Custer outnumbered and isolated. Hard-pressed on all sides, he formed his command in a hollow triangle and beat back the Gray attacks. In this peril, he remembered the demands of melodrama and when his color-bearer was shot down beside him, ripped the flag from its staff and hid it in his jacket.

Late that afternoon, Torbert was able to extricate the isolated brigade. During the night, the Confederate horse fell back to take up a stronger position on the road to Gordonsville. Sheridan, learning that Hunter's advance had been blocked by Early and that Breckenridge with heavy force was at Gordonsville, did not press the attack further but, after tearing up the railroad at Trevilian Station, returned, unmolested, to West Point on the York River and shortly thereafter to Lighthouse Point.

CHAPTER SEVEN

SHENANDOAH

WITH shell, with mine, with battering-rams of men, Grant beat upon the door of Petersburg. His blows did not burst it, yet the portal cracked and bulged. Lee sought to relieve the growing pressure upon it by striking in his turn at the vitals of the Union.

Early, the dour, with twelve thousand men went down the Shenandoah Valley, beating Hunter, beating Sigel, beating the scratch force that Lew Wallace had assembled at Monocacy Junction and actually exchanging long-range shots with the outer forts of Washington itself. His force was too light for permanent invasion, but the speech of distant guns turned political bombast at the capital into more candid squeals of panic and Grant was obliged to detach the VI Corps from the Army of the Potomac for Washington's protection.

Early retired, yet when vigilance slackened he came again. His cavalry burned Chambersburg and returned triumphantly to the Shenandoah. The mounting wail of terror threatened to wreck Grant's solid purpose and demolish the trap he was building about Lee. Some one must be sent into the Shenandoah, that valley of humiliation for so many Federal generals, and block it against further Confederate forays.

That lovely region had been, since the war's beginning, a continual threat pointed at the Union's heart. From Harper's Ferry, where the Shenandoah River joins the Potomac, it ran southeast behind the barrier of the Blue Ridge, a wide trough of farmland checkered with grain-fields, rich in orchards, dotted by comfortable dwellings whose inhabitants when the Gray columns plodded past, fed haggard soldiers from their plenty.

The gaunt foot cavalry of Jackson had ranged the valley. Among the bodies that returned to earth there were buried also the reputations of sundry Union leaders. Generals had marched in from the north with vainglorious self-confidence and shortly thereafter had emerged in a cloud of dust, with their coat-tails straight out behind. Banks, Shields, Fremont and other lesser chieftains had tasted the humiliation the Shenandoah visited on invaders and, more recently, Hunter and Sigel had joined their bruised and breathless brotherhood.

In that fair valley a festering guerrilla warfare never ended. Partizan rangers lived off the country, were sheltered by Confederate patriots, and made life an enduring nightmare for Federal commanders by a series of raids and ambushings. Generals, badgered, pestered and abased, lost their heads and embarked on reprisals that were as much personal revenge as military expediency. Early had fired Chambersburg in revenge for Hunter's house burnings.

And now, in mid-summer of 1864, spies brought word that Lee had sent Anderson to reenforce Early. There would be, so the tidings ran, a further, more redoubtable invasion of the north to break Grant's stranglehold upon Petersburg.

On August seventh, Sheridan was made commander of the newly organized Army of the Shenandoah. He became chief—over the protest of Washington authorities who said that he was too young—of eighteen thousand infantry, including the VI Corps, and thirty-five hundred cavalry. Of the latter, Torbert's First Division was the largest unit.

Perhaps the debate over Sheridan's youth—he was then thirty-three—may have led him to show special favor to the ardent youngster of twenty-four who led a brigade under Torbert. Custer worked hard and long in the subsequent months to further his chief's enterprises, creditable and discreditable alike. He emerged from that campaign with his fame enhanced, though certain portions of the increment wear a dubious tarnish. Many of the outrages committed officially by Union troops in the Shenandoah were ordered by Custer, with or without the immediate sanction but always with the subsequent approval of Sheridan himself.

Custer was young and youth is heartless. His conduct in the Shenandoah can not be dismissed so glibly. The man was emerging from the erraticism of boyhood into the enduring form of maturity. For a time this summer, he had attempted to conform to the lamentable fashion of the age and had grown a set of flaming side-whiskers. These were soon discarded, possibly because glory and such adornments were difficult to reconcile. He had cropped his flowing locks, also, though later he wore again his yellow mane. The velveteen and gilt comic-opera costume remained, but this, too, was to be discarded soon. The man of the future was emerging and to that adult outline clung more than a hint of cruelty. Custer had the beauty and the ardor and the utter ruthlessness of the sword and much of that weapon's simplicity. Whatever thwarted him, whatever abashed or discomfited that saber-like ego must suffer reprisal that was Mosaic, without even the scant mercy of Leviticus and Deuteronomy.

He was, on the testimony of his wife, a fond and tender husband. He was a sentimentally devoted son. He loved his own horses and dogs and the multitude of other pets he collected. All these were George Armstrong Custer's and therefore sacrosanct. His imagination did not reach beyond the egotistic radiance that encircled him and his possessions.

Custer still wore the sword of the first man he had killed—the man whose death throes he described so zestfully. Neither he nor the subsequent victims ever stirred in him the slightest qualm. He could have ridden gleefully and well in the ceremonious slaughters of medieval knighthood. He possessed that outworn chivalry's generosity to vanquished foeman. He had not yet acquired, indeed, he was never wholly to learn, the more modern virtue of losing gracefully. His conduct in the Shenandoah presages Washita and, more obscurely, that red Sabbath on the Little Bighorn.

Custer's heart must have sung as the Army of the Shenandoah moved out to sweep the valley clear. Ahead was rolling open country, burned brown by the drought of 1864 yet ideal for cavalry warfare. Behind him rode his red cravatted Michiganders to whom had been added the 25th New York Cavalry. The flat roar of hoofs quickened pulses and he looked, under a chief who favored him, toward Glory. He had not yet encountered Colonel John Singleton Mosby.

Union soldiers, in the months to come, were to call Colonel Mosby a ruffian and murderer. He was neither. He was a duly commissioned officer of the Confederate Army who served under the direct command of J. E. B. Stuart and, after his death, of Lee himself. In an age more given to balladry, he might have become a rival to Robin Hood.

Like his prototype's men in Lincoln green, Mosby's butternut troopers had no base for a heavy Blue foot to crush. The men of the 43rd Battalion, Virginia Cavalry, were quartered throughout the valley in the homes of patriotic residents. They met at Mosby's order, raided, ambushed or attacked, and dissolved like a spent raincloud. Far ahead of his day, Mosby envisaged the modern purpose of cavalry. His was not a weapon of strong offense but a scouting, delaying, enemy-pestering force. The rangers had discarded the romantic saber in favor of two revolvers per man. They were as evasive as fleas and they stung like hornets.

Mosby was one of the first problems that Sheridan sought to solve. Shortly after he took command of the Army of the Shenandoah he organized under Major H. K. Young of the 2nd Rhode Island Infantry a corps of scouts as a ranger antidote. In the matter of masquerade, Sheridan went at least half-way to meet Mosby.

"These men," he says artlessly in writing of his scouts, "were disguised in Confederate uniforms whenever necessary."[*]

The scouts were efficient rascals. They started the era of looting that endured throughout the valley campaign and won for the whole Cavalry Corps the half envious title, "Sheridan's Robbers." There have been less accurate epithets applied to armed forces. It is hard to teach men that the slaughter of uniformed enemies is virtuous and, at the same time, make them believe that mere theft from ununiformed foes is wicked.

---

[*] Sheridan, General P. H.: *Memoirs,* New York, 1888.

Sheridan's scouts could not check Mosby who, even while the Army of the Shenandoah was advancing into the valley, jumped the wagon train, burned a hundred wagons and vanished with a mass of mules, horses, cattle and prisoners. This and subsequent depredations ruffled the dignity and injured the pride of Union officers and quickened in Custer, at least, the exasperated anger which demands that some one, even the innocent, suffer. Sheridan, at this point of the campaign, was too worried to harbor wrath.

Early had been reenforced. Grant sent more infantry and Wilson's Third Cavalry Division and later Gregg's Second to strengthen the Blue lines. Torbert became chief of cavalry and Merritt, Custer's fellow-brigadier, took command of the First Division. Still, Sheridan refrained from weighty attack. Early and he feinted and advanced and gave way up and down the lower end of the valley like cautious boxers, while the cavalry screens before the armies met in numberless skirmishes.

On August sixteenth, a victory by Custer near Cedarville made him forget momentarily the galling attentions of Mosby's men. He charged a brigade of Anderson's command as it was crossing the Shenandoah, taking two stands of colors and three hundred prisoners, but Sheridan was in no haste to follow up this minor success and withdrew down the valley again.

As he retired, he employed for the first time the policy he and Grant had evolved. The Shenandoah Valley had been called "the granary of the Confederacy." That granary must be destroyed. Early's scouts, following Sheridan's retreat, marched through the smoke of burning barns, past farms from which all live stock had been taken. The Union cavalry did not accomplish their destruction unscathed. On August seventeenth, Confederate horsemen overtook the Third Division, beat it soundly and chased it out of Winchester.

On August eighteenth, a detail of Mosby's men penetrated Custer's camp, killed one picket, wounded two and escaped with two prisoners. At Custer's order the 5th Michigan moved out to burn in retaliation, neighboring farmhouses. There was nothing to connect the owners of these with the attack of the preceding night but there seemed no other way to spend the anger Mosby had quickened. Nor did his aimless revenge materially soothe the young General's feelings. Rangers surprised a detachment of the 5th Michigan at their houseburning and killed or wounded eighteen.

The canny sparring of Early and Sheridan endured. The Union army, after a first brief advance into the valley, had fallen back to a strong defensive line at Halltown. While the North muttered over Sheridan's lack of initiative, the little General stayed where he was. He knew that the large force at Early's present disposal could not long be retained. Soon enough the flagging man-power of Lee would make it necessary to recall Anderson's command. So he waited, while Grant's grip tightened at Petersburg and Early hesitated, reluctant to attack on ground of Sheridan's choice.

He did, on August twenty-fifth, try to get around Sheridan's right with four divisions. Merritt's cavalry met him and again was roughly handled. Two of its brigades extricated themselves in time but Custer's command was almost captured and when it broke free, was chased across the Potomac. It did not get back to the main army until the next day. Glory, in the Shenandoah, seemed as hard to capture as Mosby.

On September fourteenth, Lee recalled Anderson's command. On September eighteenth, Sheridan moved up the valley against Early at Winchester. The Confederate left flank rested upon the Opequan River. The cavalry, with Custer in advance, were to cross the stream and attack, while Sheridan thrust his infantry at Early's center. The other brigades headed for a lower ford; Custer for an upper. He found Gray troopers and infantry on the farther bank.

From the crest of a hill commanding the ford, the 6th Michigan pumped carbine bullets across stream and under this protecting fire, the 25th New York and the 7th Michigan advanced. They broke in mid-river and splashed back helter-skelter when volleys from rifle-pits, heretofore hidden on the far shore, burst the water about them.

It was Custer's voice that beat down the momentary panic and reordered the chaos of soaked and swearing troopers. It was his shouted order, more stirring than a trumpet blast, that sent his most trusted regiment, the 1st Michigan, forward. The charge foamed across the Opequan and went screeching up the farther shore. Sabers flashed and revolvers stuttered among the rifle-pits and the enemy retired to a prepared position, running back at right angles from Early's line.

Shells from Custer's horse artillery sped their withdrawal and through the banging of the guns, the cavalry could hear the unevenly pulsating roar of battle at Winchester. The other brigades of Merritt that had crossed lower down appeared on Custer's left. The line formed and went forward against the Confederate position.

You see this garishly uniformed boy with his face afire and the stridor of brass in his voice at his best now. Battle has possessed yet lifted him. His is neither the rage nor the drunkenness that blurs some minds in conflict. His passion ennobles even his body. Men who are his enemies hate him the less after they have seen him in action, so radiant is he, so divine in the absence of fear or uncertainty. You see him at his best now, when few could excel him.

Charges by the 1st and 7th Michigan and the 25th New York bucked the Confederate line. It bent and fell back toward the boiling guns at Winchester. The young centaur with his heavy saber in hand and his face like flame above his charger's blown mane trumpeted the order that swung his brigade wide to strike the enemy's rear.

Lomax's cavalry barred his way an instant. Its volleys did not check Custer's headlong charge. Union sabers slashed Gray troopers who had no swords. They broke and fled.

The Union horse goes in upon Early's endangered left flank to the jolting music of its mounted bands. Flags flutter above the advancing brigades. Below is the shine of bared sabers and the gigantic shadow that the setting sun casts before the host. The Blue wave routs the Confederate cavalry out of the ditch where it has paused to do battle and slams it in like a burst-open door upon the backs of its own infantry. Custer spurs forward, whooping and waving his hat, with the rest of Merritt's Division.

The shock of the cavalry attack breaks the back of Confederate resistance. Early flees with Sheridan in pursuit till darkness falls. On the morrow the Federal chief drives his foe from a strong defensive position on Fisher's Hill and the next day from Mount Jackson.

From Port Republic to which the shattered remnants of his force escape, Early clamors to Lee for reenforcements. Sheridan has cleared half the valley of the enemy. Custer has helped win the battle of Winchester. Each will appear presently in less heroic guise.

CHAPTER EIGHT

FIRE AND ROPE

MOSBY lay at Lynchburg with a bullet in his groin, token of a fight on September fifteenth with Colonel Gansevoort's 13th New York Cavalry. For a brief space, the Union forces believed him dead and then lost interest in that academic question for his spirit continued its disruptive way. Mosby might or might not be dead but ambushings endured, raids still struck Federal baggage trains. Such enterprises, Mosby's men told one another, would hearten their wounded leader. They were far less soothing to Sheridan and his generals.

The victory at Winchester had not entirely soothed Custer's ruffled pride. Defeat in open battle he might endure, but there was implicit mockery in the depredations of Mosby's men. They drove in suddenly. They drew blood and vanished. Theirs were the tactics of the gray wolf—or the Indian. Such bloody ridicule disparaged Custer's prowess.

His spirit had no heavy armor. It was easily hurt by derision. The corroding irritation of guerrilla warfare ate quickly through the scant protection that lay above his ego and revealed the raw actual character beneath. Mosby's modification of Indian warfare wrought small actual damage to Custer's Brigade but inflicted grievous injury on its leader's self-esteem. His dealings with Mosby's pseudo Indians afford some interpretation of his later slaughter of actual red men. The smarting of injured pride rationalizes, though it may not pardon, what happened at Front Royal, September 23, 1864.

On that morning, Captain Samuel Chapman, commanding the rangers in Mosby's absence, attacked a Union train, rolling down under escort toward Front Royal. The screaming Gray troopers were driving in the guard when Chapman marked the approach of a heavy body of Union cavalry and ordered immediate retreat. This was easier to command than accomplish, for the Blue squadrons closed in fast and the revolvers of Chapman's one hundred and twenty men had to blast a path to freedom. In the retreat, Lieutenant McMaster of the 2nd United States Cavalry was killed.

It has been said that he was slaughtered after he surrendered. It has been said that he led a detail to cut off the rangers' retreat and was killed at the head of his command, sword in hand. It has been said that he got inadvertently in the way of the fleeing Confederates, was run down and slain. Whichever tale is the truth—and none of them may be—McMaster died in the confusion and heat of battle when a sorely outnumbered force was fighting to escape.

Not all the rangers escaped. Six were captured—a man named Carter, Thomas F. Anderson, William Thomas Overby, Lucien Love, Henry C. Rhodes and David L. Jones, all duly enlisted privates in the Confederate army. Four of the prisoners were shot; two were hanged. Their execution was ordered by George Armstrong Custer, and carried out under his eyes. He apparently suffered no qualms then or later. He was one of the doomed men whose judgment always is right.

The day before, Mosby troopers had captured two couriers bearing dispatches to General Custer. They had also made a prisoner of his orderly who carried half a sheep, presumably for the General's mess.

The village of Front Royal witnessed the execution. Until recently, there were still men and women alive there who had seen it. Custer had his band play the dead march while Anderson, Love, Rhodes and Jones were shot. Carter and Overby were hanged on a tree, midway between the north end of the town and the Shenandoah River. On Overby's breast was pinned a message that read: "Such is the fate of all Mosby's gang."

Mosby's command at that time had a number of Union prisoners. Some of the rangers urged that six of these be executed at once, but it was decided to await the return of their convalescent leader before launching reprisal.

In a report to Lee from Middleburg, Virginia, October 29, 1864, Colonel Mosby proclaims his own intention. This letter also blasts any possible pretense that the men executed by Custer's order were not prisoners of war but spies or murderers. Mosby writes:

"During my absence from command, the enemy captured six of my men near Front Royal; these were immediately hung by order and in the presence of General Custer. They also hung another in Rappahannock."—This man was hanged by Brigadier-General William H. Powell, October thirteenth, and not at Custer's instance.—"It is my purpose to hang an equal number of Custer's men whenever I capture them. There was passed by the last United States Congress a bill of pains and penalties against guerrillas, and as they profess to consider my men within the definition of the term, I think it would be well to come to some understanding with the enemy in reference to them."*

This document bears endorsement by Lee, as follows: "Respectfully referred to the honorable Secretary of War for his information. . . . I have directed Colonel Mosby, through his adjutant, to hang an equal number of Custer's men in retaliation for those executed by him." J. A. Seddon, Secretary of War, has added: "General Lee's instructions are cordially approved."

At Rectortown, Virginia, November 6, 1864, Mosby assembled twenty-seven prisoners, all taken by his men in raids on Custer's command. Lots were drawn and the seven who drew marked bits of paper from the hat were condemned to die. They were sent off under guard to be hanged as close to Custer's headquarters as possible.

It was a black night, with rain, and one of the prisoners managed to escape in the darkness. Accordingly, the party halted near Berryville on the Winchester Turnpike. Five of the remaining six were hanged. There was no more rope. A ranger tried to kill the sixth with his revolver. It missed fire. The last prisoner plunged

---

* Williamson, J. J.: *Mosby's Men*, New York, 1909.

into a thicket and got away. A note written by Mosby was pinned to one of the dangling bodies. It read:

"These men have been hung in retaliation for an equal number of Colonel Mosby's men, hung by order of General Custer at Front Royal. Measure for measure."*

Mosby then wrote to Sheridan.

"General: Some time in the month of September during my absence from my command, six of my men, who had been captured by your forces were hung and shot in the streets of Front Royal, by the order and in the immediate presence of Brigadier General Custer. Since then another (captured by a Colonel Powell on a plundering expedition into Rappahannock) shared a similar fate. A label affixed to the coat of one of the murdered men declared that 'this would be the fate of Mosby and all his men.'

"Since the murder of my men, not less than 700 prisoners including many officers of high rank, captured from your army by this command, have been forwarded to Richmond, but the execution of my purpose of retaliation was deferred in order, as far as possible, to confine its operation to the men of Custer and Powell. Accordingly, on the 6th instant, seven of your men were by my order executed on the Valley Turnpike, your highway of travel.

"Hereafter any prisoners falling into my hands will be treated with the kindness due to their condition, unless some new act of barbarity shall compel me reluctantly to adopt a line of policy repugnant to humanity.

"Very respectfully your obedient servant

"JOHN S. MOSBY."†

"No further 'acts of barbarity,' " Mosby comments simply in his *Memoirs*, "were committed on my men."

There is no record that Custer's revenge, the savage reprisal of

---

* *Ibid.*
† *Ibid.*

a smarting spirit, received any reproof from Sheridan. Custer ordered the six killed, September twenty-third. On September thirtieth, he took command of the Third Cavalry Division, replacing Wilson who went to the armies in the West.

Custer was not yet twenty-five, yet in everything save actual rank, he was a major-general of volunteers. His promotion from brigadier did not come till April 15, 1865, but he was leader now of three thousand horse. Though there is little to indicate that his new responsibility sobered him, it at least modified his dress. Perhaps it was a sense of fitness, perhaps it was a hint from the shabby Sheridan, that abolished the baroque uniform of velveteen. Hereafter Custer rode in regulation blue and yellow, plus the wide hat, sailor's shirt and flaring red cravat, plus also the heavy gilt arabesques on his jacket sleeves. These, he would not abandon.

He was still his commander's willing and punitive arm. On October third, Lieutenant John R. Meigs, Sheridan's engineer officer, was killed inside Union lines by three men, possibly rangers, possibly bushwhackers. The General ordered all houses within a radius of five miles burned and it was Custer who saw to the burning.

The fires kindled that day were to spread the length of the Shenandoah, for Sheridan now sent out his cavalry to cauterize the valley, to sear it from end to end so that no army henceforth might live upon its produce. "When I'm finished," the little General boasted, "a crow won't be able to fly through the Shenandoah without carrying his own rations." Merritt and Custer undertook the mission of desolation.

Early, dourly waiting reenforcements, dared not venture far from his Blue Ridge lair to oppose the Union horse. These, under Torbert, chief of cavalry, swept the valley with a broom of fire. Confederate munitions at Staunton went up in flame and smoke. Custer and Merritt wrecked the Virginia Central Railroad. They set fire to the bridges at Waynesboro and went down the valley with scrupulous violence, burning barns and confiscating all live stock. If houses caught fire from the blazing outbuildings and innumerable civilians were made homeless, if along with the stock other more negotiable articles were taken away, that, after all, was the fortune of war. Troopers took pride in the title Sheridan's Robbers. They devastated the valley from Staunton to Winchester leaving wailing homeless behind them. Angry Confederate cavalry followed, too weak to attack the raiders until in early October their leaders, Lomax and Johnson, were reenforced by the horsemen of Rosser, a truculent general and an intimate of "Fanny" Custer at West Point.

First notice of this alumni reunion was served on Custer October eighth, when his former fellow-cadet unfraternally attacked his rear, taking some battery forges and wagons. Rosser harassed him the rest of that day while Lomax and Johnson's cavalry trod on the tail of Merritt's column. That night, Sheridan visited Torbert's headquarters near Woodstock and gave his chief of cavalry succinct orders: "Whip 'em or get whipped." Morning saw the Federal cavalry faced about to fight.

Blue and Gray horse watched each other across open country, gay with the trappings of autumn. The Confederate horse artillery crowned a low hill and before it dismounted, troopers raised a breastwork and manned a stone wall.

The divisions of Custer and Merritt wheeled into line, a long wall of restless horses and war-tried men. In the unendurable instant of waiting before the advance, Custer galloped out in front of his division on the left. He reined in his charger. The sunlight glorified the excited, quivering animal; the long-haired medieval figure, sitting him so surely. Sun flashed on Custer's bared head as he bowed low in the saddle to his old-time friend and present enemy, a gesture direct from that ancient time when battle was still a ceremony.

"That," Rosser told his staff, "is 'Fanny' Custer. I'm going to give him the licking of his life to-day."

Custer wheeled and returned to his waiting troopers. There rose the harsh sigh of sabers unsheathed. The line moved forward, at a walk, at a trot, at hard gallop, with the Boy General whooping it on from in front.

The charge swept the Gray cavalry back but did not break them.

The Confederate leaders, when the Blue squadrons had been shaken apart by swift motion, suddenly made a counter-charge. Rosser, Lomax and Johnson might have won a smart victory had they pressed pursuit, but when they had regained their lost ground they entrenched again and Custer and Merritt, coming a second time, smashed into them, tore them apart and chased Gray troopers for miles, taking everything on wheels they possessed except one gun.

Custer always spoke of this engagement as the "Woodstock Races," probably as poultice for memory of other "races" contrived by J. E. B. Stuart at Buckland.

Woodstock, like all battles in this year of Gray decline, was the victory of the strong and well-equipped many against the ill-armed, ill-fed few. With the death of Stuart, the Confederate cavalry began its decline. When food is scarce for men, horses are bound to suffer more, and food for human or beast was scarce now in the Shenandoah. Early in his report of the Woodstock fight comments:

> "The fact is the enemy's cavalry is so much superior to ours, both in number and equipment, and the country is so favorable to operations of cavalry that it is impossible for ours to compete with his. . . . Lomax's cavalry is armed entirely with rifles and has no sabers, and the consequence is they cannot fight on horseback, and in this open country they cannot successfully fight on foot against large bodies of cavalry."

Yet Early had not succumbed to despair. Reenforcements had reached him from Richmond. And Rosser still cherished toward Custer the disrespect born of early familiarity. On October seventeenth, the truculent cavalryman arranged a surprise party for his classmate.

Custer held a position on the right of Sheridan's army, now encamped at Cedar Creek. Rosser's horse and a brigade of infantry attacked his flank—or where his flank had been—early in the morning. The Gray might have rolled up and broken the Third Division, but orders received the night before had moved Custer's command and Rosser's raid gathered in only a single picket. Custer's luck still prevailed.

On October nineteenth, Early himself came against the Union left flank with greater fortune. He struck Crook and blew his division away. Screeching scarecrows ranged through the camp and the cold flame of panic enveloped Sheridan's army. It fled and in that blind stampede only the cavalry and Getty's Division of the VI Corps retained their integrity. All wagons, all guns save the horse artillery, were taken. Early might have blasted the Army of the Shenandoah out of the valley and existence if his own men had not been hungry. Abundant food, not bullets, shattered the Confederate advance.

Deaf to their officers, regiments broke ranks to gather in the blessed Union stores, and Sheridan, returning from a conference in Washington, rode up from Winchester and reformed his lines. With Custer riding hard on the right flank and Merritt on the left, he descended upon the plundering army of Early and swept it away. Sheridan recaptured all the guns, all rolling stock that had been taken and twenty-two of Early's cannon as well, with many prisoners.

The cavalry, that night, hunted the scattered Confederates as far as Fisher's Hill. Next morning, with Rosser guarding his rear, Early fell back to New Market. He tried to stand there, but Custer's and Merritt's charges and the advance of the Blue infantry routed him and he retreated, with only a remnant of his original force, beyond Woodstock. The barren Shenandoah would see him advance no more.

Thereafter, the campaign smoldered out in futile cavalry raids. As a mark of Sheridan's favor, the young General of the Third Division was sent to Washington to present to the War Department flags taken from the enemy in the Shenandoah. These were borne by the men who had captured them. The comfort that the imminence of winter always brought to a dark-eyed girl who waited in the capital, blazed into joy at tidings of her husband's approach.

Mrs. Custer hurried to the War Department to meet him and he, oblivious to his orders, sent his flag captors on to Secretary Stanton while he went to his wife's dwelling and, finding her gone, searched the city for her. When Custer finally arrived at the War Department, the banners had been presented and Elizabeth Custer, egged on by Stanton, had faltered a substitute for the address her husband was to have made.

Winter closed down. Sheridan established headquarters at Kernstown. On December nineteenth, the Third Cavalry Division moved against Early to distract his attention while Torbert with Merritt's horse raided the Virginia Central Railway. Custer was jumped by the redoubtable Rosser at Lacy's Springs and chased down the valley, losing a number of men as well as horses and equipment.

Cold rain flattened the ember heaps in the valley and mud grew deeper. Elizabeth Custer came to her husband's headquarters at Winchester. Her soft voice, her dark loveliness, the appeal of her fears, the pathos of her valor, brought admiration into Sheridan's hard black eyes. The General and his staff dined with the Custers and once, after riding back to Kernstown at night, discovered that the Third Division of Sheridan's Robbers had stolen the fine blankets and bridles belonging to their chief and his officers, leaving their own in exchange.

That winter, through deft wire pulling, Custer obtained a commission for a private of Ohio infantry and added him to his own staff. Tom Custer was less bedeviled by ambition than his elder brother. His nose was sharp and humorous. His narrow eyes were merry and his mirth had more gaiety than shrillness. He tweaked at peril's whiskers for the sheer joy of exploit rather than to win Glory's attention. The brothers rode side by side through danger all the rest of their days and in their death they were not divided.

Merriment dwelt in Custer's headquarters that winter while the rains fell. Early, like a spent wolf, clung to his lair far up the charred valley that would never again see Gray regiments swinging northward. Libby and Tom and Autie chased one another through their dwelling in wildly hilarious games of tag, while the cavalry waited for spring and about the shattered town of Petersburg, Grant's lines drew closer.

CHAPTER NINE

FIVE FORKS

IT RAINED long and hard in the spring of 1865, lifting the brick-hued rivers, holding the armies before Petersburg in the inertia of ever-deepening mud. Cannon spoke with blunted voices in the wet air. Shells that plunged into or out of the beleaguered town spread a ruin of mire, wet and red like riven flesh. Shudders of musketry ran up and down the forty-mile line of trenches.

These stretched, like a crazily drawn capital J from Ord's Army of the James that held the Charles City-Richmond Road, southward to where the Army of the Potomac had half enfolded Petersburg. On March 19, 1865, mire-daubed cavalry emerged from the downpour on the Union right flank. Haggard men, weary horses seemed molded from the sanguine earth through which they plowed. Half the troopers slogged along on foot, for the march had used up more than three thousand horses. This was Sheridan's cavalry. It had destroyed the remnant of Early's army at last; it had broken the Virginia Central Railroad, cut the James Canal and had swung around the defenses of Richmond to join Grant.

All winter the two cavalry divisions remaining to Sheridan had recruited and re-equipped. On February twenty-seventh, the superb units moved out of Winchester by the valley pike. General Thomas C. Devin led the First Division; Custer, the Third. Merritt had replaced Torbert as chief of cavalry.

The Shenandoah was abject now. The troopers splashed on to Staunton without opposition. On a ridge west of Waynesboro, Early, with a scant two thousand men far less valorous than he, barred farther advance of Sheridan's eight thousand cavalry. He had been forced, since the Shenandoah had been ravished, to send away his cavalry and most of his artillery horses. There was no forage for them. There was no heart in his soldiers.

Merritt sent Custer forward with Devin, the bulldog of the cavalry, in support. The victory was almost bloodless. Pennington's Brigade of the Third Division struck Early's left flank and the feeble Gray front gave way when Custer launched direct attack. Sixteen hundred of Early's two thousand were captured and the beaten General barely escaped across the Blue Ridge with a handful of men. Few on either side were killed in this battle that, actually, was precipitate surrender.

Floundering on through the mire, Sheridan wrecked the line of the Virginia Central for miles and cut the James Canal. Bridges across the river had been destroyed and the stream was too high to ford. The hard little General abandoned his plan to lay a pathway of ruin clear across Virginia and then join Sherman in the Carolinas. He turned instead toward Petersburg.

Movement in the mud's cohesive grip was nightmare. Mules and horses lurched belly-deep and wagons rolled on hubs when they progressed at all. The column reeled into the remount station at White House, exhausted, not by battle but by Virginia's rain-softened soil.

While Merritt refitted his divisions, Sheridan rode to City Point.

Here was Grant, grimly satisfied. He now had adequate horsemen at hand for the hunt, when Lee broke cover. With Grant was a gaunt giant whose face was as melancholy as the rain-flogged spring, whose mirth was as sudden and incredible as flashes of March sunlight, who took more joy in his little son, Tad, than in the promises of his generals. Abraham Lincoln had heard like assurance for five springs now.

The chance for victory seemed bright, yet so it had appeared each March since 1861. Sherman had come up from Goldsboro, North Carolina, present end of the furrow his army was plowing through the Confederacy. Sherman was confident. He had whipped Joe Johnston once again at Bentonville, yet the Gray army, battered but still intact, hovered about Raleigh. Sherman could unite with Grant in a few weeks' time and then——

Merritt's troopers, remounted and re-equipped rode out of White House Landing and on to City Point. There, Sheridan muttered confidences to his division commanders that drew a nod of approval from Devin and kindled odd light in Custer's blue eyes.

"Trouble ahead," troopers muttered. "Look at Old Curly."

"Drunk?" a recruit asked as Custer rode by, hair flying, face suffused and twitching.

"Drunk," a veteran scoffed. "Naw. He smells a battle."

Battle was near. Grant would not wait for Sherman. The Army of Potomac had penned Lee in Petersburg. It claimed the right to drive him into the open and finish him. Drive it must. It could not delay until the gray fox moved. Let the Blue army tarry; let the rain-dissolved roads grow passable, and Lee would be away. He would evacuate Petersburg, sacrifice Richmond and slant down into North Carolina to join Johnston. Lee knew, and Grant was aware he knew, that hope for victory was spent, but with a Confederate army still free in the field, the war might be dragged on to negotiated peace. The North was almost as sick of conflict as the South.

Sheridan's troopers rode from City Point and on March twenty-seventh camped in the mud. Crook's Second Cavalry Division, Army of the Potomac, joined them just behind the left tip of the Union fortifications. The wagon trains came in, toiling through the mire. The wine of imminent action ran through Custer. He fretted and fumed through the day, and at night sat late in his tent, writing enormous letters to his wife. Men laughed and said that this newly-wed devotion would pass. It never did.

Rain muted the voices of trumpets, calling "the General," on that twenty-ninth of March. It pelted troopers, standing to horse, and drummed loudly on the covers of supply wagons whose wheels already were deep in mire. The trumpets sang again. Mud, sucking beneath trampling hoofs, squeaking leather and the beat of metal on metal rose in a jangling roar. Whips popped in the wagon train and mules brayed. The red and white headquarters pennon of the General Commanding beat out through the storm. A great column of sodden horsemen followed, riding by fours, with rain blackened guidons and banners and the headquarters flags of Devin, Crook and Custer flapping torpidly above them. Sheridan's cavalry, ten thousand strong, was heading out again.

Their strategy was simple. Their course lay toward Lee's right flank. Theirs would be the first blow in an offensive that, Grant hoped, would smash the Army of Virginia.

West of the Confederate lines that covered Petersburg lay vital arteries—railroads and highways—which, if severed, must end secession in Virginia. The Southside Railroad, toward which Grant had fumbled only to be driven back the preceding winter, served Petersburg. West of the beleaguered city, at Burkesville, the Southside crossed the Richmond and Danville Railroad. This ran from the Confederate capital to North Carolina where Johnston feinted before Sherman's advance. Cut these railways, and Richmond must fall. Block the highways leading west and south, and Lee would be penned in at Petersburg without chance of escape.

The sodden troopers who passed through Reams Station that morning followed by an already lagging wagon train, were literally an animate stick thrust forward by Grant to prod the fox from his hole. They plowed along a horrible road through drenched land, scarred by old battles. In the rear where the wagons swayed and stuck, the Third Cavalry Division with its frantic Boy General struggled to get the mired mule teams forward. It was Custer's ill fortune this day to act as rear-guard. His shrill voice, his frantic energy could not move the wagons through Virginia's mud.

There was battle ahead. Custer could smell it. Crook's and Devin's commands would find a fight while his own troopers sank over their boot-tops into glutinous ruddy mire and heaved at the wheels of bogged wagons and swore at drivers who reciprocated, and strove to obey the shrill voice of their commander who shouted more exhortations than an army corps could have followed. Until the wagons reestablished contact with the command, Custer must stay here, clogged in the mud. Desperately, he began to corduroy the road.

All night long, axes rang and trees went down and were stripped of branches for burial in the mire. Foot by foot, the train crept forward. The troopers of the Third Division got little sleep. They swore that their frenzied commander got none. And still the rain came down.

There was cavalry skirmishing beyond Dinwiddie Court House on the thirtieth. The village, so suddenly smothered by wet and angry troopers, was the southwest point of a triangle.

North from Dinwiddie and paralleling a swollen stream called Chamberlayne's Run, a mud-stifled road ran through forest to Five Forks, the nexus of highways southwest of Petersburg. The second side of the triangle, the White-Oak Road, ran north and east from Five Forks to Lee's fortifications. The triangle's third side was the Boydton Plank Road slanting down from Petersburg to Dinwiddie. Beyond Five Forks and the White-Oak Road lay the vital Southside Railway.

The cavalry bivouacked a second night at Dinwiddie, all save the Third Division. Its troopers and their almost demented leader continued their struggle to bring the wagons through. The rain ceased. The corduroying, the hauling, the wrenching and tugging went on. On the mist-choked morning of the thirty-first, when the banging of carbines rose, was followed by the crash of musket volleys and then boiled higher, Custer must have wept in his agonized desire for deliverance from mules that bogged and wagons that rolled forward for half their lengths and stuck again. The sound of battle grew.

Release was at hand for Custer. Defeat in the first step of the campaign was imminent for Sheridan. Crook's Second Division had held the lines beyond the village that morning. At ten, out of the gray fog came more solid forms in gray, horsemen who yelled while the sparkle of gun-fire ran along their front.

For a hundred yards north of Dinwiddie, the ground is high and clear. Then it slopes down into a broad jungle of scrub pine. In these woods the cavalry of Fitzhugh Lee and Rosser have jumped Crook's command. Carbines and pistols yammer in a contest, half battle, half hide-and-seek. Infantry form behind the Gray cavalry and, charging, break through Davies' Brigade of Crook's command, blowing it back in confusion upon Devin's First Division that has been held in reserve. Panic spreads. Devin and Davies stampede to the Boydton Road, east of the court-house. The rest of Crook's troopers retire on foot in better order, slipping from tree to tree, banging away at infantry who are forming for another advance.

This is part of General Anderson's Corps—Pickett's and Johnston's Divisions and Wise's Brigade. No better infantry march with Lee, and to stay them Sheridan has at hand only the two brigades of Crook's Division—Smith's and Gregg's—that already are heavily involved in the woods below the hill-crest. There is a courier running his horse down the Boydton Plank Road, toward Custer among the wagons.

Below the hill-crest, where smoke and mist have woven artificial dusk, the rattle of firing endures. Smith and Gregg need more men. Sheridan has no more. He gives them music. The Union bands form upon the hill before Dinwiddie Court House.

"Play," the furious little General has bawled at their leaders, "and keep on playing."

The latter half of the battle is fought to discordantly blended tunes. *Hail Columbia, Johnny Fill Up the Bowl, Hail to the Chief* and *Yankee Doodle* are brayed loudly and simultaneously by the musicians upon their gray steeds. Until the sun goes down and the fight ends, these stout-lunged heroes continue their anthems.

But the fight has not ended yet. It is growing ever more violent. Smith and Gregg have been forced almost to the edge of the woods. The rebel yell soars above the clattering gun-fire. Sheridan is watching the Boydton Road, with the red battle light in his eyes.

"Hah," he exclaims at last, and curses softly in satisfaction.

The sun has burned away the fog. Its late light glorifies an advancing column of horse, moving with the deliberate haste of the mud-clogged toward Dinwiddie. It is not Devin or Davies. These still are trying to reorganize their demoralized troopers farther along the road. Yet cavalry are riding hard through the mud and at their head is a horseman with red cravat and golden hair streaming. Custer with Capehart's Brigade of his division has arrived.

Pennington's Brigade is only a little behind. Wells's has been left with the wagon train.

There is small time to lose. No one ever had need to spur Custer. Capehart's men are building a breastwork of fence rails along the hill-crest. The guns of the horse artillery, silent so far this day, are trained on the wood's edge. Smith emerges from the jungle and swarms up the slope, Gray cavalry in pursuit. A volley from the impromptu entrenchment drives the enemy back. Gregg follows Smith to the temporary safety of the barricade. Pennington's Brigade comes in on heaving mud-plastered horses and takes its place in line.

In the woods, they are lifting the rebel yell. Sheridan, Merritt and Custer gallop along the Union front. The headquarters flags above them are no more brilliant than the youngster's face. At last, he has the rôle for which his spirit has hungered. From grueling labor among the wagons, he has galloped to the rescue of his chief. No dramatic entrance could have been more spectacular or better timed. Custer waves his hat and laughs as breathless cheering from Smith's and Gregg's Brigades rises above the stubborn dissonances of the bands. Glory enfolds him and yonder at the wood's edge, where the enemy infantry is forming, waits the promise of more.

The setting sun transfigures those who strengthen the weak barricade. Brisk musket-fire breaks out in the thickets below. Sheridan's cavalry reserve their ammunition and only the garbled harmonies of the bands reply. These are made still more discordant by the wounding of an E-flat horn player.

Gray dusk and Gray regiments are gathering. The rebel yell rises. Out of the thickets sweeps a long line of infantry, bayonets shining in the odd half light. Lord's battery opens. They come on through bursting canister. Sheridan turns to Custer who nods eagerly and wheels his horse. Above the advancing tumult, Sheridan's voice snaps as he calls his headlong subordinate back.

"You understand," he reiterates, and Major Tremain of Crook's staff hears him, "I want you to *give* it to them."

Custer's gesture is half assent, half impatience.

"All right, all right, all right," he rattles. "I'll give it to them," and his charger kicks up clods as he spurs away. His strong shrill voice shouts commands to his waiting squadrons. They mount. With a whoop and swing of his hat and a wave of his sword, Custer launches his charge.

It never passed the Union line. It broke apart as it started. The troopers of Gregg and Smith stared in disbelief while the mounting yell of Custer's riders faltered and broke into howls of dismay. Horses went down and men flew headlong. Custer's thunderbolt sputtered out in a riot of bogged animals and overthrown men.

He had paid no heed to the soggy slope, pocked with mud-holes, that lay between him and the onsweeping wave of Gray. No cavalry could move over such a quagmire. Custer had seen only the enemy infantry toward whom he yearned, and now, two-thirds of his effectives were in a hopeless welter of mired and floundering horses. Yet, his luck held.

"Some prudent and better informed subordinate," Tremain records, "forseeing this emergency, had prepared a dismounted battalion to meet the advancing rebels and they were yet held at bay. Custer withdrew his troopers and quickly disposed them to fight on foot."*

They fought well, to compensate for earlier ignominy. The repeating Spencers spouted, "like Roman candles" in the twilight. The Gray charge faltered and withdrew.

The Confederate infantry had accomplished half their purpose. They had driven back the presumptuous column that Grant had thrust out to get behind Lee's right flank. Now they held it at bay. To-morrow . . .

That night, Grant moved to meet the morrow. Mackenzie's cavalry from the Army of the James and Warren's V Corps from the Army of the Potomac marched toward Dinwiddie, where Custer held the lines beyond the court-house, and behind his brigades, creaking and rumbling, the accursed wagon trail rolled in.

Lee's men had come against Sheridan, that afternoon of March

---

* Tremain, H. E.: *Last Hours of Sheridan's Cavalry*, New York, 1909.

thirty-first, from entrenchments they had raised along the White-Oak Road to shield the vital highway junction at Five Forks. As the morning of the first of April dawned, with stars above and mud below, the slow advance of Warren's V Corps imperiled the left of the temporary line the Confederates held beyond Custer's outposts. The Gray fell back deliberately from Dinwiddie and along their retiring front, Merritt's Cavalry Corps—the bulldog Devin and the staghound Custer—skirmished.

The Confederate retirement was the deliberate withdrawal of the roused bear. Battle flared and died and blazed again in the murky woods as Pickett's and Johnson's infantry turned and stood and fell back again. Ahorse when possible, dismounted when the jungle was too thick, the men of Devin and Custer drove the foe along with nagging carbine fire, but the Gray regiments presently would be driven no farther. Across the Union front rose the fortifications at Five Forks. Cannon and musketry checked the Blue advance.

Warren's Division groped toward the Confederate left flank. There was delay that reiterated appeals from Sheridan's aides and, presently, the blistering words of the little warrior himself did not hasten. Merritt's troopers held the front. Warren's attack hung fire.

Late in the afternoon it was launched. The cough of musketry volleys was signal for Devin who held the center, and Custer on the right to redouble their fire. The Gray reply was vigorous. Powder smoke rolled in a thickening cloud over the White-Oak Road. The din elated the youngster. He fumed and begged Merritt for the order to charge.

In the woods on the Confederate left, Warren's infantry blundered. Panic rose as Gray volleys blasted Ayres' Brigade. There was delay and further confusion that Sheridan himself beat down. He relieved the sluggish Warren of his command and put Griffin, a divisional general, in his place. The reformed Blue columns, with Mackenzie's cavalry in support, overwhelmed the eastward end of the Confederate entrenchments, and moving westward, rolled up the defense.

Before Merritt's dismounted troopers, the firing faltered. To the grim Devin, to the fidgeting Custer, came the command to attack, dismounted. Devin obeyed completely. His division and one brigade of Custer swept forward to the works. The Boy General chose to misunderstand or revise his superior's order. Glory never shone most brightly on a mere infantry charge.

> "Custer," writes Major Tremain who saw the battle, "was ordered to dismount his division and send them forward. He dismounted enough to comply with his orders, pressed them to the front and sent two mounted brigades still further to the left, to strike the enemy's rear."*

It is hard to understand how one-third compliance can be construed as military obedience. Here was insubordination as grave as that for which, earlier, General Warren had been deprived of his command. Warren's delay threatened Sheridan's plan. Custer's cavalry charge brought no later, verbal reproof from Sheridan. It won him instead fresh glory.

The Blue horsemen who galloped at the Confederate line found themselves opposed by cavalry under Fitzhugh Lee and the Confederate infantry of Terry and Corse. These checked and flung back Custer's charge.

"Custer," Sheridan says in his *Memoirs,* "gained little ground, until our troops, advancing behind the works, drove Corse and Terry out."

But thereafter in the hunt of fugitives through the gathering dusk, the men of the Third Cavalry Division, being already ahorse, surpassed all other troopers. His completion of the Confederate rout mitigated Custer's offense. Custer's luck still held. All his days Sheridan was to make excuses and allowances for his headlong, headstrong junior. For his semi-insubordination at Five Forks Custer received the brevet rank of Major-General, United States Army.

The pursuit returned at last to an army rocking with the exulta-

---

* Tremain's *Last Hours of Sheridan's Cavalry.*

tion of victory. Already Colonel Newhall of Sheridan's staff was hurrying with the tidings to Grant at Dabney Mills. Six thousand prisoners with all their train and artillery taken; muskets in such numbers that they were being used to corduroy roads. More than this, the defense that had shielded the Southside Railroad had been stripped away. Lee's right flank would be turned if he remained in Petersburg.

Cannon roared along Grant's line as Newhall rode back to Five Forks. Their distant tumult could be heard in Sheridan's camp, where fires blazed and battle-scattered commands reunited and Custer, scribbling fast, informed an anxious woman who waited in Washington of his part in the day's victory.

Early on the morrow, April second, Meade's frontal attack went up over Lee's Petersburg fortifications.

CHAPTER TEN

VIEW HALLOO

LEE was loose. His front had burst in and Sheridan's horse and foot threatened the Gray right flank. This was defeat. It was not yet complete disaster. Much must be sacrificed, but the Army of Northern Virginia might still be saved.

There was fighting in Petersburg all that bright Sunday. There was fighting to the west of the doomed town where Miles's Division of the II Corps, temporarily under Sheridan's command, went forward cheering beneath blossoming fruit trees to break a Confederate force at Sutherland Station and cut the Southside Railway.

In Richmond, an aide tiptoed up the aisle of St. Paul's church to the pew where Jefferson Davis prayed and whispered in his ear. Petersburg was falling. The capital of the Confederacy must go too.

Across open farming land west of Sutherland, Griffin's VI Corps trudged at Sheridan's order to Ford Station on the Southside Railway, driving in farther against Lee's right flank. Before the exultant infantry, Merritt's horsemen skirmished over drying meadows with Confederate cavalry who would not stand long enough to gratify a Glory-Hunter's craving. The cavalry camped that night beyond the Southside, where Namozine Creek flows turgidly north to the Appomattox River. Bands played triumphantly in the bivouac and men wrung one another's hands and proclaimed that the war was over. Not while Lee was loose.

Smoked from his lair, hard pressed but not yet desperate, the gray fox was loose and running. Fainter-hearted men saw more clearly the impending doom. Lee still strove to shake his army free from the pursuit. No time for feint or stratagem now. Haste

100

was the only expedient whereby the Grays' forty thousand might be saved from a hundred thousand foot, horse and artillery that closed in. By haste, the few might outstrip the many and, circling south beyond Sheridan's advance, unite with Johnston in Carolina.

Three roads had led thither and even now, one of these had gone. The Southside Railway from Petersburg had been cut thrice by Miles, Griffin and Merritt. The Richmond and Danville Railroad farther west had not yet been reached by the Blue advance. Beyond that as a last possibility, the Prince Edward-Danville Pike offered escape by foot to the south.

It was the Richmond and Danville for which Blue and the Gray raced now. Lee marched rapidly west along the Appomattox River. Behind him, trudged Grant's heavy columns and on the Confederate left flank, Sheridan hovered. Musketry of the Gray rear-guard brawled with Union skirmishers early on the morning of April third, as the last of Lee's regiments swung out of Petersburg. Shoulder to shoulder, Sheridan and the Army of Northern Virginia ran for the Richmond and Danville line.

On the morning of April third, General Weitzel's Blue regiments marched in through the gloom of burning Richmond. All that day, the Army of the Potomac trod on Lee's heels and, south of the Gray retreat, Sheridan's horse and the V Corps went westward.

From the fleeing army, stragglers and deserters by the thousand fell into Sheridan's hands. Lee's host was crumbling away as it marched. Custer gathered in many and found the still organized units his division attacked discouragingly eager to surrender. At Namozine Church, he skirmished with Gray horse who fell back, but not before Tom Custer, whooping through the fight, had captured a Confederate battle flag.

Much of the Union cavalry's prowess in this last campaign was due to the shattered morale of the Confederate horse. The sword that Stuart had wielded was blunt. Animals and men were gaunt and tired. Heart remained in the Confederate infantry. This arm kept until the end a surly dangerous élan, but the splendid Blue squadrons scattered the Gray with little effort.

"At this stage of the war," Colonel Newhall writes, "it was not considered necessary for our cavalry to make very elaborate preparations to meet the enemy's horse; we outnumbered them and 'had the morale on them.' "*

That night, Sheridan camped on Deep Creek, still between Lee and possible escape to the south. So lax was the starved army that Young's Scouts were able to take a leaf from Mosby's book, kidnap Brigadier-General Barringer, and bring him into the Union camp. Meade with the VI and II Corps and Ord with the XXIV from the Army of the James were pressing Lee's rear. Scarcely a day's march ahead of Sheridan lay the vital line of the Richmond and Danville.

He marched at dawn. Crook's Division hurried on to cut the railway. The V Corps followed. Merritt with Devin and Custer slanted away to the north to strike the Gray army and, if possible, delay its flight. At Tabernacle Church, they attacked Lee's toiling wagons guarded by infantry and cavalry. Custer charged; Devin charged. They could not break through that slowly moving wall and drew off at last, shaken by the bitter gun-fire.

That afternoon, Crook reached the railway, tore up track, and halted at Jetersville Station. The V Corps and Merritt's cavalry joined him there. The second possible line of Lee's escape was closed to him now, unless he attacked in force. All night, while his men entrenched, Sheridan feared Lee would come. At dawn, when the first regiments of the Army of the Potomac that had marched all night, reached Jetersville, Sheridan hoped Lee would attack. The Union army, well fed and equipped and uplifted by imminent victory, was outmarching its enemy. Lee was too canny a soldier to send his starved legions against the massed strength of the Blue at Jetersville.

The gray fox is almost spent. His sides are heaving. He runs on, ever to the west. He can not turn south. The pursuit has blocked his passage thither. Only the road through Farmville to

---

* Newhall, F. C.: *With Sheridan's Cavalry in Lee's Last Campaign*, Philadelphia, 1866.

Danville remains equivocally open and Blue infantry are outfoot-
ing Lee. Ord and his corps, with Gibbon second in command, is
ordered to hurry north and west to Farmville. Capture of this
village will shut off Lee's escape. The Army of the Potomac follows to crush him and Sheridan's cavalry, emancipated at last
from the pace set by foot sloggers, is sent to harry the Confederate
retreat, delay it as much as may be or get ahead of it and hold
it for Meade to finish. Wright's VI Corps, comrades of Sheridan's
Robbers in the Shenandoah campaign, will follow the course of
the horsemen and attack whatever segment of the retreat the cavalry succeeds in halting.

Light rain envelops Jetersville on the morning of the sixth.
Crook has the advance. His squadrons slop away into mist while
Devin of the First Cavalry Division and the eager commander of
the Third, wait Sheridan's order to advance. It comes at last. The
fours move out through the falling drizzle and the regiments of
the VI Corps take their hoof-churned trail.

The rain ceases. A red spring sun looks down on a steaming
land. Custer's nostrils twitch and he writhes in the saddle as
ahead, through thinning mist, sounds yelling, the brisk popping of
carbines and the brusk retort of musket volleys. Crook has struck
Lee's line of march. He has charged it and has been repulsed, for
the men who convoy the mire-dappled, hurrying wagons are veteran, truculent infantry of Ewell's Corps.

These tried regiments guard Lee's rear. Humphreys' II Corps
is on their trail. Their surly lines are too strong for cavalry alone
to break. From a hilltop, Sheridan surveys the long Gray serpent,
twisting away down Deatonville Road, nagged in the rear by Humphreys' skirmishers. Somewhere in that hurriedly crawling line,
there must be a flaw that cavalry can find and, charging, crack open
into disaster. Sheridan keeps Stagg's Brigade of Crook's Division
and Miller's Battery but sends the rest of his horse and guns ahead
to test the Confederate line. The burly little commander grins as
the Third Division moves off with Custer, whooping like a boy released from school, riding magnificently at its head. Then Sheridan goes into action with his single brigade and battery.

Shells from Miller's guns burst on the Deatonville Road. Men and mules fall, wagons break above fountains of mud and fire. There is confusion. There is delay. These are heightened by a charge from Stagg's Brigade. A blaze of musketry throws it back. As the scorched cavalry retire, Seymour's Division of the VI Corps reaches the field, deploys and goes into action.

The attack is too heavy for the Gray rear-guard to stand. There is a four-corners on the Deatonville Highway. Some of Ewell's regiments fall back along a road at right angles to the course Lee's main command is pursuing. This, Sheridan learns, leads to a village north and west called Appomattox Court House.

The General leaves Humphreys to chase this fragment onward and, with the VI Corps, hurries along the highway the wagon train has taken. There is the reiterant roar of firing far ahead. Custer, Devin and Crook are trying to smash the moving Gray line.

The VI Corps and Stagg's Brigade emerge from a woodland. They are at the foot of a wide plateau that rises to a tree-crowned crest beyond the ruddy waters of Sailor's Creek.

Gray skirmishers swarm along the creek. The wagon train is stalled on the Deatonville Road. Across the plateau to bar a farther Union advance, Ewell's Corps deploys for battle. Starving and weary, they can run no farther, but they can still fight, breaking the Blue pursuit, if possible; holding it in check long enough, in any event, for the train to get away. Bread they have not, but there are still powder and ball. Legs and lungs are spent; not hearts.

The sputter of musketry swells into the crackling roar of battle. Wright's Corps crosses the creek. The Gray line bends, stiffens and moves forward, yelling. Sheridan swears sulphurously as Seymour's Division is flung back. Ewell's starvelings are breaking the Union line.

Above the battle-cloud, where gun-fire flares, a distant pillar of black smoke rises into the cleaner upper air from wagons ablaze on the Deatonville Road, and some one shouts that Blue cavalry have appeared on Ewell's right and rear. . . .

Meanwhile Custer, Devin and Crook have moved along the flank of the retreat, each division charging in turn and when beaten back by the blaze of gun-fire from Anderson's dogged infantry, passing behind its brother divisions, to reform and charge again, farther along. Repeated blows halt the wagons but fail to uncover a weak spot. By noon, Custer believes he has found it.

The Third Cavalry Division is well ahead of Ewell's rear. Gray infantry, defending the stalled train, seem fewer here. Custer's two light field pieces open. He dismounts one regiment that blazes away while the rest of his command forms for the charge. Out of the scrub it comes, a screeching tumult of horsemen, red cravats fluttering behind the sheen of steel. Ahead, whooping shrill glee and swinging his heavy sword rushes a stripling, splendid as a figure from Froissart. Across the downward slanting field, Custer leads his squadrons at the enemy line.

This holds its fire until the first ranks almost reach the wagons. Then flame and smoke spout, thundering. Horses go down; men pitch from the saddle. The charge is blown away. The rebel yell rises, shrill, defiant, as the Third Division reels back to the protection of the woods. Behind the discomfited troopers, their leader rides, his trumpet voice already exhorting them to another charge.

It is not mounted men who break the wagon train's defense. West of the field over which Custer has charged, the soberer, cannier Crook had dismounted Gregg's Brigade of his division in woodland close to the Deatonville Road. As Custer retires, Gregg's troopers pump their seven-shot Spencer carbines into the train and then charge afoot. There is screaming and the rattle of pistols among the wagons. Mules with traces cut gallop out of the woods and a smoke pours up where Gregg's men are burning the train. Cavalry, galloping in, gain the road. There is brief fierce fighting among the wagons. Out of it, a horseman who reels in the saddle, whose face is masked in scarlet, trots toward Custer, shaking a Confederate battle flag.

"He shot me," Tom Custer babbles to his brother, "but I got it."

The ball of the Confederate color-bearer, now dead, has driven through his cheek and come out behind his ear. Tom waves the

tattered banner about his head and is deaf to his commander's plea
that he seek a surgeon. Custer has to place his wounded brother
under arrest to get him off the field. For this trophy and the flag
he took single-handed at Namozine Church, Tom later is awarded
two Congressional Medals of Honor.

Fellow staff members drag him away, still protesting, and Custer
turns to gathering up his command. There is no time for plundering now. Beyond the hills to the north, battle boils along Sailor's
Creek. Flame climbs up the wagon covers. Crook, Devin and Custer assemble their divisions and ride toward the sound of the guns.

These were raging furiously on either side of the roiled waters
of Sailor's Creek. Seymour's Division had been thrown back across
the rivulet in confusion, but on both flanks of the Confederate line,
the rest of the VI Corps was closing in. There was bayonet work
in the powder fog. The fight was nearing that taut battle moment
when one or the other contestant breaks. A member of Sheridan's
staff looked up to the tree-crowned crest beyond the creek, exclaimed and pointed.

Over the hill they came, steel-tipped lines of cavalry. Guidons
shone in the afternoon light and a great cheering rose as they saw
the hard-pressed enemy. The foremost horseman swung his hat
and yelled. His bared head was gold in the sunlight. With Custer
in the lead, Sheridan's cavalry flung itself on the backs of Ewell's
command.

It was over quickly. There was brief confusion and a dying
gun-fire. Then, by companies, regiments, brigades, the cornered
men threw down their arms and Sheridan rode forward to a little
group on the hillside. There, amid hunger-sick infantry who held
musket butts aloft in token of surrender, stood General Ewell.
Elsewhere on the field Generals Barton, Corse, Kershaw, Custis Lee
and Defoe were taken. Besides thousands of prisoners, there were
fourteen guns and many wagons, and innumerable mules and
horses. From among the last, Custer, once more enveloped in
glory, obtained a blooded Virginia gelding that he renamed "Custis Lee."

Next day, April seventh, Sheridan's cavalry moved out ahead of the infantry, riding through a drizzle to Prospect Station on the road to Appomattox. In Lee's rear, Humphreys had taken many prisoners and eighteen cannon. Griffin's VI Corps and Ord's Divisions had occupied Farmville, blocking the Gray's last hope of escape to the south.

That evening, Grant wrote Lee, urging his surrender to prevent "further effusion of blood."

Chapter Eleven

CLIMAX

Fruit trees burned white against green hillsides. April's sky was tender and in a land lovely with vernal promise, Lee's hope withered.

Columns of singing Blue infantry filled Virginia's drying roads. The lilt of victory was in their voices and their pace. There were brief rages of gun-fire that pleasant April eighth, as Meade's advance-guard struck the Confederate rear and drove it farther.

Northward on the Prince Edward-Danville Pike, Griffin's V Corps and Gibbon's XXIV from the Army of the James were swinging, and ahead of them, with rattle and jingle and excited voices, Sheridan's cavalry rode toward the west.

Along the north bank of the Appomattox River, Lee's army staggered, hungry and sleepless, toward Lynchburg, sole remaining refuge. Sheridan would set ten thousand horse across the Appomattox-Lynchburg Road, blocking it, holding Lee until the infantry could get up. The V and XXIV Corps turned off the Danville Highway and followed the cavalry.

Sheridan rode with Pennington's Brigade of the Third Division, which had the advance. Sunlight flamed on Custer's long yellow hair and spun from the golden arabesques of his sleeves. His lean face had burned to the hue of his scarlet cravat. The fretting charger and he were one in resentment of the column's deliberate pace. Those who saw him pass, stridently gay, must have fancied him the leader of the column and scarcely have heeded the squat shabby person in the disreputable hat who was Sheridan.

They marched all day toward Appomattox Station on the Petersburg-Lynchburg Railway, a few miles from Appomattox Court House, and Union plunderers swept a stock farm clean of horses including a dark bay stallion, Don Juan, that Custer later bought from the government. Then the monotony of that journey through a rolling land of rough plenty was broken. The sun was well in the west when scouts galloped back with tidings.

At Appomattox Station four trains of supplies, sent from Lynchburg at Lee's order, waited for the starving Gray army.

Sheridan conferred briefly with Merritt, who barked an order to Custer. The word set the youngster's smoldering excitement ablaze. The torpid clatter of the march swelled as the Third Cavalry Division moved quickly ahead and in its wake Devin's and Crook's troopers hurried. They could not keep up with Custer. Even the rear regiments of his own command lagged behind the 2nd New York and 3rd New Jersey who followed their General. It was only an hour before sunset when the breathless regiments saw through trees the single building that was Appomattox Station and against the woods beyond it, the smoke of locomotives, towering golden in the afternoon light. Custer sent a detail toward Lynchburg to tear up track, lest any of the trains escape, waved his hat about his head and whooped his command to charge. The cavalry followed their leader in a yelping, disorganized race for the trains. "Custer," writes Colonel Newhall of Sheridan's staff, "might not well conduct a siege of regular approaches but for a sudden dash, Custer against the world."

An army might have been hidden in the woods beyond the railway. Custer, with a quarry in view, rarely consulted prudence.

The scream of a locomotive rose above the yells of the troopers. As the first horsemen reached the station, the foremost engine uttered panicky coughing. Its driving wheels spun and caught. The train jerked, moved and halted as Private Blodgett, sixteen, of the 2nd New York reined in his horse beside the cab and thrust a pistol in the engineer's face.

The 3rd New Jersey swarmed down in the wake of the 2nd New York. There was a welter of plunging horses and cheering men about the captured trains. Then the rising triumph was blasted by the double clap of a cannon shot from among the trees and the burst of a shell overhead.

Those woods were not empty. They were crammed with guns and wagons that had been hurried forward by Lee in an effort to get them to Lynchburg. They had parked here for the night. By ones, by twos, by batteries, the guns opened on Custer. He may have struck, for all he knows, the whole Army of Northern Virginia. He does not hesitate. Men are dismounted and flung out as skirmishers beyond the track. Successive regiments as they arrive are thrust into the line on foot. Custer shouts for engineers to draw the trains out of the line of fire. Four men of the 2nd New York volunteer. Locomotives cough. The cars groan and roll away amid triumphant tooting and the increasing thunder of cannon. With Pennington's and Capehart's Brigades, dismounted, Custer charges the woods.

These are not heavily held. Lee has not dreamed of cavalry on his front, yet the convoy of his train and the few gunners fight so sturdily that, even after the arrival of Wells's Brigade, Custer can get no foothold in the woods.

Sheridan appears and sends word to Merritt to hurry up Devin's Division which goes into action on Custer's right. Sheridan does not object to the tumult of battle but the tootling of the triumphant volunteer engineers rasps his nerves. He sends word that the annoying whistling must be stopped, or else the trains will be burned. It ceases. Custer goes forward as Devin's troopers strike the Confederate left flank and roll it up.

Carbine-fire, banging and sparkling, silences the cannon in the woods. The Gray force there takes flight. Devin and Custer swarm across the road from Appomattox Court House to Lynchburg. This is choked with abandoned guns and wagons. Custer drives ahead with a mob of dismounted troopers toward the courthouse, meets organized infantry resistance and falls back. Devin holds the road while the breathless, triumphant youngster reforms his command, and assembles the booty, which includes twenty-five cannon and more than two hundred wagons.

Lee's last possible way of escape is barred now, by only a few thousand cavalry, but barred nevertheless.

That night Sheridan wrote Grant that if Gibbon's and Griffin's

Corps could get up by morning, "we will perhaps finish the job."
Before the dawn of April ninth, the hard-marched infantry came
in. That dawn was clear and serene. It had not endured long before carbines spoke on the Lynchburg Road. There, Crook's Division had replaced Devin's and Custer's battle-tangled commands
which, reorganized, were in support on the right. Light and the
guns' stammering increased together.

The door of the trap had slammed upon Lee. He was to try to
break it down. Crook still held that door, but heavier battle was
spawning. Gray lines formed on the Appomattox Road, infantry
of Gordon, cavalry of Fitzhugh Lee. Above their soiled ranks was
the tattered brilliance of many flags. Regiments had shrunk to
company strength, and yet each went forward under its own
colors.

The quavering rebel yell rises. Crook's carbines blast the first
advance. Beyond range, the weary Gray reforms to come again.
On the right behind Crook, Custer frets. Over the road from the
station, Gibbon's infantry are hurrying to the firing line. Crook,
Gibbon and Custer are blocking Lee's last break for freedom—
Crook, Gibbon and Custer! In this high hour, has the present worn
thin to reveal the future's underlying warp and web?

Sunlight dwells, beyond the powder fog of Crook's front, on
rolling green hills, with the little court-house village in the background. The smoke of Lee's camp-fires rises through still air to
blur farther ridges. Gray infantry reenforced by Longstreet are
ranked in the middle distance and, nearer at hand, Fitzhugh Lee's
horse prepares to charge Crook's center.

There is cheering from the line of powder-grimed troopers in
blue and yellow as Gibbon's Corps comes up. Fitzhugh Lee sees
the infantry deploy and gallops off to make a vain attack upon the
Union left flank, held by Davies' Brigade of Crook's command.

There is a banging of musketry and yelling in the Lynchburg
Road, as Gordon and Longstreet beat along the Union line but
can not break it. The Gray falter and withdraw. The infantry of
Gibbon and Griffin move forward, driving Lee's men back toward
where the massive columns of Meade are rolling up from the east.

On the right flank of the Blue advance, Merritt's Cavalry Divisions form.

Devin, the dour hard-hitter, sits stolidly ahorse. Custer is straining at the invisible leash. The order to trot is no appeasement for his mounting desire. Ardent as the morning, he leads his brigades forward. He is shaken by the ripple that runs through the ranks as they reach the threshold of the charge that will end the war. Men who cherish the harsh beauty of battle remember him in that moment. Newhall rears a monument of baroque phrases in his honor.

"At the head of the horsemen rode Custer of the golden locks, his broad sombrero turned up from his hard bronzed face"—Custer never tanned; he burned a violent scarlet—"the end of his crimson cravat floating over his shoulders, gold galore spangling his jacket sleeves, a pistol in his boot, jangling spurs on his heels, and a ponderous claymore swinging at his side—a wild, daredevil of a general, and a prince of advance guards, quick to see and act."*

So a veteran saw him. It is well to remember him thus, with his massed troopers behind him and ahead the greater fame this last charge promises. Custer's eager gesture as he draws sword is a salute to Glory.

He can not know that in this brilliant moment, his life has reached its crest; that from this height, lit by the glare of unsheathed sabers, his road will wind slowly down to tragedy that later years will transform into greater renown. The moment passes. Glory, the capricious, the long indulgent, averts her face. The shout dies in Custer's throat. He stares at a horseman in soiled gray, galloping up out of the battle murk; a horseman who waves above his head a towel bound to a stick.

Custer's voice as he greets Captain Simms, bearer of Longstreet's flag of truce, is flat with anti-climax. The cavalry halts. Sabers are resheathed. In the meadows below, musketry sputters out into an

---

* Newhall's *With Sheridan's Cavalry.*

odd silence. Colonel Peyton arrives with a second white flag from Gordon. Custer and Colonel Whittaker accompany the emissaries to Sheridan. Later, the Boy General rides with Simms to Longstreet, who takes small pleasure in his visit. Longstreet wrote later:

"General Custer's flaxen locks were flowing over his shoulders and in a brusque excited manner he said:
" 'In the name of General Sheridan I demand the unconditional surrender of this army.' "*

Longstreet, by character and present mood, was not to be bullied. His reply deflated the youngster who had been carried off his feet by the moment's excitement. Severity, properly applied, always quenched Custer.

"He was reminded," Longstreet writes, "that I was not the commander of the army and that he was within the lines of the enemy without authority, addressing a superior officer, and in disrespect to General Grant, as well as myself; that if I were commander of the Army, I would not receive the message of General Sheridan.
"He then became more moderate, saying: 'It would be a pity to have more blood upon the field.'
"Then I suggested that the truce be respected, and said: 'As you are now more reasonable, I will say that General Lee has gone to meet General Grant and it is for them to determine the future of the armies.' He was satisfied and rode back to his command."

He did not return at once to his division. Chastened by Longstreet's stern reproof, Custer rode more decorously to Gordon who recalled him favorably later as "an officer of strikingly picturesque appearance."

"This Union officer was slender and graceful and a superb rider. He wore his hair very long, falling almost to his shoulders. Guided by my staff officer, he galloped to where I was

---

* Longstreet, General James: *From Manassas to Appomattox*, Philadelphia, 1895.

sitting on my horse and with faultless grace and courtesy"—
for this, Longstreet is entitled to some credit—"saluted me
with his saber and said: 'I am General Custer and bear a message to you from General Sheridan . . . !' "

Later, when Sheridan came up, Gordon found the squat, brusk
general an anti-climax and a disappointment. They rode on together toward the court-house. Behind them the rattle of firing
rose briefly where General Geary and his brigade boasted that
South Carolinians never surrendered. Merritt's cavalry, closing in,
changed the minds of the vainglorious handful, and the guns of
the Army of Northern Virginia had spoken for the last time. This
was Custer's mild compensation for the charge he had been denied.

Generals of the Union army gathered before the oblong brick
house of Wilmer McLean in the little town that dreamed in the
Sabbath noon, unconscious of its new abiding place in history. Orderlies held Grant's Cincinnati, Sheridan's Rienzi and other chargers in the road and, a little apart, a gray horse named Traveller
cropped the grass about beds of daffodils.

Men moved softly before the wide steps of the McLean house
and spoked in hushed voices, as though church services instead of
military negotiations were proceeding inside. Through the mud-
stained, battle-weary group, Custer moved like a flame above embers. Shadows crept across the lawn. Inside the brick house the
hum of speech rose and fell and was broken occasionally by the
scraping of chair legs. Horses stamped and shook themselves in
the street, with a loud clatter of equipment.

It was four, that afternoon of April ninth, when the rumble and
clinking of many spurred boots rose in the hallway of the McLean
home. Those who had squatted on the porch steps sprang up.
Traveller lifted his head from his grazing.

A gray-bearded man in a gorgeous gray uniform with a jeweled
sword still hanging at his side, came out upon the porch. His be-
spectacled military secretary followed him and at their heels, like
mourners emerging from a death chamber, Grant and his generals
followed.

At the top of the steps, Robert E. Lee paused. He signaled for his horse and, while the orderly hastily strapped the bit into Traveller's mouth, looked across the valley toward where his army lay. So he stood, softly smiting one gloved hand in the palm of the other, until his charger was brought forward.

Lee mounted. Grant, standing on the steps, lifted his hat. Gravely and silently Lee doffed his. Then he passed between bareheaded soldiers into the sunlit road beyond.

Grant and his staff rode away. As they departed the spell broke. Union officers charged into the room of the surrender. The bewildered McLean was caught, pulled a dozen ways at once, offered incredible amounts for objects that, until history's hand had touched them, had been of no value.

For twenty dollars in gold coin, Sheridan bought the table at which Lee had sat and turned it over to his favorite as a gift to Mrs. Custer. Her husband strode away to his division's bivouac with the trophy on his shoulders while the less fortunate bawled "Sheridan's Robber!" after him. His wife kept the relic all her days. More precious to her was the letter from Sheridan that accompanied his gift.

"My dear Madam: Permit me to present to you the table upon which were signed the terms of surrender of the Army of Northern Virginia, under General Robert E. Lee; and in conclusion let me add that I know of no person more instrumental in bringing about this most desirable event than your most gallant husband.

"I am, madam, most truly your friend
"PHILIP M. SHERIDAN, Mj. Gen., U. S. A."*

Slowly the bartering group in the McLean parlor broke up. As they left, the far sound of cheering came across the valley from where haggard men swarmed about Lee, riding to his own tent with his eyes fixed on Traveller's ears.

---

* Ronsheim, Milton: *The Life of General Custer*, Cadiz, Ohio, 1929.

CHAPTER TWELVE

AFTERMATH

THE Cavalry Corps was ordered back to Petersburg on the morrow of Lee's surrender but while they tarried at Appomattox, Custer composed a congratulatory general order to his division. There is a florid Napoleonic flavor to this document. The Boy General was an admirer and student of the Little Corporal.

"Soldiers of the Third Cavalry Division: With profound gratitude toward the God of battles, by whose blessings our enemies have been humbled and our arms rendered triumphant your Commanding General avails himself of this, his first opportunity to express to you his admiration of the heroic manner in which you have passed through the series of battles which today resulted in the surrender of the enemy's entire army.

"The record established by your indomitable courage is unparalleled in the annals of war. Your prowess has won for you even the respect and admiration of your enemies. During the past six months, though in most instances confronted by superior numbers, you have captured from the enemy in open battle one hundred eleven pieces of field artillery, sixty-five battle flags and upward of ten thousand prisoners of war, including seven general officers. Within the past ten days and included in the above, you have captured forty-six pieces of artillery and thirty-seven battle flags. You have never lost a gun, never lost a color and never been defeated and notwithstanding the numerous engagements in which you have borne a prominent part, including those memorable battles of the Shenandoah, you have captured every piece of artillery, which the enemy has dared to open upon you.

"The near approach of peace renders it improbable that you will again be called upon to undergo the fatigues of the toilsome march, or the exposure of the battlefield; but should the assistance of keen blades, wielded by your sturdy arms be required to hasten the coming of that glorious peace for which we have been so long contending, the General commanding is firmly confident that, in the future as in the past, every demand will meet with a hearty and willing response.

"Let us hope that our work is done and that blessed with the comforts of peace, we may be permitted to enjoy the pleasures of home and friends. For our comrades who have fallen let us ever cherish a grateful remembrance. To the wounded and those who languish in Southern prisons, let our heartfelt sympathy be tendered.

"And now, speaking for myself alone, when this war is ended and the task of the historian begins—when those deeds of daring which have rendered the name and fame of the Third Cavalry Division imperishable are inscribed upon the bright pages of our country's history, I only ask that my name be written as that of the Commander of the Third Cavalry Division.

"G. A. CUSTER
"Brevet Major General Commanding."

This is more ornate but scarcely more accurate than other battlefield proclamations. By limiting himself to the last six months, four and a half of which had been spent chiefly in winter quarters, Custer is able to ignore sundry earlier retreats and humiliations. It is doubtful, furthermore, whether at any time during the 1865 campaign, he and his men had gone forward against superior numbers. At Waynesboro, for example, which was more a precipitate surrender than a battle, he and Devin had faced Early's faint-hearted two thousand with eight thousand men.

Most of the prisoners, some of the battle flags and many of the guns taken by his division came into their hands through the wholesale desertions and abandonments that accompanied the flight of Lee's army. A leader's praise of his own command when uttered publicly for posterity's notice is apt to be fulsome.

When the corps returned to Petersburg, Custer received word of his promotion to major-general of volunteers. He was twenty-five years old, youngest man in the army to wear twin stars.

More glory yet might be squeezed from the failing war. The cavalry, with the VI Corps, old companions in battle, marched south and west toward Danville to strike the rear of Joe Johnston's army which still evaded Sherman in North Carolina. Crook's Division had crossed the Dan River, Devin's and Custer's were about to follow, when, on April twenty-eighth, Sheridan received dispatches telling of Johnston's surrender and ordering his own command back to Petersburg. The Cavalry Corps had ridden toward battle for the last time.

Custer had sent for his wife. When the chance for fresh glory was spent, his first thought always was of her, and she who asked little more of life than his presence, met him beyond Petersburg. Thereafter, she rode beside him on the march.

There was a review in Petersburg. Then Sheridan was summoned to Washington and Crook led the Cavalry Corps northward. It swung wide of the direct route to the capital for the main highways were filled with Sherman's army, moving toward Washington for the grand review.

Sheridan's Robbers rode through places whose names they had glorified—Yellow Tavern, Trevilian Station, Culpeper. These hamlets, meek and shabby even in the full glamour of spring, may have dismayed the Boy General by their indifference to their new fame. He went through them toward peace. Where, henceforth, might the Glory-Hunter find surcease for his eternal desire? How, hereafter, might he keep brightly burnished the splendor of his name?

So he may have thought, as the cavalry moved by easy marches toward Washington. He never underestimated his own prowess and honors, and those who have written of him have followed his example. Had they been less willing to accept his, or his wife's, estimate of George Armstrong Custer, we might see him more clearly as he leads his division toward the final triumph at the capital.

Men have been so fascinated by the tragedy of his end that much material concerning the years when a haphazard negligent youngster was beaten into enduring form by the war's sledge has been lost. The men who knew him then are gone now. Old soldiers, spending their retirement in setting down recollections, speak of him only briefly. Perhaps their scant comments were candid. It is possible they stifled criticism for the sake of the woman who spent her widowhood glorifying a memory. We know men acknowledged his bravery. We know many thought him bewilderingly lucky. That is all we shall ever learn certainly from his companions in arms during the Civil War.

He rides north, a swaggering, restless horseman. A big white hat shields an eager sunburned face with deep-set bright blue eyes, hawk nose and yellow drooping mustache and chin tuft. His thick curls fall to his shoulders. His scarlet cravat flows from beneath the wide, star adorned collar of his blue shirt. Intricately looped strands of gold braid glitter on his sleeves. A trooper bears his personal flag of red and blue horizontal stripes, with crossed silver bars superimposed, and back of him clatter three thousand horsemen who follow the youngest major-general in the service.

He craved the romance and the splendor of war and he clothed himself in these. He loved the shock of combat, was thrilled by the charge. His fondness for drama urged him to stretch his orders and fight ahorse when dismounted battle would have served better. Those who came after were dazzled by his beauty and sentimentally entangled by the glamour of his end. They saw him, splendid at the head of his horsemen, and looked no further. History helps but little in the effort to comprehend this swashbuckling youngster, this headlong, fantastic cavalry leader. There are gaps in the record that no one now may span.

There is the puzzle of his rocket-like elevation to the command of a brigade. One day, he is a first lieutenant of regular cavalry, assigned to Pleasonton's staff; the next, a brigadier-general of volunteers. His contemporaries grumbled that this was rank favoritism plus political influence. After the reticence of seventy years, no better explanation remains.

Nothing indicates that he had ever displayed any striking qualities of generalship. A staff lieutenant has small chance to exhibit such abilities. It is doubtful, in Custer's case, whether they existed. He had immense self-confidence and a flawless valor, but his fame as brigadier and division commander is due more to a vivid personality than to great professional skill. He was to war correspondents and through them to mankind in general, "the Boy General with the Golden Locks" and "the Murat of the American Army." Colorful phrases like these may be a substitute for merit.

He fought with headlong courage at Gettysburg, under Gregg's command. His charge won a victory at Cedarville, but Torbert was his superior here. Merritt directed his fine advance at Winchester. It was Torbert who directed the battle of Woodstock. Sheridan guided him at Yellow Tavern, Dinwiddie and Five Forks. It was Crook, not he, who broke the Confederate line on the road beyond Sailor's Creek. Whittaker, his first biographer, speaks of these conflicts as though Custer had won them independently. Always, there were other units of the Cavalry Corps in the fight. Always, a superior in the field directed the victory.

While Custer's luck held, it took the place of generalship. While fortune still favored him, his later self-directed Indian campaigns though strategically bad, were successful. Before his last battle, luck had deserted him. He was lucky but not as fortunate or as skilful as his eulogists say. It was sheer accident that Fitzhugh Lee and Stuart did not annihilate his brigade and the rest of Kilpatrick's Division at Buckland and despite this whim of chance, the Gray horsemen sent him running for dear life to the protection of infantry. At Trevilian Station, his rashness got him caught between two Confederate commands. He lost his baggage train and almost lost his brigade.

At Shepherdstown in the Shenandoah, Early chased him from the field and across the Potomac. Other Union cavalry engaged managed to get out of a tight spot less ignominiously. Rosser beat him on the day before Woodstock. Rosser and the feeble Confederate horse of 1864 jumped him at Lacy's Springs and beat him again.

It was his luck that saved him from additional defeats. Rosser's plan to capture his entire command was thwarted, not by Custer's generalship, but by orders that had caused him to shift his position. At Appomattox Station, his wild dash for Lee's supply trains was successful, yet if the woods behind the tracks had been occupied in force, his whole command might have been destroyed.

"If" is a potent word in war. It wins or loses most battles. The fact remains that Custer was not invincible. Nor was he, as far as the testimony of history can be trusted, a strategist comparable to Sheridan or even Merritt or Torbert. He was a fair tactician and a smart disciplinarian. Throughout the war and even thereafter, he who had been a slovenly and inept cadet at West Point visited upon the inept or slovenly the harshness of the convert. He made his brigade and later his division the equal of any in the field, but the constant hammering by which this was accomplished did not endear him to his commands. Tireless himself, he made no allowances for the fatigue of lesser men.

He was plunged, fresh from an insurgent career at West Point, into the haphazard and scrambled first years of the war. He seems in the Peninsular campaign to have roved about much as he pleased. He was accepted by McClellan as a staff officer and, in return for the adolescent devotion he paid his chief, received many privileges. Thereafter, he was assigned to the cavalry, that neglected and disheveled stepchild of the army which did not become an effective fighting force until after Sheridan's arrival.

Those years of loose discipline seem to have preserved the youthful insubordination that remained a characteristic all his life. His neglect of responsibility flares up clearly again and again throughout the war.

In the attack on Brandy Station, September 13, 1863, Custer leads his brigade until he sees trains at the station that he wants to capture. He deserts his command and gallops off in a vain attempt to take them.

Neglect to determine the position of the enemy plunges him up to the neck in trouble at Trevilian Court House.

He disobeys orders, lets flags captured in the Shenandoah be presented to the War Department by underlings and meanwhile ranges the city in search of his wife.

At Dinwiddie, his headlong haste bogs down in mire the charge he tries to launch. His editing of orders from a superior at Five Forks, whereby he advances mounted instead of on foot, holds up the left of the Union advance.

Such sins, while luck held, were concealed under the bright mantle of victory. It was only when fortune at last deserted him that they wrought his destruction. Men were relieved of their commands in the Civil War for scarcely more flagrant insubordinations and mistakes than Custer displayed and, thanks to luck, survived.

You can determine the flavor of his strange personality no more accurately now than one may fix the taste of wine by examining its long deserted bottle. Many men disliked and distrusted him. A few gave him great devotion. Sheridan cherished an enduring fondness for his daredevil. Godfrey and Varnum and other subordinates paid him in their old age a clear, unwavering, beautiful loyalty. We see him most completely in the reiterant tributes of his widow's books. These naturally prejudiced volumes do not reveal the fascination that she and some men found in him.

Utter bravery, in soldier or civilian, hides a multitude of defects, and George Armstrong Custer was as physically valiant a man as ever drew sword. Even the defects that were solidified during the molding years of conflict were those that, in time of war, may well be mistaken for virtues: brutality that served Sheridan well in devastating the Shenandoah; ambition that was twin brother to ardor; hard-driving discipline that might be hailed as zeal for a cause when, more probably, it was a frantic, never-ending search for fame. All his days, he was to pursue Glory and when she denied him, his efforts to regain her favor were the wild expedients of a rejected lover.

This, at the range of seventy years, is all we can see of the gorgeously uniformed, hot-headed young man who rides north with his division and camps at length midway between Washington and Alexandria, to wait the grand review in Washington.

Her husband had come back to Elizabeth Custer, crowned with

glory. She was soon to learn how briefly such adornment kept its luster for him. All his life she was to face with secret tears and the nagging bedevilment of actual and fancied terrors, the difficult fact of his martial ambition. Hereafter, she was to follow him wherever she might—with his cavalry on the march, through the cold and the heat of the frontier. Physical privations were privileges to the woman who had been reared with the elaborate delicacy of mid-nineteenth-century wealth, as long as she might share them with her husband. She paid for that joy by the torment of their separations and found the price ridiculously small. The love his wife bore him and he bore her may be George Armstrong Custer's most intrinsically sound fame.

Even now, a possible new separation trod on the heels of reunion. There was trouble north and south of the Rio Grande. Beyond that river, Maximilian's fantastic ambition affronted the Monroe Doctrine. Above the stream, Texas was sagging toward anarchy. Sheridan, statecraft decided, must go to the border at once, foregoing the privilege of leading his horsemen in the review. As soon as that triumph was over, Custer and Merritt were to follow him to assume command of cavalry units that were concentrating in Louisiana and to march into Texas. To woman and man alike, thought of another parting was unendurable. It was decided at last that not only Custer's personal staff and his cook, Eliza, but his wife as well would accompany him to Texas.

Meanwhile, the cavalry cleansed and polished itself for the imminent grand review. On Monday, May twenty-second, the day before he might have led his horsemen in parade, Sheridan was to leave for New Orleans. He waited grumpily that Sunday, apart from his command, at Willard's Hotel. The cavalry had been ordered to shift its camp to another nearer Bladensburg. They chose, in obeying, to march past their chief's hotel. It was raining hard—reminiscent weather for Sheridan's Robbers. Horse, guns and train moved through the storm to the valiant blaring of their bands and Sheridan, surprised and touched, hurried to the balcony of the hotel and received the salute of his corps for the last time.

There was rain, too, on the morning of May twenty-third. A

hundred thousand men from the armies of the East moved to their places appointed in Meade's order of the day. Shortly after sunrise, the storm ended and a brisk north wind tore the clouds away from the freshly washed city. The Cavalry Corps formed on Maryland Avenue with the head of the column abreast of the north entrance to the Capitol.

Promptly at nine, Meade, his staff and an escorting squadron of the 1st Massachusetts Cavalry rode away. The General's punctual fulfilment of his own orders caught Washington napping. Meade arrived at the reviewing stand in front of the White House before the President, the Secretary of War or even Grant had taken their places.

Trumpets' voices broke into echoes against the Capitol's walls. The column of Blue horsemen stirred, grew rigid. The trumpets sang again. The harsh roar of hoofs answered. With Merritt and his staff at its head; with Custer leading the Third Division, followed by Davies with the Second and Devin with the First, the Cavalry Corps moved out.

Eight thousand riders fill the street, swinging along at the mile-eating walk Sheridan has enforced. Sunlight flares on the hides of carefully groomed chargers; spins from the buckles of polished belts that are strapped over faded blue and yellow uniforms; flashes from saber blades and carbine locks. Guidons are wind-tormented color against the rain-washed sky. The school children of Washington, filling every window of the Capitol, pelt the column with flowers. Above the dry clamor of hoofs rise their piping voices. Custer, controlling his charger, Don Juan, with the skill of the perfect horseman, waves his hat to the youngsters through a shower of blossoms.

The column goes down Capitol Hill in a slow blue flood. It turns into Pennsylvania Avenue. From sidewalks, stands, windows and housetops, a hundred thousand civilians watch. Hoofs clatter more loudly on the pavement. The jangle of arms is gay as the wind-swept morning. The bands blare and a great shouting rolls in upon the troopers. Sheridan's Robbers are on the march once more.

Never again will they ride together. At the far end of the avenue the White House gleams. There is the end. Beyond the reviewing stand, they will ride into history. "Never again" is a trite phrase now for the sun is bright, the wind hunts small clouds across the sky and the mass movement and the din weave their spell. Life will be mild and sweet. Who will miss the absent tang of danger?

The hoofs are flat enduring thunder on Pennsylvania Avenue. The cheering soars into hysterical screeching.

Never again the empty calm when the fight is over; never again the camp-smoke drifting across a stream; never again the stamp and reek from the horse lines and the voices of trumpets drawing in the night.

Merritt and his staff move soberly ahead. The bellowing of the spectators makes Don Juan shy. Few men can ride like Custer. Old Curly! Forget envy and grudges now. We are riding behind him into history and yonder is our end.

Never again the distant summoning guns. Apples are born on Shenandoah's trees. We shall ride that way no more. Grass heals the battle wounds on Virginia's soil; grass covers many of us there. The rest will wait its investiture in peace.

The bands' pumping can scarcely be heard through the tumult. Hats are waved, flowers are flung. The corps moves upon a wave of sound. Strange that Custer's horse should flinch so from mere shouting!

Never again the hoofs' blunt, mounting tumult; never again the harsh ecstasy of the charge; its wind that blows upon the coals of valor. Beyond the White House reviewing stands, is the soft safe life we had half forgotten. We shall grow old with its sweetness on our lips.

Never again to quaff the tingling draught of peril; never again to follow that yellow-haired leader.

The Cavalry Corps fills Pennsylvania Avenue. The horse batteries follow and, behind, the bayonets of the IX Corps are a rough river in the sunlight. Cheering, impartial, impersonal, envelops foot, horse and guns. There is no place for individual tribute here.

The acclaim is for an army, not for any man, not Merritt, nor Davies, nor Devin, nor Custer himself, so gallant on his fretting steed.

When a hundred thousand march, who can hope for personal notice from a frenzied crowd? Even the perfect horseman, the devotee to fame, the Boy General must be content to share the uproar with many. Must he? The reviewing stand is close and Don Juan is running away.

Don Juan is running away with a man no horse ever outwitted. Custer's hat blows off. Merritt and his staff scatter before the frantic animal's rush. Rider and charger flash by, to the panic beat of hoofs and the streaming of wind-blown curls. They pass the grandstand, the President, his Cabinet, the generals and the ambassadors at a hard run. The yelling is not for the Army of the Potomac now. It is personal at last. It proclaims the glory of one man, of George Armstrong Custer who, beyond the stand, masters his rebellious steed and amid wilder cheering, gallops back to his place in line. When he passes a second time, erect and soldierly at the head of his division, all men know him and call his name.

Custer's wife always spoke of the outburst as an accident. Major Tremain, who saw it, does not seem so certain. He refers to "that notorious incident" that carried Custer "past the reviewing officer, the President of the United States, his Cabinet, the military, civil and diplomatic functionaries of this and many other countries, not in the stately and sedate manner of a warrior chief on his prancing charger, but shooting like the wind. Was this," Tremain asks, "a disappointment or was the sensation agreeable? Who among the spectators or performers at this state occasion will forget 'how Custer's horse ran away with him'?"

The whole man with his flaws and flairs is epitomized in that dash. He has been, he will ever be, prone to spectacular outbursts against ordered regularity; insurgent in his hunt for Glory. That runaway is at once his biography and his epitaph.

CHAPTER THIRTEEN

MUTINY

THE Third Division camped at Arlington. In the late afternoon, that twenty-second of May, Custer bade his command farewell. The shadows of massed regiments stretched far across the grass. In the background Elizabeth Custer waited ahorse with the staff while the General rode through the rich sunlight, down the line of troopers for the last time. They cheered him. They yelled for Old Curly, avatar of their glory, with the enthusiasm of men for whom the nightmare of war at last had ended, and Custer, enveloped by their hoarse acclaim, fought to keep back the tears.

He wept easily. Pathos in book or play would make him cry. His wife extolls the stormy grief that shook him whenever he had told his mother good-by. Sentiment could stir him. Tragedy, unadorned, could not reach him, or else it reached beyond him. Suffering must be dressed in the elaborate furbelows of his era, were it to quicken his sympathy. He could hang Confederate troopers and shoot a fleeing officer in the back with no compunction, yet the plight of the waif, Johnny, woke his compassion, and Joe Jefferson in *Rip Van Winkle* dissolved him in tears.

Now, as he rode past his cheering brigades, he fought for self-control. The adoring eyes of his wife marked the struggle and when the regiments shouted for her to ride forth and take their tribute she refused, half weeping, herself. "I was too overcome from having seen the suffering on my husband's face to endure any more sorrow." *

They left, next day, by train for Louisville—Custer, his wife, his

---

* Custer, Elizabeth B.: *Tenting on the Plains,* New York, 1887.

staff and Eliza. Sheridan was on his way to New Orleans and, thereafter, Texas. At Shreveport, a new First Cavalry Division was massing for Merritt to lead to San Antonio. Other units, to be called the Third Division, were assembling in Louisiana at Alexandria. Custer was to march them to Austin.

The ostensible purpose of this move was to regulate a commonwealth left leaderless by the war's end; actually, the advance was the government's first step toward possible war with Maximilian and his sponsor Napoleon III.

Not until the possibility of intervention had passed did Custer ever speak of it to his wife. Her timid heart had been too relieved by the return of peace for him to darken it by talk of further conflict. He refrained from curdling her happiness during that southward journey. Long afterward, she wrote of its merry vicissitudes.

She remembered the clamorous train, filled with joyous dis, charged soldiers going home and the music and shouting at each station that welcomed returning warriors. She recalled how all Custer's staff managed to get into the car reserved for ladies and their escorts by each taking a bit of her luggage and presenting these as passports.

Once only was she frightened. That was when they dined in a railroad station restaurant and a surly proprietor refused the negress Eliza food, and her husband, chivalrously angry, compelled him to serve her.

From Louisville, the steamer *Ruth* bore them to New Orleans. Summer came up the river to meet them. The nights were softly bright and they sang on deck to the music of a staff officer's guitar. The Confederate General Hood took passage on the *Ruth* and Custer's wife banished momentary fear when her husband and his late foe greeted each other as friends, and Hood, who had lost a leg, admitted to her that he had tried English, German, French, Confederate and Yankee artificial limbs and that the Yankee was the best.

Custer reported to Sheridan at New Orleans and learned that war with France still was possible, though the massing of troops above the Rio Grande probably would bring about a withdrawal of Napoleon's support from the puppet Emperor. The General and his wife ranged the city together, visiting shops, markets and restaurants where Custer amazed Creoles by the prodigious amounts of coffee he consumed; calling on the vast General Scott who had given the Boy General his first orders as a combatant; spending their money with the recklessness of children.

They were almost penniless when they at length boarded the steamer *Indiana* that was to take them up the Red River to Alexandria. They made only the most feeble protest when Captain Greathouse insisted that they ride free. When they landed, he presented them with a hogshead of ice, the last they were to see for many weeks.

Alexandria offered them no further luxuries. It was a dismal place that had been half burned during the war. Its water was brackish, its residents hostile and it swarmed with tarantulas and centipedes. These filled Mrs. Custer with dread which she was soon to forget in the face of more actual peril. The discipline her husband tried to impose upon the turbulent regiments assembled there bred immediate trouble.

No command that Custer ever held esteemed him until it had followed him into battle. Memory of his dazzling bravery in conflict thereafter was partial compensation for the ordeal of serving under him. He was a commander whom, at best, the rank and file admired rather than loved; a martinet who expected all to possess his own inexhaustible energy and spirit. As a leader of regulars, he brought the 7th Cavalry into hard efficiency. As a chief of volunteers with the civilian soldiers' independence and lack of reverence, he was less successful. The Michigan Brigade muttered and resented his stern enforcement of the minutiæ of discipline when he became its general, but the war was at its height and shortly after taking command Custer was able to display the compensating splendor of his valor.

The war was over now and the grumbling troopers assembled at Alexandria came from western armies that had not known Custer. They were volunteers, all of them. The best volunteers, when no enemy is available, are likely to display a profane disregard for military sacraments.

These troopers may not have been the best volunteers. Mrs. Custer, ever the devoted advocate, writes of them as though they were the sink scourings of the army. They were hardly that. They were middle-western civilians who had turned soldiers in a crisis. That crisis was past. Other regiments throughout the North were being disbanded and sent home. These men had been exiled to the South on duty that promised small excitement and much toil. They were resentful; they were insubordinate, but the regiment that flared up into mutiny under Custer's harsh command was the 3rd Michigan Cavalry, brothers of the troopers who had followed their Boy General in the Michigan Brigade.

From the beginning, the rigors of Custer's discipline bred heat. He could not, he would not, endure slovenly soldiers—he who as a cadet had been a chronic sloven himself. To homesick resentful men, his harshness was challenge. There was grumbling that fermented into threats, uttered so loudly and frequently that, at his terrified wife's behest, Custer slept with a pistol under his pillow— and did not tell her till later that it never had been loaded.

A soldier, tolerant of the vagaries of volunteers, a general with a facile sense of humor, might have met and scattered the growing resentment. Custer was without these saving qualities. He struck at insubordination with brutal reprisal. He had insurgents flogged. He shaved the heads of the more vociferous protestants and drummed them out of camp. Mrs. Custer tells with awe, in which there is unwilling trace of mirth, how one trooper, thus disgraced, ordered a hack to wait for him at the camp limits. Into this he climbed, clapped a wig on his shaven pate and drove away with derisive sounds and gestures.

Some officers completely lost control of their commands. A colonel complained bitterly to Custer that "the boys" had acquired the habit of shooting at his tent after Taps every night. The mounting disorder, the lack of a battle into which he could lead his heretical command and there win its admiration drove the General frantic. He wrote of his plight to Sheridan who returned authorization for his subordinate to use "such summary measures as you deem proper to overcome the mutinous disposition of the individuals in your command."

That disposition was made glaringly evident soon thereafter, not in the most turbulent of the regiments but in the ranks of the 3rd Michigan, best drilled of the volunteers, and even this revolt was more a citizen-soldier's idea of jest than deliberate mutiny.

The 3rd Michigan Cavalry during this ordeal had most nearly kept its morale but the men were bitterly homesick and longed for discharge. The regiment's "mutiny" was precipitated by incautious praise. After review one day, an inspecting officer congratulated the troopers upon their smart appearance and added that it was just such fine alert soldiers who were needed in Texas. Forthwith logicians in the regiment deduced that if smartness kept them in Texas, it were better not to be smart. The mutiny that ensued was really a practical joke, but Custer had scant appreciation of practical jokes unless he was their instigator.

At the next review, the erstwhile soldierly appearing 3rd Michigan was a grievous sight. Ninety clowning troopers in preparing for it had violated every tradition of smartness that they knew. Their uniforms were awry. Jackets were turned inside out; trousers were on hindside before; hats were worn backward, sabers at wrong hip, horses and horse equipment were as disreputable as earnest buffoons could make them. If lack of smartness brought them nearer discharge, the 3rd Michigan was eager to supply that lack.

The wrath of Custer, when he saw this unholy exhibition, was dire. He declared the entire regiment mutinous and placed the ninety masqueraders under arrest. A sergeant, said to have been ringleader, was court-martialed and sentenced to be shot.

Contrite over a jest that had gone too far, the whole regiment signed a round robin pleading for the miscreant's life. Custer was adamant and his vindictiveness bred threat of genuine mutiny. Word came to headquarters that sullen erstwhile jokers had sworn that, if their comrade died, Custer would be shot on the field of execution.

Whatever other virtues he had or had not, the General was not one to quail before a threat. His steel nerve on the day set for execution almost excuses his perpetration of its brutal melodrama.

The threats of the 3rd Michigan had a candor that alarmed even Custer's staff. His wife was frantic. His officers begged him not to attend the execution at which the sergeant and a deserter were to be shot. Custer laughed. His aides implored him, if he insisted on being present, to wear side-arms. Custer refused and forbade his staff to carry weapons.

On the morning of the execution, the turbulent division was drawn up on three sides of a square. Instead of taking his post the General wheeled his horse and followed by his apprehensive staff, rode slowly along the entire front of his command. Troopers glowered under the challenge in the bright blue eyes but no one stirred. There was no sound save the thump and scuff of hoofs.

A four-horse wagon, escorted by the firing party with reversed carbines, drove into the square. It bore two men—the sergeant and the deserter—sitting upon their coffins. Graves already had been dug at the square's open end. At the foot of these, the sentenced men squatted upon the boxes in which they would be buried, while the provost marshal received the carbines of the firing squad and loaded them, seven with ball cartridges and one with blank. There still was no sound among all those waiting resentful hundreds save the loud clatter of breech blocks. This was followed, after the eyes of the prisoners had been bandaged, by the strained voice of the provost marshal reading the warrant for the execution.

The firing party took position. The prisoners stood beside their coffins. There was an instant's pause before the command to fire. The yellow-haired general, so stiffly correct at his post, looked down the sullen line of the 3rd Michigan. He had called their bluff. The provost marshal took the blindfolded sergeant's arm and led him aside. At the crash of the volley, the deserter pitched forward and the sergeant, saved at the last moment by Custer's melodramatic plan, collapsed at the provost marshal's feet.

The General had challenged the temper of his command and had won. He had found in the execution a substitute for battle in which to impress men with his bravery. Thereafter, the uproarious elements in his division subsided and when the column reached Hempstead, Texas, Sheridan congratulated Custer on the condition of his men and horses. The comments of the not particularly felonious sergeant have not come down to us.

Mrs. Custer rode with her husband to Hempstead. The route lay across drought-smitten pine barrens and plains. It was here that she first became fully aware of the tireless energy of Custer at which all men marveled and some cursed. He was made, so his subordinates swore, of rawhide and rubber and steel springs. Leisure irked him. In garrison he might become harsh and short-tempered, but on the march, no matter whither that march led, he was the embodiment of cheerful vitality.

This endless physical resilience laid him open later to charges of cruelty that were sometimes only lack of imagination. He failed to remember that other men were not so built that they could go through a whole day's hot and dusty march with no liquid save the cold tea or coffee he drank at noon. He could throw himself from the saddle, curl up in the meagerest shade like a dog and go instantly to sleep. He could endure the heaviest march, bring his weary horse into camp, have another saddled and be off at a gallop to hunt or else inspect the next day's route. Thereafter while others ate and went soddenly to sleep, he would sit late in his tent, writing enormous letters.

Like Antæus, close contact with earth invigorated him. He was one of the healthiest, most vital men who ever lived, almost immune to hunger and thirst, heat and cold, sleepiness and fatigue. Even mosquitoes did not trouble him. Part of the dislike many felt for George Armstrong Custer may have sprung from his failure to see that other mortals were not as tireless as he.

That inexhaustible vigor and lust for prowess made the General the most ardent of hunters. When the chance for battle failed, this became his chief joy. Deer and smaller game were plentiful about Hempstead and hospitable planters gave the General dogs, the nucleus of the pack that, hereafter was to accompany him, in whole or in part, wherever he went.

Custer liked dogs and horses and after them all furred and feathered creatures. He adopted wolves and beavers, opossums, raccoons, prairie dogs, even a buffalo calf. He was of that scornful or maladjusted clan which displays more affection for lesser creatures than for its fellow beings, yet he was a ruthless hunter. To a soldier there may be no paradox in a code that relishes slaughter of a species and lavishes fondness on the individual.

All animals were Custer's delight, when he was not hunting them, but his deepest love—save for that he lavished on a few humans—went out to his dogs. He cherished them, talked with them, slept with them. His wife did not share his passion. They swarmed to his quarters. They packed his tent on the march and shared his bed. Some of the more savage frightened her, but she endured them all. She was always holding more tightly to her beloved because of the intrusion of some new terror.

Others were less tolerant of the General's devotion. His bulldogs and his beagles, his fox-hounds, staghounds, wolfhounds, the whole clamorous pack were cursed long and often by his command, and soldiers returning from the Black Hills expedition in 1875 grumbled that when Custer's dogs suffered sore feet, he ousted ill men from ambulances so that his animals might ride—a charge probably no more factual than many of the fantastic tales, pro and anti, that have been spun about him.

Hunt bugles of cowhorn were common in Hempstead. Custer and his brother, Tom, practised on these, with antiphonal discords from the hounds. Tom shot at a deer, killed a dog by mistake and was reminded frequently of that mishap all the rest of his life. A Captain Lyon slew his first buck and was immediately pinned down by the Custer brothers and drenched in the animal's gore. Custer wit was not cerebral. Emmanuel Custer came to visit his sons and immediately was made the butt of endless practical jokes.

Sheridan, on the border, was conducting an involved game of bluff, massing troops here and there, ostensibly preparing for an invasion of Mexico and endlessly complicating the worries of the hapless Maximilian. Custer's division was moved from Hempstead to Austin in November. The government was pouring troops into the state and the General was at one time commander of thirteen regiments of infantry and as many of cavalry. Hunting was scant at Austin and Custer turned to horse-racing. He spoiled the Texans when his bay beat the best Austin could offer, but Jack Rucker, another of his horses, was drugged just before a race and the natives got back their own and more.

Slowly the possibility of intervention in Mexico died away. Christmas came and Custer, attired as Santa Claus, delivered gifts from a tree to his family and members of his staff. Reconstruction made headway in Texas. Troops gradually were withdrawn and toward the end of that winter, Major-General Custer was mustered out of the volunteer service. Thanks to his brevet rank, he still retained his sounding title, but on the army lists he stood a mere captain of the 5th United States Cavalry.

PART TWO
INDIAN FIGHTER

PART TWO: INDIAN FIGHTER

CHAPTER ONE

INTERLUDE

THE youngest General in the American Army had become, overnight, a mere troop commander. His star had paled with the dawn of peace and now seemed quite extinguished. Sheridan's border maneuvers and Seward's peremptory demands had awed Napoleon. French troops were evacuating Mexico and with their departure vanished the chance of intervention, of new war, of fresh fame. Glory did not linger at a company officer's quarters. Furthermore, the pay of Custer, the lavish, had dropped from eight thousand dollars to two thousand dollars a year.

Before he left Texas, the erstwhile General had launched a harebrained scheme to improve his fortunes and regild his fame. Juarez, Diaz and Carvajal, leaders of the Mexican Army of Liberation, lingered across the Rio Grande, waiting for the departure of the French before they marched against the unhappy Maximilian. Russet gentlemen whispered magniloquent offers in Custer's ear. He considered these ever more seriously during his trip north.

He, the water hater, was wretchedly seasick when storm smote the converted blockade runner in which he, his wife, his father and his staff voyaged from Galveston to New Orleans, but by the time the steamer that carried them up the Mississippi was well under way, the tawdry promises of the Juarez emissaries seemed more alluring. Gaiety returned and he spent his surplus vitality in bedeviling Emmanuel, his father.

None of the reverence Custer paid his mother tinctured his attitude toward his sire. From his sons, the white-bearded patriarch

139

received the same rough treatment they would have accorded friends of their own age—a tribute more precious perhaps than filial respect. Emmanuel was a tough old gentleman. He had to be, for his sons' play was strenuous and physical. The laughter of George Armstrong and Thomas Custer had the paleolithic quality that demands, for inspiration, the spectacle of an abashed or discomfited victim. While in Texas, one of their typical jokes had been to assail their mounted father, pull his cape over his head and spur his horse, in the hope that the frightened animal would throw the old man. Their pranks aboard the river boat had the same flavor. They stole his dinner and picked his pocket and doused him with water from a door transom. The things at which men laugh are self-revealing.

At Cairo, part of Custer's staff told him good-by. The remainder dispersed at Detroit. The General and his family went on to Monroe for the summer. In April of 1866, he received leave of absence "until further notice."

Meanwhile, George Armstrong's influence and the two Medals of Honor his brother wore had won for the light-hearted Tom a commission as second lieutenant in the 1st Infantry.

Men with brilliant war records were in political and business demand. Custer was besieged by enterprises willing to pay well for his name on their letterheads. Adherents suggested that he run for Congress, for governor. There was tentative talk of a diplomatic post. The General listened apathetically to such suggestions. Glory dwelt in none of them. He was lonely without her presence, and she waited below the Rio Grande. The siren song of the Juarez junta drew him to New York.

There, hints and vague promises of the emissaries in Texas crystallized into a definite offer. Custer could have the rank of adjutant-general in the Mexican Army. His pay would be sixteen thousand dollars yearly, in gold. He was to raise a personal command of not less than one thousand cavalry in the United States, for which the Juarez government would supply funds.

Fortune seemed to smile, though Elizabeth Custer wept. Her husband, since Sheridan was out of reach, consulted General

Grant. Custer wanted a year's leave of absence with permission to take service abroad. To this odd request, Grant showed sympathy. He was never too scrupulous about international ethics. He gave Custer a letter to Ambassador Romero in Washington. In this the General of the army praised Custer's record as a cavalryman and added:

> "There is no officer in that branch of the service who had the confidence of General Sheridan to a greater degree and there is no officer in whose judgment I have greater faith than in Sheridan's. Please understand that I mean by this to endorse General Custer in a high degree."*

In the years ahead, both Grant and Sheridan were to alter their opinions of George Armstrong Custer. Despite their present endorsement, President Johnson refused to sanction a filibustering vacation by an officer of the army and, faced by the choice of abandoning the United States service or relinquishing the glamourous Mexican adventure, Custer elected to retain his commission.

The prospect of a dull and frugal life as a cavalry captain had altered and brightened. Congress was about to increase the standing army to forty-five regiments of infantry, five of artillery and ten of cavalry. This would mean the selection of fifteen hundred new officers and the consequent elevation of those already in the regular service.

On May 17, 1866, Judge Bacon died. His daughter writes, remembering her father's earlier hostility to her husband, that the Judge's last words bade her to be guided by Armstrong and follow him everywhere. She needed no such admonition.

The death of her father brought Elizabeth Custer sufficient inheritance to temper the niggardly pay of an army captain. She and her husband tarried for a time in the Monroe mansion that now was hers. The placid existence must have galled her high-strung mate and rekindled his longing for the Mexican adventure, for in July he and she left for Buffalo.

---

* Whittaker's *Life*.

Johnson was deep in his tragic struggle with a vindictive Congress. He was to speak in Buffalo at the beginning of the vain "swing around the circle" whereby he hoped to enlist popular support for his reconstruction plans. Custer begged again for the withheld leave of absence, and once more Johnson denied it.

The Chief Executive must have felt the charm which the young soldier exerted on certain men, for he invited Custer and his wife to accompany the presidential party on its tour. It has been said that Johnson feared assassination and selected Custer as his bodyguard. Whatever the cause of his invitation, the General and his wife accepted and enjoyed the oratorical junket, which included beside the unhappy President's attempt to persuade a still hostile people, the dedication of a Lincoln monument in Springfield, Illinois. Johnson seems to have enjoyed Custer, too, for before the tour ended he offered him the colonelcy of the new 9th Cavalry, a negro regiment. Custer declined. Elsewhere at about this time, a colonel of volunteers with a brilliant war record was declining a majority in the same regiment. His name was Frederick W. Benteen. He was to play a part in Custer's subsequent career.

On the presidential tour Custer visited the region of his birth for the last time. His family had left New Rumley and settled in Monroe. Johnson was scheduled to address the General's erstwhile neighbors at New Market railway station some two miles from Custer's old home. When the presidential train stopped, the platform was affrontingly empty and the walls of the station blazed with denunciatory placards.

"This is my native place," the bitterly embarrassed young soldier said to Johnson, "but I am ashamed of it."

He never returned, but a bronze statue of him, unveiled in 1932, now dominates an acre there, known as "Custer Park."

Shortly thereafter, the extended leave which had been a respite to his wife and an ordeal to Custer came to an end. In the army expansion, Sheridan saw to it that old leaders of the Cavalry Corps had their reward. Custer, Merritt and Devin were raised to the rank of lieutenant-colonels. The first of these on July 28, 1866, was assigned to duty with the still unborn 7th Cavalry.

The calm of the Bacon home in Monroe was shattered by uproar when the tidings of his promotion and imminent restoration to active duty reached the leave-surfeited officer. Custer's self-control was a brittle shell beneath which lay tumultuous emotions. When the impact of events cracked that thin armor, passion sprouted, shameless and wild. Enemies who in his lifetime called the man "crazy" may have seen him at such moments. To the uninformed spectator, the General's outbursts of glee must have been alarming but his wife's love of him transformed them into charm. She writes:

"From the first days of our marriage, General Custer celebrated every order to move with wild demonstrations of joy. His exuberance of spirits always found expression in some boyish pranks before he would set to work seriously to prepare for duty. As soon as the officer announcing the order to move had disappeared, all sorts of wild hilarity began. I had learned to take up a safe position on top of a table; that is if I had not been forcibly placed there as a spectator. The most disastrous result of the proceedings was possibly a broken chair, which the master of ceremonies would crash and perhaps throw into the kitchen by way of informing the cook that good news had come."*

There must have been raving and chair smashing in that Michigan homestead on the day when Glory, the long neglectful, relented and smiled once more. That smile held promise. No young officer, galled by inactivity, restlessly eager for fame, could have asked more of her than Custer had just received.

The nation clumsily readjusted itself to peace, but on the frontier the promise of battle remained. Custer, so the original orders read, was to report to Fort Garland in the heart of the Colorado Rockies. He found it at last, a tiny point on the atlas's page. His imagination took fire and he babbled to his wife, not of warlike Indians whom already she dreaded, but of the fishing, the hunting, the scenery and the glamour of this outpost of empire.

---

* Custer, Elizabeth B.: *Boots and Saddles,* New York, 1885.

When later, these orders were countermanded and the new Lieutenant-Colonel was directed to proceed instead to Fort Riley in Kansas, that post also was glorified by Custer's unbridled fancy. On the frontier waited romance and further pursuit of Glory. Where he met her made no difference.

The end of four years of conflict had turned the nation toward the West. Along the Platte Valley that had seen the wagon sails beat out to Oregon, to California, to Colorado, the Union Pacific thrust its steel westward. In Kansas, the Kansas Pacific reached toward Denver.

These lines, a few rivers and trails, the eruptions of mining camps where the adventurous sought gold and a pepper sprinkling of frontier forts were certainties on the maps of territory beyond the Missouri. Otherwise, the land that whites had sworn was to be Indian for all time was a provocative blank. Stretches of virgin paper could be filled with wonder by imaginations quick as Custer's. Here roamed herds of bison, so vast they were immune to slaughter; bear and elk, deer and antelope. Untold marvels dwelt in the maps' reticence. There were incredible hills and unimaginable valleys waiting the explorer and, through this mysterious land, ranged horsemen of a stone-age chivalry, splendid in paint, magnificent in feathers, terrible in war.

The West men imagined then was as fantastic as western novels and moving pictures of the present.

So Custer and a million other restless men of the late 'sixties dreamed of the Indian country. Many who sought to test the reality of their vision broke their hearts in that bright bare land. The 7th Cavalry's second in command found no disillusions there. He, who theretofore never had been beyond Illinois, took to the hard demanding life of the West like a seal to the sea. Ardent hunter, merciless foe, endlessly inquisitive pathfinder, remorseless driver of men—the West offered surcease to all the cravings of his tireless body, rapacious spirit and glory-hungry heart.

His wife had resolved to go with him. Only rarely from now on were they separated. For her, the promise of calm domesticity that peace had offered was gone forever. Her Glory-Hunter had found a new trail. He was to follow it with a few respites all the rest of his days, and Elizabeth Custer followed him. It was not her dying father's counsel that impelled her, but the valor of a timid adoring nature that placed love above terror.

The preparations for the journey were vast and complicated. A young woman friend of the General's wife was to accompany them, as companion to Elizabeth Custer and challenge to the hearts of subalterns. In addition to personal belongings, Custer took the beginnings of a circus with him—the thoroughbred racing mare bought in Texas, Jack Rucker and Phil Sheridan, his own chargers, and Custis Lee, spoil of the Appomattox campaign and now his wife's saddle horse. There were also Turk, a bulldog, Byron, a greyhound and several other dogs, as well as smaller pets, and Eliza, their cook, and other servants.

They left on October seventh; Custer, having bidden his mother good-by, cried on the way to the station. Thus he always parted from her. His wife writes that after each farewell, "the General would rush out of the house, sobbing like a child and then throw himself into the carriage beside me, completely unnerved."*

The Custers lingered in St. Louis. The city's gaiety was a grateful respite to a man who had grown heartily weary of the placidity of a little Michigan town. He and his wife visited a fair and she remembered, long afterward, how enraptured he was by the hogs on exhibition and how he recalled the pig his father had given him to raise, long ago.

They were present at the tournament in the amphitheater and the subsequent banquet and ball, into the glitter and splendor of which Custer, the practical joker, led the actor, Lawrence Barrett, attired in a gray business suit.

Barrett was appearing in *Rosedale,* and Custer, having sobbed through the performance, went backstage afterward to meet the star. Ardent friendship sprang up between them. During his rare sojourns in the East thereafter, Custer saw Barrett whenever possible.

---

* *Tenting on the Plains.*

"It is hard," Mrs. Custer writes, "to speak fittingly of the meeting of those two men. They joyed in each other as women do and I tried not to look when they met or parted, while they gazed with tears into each other's eyes and held hands like exuberant girls."*

The railroad carried Custer, his wife, her friend, his servants, horses and dogs to Leavenworth where frontier furniture was purchased. A train bore them, thereafter, across prairie to within ten miles of Fort Riley. Where the railroad momentarily ended they saw General Sherman, on an inspection tour, drive the spike which completed that division of the Kansas Pacific. A horse for Custer, an ambulance for the women and wagons for his baggage bore the party the rest of the way to Riley, November 3, 1866.

The fort was a square of story-and-a-half buildings set about a parade-ground. It stood on a plateau at the junction of the Smoky Hill and Republican Rivers and from it to the sharp horizon line rolled the brown desolate sea of the plains. In this raw new post Custer met the new raw regiment with which his fame is most closely linked.

On the frontier, where encroaching whites faced increasingly desperate red men, there tarried a peace that was only the aftermath of storm. Far-sighted men of the Indian Bureau strove to pacify and stabilize the outraged tribes, while settlers pressed forward into lands, forsworn by treaty, and Hancock, now commanding the Department of the Missouri, prepared to wrest the Indian problem from civilian hands.

---

* *Ibid.*

CHAPTER TWO

RED BACKGROUND

THE story of the Indian Wars is a tale of prodigious grand larcenies, wholesale retributive assassinations and subsequent mass lynchings. No comprehensive narrative yet has been written of this westward thrust of one race and the consequent eviction and practical extinction of another and weaker. It is probable that never will it be set down with entire accuracy, for white men on the frontier kept few records and red men, none.

It is a complex recital with all the aberration and confusion of nightmare. For the sake of national self-esteem oblivion might be the best tomb for a passage in history more foul than many that Americans survey with smug disapproval in the annals of other lands.

The threads of the tragedy are tangled. Already some of them have been lost, but in the marred pattern remaining you still may follow the major themes. There is the movement of a greedy people toward land they had forsworn because they had believed it worthless. There is the just and volatile resentment of far feebler folk who are split into mutually antagonistic, loosely organized tribes; a people wedded to a stone-age, individualistic chivalry; a proud, a war-loving and, eventually, a desperately frightened people. There is an Indian Bureau to which the fate of these folk is entrusted and, within that bureau, men who break their hearts in the vain effort to save their charges and men who outrageously plunder their wards.

Opposed to this unreliable force for frontier peace is the army, designed for war, justifiably distrustful of the Indian Bureau's integrity, jealously challenging its authority and, when this has been

147

successfully defied, indulging in ghastly reprisals on the red men. Technically, the troops on the frontier were stationed there to maintain peace and uphold treaties. The prime purpose of a military organization is battle. When placed in judgment between indignant savages and angry members of their own race, soldiers are not equitable police.

Innumerable outrages were committed by reds upon whites. These the army punished by blind retribution. There was also at least an equal number of white outrages upon the Indian. There is no record of the army slaughtering whites in reprisal.

There are innumerable minor strands in this insane design. There are the aggressive frontier folk who wail inordinately over Indian aggression, and humanitarians in the East who deplore with minor, unheeded protest the reiterant sullying of national honor by the violation of treaty after treaty with the red tribes.

There are Indian chiefs who are bribed or frightened into selling the land of their people, and other leaders who deny the legality of such a sale.

There is the blundering of a government that never lets its right hand know whom its left hand plunders. Here is the record in brief:

By 1825, it had been established that beyond what are now the western boundaries of Wisconsin, Illinois, Missouri and Arkansas began the Great American Desert, a parched, worthless land, obviously fitted for Indian occupation. Accordingly, all earlier treaties were torn up; eastern tribes were transported into that area, and in 1835 Jackson announced to Congress that the work of removal had been completed, adding, "The pledge of the United States has been given by Congress that the country destined for the residence of this people shall be forever secured and guaranteed to them."

For a little, this arbitrarily raised dam held back the whites but rivulets filtered through, flowing to Oregon, roaring to California, moving into Minnesota.

In 1851, the Sioux in that last territory were forced to cede most of their land. Before the treaty was ratified they were hustled out by an influx of settlers. Soldiers at Fort Snelling refused to interfere. The Sioux, furthermore, never received a cent of the cash compensation promised them.

In 1853, the tribes in Kansas and Nebraska were compelled to sell most of their holdings there. Tidings of gold in Colorado sent, in 1859, a stampede into the heart of the Cheyenne-Arapaho country. In 1861, some chiefs of these tribes made a treaty at Fort Wise, selling the western half of their range which the whites had already taken.

The mounting pressure of the invaders bred heat. There was an uprising of desperate Sioux in Minnesota during 1862. There was trouble on the plains, as indefinite in origin and as unscrupulous as a dog fight. Stage lines were strangled, settlements burned. In 1864, Colorado militia attacked White Antelope's and Black Kettle's band of Cheyennes, dwelling peaceably on Sand Creek. Under the leadership of Colonel John Chivington, a Methodist minister, and Major Scott Anthony, brother of Susan B. Anthony, they wrought indescribably hideous massacre of men, women and children.

Tidings of this deed swept like wind-blown sparks across the plains and, where they lit, fire blazed. The Sioux, allied with Cheyennes and Arapahos, struck against guilty and innocent alike and the white men retaliated in kind. Indian wars had the aimless savagery of a blindfold battle. On either side the blameless suffered. To settlers, even to soldiers, all brown men on horses looked alike. Indians believed in the tribe's responsibility for the sins of individual members, and to them outrage by white men was a debt due in blood from the next whites encountered.

In 1865, the haphazard war moved north into the heart of the Sioux country. In crass violation of still another treaty, the government began a fort-guarded road from Fort Laramie to the mining camp that had been established at Bozeman. For a year thereafter, patriots under Red Cloud fought for their land and, at last, won. The road and its protecting forts were abandoned.

Meanwhile, in the land south of the Platte, the war against Cheyenne and Arapaho continued to smolder. It had taken heavy toll in lives and property from the whites. It had shaken the once mighty Cheyenne people by the Sand Creek slaughter. In October of 1865, war-weary chiefs, Black Kettle among them, assembled on the Little Arkansas and agreed to another treaty. This granted them a new reservation, partly in Kansas, partly in what is now Oklahoma. That treaty was never confirmed by the Senate.

Until 1867, when a further treaty was drawn, the Cheyennes and Arapahos had no home. During this interlude they were as panicky as hard-hunted animals. The tribes were scattered piecemeal over a vast territory and one of the warrior fraternities of the Cheyennes, the Dogs, opposed the Little Arkansas treaty and wished to continue the war. Colonel E. W. Wynkoop, agent for the Arapahos and Cheyennes, and an honorable and patient man, gradually overcame the fears of his savage charges and by tact and fair dealing eventually concentrated many of the Cheyennes, including the insurgent Dogs, about Fort Larned.

Gradually, during 1866, the war south of the Platte died away, not into lasting peace but another precarious truce. There could be no peace while a weak yet valiant barbarism held territory that a stronger race craved and invaded over trampled treaties.

Certain pages in our history might to-day be less soiled if the whites had continued Massachusetts' early war of extermination against the Pequods until the continent had been swept clean of obstructive savages. That course would have had no more brutality than the protracted piecemeal cruelty of the system pursued by sentimental hypocrites. It would have possessed at least a wholesome honesty. The army, with its hard logic, was willing to follow some such remorselessly consistent plan for the settlement of the Indian question. It was Sheridan who said: "The only good Indian is a dead one."

The regiment that was born at wind-ravaged Fort Riley in September, 1866, was to do its part to fulfil this aphorism.

The 7th Cavalry, when Custer joined it seven weeks after Major John W. Davidson of the 2nd Cavalry had begun the work of organization, was still a haphazard assemblage of ragamuffins and their betters. An outfit more catholic probably never gathered anywhere. Among the rank and file were Civil War veterans, some of whom had held commissions during the conflict. There were "gentleman rankers" and men who had turned to the army as a refuge from the law. There were brave and competent soldiers and a most egregious collection of drunkards and shirkers in that half orphan regiment which was destined to be guided during its formative years by a stern stepfather.

The officers of the command were almost as heterogeneous a lot. The colonel was Andrew J. Smith, old Indian fighter and commander of the XVI Corps in the Armies of the West. He, Custer and the senior Major, Alfred Gibbs, leader of a brigade in the First Division of Sheridan's cavalry, were the sole West Point graduates in the original officer personnel. Gibbs suffered from a lance wound incurred in an earlier Indian war and died at Fort Leavenworth in 1867. It was he who organized the 7th's band and first drilled it in the ditty Custer had selected as its warsong.

Garry Owen, divorced from the glamour that history and regimental tradition have cast upon it, is a tune chiefly notable for its plagiaristic resemblance to *The Campbells Are Coming.* Its words, which proclaim it a drinking chorus, celebrate the delights of knocking out the Limerick street-lights and beating up the bailiffs. Its music has, however, the lilt of galloping horses and it is possibly for this reason that Custer chose for future immortality so otherwise inappropriate a song.

The junior majors were Wickliffe Cooper, erstwhile colonel of the 4th Kentucky Cavalry, United States Volunteers, and Joel H. Elliot.

Elliot was a pleasant and earnest youth, with a high fair forehead beneath wavy hair and a studious face, framed by sideburns. He had served inconspicuously as a captain of volunteer cavalry in the war. At its conclusion he had become superintendent of schools in Toledo, Ohio. He took the army examinations, hoping at most for a commission as first lieutenant. To the youngster's consternation, the board scanned the almost perfect record he achieved and forthwith made him a major. He was younger than any captain in the 7th Cavalry and the junior of many of the lieutenants.

The Custer caravan arrived at the post when its normally cramped quarters were terrifically overcrowded. The 7th was still too young to take over the fort and the original garrison lingered. The advent of the new Lieutenant-Colonel was heralded by a dogfight in the ambulance where Mrs. Custer, her friend, the cook Eliza, and some of the General's favorite animals were riding. The events of the next few months were equally impromptu and disheveled.

The elderly Colonel Smith appeared, tarried for only a little while and departed. From then on, throughout almost all the rest of his service, it was the Lieutenant-Colonel's lot to guide and mold the regiment in which he was always, nominally, only second in command. This, at the outset, was a difficult task. The material that he had to handle was no more reverent than the volunteers he had disciplined in Alexandria. Before the first year of the 7th's existence was spent, Custer had another mutiny on his hands.

At the beginning, the morale was low with little at hand to lift it. The War Department had chosen a God-forsaken spot in which to give birth to the regiment and it had sent to lead it a wide variety of officers.

Among them was a Frenchman, a Prussian, an ex-Montana judge, a former member of Congress, and a half-breed Indian, Lieutenant McIntosh. There was Captain Myles W. Keogh, once a Papal zouave, a devil-may-care Irishman with mustache and imperial and an unholy thirst which he could curb only by placing all his cash in the hands of Finnegan, his striker and actual guardian. Keogh died at the Little Bighorn.

So did William W. Cook, a gigantic Canadian soldier of fortune with long black Dundreary whiskers that won for him the nickname of "Queen's Own," and Tom Custer who had been transferred from the infantry to his brother's regiment. These were lieutenants on the original roster of the 7th Cavalry.

Other captains included Louis McLane Hamilton—a soft-voiced

CAPTAIN AND BREVET BRIGADIER GENERAL FREDERICK W. BENTEEN
Copyright by Barry

aristocrat with a little mustache and features faintly resembling those of his grandsire, Alexander—and Frederick W. Benteen.

Beneath a shock of prematurely white hair, Benteen's prominent eyes looked out upon the world from a rugged rubicund face. There was challenge in their stare. There was, it seems, a chronic challenge in his nature. A Virginian by birth, he had cast his lot with the Union when secession came and had led with distinction the 10th Missouri Cavalry and later a brigade in the West. Men who had fought beside him in the Union army knew him for a brave and an able officer. Men who served with him in the 7th Cavalry, confirm that judgment. General Hugh L. Scott recalled Captain Benteen as one of the most competent leaders he ever knew, a bluff and genial man when sober, a rancorous reviewer of old grudges when in liquor. General E. A. Garlington, who joined the 7th immediately after the Little Bighorn campaign, has this to say of Benteen:

"From what I saw of him and from the impression of the current opinion of his old comrades in the regiment, I regarded him as a fine, practical field soldier. From my own observation, and remarks made by officers who had served with him since the organization of the regiment under all sorts of conditions, I should say that his chief asset as a soldier was demonstrated in action when the bullets began to sing—coolness, poise, self-command under stress.

"Taken by and large, he was rather a singular character, proud and a little vain perhaps. He had made an excellent showing as a cavalry officer in the Western Army during the Civil War. He was older than the majority of the officers in the regiment. He was not an habitual drinker but once or twice a year he would begin and keep it up for days, would not go home and would finally be given harbor by some sympathetic bachelor until he was ready to face his family. It was during such periods that he became abusive and insulting to those whom he disliked or disapproved of. He was much liked by most of the officers in the regiment and they took care of him in such periods."

The estimate of Colonel C. A. Varnum, sole surviving officer of the Little Bighorn fight, parallels General Garlington's. He remembers that "Benteen drank and played poker and when under the influence of liquor would utter sneering remarks. He was a law unto himself and a soldier of undoubted courage."

An enlisted man's opinion confirms that of Benteen's brother officers. Theodore Goldin, one of the few remaining troopers who rode into the Little Bighorn Valley that tragic Sunday, said this:

> "I always regarded Benteen as one of the very best officers in the regiment and so far as my acquaintance with him went—and I knew him better perhaps than any other officer of the regiment—I found him inclined to be outspoken in praise or criticism but on the whole regarded him as a soldier and a gentleman. Strong in his likes and dislikes, perhaps, but usually prepared to give good reason for either."

This, as clearly as we can see through the haze of almost sixty years, is the authentic figure of the man. Of all the 7th Cavalry's officers, only Custer himself has been more obscured by fable and half-truth. Romanticists, who have insisted on turning the tragedy of the Little Bighorn into conventional drama, arbitrarily have cast Benteen as a villain in the piece.

Evidence that Benteen did not like Custer is plentiful, but the army and even the officer personnel of the 7th Cavalry was well supplied with men of that same mind. Benteen was a hard intemperate realist; Custer, an abstemious, picturesque romanticist. Injustice, real or fancied, to himself or another, rankled in Benteen's mind. Custer could not cherish grudges. His immediate response to affront might be fiery indignation or cruel reprisal, but by the morrow the offense would be forgotten.

He had the romantic magnanimity of youth. His wife writes, omitting further identification, of one who had been her husband's bitter enemy in his earlier years. Misfortune smote this man and he sought a commission in the army. Custer, learning of this, exerted his influence on his foe's behalf and helped him into his new profession.

Myles Moylan, during the Civil War, had been captain in the 4th Massachusetts Cavalry. He enlisted in the 7th Cavalry as a private, rose swiftly to regimental sergeant major and in 1867 received a commission. The bachelor officers' mess declined to admit the former ranker, and Custer, learning of this, invited the bewildered Moylan to become a boarder in the Custer home and made the new officer his adjutant.

Acts such as these were picturesquely generous. Benteen was neither romantic nor forgiving. He and his young superior were as antipathetic as water and fire.

From their first meeting, Benteen disliked Custer. He deemed the other's love of display cheap pose and his grandiloquent speech, boastful. In a letter, now in Dr. Philip G. Cole's collection, Benteen describes his first official call upon his new Lieutenant-Colonel and says that Custer spent much time reciting his own prowess in the Civil War, interspersed with readings from the Third Cavalry Division order book. "I had been," writes Benteen, "on intimate personal relations with many great generals and had heard no such bragging as was stuffed into me that night."

Apparently, this was the beginning of a dislike that subsequent events magnified into lifelong hatred by Benteen. Jealousy also may have increased the captain's animus. He had been a distinguished soldier in the Civil War and now, in the topsyturvy organization of the 7th, men whom he considered less able—and among them he included Custer—were placed above him. Others felt similar grievances.

Former colonels who were now lieutenants, men who had commanded brigades and now were captains, grumbled to each other about their spectacular junior who was the regiment's second in command and soon to become its actual leader. The sublime self-confidence of Custer, the rasping strictures of his discipline, the very intemperance of his temperance galled his brother officers. When the Lieutenant-Colonel actually assumed command, these traits pressed sorely on the rank and file, too.

Custer tarried with the 7th only briefly at their first meeting. Soon after reporting, he was summoned to Washington to appear before the Examining Board and did not return to Riley until December eighteenth. From then until February twenty-sixth, he was ranked by Colonel Smith. He first commanded the regiment February twenty-sixth to March fourth, and again took charge March twenty-sixth, when the 7th rode out on Hancock's grandiose, trouble-making expedition.

From the first, the men were not happy at Riley and there was a steady trickle of desertions. Singly and in squads, disheartened troopers vanished. One set of sinners, jammed into the guardhouse for drunkenness, edified the post by gospel hymns and loud prayers while they dug their way out of their prison's rear and then went over the hill.

In addition to loneliness and cold, there was the further morale-lowering factor of abominable rations. Surplus food, foisted on the government by crooked contractors during the last part of the war, was shipped to the unhappy regiment—weevily hardtack, thick sides of bacon which, when unwrapped, were found to contain lean and moldy meat with a flat stone included to increase weight. The men at Riley and those detached to garrison other frontier posts spent a wretched winter. The wind blew ever colder. Snow brought further isolation. The sutler's liquor was sole respite from monotony for officers and men.

Custer's quarters had no sink, no closets. The water was hard and drawn at need from a barrel that stood by the kitchen door. The wind blew clothes on the washline to ribbons. Eggs were a dollar a dozen; butter a dollar a pound.

Elizabeth Custer was happy. If she mothered her husband, he spent upon her more than paternal care. He frowned upon her when she attempted housework and bade her leave this to the servants. She writes of how he warmed her clothes before the fire and poured the water for her morning bath. Never, while he was near, could she remember buttoning her own shoes.

Always the cruel winters of the plains were the happiest part of the year for her. While they endured, there was peace on the frontier. She looked forward with dread to the advent of every spring, for it brought, not respite, but the possibility of another campaign. She must have prayed that the winter of 1866-67 might never end for when it had passed, the pompous and obstinate General Hancock, deaf to the protests of agents who were doing their utmost to reassure and pacify the panicky Cheyennes and Arapahos, was resolved to march the 7th Cavalry, infantry and guns, deep into Indian country for no more plausible reason than to frighten the already terrified tribes.

Fear all that winter chilled the hearts of Indians whose range was south of the Platte—dread born of a treaty not yet endorsed by the government, quickened by the mounting pressure of the white thrust westward, lifted toward panic by rumors of the new army that was coming in the spring to perpetrate a vaster Sand Creek massacre.

In the north, the Sioux still raged about the forts Carrington had built illegally to guard the treaty-breaking Bozeman Road. On December 21, 1866, Red Cloud's warriors wiped out Captain William J. Fetterman and seventy-nine men who essayed a sortie from Fort Phil Kearny. On December twenty-eighth, Sherman sent his prescription for restoring peace in the north to Grant: "We must proceed with vindictive earnestness against the Sioux, even to their extermination—men, women and children. Nothing less will reach the root of the case."

"The army," Custer assures us, on page 21 of his *My Life on the Plains,* "is the Indian's best friend."

CHAPTER THREE

HANCOCK MARCHES

WARM winds came up from the south to Fort Riley and at their touch the drifts shrank. Each day Elizabeth Custer marked the snow's withdrawal; each day her husband fretted at its maddening deliberation. When the plains were clear, he was to ride out on Glory's trail again.

Eight troops of the 7th Cavalry were to accompany Hancock's bellicose expedition and Custer, not the elderly colonel of the regiment, was to lead them. He itched, this blacksmith's son, to grasp his still untempered regiment and hammer, hammer, hammer it into a weapon, fit to meet whatever adventure or battle lay beyond the provocative horizon. Already the spell of the West had laid hold on him. He was never to shake it off.

There was psychic kinship between the man and the land, the glamourous and harsh Indian country, to which his remaining years were dedicated. The West was the appropriate background for him. Against it, his personality shone so vividly that men to-day only half remember his Civil War prowess in the stronger brilliance of Custer in Kansas, Dakota, Montana.

By adoption, the West made him her own. He was a precocious child, quick to learn her ways. Most generals, bouncing miserably along in ambulances, remained forever outlanders. Custer, riding his charger at the head of the 7th Cavalry, turned himself into an able scout, a competent guide, a daring and level-headed explorer, a warrior as unscrupulous as the dark horsemen who opposed him.

No trace of that adaptability can be found in his wife. For the love she bore her husband, she endured the frontier's privation and peril—and all her days thereafter, looked back with reminiscent shudders on the danger and discomfort and most of all upon the dread of parting that each spring brought. "I used to be glad that ours was a mounted regiment. If we had belonged to the infantry, the regiment would have been sent out sooner." She learned, that spring of 1867, to invest with terror the cheerful sounds of a cavalry post on the eve of campaign—the flat chiming of blacksmiths' anvils, the rumble and clatter of wagons and the whine of sabers on the grindstone.

At Leavenworth, Hancock, the bull-headed, was organizing the infantry and artillery and vast wagon train of his command. Fourteen hundred men, the largest military force ever seen on the plains, were to comprise this expedition. There was no reason for it. In the north, where Carrington held the Bozeman Road forts, hard fighting still endured. In the land that the army prepared to invade, there was almost complete peace.

The still unconfirmed treaty of the Little Arkansas was at work. The Cheyennes, enraged and frightened by the slaughter at Sand Creek, were turning with increasing confidence to their agent, Colonel Wynkoop. The scattered remnants of what had been the most powerful in battle of all plains tribes were assembling gradually about his headquarters at Fort Larned.

Wynkoop had warned the Department Commander that the march of armed forces toward the Cheyennes would be regarded by the survivors of Sand Creek as prelude to further massacre. The agent of the Kiowas and Comanches added his persuasions, to no effect. In a blustering letter, Hancock explained that his expedition's purpose was to awe and impress the Indians with the martial might of white men. He was not seeking war, but he implied that he would not be reluctant to engage therein. "No insolence," he wrote, "will be tolerated from any bands of Indians whom we may encounter. We wish to show them that the government is ready and able to punish them if they are hostile, although it may not be disposed to invite war."

The upper millstone of the War Department, the nether of the Indian Bureau, were grinding again with the Cheyennes between them.

Late in March, Hancock, in his ambulance, with six companies of infantry, a battery of light artillery and a train that included pontoons arrived at Fort Riley. On March twenty-seventh, having been reenforced by another company of infantry and Troops A, D, H and M of the 7th Cavalry under Lieutenant-Colonel Custer, he marched to scare the Indians into abject surrender.

Included in the army were five hounds belonging to Custer. These shared his Sibley tent and his bed at night. Elizabeth Custer saw him depart, stridently gay upon his charger, Phil Sheridan. As much of herself and of her thought as she might send went with him—her heart and a barrel of apples and another of onions. He loved these last and she hated them, so he ate them only on campaign.

Hancock's column crawled over the horizon and vanished, leaving the woman the desolation of waiting, taking her husband for the first time into the brown bright waste for which fate seemed to have formed him; that hard and perilous land he was to love.

From the first, he took to Indian campaigning with an ease beyond the rest of the blundering regiment. On the march the bubbling energy that activity seemed only to set more violently boiling, found release in imposing extra drills to harden and smarten his command; in chasing jack-rabbits with his hounds; in sitting up long after the rest of the camp was asleep to write prodigious letters to his wife. He kept her most recent in his pocket and re-read it often.

Despite the skepticism of his comrades, who predicted that he would outgrow in matrimony his epistolary fervor, the size and frequency of his letters never diminished. The last of them was written on the day, still nine years hence, when he led his regiment up the Rosebud toward the Little Bighorn battle-field.

In these epistles are glimpses of the paradoxical essence of the man. Their dominant note is pride, not the weathered and dignified balance of the mature who have evolved formulæ for life, but the prowess-loving boastfulness of the very young.

Custer has ridden so many miles and is still untired. Others have gone to bed, utterly fatigued, but though it is nearly morning he is still unwearied. He and his dogs have wrought spectacular slaughter on a hunt. His companions marvel that he is so immune to cold. General So-and-So has paid him this or that compliment.

They are artless letters to have been written by a man in his late twenties and early thirties, in whose hands the lives of many other men rested. In their youthful strain one may find the strength and the weakness which seemed to stir in others a great devotion or hatred. George Armstrong Custer never became completely adult and it may have been this protracted adolescence with its aberrations, its yearnings for glory, its spectacular generosities and cruelties that his associates found infinitely charming or equally intolerable.

He wrote while the Hancock column marched toward Fort Larned.

> "Often, so very often, when meditating on my past eventful life, I think of the many reasons why I, above my fellow men, should be thankful to that wise and good Being who has borne me through so many scenes of danger, unharmed, and through whose benefices I have been recipient of honors and pleasures seldom heaped so bountifully on one so young and unassisted by family, wealth and political influence."*

And in another letter, written on the same march, Custer, the critic, looks approvingly over the shoulder of Custer, the writer, who reveals the prime motive force of his whole career:

> "In years long numbered with the past when I was verging upon manhood, my every thought was ambitious—not to be wealthy, not to be learned, but to be great. I desired to link my name with acts and men and in such a manner as to be a mark of honor, not only to the present but to future generations."

This is not a march-worn husband writing to his wife. This is adolescence engaged in autobiography. Further in the same letter:

---

* *Tenting on the Plains.*

"My ambition has been turned into an entirely new channel. Where I was once eager to acquire worldly honors and
distinctions, I am content to try and modestly wear what I
have and feel grateful for them when they come, but my desire
now is to make myself a man worthy of the blessings heaped
upon me."*

So, in his snow-surrounded Sibley, George Armstrong Custer extols his own humility. Whatever inspired this pious mood did not
endure. Within a few months after forswearing mundane pomps
and vanities, part of his regiment had mutinied against him and
his own insubordination had brought about his court martial and
punishment.

The Hancock expedition picked up Troops F and G of the 7th
Cavalry at Fort Harker and on the seventh of March reached Fort
Larned where Troops E and K joined and where Wynkoop once
more attempted to dissuade Hancock from approaching closer to
the terrified Cheyennes on Pawnee Fork, some forty miles away.
He sent runners out to summon chiefs to a council at the fort.

On the morrow it snowed. The cold was so bitter that pickets
on the horse-lines whipped the animals all night to keep them from
freezing and one hitherto scornful subordinate who had mocked
at Custer's habit of sleeping with his dogs, humbly borrowed a
hound from him as a bed warmer.

The storm was not the only reason for the Indian's delay. With
the memory of Sand Creek scarcely three years old, they were profoundly reluctant to place themselves within reach of troops again.
Spurred on by Hancock, Wynkoop sent further summons on the
eleventh and received word that there was a buffalo hunt afoot on
Pawnee Fork and the chiefs begged to be excused. Despite the
agent's protests, Hancock announced that he would march upon
the village, March thirteenth. On the evening of the twelfth, a few
of the more valiant chiefs came in, among them Tall Bull, leader of
the Dog fraternity, who was to die at Summit Springs with fifty-one
of his brotherhood when Carr massacred them in 1869 at the cost
of one trooper wounded.

---

* *Ibid.*

"In years long numbered with the past," he wrote, "my every thought was ambitious—not to be wealthy, not to be learned, but to be great . . . to future generations."

Hancock insisted on holding a council that night, a sinister time to the Indian mind, and the General's baleful statements did little to quiet apprehension. Hancock accused the Cheyennes of having white prisoners and demanded their return. The village on Pawnee Fork had none.

With a fine disregard of promises, uttered or implied, Hancock overrode the protests of Wynkoop and marched upon the village, April thirteenth. All that day the column was watched from a distance by brown, feathered horsemen. Edmond Guerrier, the scout, whom men called "Geary," informed Hancock that the smoke ahead was caused by Indians who burned off the grass to keep the cavalry from coming too close to their camp.

That night, Pawnee Killer, chief of a band of Sioux who were visiting the village, and White Horse, a Cheyenne leader, came to Hancock's tent and promised a conference on the morrow at this point if the soldiers would only stay away from the Indian camp. When the conferees had not arrived by eleven the following day, Hancock pressed forward and met them, coming in.

This probably was Custer's first sight of Indians in mass. The advance of the barbaric horsemen awed him, as it did all novices and many veterans, into overestimating their numbers. He writes of them in *My Life on the Plains* as though they were a great host. Actually, there were not more than three hundred.

Hancock's welcome to his invited guests was at least equivocal. Infantry was deployed, the battery wheeled into position and the 7th Cavalry, sabers drawn, galloped to the flank of the hastily formed battle line. The Indians halted. A few chiefs rode out into the wind-swept land between the forces and held a brief conference there with Hancock and Custer.

The chiefs explained that their women and children were frightened—from the tactics of the force opposing them it must have seemed at the moment that fright was wholly justified—and begged Hancock to come no nearer the village. The General insisted on approaching but promised that his soldiers would keep away from the lodges.

They found the Cheyenne camp at the foot of a line of bluffs along the Pawnee Fork and set their tents a half-mile distant. At midnight, Hancock ordered Custer to surround the village.

A pledge given to Indians was a pledge unuttered. Word had been brought in that the Cheyennes were running away. Hancock ordered the 7th Cavalry out to hold the frightened savages. Twelve hours after he had given his word that his soldiers would not enter the Cheyenne camp, his troopers were moving against it.

The Indians had absolute right, as far as any red man had rights, to be where they were. Their village site had been sanctioned by their agent. They had been quiet all winter and the army had no cause whatever to interfere, but the squadrons of Custer marched on the camp.

The Cheyennes already had fled. What might have been the outcome otherwise, those who have read of Sand Creek and Washita and other massacres called "battles" by the victors may guess. If Indians had remained; if, waking, they had marked the stealthy approach of soldiers, their instinctive resistance would have been prelude to slaughter.

"They feared us; feared another massacre like Chivington's," Custer wrote his wife immediately after the flight had been discovered.

Hancock was furious and on the morrow sent Custer and his troopers to run down the fugitives. Pursuit inevitably confirmed the Cheyennes' worst fears. They scattered and left for the cavalry a hundred trails, spreading out like fan sticks. Thereafter, when they had shaken off pursuit, they returned to the war-path from which Wynkoop had lured them with much tact and patience.

A raw regiment and a leader still inexperienced floundered deplorably in pursuit despite the guidance of Wild Bill Hickok and other scouts. Winter had left the men soft and they were still little more than recruits. An entire troop, sent out to ride to the nearest stage station on the Smoky Hill Road, got lost and reapproaching the main command by accident, mistook it and was mistaken by it for hostile Indians.

Some blunderers in a hunting party killed one of Custer's hounds, and the Lieutenant-Colonel himself, while pursuing a buffalo, managed to shoot his own horse, Custis Lee, whom his wife adored, and had to walk, burdened with saddle and bridle, a number of miles back to his regiment. These were the only fatalities in Custer's first foray against the Indians.

He returned to Pawnee Fork, however, with news that the Cheyennes had attacked the stage line stations. Hancock in retaliation burned the deserted village. He had managed, for no legitimate reason whatever, to start another war.

Hancock proceeded to Fort Dodge, where he conferred with Kiowas and Arapahos. The 7th Cavalry marched to Fort Hays. There was no apparent need for Custer's haste, but he drove his men hard, handling his novices as though they were veterans of his old Third Division. "One night," he pridefully writes his wife, "we were marching till daylight."

He tarried for a time at Hays and Mrs. Custer joined him there. The peril of her trip deep into country rekindling with Indian peril did not daunt, though it frightened her sorely. "It seemed to me the end of all the troubles that would ever enter my life had come when I was lifted out of the ambulance into my husband's tent."

They were together for a blissful week or so. It may have been that their love for each other burned so ardently because it was always bounded by separations.

Hancock had placed Custer in command of all the troops on the Smoky Hill Road, and the government had solemnly declared a war, which already it had started, upon the Cheyennes and those bands of Sioux who ranged south of the Platte. Troops G and F were detached from Custer's command for special duty while the regiment camped on Big Creek near Fort Hays. The six troops remaining prepared for further campaign.

Officers and men alike still were unfit to cope with the hard task of Indian chasing or the harder discipline of their leader. While at Hays, four officers started off on a buffalo hunt, lost themselves completely and turned up, twenty-four hours later, at a distant stage station. In the rank and file there was resentful muttering. Custer's inexhaustible energy was winning him the hatred of lesser men.

That energy in time became Satanic. On June first, the six

troops of the 7th Cavalry marched to scout along the Platte. Custer tarried at Hays with his wife until midnight. Then with two orderlies, Will Comstock, the scout, and four Delaware trackers, he rode after his command, reached it at daybreak, breakfasted, led it at a smart pace all day; that evening when the weary regiment camped, rode two miles farther, scaled a hill to inspect an Indian burial scaffold and wrote thereafter to his wife before he slept.

The troops found no Indians on the march to Fort McPherson on the Platte. It was summer now; grazing was good and the feathered light cavalry of the plains never were seen unless they wished to be. While their ponies fed well and were strong, they could outmarch, outfight and infinitely outmaneuver the plodding troopers.

It was like trying to run down wolves with artillery. Custer marched his men hard, and, as the galling sense of impotence grew, harder still. He replied to their mutterings, to the protests of wiser officers, with still more vigorous pursuit of a derisive enemy that would not stand still to be defeated. This was a foe as evasive as Mosby himself. From the Platte to the Republican and the Smoky Hill, then back toward the Platte again, he pushed his increasingly tired command. His sole response to the ripening mutiny in their ranks seems to have been "If I can stand it, they can." He was not made of the same material as other men.

For long, the column's gropings were so barren of battle that Custer bade his wife join him in the field. She had returned to Fort Riley from the camp at Hays. Now she hurried to Fort Wallace, still farther west, whither Custer was sending his wagon train for more supplies. She was to go to him under escort of Cook, the gigantic, side-whiskered Canadian-born.

Colonel Smith, now commanding the Department of the Upper Arkansas and tarrying at Fort Wallace, flatly refused her permission. Her agony of disappointment saved her a more hideous ordeal, for the Indians knew that Custer had divided his command and for the first time, struck.

At dawn of June twenty-fourth, Pawnee Killer's Sioux rode down screeching upon the 7th's camp on the Republican, hoping to stampede the horses. They failed, but there was a brisk fight in which Custer joined, attired in a red nightshirt, before they were driven off. The warriors trotted away with such provocative deliberation that Captain Hamilton's troop was ordered in pursuit, and driving the taunting enemy before them, walked deep into an ambush laid by further Sioux, from which the remaining troops rode to extricate him. The Indians withdrew. They had afforded Custer his first lesson in red strategy.

On June twenty-sixth, the train that was to have brought Mrs. Custer to her husband's camp was assailed by Indians, midway between Wallace and the Republican. For hours, a running fight endured and was ended only by the appearance of reenforcements, sent out by Custer to insure his wife's safety.

Thereafter the hostiles vanished completely and were seen no more while the weary column blundered along the Republican and then crept northward again toward the Platte. They had accomplished nothing whatever of military worth. They had ridden out to subdue hostile Indians and had succeeded only in prodding the smoldering fire of war into fiercer blaze.

The yellow-haired leader of the ragged squadrons, whose ardent face now was masked by a stubble of red beard, had learned the elements of Indian warfare which were those of the wolf against the buffalo—leap in, slash and dodge away unhurt—but he had evolved no military counter-offensive. The exhausted troopers of Custer's command also had had their first lesson in the ordeal of his leadership, and the ferment of mutiny was at work in their sullen ranks.

CHAPTER FOUR

COURT MARTIAL

THE flawed imagination that blinded Custer to the sufferings of other men was the chief of many afflictions his command endured. This myopia plus incredible stamina, plus egotism, that esteemed no pronoun save the first person singular, wrought havoc with the not too lofty morale of trail-weary troopers.

In the years to come, when the unfit in spirit and flesh had been more thoroughly weeded from the 7th Cavalry, that regiment consisted of men whose hearts beat in the rapid measure of Custer's and of other stout souls who were able to endure what they did not admire.

It was one of the best cavalry units in the service that Custer led along the Yellowstone in 1873; that explored the Black Hills in 1874; that marched behind singing bugles up from the Rosebud's mouth on June 22, 1876, toward the vain tragedy of the Little Bighorn.

The gaunt resentful troopers who fumbled along the Platte and Smoky Hill Rivers in the summer of 1867 were not of that later durable and competent strain. Their lips were cracked by alkali water, their faces flayed by sun, their spirits depressed by the tactics of their commander. They had jolted interminable miles through a parched and shadeless land to find an enemy who was visible only when he preferred to be and declined, derisively, to be abolished.

Custer had led his squadrons out to break the power of the hostile Cheyenne and Sioux and to herd the stricken remnants of vanquished tribes into captivity. Whatever hope he cherished of the glory to be found in chasing Indians wilted in the pitiless heat of that June and July. Whatever more humble delusions his command had entertained of the joys of scouting vanished even more swiftly. The spirit of his men soured. Custer's disillusion was more volatile and vindictive.

There was an implicit disparagement in the strategy of the Indians. Their facile shifting before him sullied the fame of the Murat of the American Army. It was not the speed of panic that the Cheyennes and Sioux displayed. They moved so easily, so imperceptibly, that scouts and Delaware trackers found no trace of them. And then, when confidence slackened the vigilance of the dusty Blue pursuers, they turned and struck.

The red horsemen were by training and inheritance better cavalry than Custer led. That knowledge galled the column's commander and a foe's obliviousness to his fame irked him further. The kindred tactics of Mosby's men had stung him into similar wrath but he had been able then at least to catch and hang certain of his implicit defamers. He could not catch any Indians, at all. They harmed him but little. In return he had slain only a very few. His enterprise, that was to have burnished his fame, was crumbling away into ridiculous failure.

Knowledge of this tightened still further the curb of discipline with which he managed his men. It was almost six weeks now since he had marched from Fort Hays. It was nearly four weeks since any but guards of the wagon train had had contact with even the equivocal civilization of a frontier fort. They were playing an aimless pussy-wants-a-corner game against a will-o'-the-wisp antagonist. The food was vile, the heat remorseless. Dysentery and scurvy tortured the weary men and the premonitory symptoms of a more dangerous ailment appeared. Nevertheless, Custer drove them with the same indiscriminate vengeance that had impelled him to burn Shenandoah farms when Mosby had flouted him.

Custer chose to move up to the Platte from the north fork of the Republican. The route he selected was sixty-five miles long. There was no water in all its sun-beaten miles. The march would have to be made in a single day.

In the leader's own account of that trek, no adequate military reason is given therefor. The column left the Republican at dawn. All day it crept through corrosive alkali dust, over dun dry land, unsteady in the blaze of sunlight. Men suffered, horses suffered more. Many of the dogs that were the troopers' pets dropped and died in the bright heat that sucked all moisture from men's bodies; that seemed to penetrate and shrivel vitals so that mortals became light and giddy husks whose speech was hoarse whispering.

The torturing sun set at last. The moon came up. The Platte still lay miles ahead. Custer, who had led his column through torment, deserted it now. Whether this was further vindictiveness, or his odd lack of imagination, no one can tell. He turned command over to Major Elliot and with Lieutenant Moylan, Doctor Coates, the surgeon, and an orderly, rode ahead to water.

The Lieutenant-Colonel explained later that he had gone on to select a camping-place for his command. When he reached the river's edge, at eleven P. M., neither he nor his companions attempted to reestablish contact with the troops. They drank, thrust sabers deep into the turf, picketed their horses to the weapons' hilts, and slept so soundly all night that Indians raided a stage station less than a mile away and killed three men without rousing the slumberers.

When they woke they found, three miles down-stream, the command they had deserted. Some of the exhausted troops had not reached water until dawn. There is no record of the welcome they accorded their truant leader.

There was a near-by town called Riverside. It consisted of a stage station and barns. Here Custer learned of the Indians' attack. Here, also, he telegraphed to Fort Sedgwick, fifty miles east, for instructions and learned that Lieutenant Kidder of the 2nd Cavalry, with an escort of ten troopers and Red Bead, a Sioux guide, had left Sedgwick more than a week earlier, bearing dispatches to Custer on the Republican. These orders, summarized by wire, instructed the Lieutenant-Colonel to march to Fort Wallace for further supplies. Before his command was fit to move again, the troopers had turned from angry muttering to actual mutiny.

Ever since the command had taken the field in April, there had been a dribble of desertions. More than a hundred troopers had considered the peril of flight with the hand of red man and soldier alike against them, better than the ordeal of further service. While they had been deep in hostile country, desertion had been too dangerous for many to essay, but Custer's camp now was pitched on the Platte and beside the river ran the great highway west. The column was to march back toward Fort Wallace on July seventh. On the night of July sixth there was wholesale desertion.

Custer says that "upwards of forty men" vanished between taps and reveille. He had an Old Testament disregard for numerical accuracy. Rolls, later inspected, revealed that in the entire week ending July seventh, only thirty-four troopers in all deserted. Forty, or thirty-four or fewer still, this apparently was only forerunner of further, graver defection. Quartermaster-Sergeant MacMahon confided to his commanding officer that a larger number of malcontents had planned on the following night to take the best horses and escape.

At noon of June seventh, while the column was halted, seven mounted men and five on foot left the camp and started back toward the Platte. Such flagrant insubordination not only was desertion but derision, and Custer, stung by the affront, appears momentarily to have lost his head. He yelled to Lieutenant Jackson, officer of the day, to pursue the fugitives and "to bring in none alive." On this count, the Bureau of Military Justice that reviewed his court martial debated whether Custer should not be turned over to the civil authorities to stand trial for murder.

Jackson's horse was unsaddled, but the chargers of Major Elliot and Lieutenant Cook stood ready. These officers gave chase. The mounted deserters got away. Three of the runaways on foot were shot down. Two others saved themselves by shamming death. One of the shot, Private Charles Johnson of E Troop, died at Fort Wallace, July seventeenth. The wounded were bundled into an army wagon. The column resumed its march and that night the company officers patrolled the camp with orders to shoot any trooper who emerged from his tent.

"From that date onward," Custer says with more complacence than accuracy, "desertion from that command during the continuance of the expedition was never attempted."

The fact that, as the column marched toward Wallace, the Platte road grew ever farther away and the danger from Indians increased, no doubt stimulated the troopers' temporary fidelity. That danger was exemplified on July twelfth, when Jack Corbin, the scout, picked up the tracks of Lieutenant Kidder's party.

This young officer, fresh from the East, had mistaken the trail made by Custer's wagon train on its trip to Fort Wallace in late June for the route of the column itself. The man to whom he bore dispatches found Kidder at last. The youngster's stripped and mutilated body lay with the corpses of his escort and Red Bead, the Sioux, where the hostiles had enveloped and abolished them. They were buried beside the trail. Custer then pressed on and reached Fort Wallace on July fourteenth.

Captain Barnitz with two troops of the 7th Cavalry, in scarcely better condition than their sun-flayed, trail-worn comrades, garrisoned Fort Wallace. They had been attacked repeatedly by Indians. Rations were scant and there was cholera in the fort. There was cholera, too, at Fort Hays. Rumor said that cholera was raging also at Fort Riley where Elizabeth Custer waited for her beloved. There were no telegraph wires from Fort Wallace whereby her husband might be reassured. There were, however, definite instructions from Hancock forwarded to Wallace by Colonel Smith. On these, further counts in the subsequent court martial rested. Hancock's orders were specific.

Custer's column, his commanding officer directed, "until further orders will operate through Fort Wallace as a base between the Arkansas and the Platte. He will habitually draw his supplies from Fort Wallace." Thereafter follow sundry details for the guidance of Custer's further campaign and the concluding sentence: "The cavalry will be kept constantly engaged."

On receipt of these orders, Custer, who had commanded that no deserters should be brought in alive, deserted his own command. He chose, as pretext, the fact that supplies were low at Fort Wallace. He determined to ride with an escort through cholera-smitten Fort Hays to Fort Harker where a ration train could be assembled and sent back to Wallace. Meanwhile, he would go on to Fort Riley where men said cholera raged; Fort Riley, where Elizabeth Custer waited and wrote him pitiful letters filled with loneliness and love:

"I know you are wondering why this letter is cut up so. Well, I began to try and cut out the tearstains, for I know I ought not to send you such doleful letters, but I had to give up cutting as a bad job, for I soon would have nothing to give the messenger."

And again:

"Eliza's darky beaux planted us a little garden and I let them do it to please them, feeling sure in my heart, though, that I should have something better than gardens by the time the seed came up, for I was certain I would be with you. But the seeds are coming up. I hate them."*

It was six weeks since Custer had seen his wife. Men said there was cholera at Fort Riley. He could not know that men lied. Each scout who had brought mail through had borne heart-stricken pleas from his darling. But Custer had his orders to stay at Wallace and pursue a campaign that promised only further aimless groping, far from even the faintest smile of Glory.

He had his orders when he took the captured Shenandoah flags to Washington. He neglected them then to search for his wife. He has his orders now. He will have equally explicit orders when he rides, nine years hence, up the Rosebud from the Yellowstone. He was able always to discipline subordinates so much more stringently than he could control himself. Now, he casts Hancock's instructions aside and, selecting the least exhausted seventy-five horses of his command, rides with them and their troopers as escort and Captain Hamilton, Lieutenant Cook and Tom Custer for compan-

---

* *Tenting on the Plains.*

ions, eastward. Ostensibly, he is going to Fort Harker for supplies. It is scarcely the duty of a commanding officer to ride on such an errand. Actually, he is hurrying to Fort Riley as fast as weary horse-flesh can carry him. This insurgent dash was launched from Fort Wallace on the evening of the fifteenth. The way was set with peril. For the unhappy troopers who had no wives waiting at the road's end, it must have been untold agony.

The plains were swarming with hostiles, prodded into fiercer indignation by Custer's futile campaign. Enough warriors might lie along the way to enact a larger version of the Kidder tragedy. The stage stations were garrisoned and barricaded. Men hearing the approaching storm of hoofs shot first and asked questions afterward. With only scant food and less sleep, Custer drove his men on. He seemed to have cast away along with Hancock's orders, all mercy, all sense of duty. Near Downer's Station, the lagging rear of his escort was jumped by Indians who shot two. When the survivors brought word of the attack, Custer did not turn to exact reprisal. He did not even tarry to recover the bodies of the dead but ordered Captain Carpenter, 37th Infantry, commander of the station garrison, to bury them and hurried on.

Horses and men, already worn by the long campaign, marched one hundred and fifty miles from Wallace to Hays in a total elapsed time of fifty-five hours in which they had six for rest and sleep. At Hays, since his escort was almost spent, Custer left Hamilton to bring it on more slowly to Fort Harker and rode ahead with his brother, Lieutenant Cook and two orderlies.

Custer boasted later that his shooting of deserters near the Platte checked further defection during the expedition. Twenty of the seventy-five in his escort deserted at Hays or Harker.

The three officers and the orderlies did the additional sixty miles to Fort Harker in less than twelve hours. There, Custer reported at once to Colonel Smith, routing that elderly gentleman from his bed. Smith, bemused by slumber, or else bewildered by the hot rash voice that rattled through the tale of the Kidder slaughter, the need for rations at Wallace and its owner's desire to go on at once to Fort Riley by train, granted him permission to proceed. Next morning, when Custer's disregard of orders became clearer to his superior, Smith sent him a telegram, ordering him to return at once to his command. Meanwhile, tidings of this insubordination had reached Hancock, who was far less indulgent.

On July twenty-eighth, Custer was placed under arrest by his Department Commander. The court martial that tried him assembled at Fort Leavenworth, September fifteenth. The accused pleaded not guilty on all counts and later alleged that the court had been packed against him. There were seven charges preferred. In each instance, a verdict of guilty was returned. According to the court's findings, George Armstrong Custer had committed the following military crimes:

He had disregarded orders and had deserted his command on July fifteenth;

By his insurgent dash he had damaged horses belonging to the government;

He had neither pursued Indians who had attacked his escort nor had he recovered the bodies of soldiers killed;

On July seventh, he had ordered officers to chase and shoot down deserters and bring none in alive;

The obedient officers actually had shot these deserters;

One of the shot, Trooper Johnson, had died of his wounds.

The court also found him guilty of neglecting and refusing to permit the wounded men to receive medical attention thereafter, but attached no criminality to this.

Custer was sentenced "To be suspended from rank and command for one year and to forfeit his pay proper for the same time."

The Bureau of Military Justice, in reviewing the court martial record on November 8, 1867, endorsed all the findings and concerning the charges that he deserted his command commented:

"The conclusion unavoidably reached under this branch of the inquiry is that Gen. Custer's anxiety to see his family at Ft. Riley overcame his appreciation of the paramount necessity to obey orders, which is incumbent on every military officer; and that the excuses he offers for his act of insubordination are afterthoughts."

In regard to Custer's suppression of the mutiny, the review board is still more gravely concerned. It comments on the leniency of the punishment and after involving itself in many ponderously complex sentences, whereby it suggests the possibility of bringing the accused "before a court of competent jurisdiction" on a charge of murder, passes along responsibility for any such step to the President himself.

Apparently, the Chief Executive had no desire to tamper with the verdict for, also on November eighth, the findings and sentence of the court were approved by General Grant, "who directs the necessary orders to be issued by the Adjutant General, in which the leniency of that sentence, considering the nature of the offenses of which Gen. Custer is found guilty, is to be remarked on."

No one knows, since all who were his intimates then are dead, how the vain and high-strung man endured the stripes of verdict and sentence. The punishment must have been bitter to him, whose career heretofore had been so haloed in fame, so resonant with praise. In the three large volumes in which his wife celebrated the prowess of her dead hero, she mentions only with curtest reticence that court martial. We can not tell whether Custer plunged like the colt who first feels bit and spur, or endured the disgrace with a philosophy born of magnanimity or callousness. In Custer's own book, *My Life on the Plains,* he refers to his sentence with the determined lightness of a whipped small boy who boasts that the punishment didn't hurt much. There is no evidence that he ever attempted reprisal on any of the court members or the witnesses that wrought his temporary downfall.

And perhaps that unscrupulous rebellion against authority, that long mad ride through concrete peril and the more imperceptible barriers of military duty, had its compensation. His wife tells of the instant when the racer reached his goal.

"After days of such gloom, my leaden heart one morning quickened its beats at an unusual sound—the clank of a saber on our gallery and with it the quick, springing steps of feet, unlike the quiet infantry around us. The door behind which I paced uneasily opened and with a flood of sunshine that

poured in, came a vision far brighter than even the brilliant
Kansas sun. There before me, blithe and buoyant, stood my
husband. . . .

"There was in that summer of 1867, one long, perfect day.
It was mine and—blessed be our memory which preserves to
us the joys as well as the sadness of life—it is still mine for
time and for eternity."*

To them, the price exacted for that reunion may have seemed
small indeed.

---

* *Tenting on the Plains.*

Chapter Five

REINSTATEMENT

THOSE who hated the man must have been downcast in their moment of triumph by George Armstrong Custer's outward calm beneath punishment. Men who loved him—they were fewer, yet even more ardent than his enemies—saw in his fortitude still another evidence of greatness, still further warrant for worship.

Glory's unappeasable pursuer, the emotional, high-keyed egotist, surprised friend and foe by his conduct in disgrace. He did not, as many had expected, resign his already suspended commission and embark thereafter on reckless reprisal. Neither did he withdraw like a proud and sensitive spirit, from the scene of his disgrace. He continued to dwell, unabashed, at Fort Leavenworth, where he had been tried. Unwonted fortitude and philosophy may have stayed him. It is more likely that once more Custer had been tamed by superior power, ruthlessly applied.

The court martial's verdict did not crush, but it subjugated the man, who forever identified tolerance with weakness and in its presence comported himself like a calculating pupil who tested how far he dared plague the professor. When the professor visited stern reprisal upon insurgence, Custer grew meek.

He was docile and penitent later when he crossed wills with Grant and was utterly worsted. He accorded Terry no great respect or loyalty, for Terry was a mild and generous man. He strove to dominate General Stanley on the Yellowstone expedition until that surly old war-dog turned upon him savagely. Thereafter Custer was contrite and obedient. He was a tumultuous subordinate to Kilpatrick, a man of his own breed, but he respected the iron will of Sheridan and made himself one of that general's most trusted

178

officers. Judge Bacon's firm dislike had awed him into placating meekness. All his days, he remained ebulliently youthful—a high-spirited colt who took advantage of slack rein and irresolute voice, yet was docile when the curb drew tight and the righteously wielded whip came down.

Now, while he remained at Leavenworth and puzzled adherent and enemy by his conduct, mitigation of his plight drew near in the person of Sheridan himself. Hancock had raked the embers of frontier war into fresh blaze. Sheridan, the brusk and bitter, had made himself immensely unpopular as head of the Fifth Military District, comprising Texas and Louisiana. Hancock was transferred in September, 1867, to Sheridan's post in the South and the hard-handed little General replaced Hancock as commander of the Department of the Missouri. When he arrived at Fort Leavenworth, Sheridan found his favorite officer in trouble.

The new head of the department could do nothing to alter the verdict of the court martial Hancock had ordered, but he showed his esteem for his old subordinate at once. Quarters were reserved for Sheridan at Fort Leavenworth. He turned these over to Custer and his wife who occupied them all winter. This was as much as even the General Commanding could do toward opposing a sentence that Grant so positively had affirmed.

There were other problems to afflict Sheridan. The Indians, stirred up so violently by Hancock's and by Custer's campaigns, still were rebellious and were buffeted by the insane cross-purposes of the army and the Indian Bureau. These organizations were indulging once again in a war of their own. Agents were calling generals "butchers" and generals were branding agents "thieves," with a modicum of truth on either side.

Since the summer's campaign had won no victory, the whites, that fall, had turned once more to treaty-making. The treaty signed on the Little Arkansas in 1865 and never confirmed, was torn up. Another was made October 28, 1867, on Medicine Lodge Creek. Generals Terry, Augur and other officers with representatives of the Indian Bureau and a handful of chiefs of the Cheyenne, Arapahos and Kiowas signed one more eternal agreement, with the honor of the United States pledged thereto. By this, new reservations were apportioned the various tribes, largely in what is now Oklahoma, and the Indians in turn forswore all right to their old lands on the Smoky Hill and the Republican. The Kansas Pacific wanted these.

Many of the Cheyennes had fled north to the country where their allies, the Sioux, still hacked away at the perishing Bozeman Road. The chiefs at the conference had no right to speak for the absent, yet the majority of the Cheyennes accepted the treaty. The warrior fraternity of the Dogs rejected it scornfully. Most of the subsequent violence on the frontier was due to them. An Indian tribe was not a nation. It was merely a vast family, held together by community of speech and tradition. No chief could impose his will upon all his fellow-tribesmen. One might as well expect all nephews to be wholly obedient to an uncle's opinion.

Yet the treaty was established. Peace was more difficult to attain. Newspapers, telegraph or postal system were no part of a savage culture. It took time for word of the new agreement to spread over the plains. Meanwhile, angry barbarians continued their depredations. These were avenged blindly by the whites, soldiers and frontier folk alike, and peace had become a mockery by the time the ink on the treaty had dried. Winter hampered the depredations of either race. Spring promised a fresh campaign. Meanwhile, Colonel Wynkoop at Fort Larned and other sincere agents worked desperately to lure their charges away from the war the army expected, and Custer at Fort Leavenworth tried to ignore military preparations in which he might not share.

The court martial had one further repercussion over and beyond post gossip. The reviewing board's reference to the possibility of turning the deserter-killers over to the civil authority bore short-lived fruit.

On January 3, 1868, Judge Adams of Leavenworth issued a warrant for the arrest of George Armstrong Custer and W. W. Cook on a charge of murder. They were arraigned before Adams on January eighth. At the hearing's conclusion both officers were discharged from custody.

As spring approached Custer and his wife retired to her home in Monroe. There, he wrote later, they passed a delightful summer. This is characteristic bravado. There was trouble on the plains. His regiment was in the field. He was probably as miserable and restless as a caged mountain lion. There were raiding and burning along the frontier, and in sleepy Monroe, smug men and women asked Custer what the outcome would be and veered away from the subject of why he tarried there.

On August tenth, the Indian Bureau, through Wynkoop, issued arms and ammunition to the supposedly peaceful Cheyennes and Arapahos who had gathered at Fort Larned. The howl of protest that rose from the army was a logical response. There was little sense in a system under which one department of the government gave weapons to savages who were potential enemies of another department. There was scarcely more truth in the army's claim that, due to such gifts, the Indians always were better armed than soldiers.

As a rule, only the most decrepit and outmoded guns, and few of these, found their way into Indian hands. Their firearms were usually poorer and fewer than those of the troops. Ammunition was pitifully scant at the best of times. P. E. Byrne, who has made exhaustive study of the Sioux wars, exposes the fallacy of the old army claim of the superior quality of Indian guns. George Bird Grinnell, most patient and thorough of white students of the Cheyennes, believes that eight years after this period, in the Little Bighorn fight, only half the warriors had guns of any sort and that the best of these were old Sharps rifles. If the Indians ever had possessed one-third the firearms soldiers believed were theirs, the conquest of the West would have had a longer, even bloodier, history.

At Fort Larned, the entire Arapaho tribe received eighty Lancaster rifles and one hundred pistols. The Cheyennes got about an equal number. No mention is made of anything as modern as a revolver and the Lancaster rifle was a whimsical and archaic weapon, last manufactured in England during 1857, eleven years earlier.

Immediately after the first issue, Indians, probably the Dog fraternity, raided the young settlements on Walnut Creek and the Solomon River in Kansas. On September first, Brevet Brigadier-General Alfred Sully, with eleven troops of the 7th Cavalry, under Major Elliot, and a few companies of the 3rd Infantry marched out to punish the offenders, or whatever Indians they might encounter. News that his regiment had taken the field without him must have been anguish to the man for whom, so he writes, "time passed pleasantly enough" in Monroe.

Sully, directing his clumsy command from the ambulance in which he rode, was tricked, bewildered and outfought by the Indians. He groped toward the Cimarron from Fort Dodge and then, pestered and stung on all sides by evasive warriors, turned tail and hastened back to Dodge with panicky speed.

On August nineteenth, the Medicine Lodge treaty was ratified by the Senate.

There remains no record of how Sheridan greeted his defeated subordinate but it was General Godfrey's belief, years later, that Sully laid part of the blame for failure on the shoulders of the young Major Elliot, whom he disliked.

Somewhat tardily on September nineteenth, Sherman proclaimed from St. Louis that a state of war existed with the Cheyennes and Arapahos. He suggested, furthermore, that since all Indians looked alike, those peaceably inclined should be conducted by their agents to their reservations "within the Indian territory, south of Kansas, there to be provided for under their supervision, say about old Fort Cobb."

In a later letter to Secretary of War Schofield, Sherman writes:

"I have dispatched General Hazen to the frontier with a limited amount of money wherewith to aid the said agents to provide for the peaceful parts of those tribes, this winter, while en route to and after their arrival at their new homes."

Years earlier at West Point, Hazen had arrested Cadet Custer for his negligence as officer of the guard.

Sully's failure had galled General Sheridan. It had demonstrated, once more, the inanity of sending troops against innate strategists at a time when grass was plentiful for hard little Indian horses and game kept the bellies of their riders full and a thousand miles of wilderness lay behind the war-parties as a refuge. In winter, ponies grew gaunt and weak. Indians had no granaries. The red men, when the snows came, endured them in villages, pitched for the winter's duration in some sheltered spot. Cold destroyed Indian mobility. Sheridan determined to strike in the winter and he knew whom he wanted to deal that blow.

Sully agreed with Sheridan that Custer was the man. Sherman, in endorsing Sheridan's plea that the exile's sentence be terminated, wrote that Custer was "young, very brave even to rashness, a good trait for a cavalry officer, and ready and willing now to fight the Indians."

On September twenty-fourth, screechings and chair-smashings in the Bacon house at Monroe proclaimed that a tormented man at last had his release. The telegram which he waved while he pranced and howled read:

"Generals Sherman, Sully and myself and nearly all the officers of your regiment have asked for you and I hope the application will be successful. Can you come at once? Eleven companies of your regiment will move about the first of October against the hostile Indians, from Medicine Lodge Creek, toward the Wichita Mountains.

"P. H. Sheridan, Major General Commanding."

Custer did not wait for further word. He took train at once and the Adjutant-General's dispatch restoring him to duty overtook him en route. He departed from Monroe in great haste but he tarried long enough to choose two dogs from his pack, the staghounds Maida and Blucher, to accompany him.

He found Sheridan at Fort Hays, deep in plans for the forthcoming campaign. A base camp was to be established close to the border of the new Indian reservations. From this, a column consisting of eleven troops of the 7th Cavalry and the 19th Kansas

Volunteer Cavalry under Colonel S. J. Crawford who had resigned
the office of governor to lead it, would proceed against the Indians.

After his conference at Hays, Custer and an escort rode in haste
to Fort Dodge, where he reported to Sully, who was to be commander of the column in which the 7th Cavalry was to ride southwest. Thirty miles from Dodge, on Bluff Creek, the tents of his
command were pitched. There it had been camped ever since its
return from the Sully fiasco. Early in October, Custer rejoined it.

If the morale of the 7th had been low when he had deserted
it at Fort Wallace, the preceding year, nothing thereafter had contrived to lift it. Major Elliot who had commanded it was an even
younger and a far less experienced soldier than Custer. What relief Elliot felt in relinquishing leadership must have been tempered
by the implicit disparagement of the wholesale reorganization the
regiment endured at the hands of its Lieutenant-Colonel.

The men were shabby, weary, poorly mounted, disheartened.
They had been mocked and flouted by the Indians, who had even
dared during Sully's march to ride down upon the rear-guard and
kidnap two troopers. In their camp, they were beleaguered by derisive warriors. Custer barely had rejoined his regiment when another attack against it was launched. A wave of red horsemen bore
down upon the tents, arms and trinkets sparkling, feathers and
paint ablaze, shrill voices raised in fearful screeching.

Pickets dutifully pumped their Spencer carbines into the advancing host. Others joined them on the firing line. The shower
of bullets hit a pony or two. The charge split and tore screeching
past, unharmed, unharming. For a time thereafter, warriors lingered at extreme carbine range, taunting the clumsy troopers. This
derision lent bitterness to the triumph of Custer's return. His energy, which had mounted in the months of enforced idleness, laid
hold upon the regiment, tearing down and rebuilding.

That night, four columns left the Bluff Creek camp to scout up
near-by streams and find if possible the village where the pestifer-
ous and irreverent warriors lodged. They found nothing, due to
the conduct of California Joe, born Moses Milner, whom Custer incautiously had created chief of scouts. Joe drank deep in celebra-

tion of his promotion and mistook the column he was supposed to be guiding for a hostile horde against which he suddenly advanced, shooting and screaming, and incidentally, losing his briefly held rank. The varied descriptions of California Joe are typical of the uncertainties that confront historians of this period. Among the supposed acquaintances of the man who have written of him, one says that his hair and beard were black; another, that they were flaming red, and the third, Custer, that they were brown.

After further scouting against the Indians, the regiment made camp on October twenty-first, within a few miles of Fort Dodge, to prepare for the coming campaign. Here by drill, by reorganization, by target practise, Custer strove to stiffen the 7th's morale and efficiency.

Horses were reclassified and each troop received mounts of a uniform color. Troopers were taught on the range to aim at what they intended to hit and the forty best shots in the regiment were banded together in a sharpshooters' corps under Lieutenant Cook. The band, in deference to Sheridan, whose Cavalry Corps musicians always were so mounted, received gray chargers.

The troopers were issued equipment for the winter campaign. Early and late, the brilliant figure of their Lieutenant-Colonel moved through the regiment, his quick intemperate voice rattling criticism and counsel. By example, by exhortation, by the pressure of discipline, he made the slouching, disheartened men into soldiers who, when the column moved out on November twelfth, rode with a swing and confidence and looked forward to the battle they believe waited for them.

The army was in the ascendant. The Indian Bureau had failed to keep the peace and temporarily was discredited. It remained now, only to punish the Indians themselves. From Sheridan down, officers were too concerned in furthering this purpose to examine it ethically or to answer questions concerning its legality had any one on the vindictive frontier been inclined to ask them.

There had been hostiles abroad on the plains all that summer, but hundreds of Kiowas, plains Apaches, Arapahos and Cheyennes had come to the forts in compliance with the treaty and had been sent to land reserved for them thereunder. It was toward this land that Sheridan's little army now was marching, to catch Indians in their winter-bound lodges and exact bloody pay for past raiding.

What Indians had done the raiding? Where were they now? How were the troops to distinguish between peaceful bands in their winter villages and possible hostiles in theirs? There was no sound answer to these queries. Dead Indians, to Sheridan, were good Indians.

The army was in the dangerous mood of a man too long derided. In the north, Red Cloud's warriors had whipped it and forced abandonment of the Bozeman Road forts. In the south for two summers, brown men on quick ponies had mocked the armaments sent against them. Further humiliation was insupportable. Wherefore, Sheridan and Custer were marching toward those reservations to exact from residents toll for past misdeeds of unidentified hostiles. If they could not get the guilty Indians, any Indians would do. Men who had hanged and burned through the Shenandoah campaign would not be squeamish over the possibility of punishing the wrong red men.

Veterans of that campaign liked to refer to "the glory of the Washita." Peering past that phrase, one finds little glory there for any white man, even for George Armstrong Custer, whose fame as an Indian fighter grew from that blind and vengeful massacre so strangely stained with callousness or a cowardice stranger still.

Chapter Six

WASHITA

THE bright days grew colder. Cottonwoods shed their leaves and frost blanched the ground each morning. Winter, immobilizer of the red man, preparer of white vengeance, crept near. On the plain near Fort Dodge, Custer hammered his command. The rest of his life was to be spent with all or part of his regiment. He never ceased his remedial pounding and at last he made the 7th Cavalry, in drill at least, the best horse soldiers on the plains. Officers in rival units admitted this.

General Charles King, then a captain of the 5th Cavalry, wrote of his encounter in 1876 with the mauled and battered remnant of the regiment that had survived the Little Bighorn fight.

"Each company as it comes forward opens out like the fan of a practiced coquette and a sheaf of skirmishers is launched to the front. Something in the snap and style of the whole movement stamps them at once. There is no need of fluttering guidons and stirring trumpet calls to identify them. I know the 7th Cavalry at a glance."*

The purgatory of idleness suffered at Monroe was over. Custer was on his beloved plains and chief of the 7th once more. He had returned to his element and, so returning, had resumed all his normal characteristics including his knack for superior-baiting.

Sully was to command the vast supply train—four hundred white-topped wagons—the infantry companies and the 7th Cavalry that were to march to Camp Supply at the junction of Beaver and

---

* King, General Charles: *Campaigning with Crook*, New York, 1890.

Wolf Creeks in what now is Oklahoma. The column moved from Dodge on November twelfth. A few days later, at Beaver Creek, it crossed an Indian trail and Custer at once demanded permission to pursue. Sully's refusal apparently rankled, for when the troops and train reached Camp Supply, Custer and he became embroiled in the old army dispute concerning relative rank.

Sully and Custer had been commissioned lieutenant-colonels in the regular army on the same day. The former had been placed in command of the column on its march to Camp Supply. Now that the base had been reached, Custer insisted that his brevet of major-general outranked Sully's brevet of brigadier.

Two or three days later, when Sheridan approached under escort of two companies of the 19th Kansas, Custer rode out to meet him and laid the dispute before him. Sully was ousted and sent back to Fort Dodge. He had been one of those who had urged Custer's reinstatement. That night the 7th's band serenaded Sheridan.

On November twenty-second, the 7th Cavalry made ready for war. The 19th Kansas, which was to have accompanied it, had got itself lost on the march from Topeka and did not reach Supply until almost a week later. Custer was unwilling to wait. His regiment, he was sure, could whip all the Indians on the plains. This belief endured till his death. Now, he talked over plans with Sheridan and prepared to march. His instructions were simple.

"To proceed south in the direction of the Antelope Hills, thence toward the Washita River, the supposed winter seat of the hostile tribes; to destroy their villages and ponies; to kill or hang all warriors and bring back all women and children."*

No one explained how the troops were to tell hostiles from friendly red men. Sheridan's expedition cherished his definition of a good Indian. It was to march into Indian country for the simple purpose of slaughter.

It is well, for a moment, to consult the Medicine Lodge treaty of 1867, which now was in effect. This set aside definitely limited

* Keim, DeB. Randolph: *Sheridan's Troopers on the Border*, New York, 1870.

ranges in Oklahoma for Cheyennes, Arapahos, Kiowas, but Indians not on these reservations were not necessarily to be considered hostile. They were, it is true, bound to keep away from settlements and the highways, but south of the Arkansas River, so the treaty said, they were to be allowed to range unoccupied land much as they pleased.

By Article II, the tribes promised to relinquish title to territory outside their reservations, "but," the text reads, "they yet reserve the right to hunt *on any lands south of the Arkansas* so long as the buffalo may range thereon in such numbers as to justify the chase."

There still were many buffalo south of the Arkansas River. Many Indians were wintering there, too. Camp Supply itself was far south of the stream. Custer's punitive force was to march still farther. The expedition was as blindly savage and ruthless as the random discharge of a gun in a crowded room where a criminal may or may not be hiding. Men are prone to overlook what happened on the Washita River in admiration of Custer's leadership in getting his regiment thither.

He was the ideal spirit to carry out the frontier's desire for revenge. The frontier, and Sheridan and Custer did not admit the existence of innocent Indians. On September 3, 1868, *The Council Bluffs Bugle* published this prescription for the problem's solution:

"Offer a reward of $500. for each Indian's scalp brought in and in less than six months we will have an end of the Indian war and will have peace with the red devils on a permanent basis."

Reveille's trumpets at four the morning of November twenty-third came dull through snow-filled air. They roused Custer who had sat up until two, writing to his wife. Troopers and teamsters floundered mid-shin deep, as they saddled and harnessed. Dawn had a livid uneasy light. Great sticky flakes swarmed, plastering and turning spectral the struggling men. The gray tumult of the morning daunted Sheridan, but Custer insisted on marching. At six the column lurched out into the quickly enveloping storm—eleven troops of cavalry, seven hundred-odd men, with the band bravely pumping *The Girl I Left Behind Me*. Custer, in buffalo shoes, buffalo vest and a fur cap, gifts of Sheridan and his staff, led the way. With him rode California Joe, Jack Corbin, other white scouts and eleven Osage trackers with their war chiefs, Little Beaver and Hard Robe. In the rear, the wagon train rumbled to the snow-blunted popping of whips. The column dissolved in the turmoil of the storm that blotted out quickly even the braying of the band. George Armstrong Custer again was off on the trail of Glory.

It was a blind and difficult trail, that snow-smothered morning. All landmarks were abolished. The column groped a little way through troubled opacity and halted. The white scouts had lost their way. The Osages cast about and returned, as ignorant as the others. Aborigines and men long skilled in plains craft did not know where they were, or in which direction they moved. It was Custer who led the march that day. Riding in advance with a compass in his hand, he guided his guides and his command fifteen miles through eighteen inches of snow to camp in the timber alongside Wolf Creek.

Sun glared next morning on a white world, through which the slow black snake of the column crept southward. On all that dazzling expanse, scouts marked no other human trail. The troops killed many rabbits and some buffalo, and Custer was delighted with the prowess of the staghounds who tore at a snow-bogged calf until, "watching a favorable opportunity, I succeeded in cutting the hamstrings."

They were still following Wolf Creek upward and, on the morrow, left the dwindling flow and crossed a divide into the basin of the Canadian, camping that night on one of its tributaries. This was Thanksgiving Eve. They had seen no Indians or Indian trails. On the morrow, November twenty-sixth, the column reached the Canadian which carried a burden of slush and ice. Osages told Custer there was an Indian crossing some miles above. He sent Major Elliot and Troops G, H and M to scout in that direction.

PLAINSMAN
Custer in frontier garb, 1872
From the collection of E. A. Brininstool

The rest of the column negotiated a ford found by California Joe.

The last of the wagons, double-teamed and urged on by screeching troopers, had crept up out of the river and the rear-guard was crossing when Corbin came back. Elliot had found an Indian trail leading southward. He was following it.

A trumpet stuttered officers' call. Corbin on a fresh horse loped away bearing orders to Elliot to follow the trail until eight P. M. and then wait until the rest of the regiment joined him. Custer's eyes sparkled. His voice cracked about his assembling subordinates. The hunt was on. No time must be lost.

Seven wagons and an ambulance under the command of the jovial, neck-whiskered Captain James M. Bell, quartermaster, were to accompany the column. The rest of the train would follow, escorted by troopers on the eighty most nearly spent horses, and led by the officer of the day. No tents, no blankets were to be taken. In twenty minutes, the chase would start.

Part of that twenty minutes was occupied for Custer in parrying the frantic appeals of the officer of the day. This was Captain Louis McLane Hamilton, his devotee and a sunny-tempered, expert soldier who had made his troop the best in the regiment. There was the prospect of a fight ahead. Hamilton almost wept in his beseechings not to be left behind. When he appeared dragging the snow-blind Lieutenant E. C. Mathey who was willing to remain with the train in his place, Custer permitted the exchange. Men recalled later that Hamilton often had said, "When my time comes, I hope I am shot through the heart in battle."

In twenty minutes the lightened regiment was on the march, drawing on the blank white page of the plain an hypotenuse to cut Elliot's trail. It marched all afternoon, to the steady underlying growl of crusted snow, hoof broken. A cold red sun slid down a leaden sky. It was dusk when they turned into the jumbled furrow plowed by Elliot's three troops. A lopsided moon was rising when they overtook the Major, waiting beside a creek whose high banks afforded shelter and concealment. Small fires were lit, coffee was brewed. The hunt pressed forward.

It followed through timber and open glades the path stamped

on the snow by pony hoofs. In the moonlight, black trees cast blacker shadows and, silent as these, Hard Robe and Little Beaver slid along on foot before the advance. After them came Custer and the rest of the scouts, mounted, and a half-mile behind, lest the loud crunching of the snow crust betray their presence, the long dark column.

They were moving down-hill now, into the valley of the little river, Washita, where Fort Cobb stood and General Hazen, temporarily serving as agent, fed his Indian charges. Hoofs were trampling on still another treaty. No thought of that defilement seems to have troubled the hunter who with his soldiers followed the shadow-filled tracks, stamped on whiteness by ponies' hoofs.

Trailers said that the enemy—so arbitrarily they named the quarry—could not be far ahead. Osages smelled smoke, stiffened like pointing dogs and, creeping forward a half-mile, found, some seventy-five yards to the left of the trail, remnants of a fire kindled by herd boys during the previous day. A village must be near.

Custer, ahorse, the Osages on foot, went forward. In the moonlight the white slope rolled downward in frozen billows and as they neared the crest of each, an Osage crept forward on hands and knees to peer over before advancing farther. At length, Hard Robe crawled up a ridge and did not withdraw. Custer dismounted and joined him.

Before them, dim land swimming in moonlight fell into a valley. Darkness in the distance might be trees, nearer sluggish movement might be buffalo, or a pony herd. As Custer stared, up through the silence came the tinkle of a herd bell and the shrill wail of a child.

"Savages though they were and justly outlawed by the number and atrocity of their crimes and depredations on the helpless settlers of the frontier, I could not but regret that in a war such as we were forced to engage in, the mode and circumstances of battle would possibly prevent discrimination."*

* Custer, General George A.: My Life on the Plains, New York, 1874.

So he writes later. Now, he has found his Indians. He has no knowledge of what band, what tribe sleeps in the tree-shielded lodges beside the Washita, on land secured by treaty. Kiowa? Cheyenne? Arapaho? Hostile? Friendly? Custer does not know, but he sends a scout back to halt the column and summon all officers to prepare retribution for "the number and atrocity" of the slumberers' crimes. Meanwhile, the Osages, better strategists than he, urge him not to attack.

It was the village of Black Kettle, the Cheyenne, which the council of war, held that midnight, planned to abolish. Half of Black Kettle's people had paid their lives for their chief's love of peace in the Sand Creek slaughter. Black Kettle had been among those who had signed the Medicine Lodge treaty. Black Kettle, when seven hundred troopers swept down at dawn on his village of less than a third that number of men, was one of the first to die.

The attack was satisfactory spectacle if strategically reckless. Custer had no knowledge whatever of the village's size. Trees in the river bottom hid most of it from view. California Joe and the Osages feared the village might be too big to handle. It might have been as vast as that which, later, he rode against to his annihilation on the Little Bighorn, and here, as there, Custer divided his command. Here, as there, he made no reconnaissance. Here, as there, he sent fractions of his force beyond his control.

At daybreak, the band struck up *Garry Owen* and continued to play until the keys of the instruments froze. From the positions they had taken during the night, on four sides of the village, the troops charged—Elliot, with G, H and M from the left rear; Captain Thompson with B and F from the right rear; while Captain Myers with E and I, Hamilton with A and C, West with D and K and Cook with his sharpshooters, closed in from the front, under Custer's leadership.

It was over quickly. The village was captured at once. Black Kettle perished at his lodge door and Captain Hamilton fell at the head of his men, shot through the heart. The raving of Spencer repeaters blew the dawn stillness to screeching fragments. Powder smoke respread dusk on the trampled snow where lay Cheyenne men, women and children who had died as they rushed from their dwellings.

Between the squadrons of Elliot and Thompson as the attack was launched, a gap appeared and through this a horde of screaming Indians fled down-stream. The boyish Major marked their flight and turned in pursuit. Lieutenant Owen Hale recalled that Elliot cried as he drove spurs into his charger: "Here goes for a brevet or a coffin!" Sergeant-Major Kennedy and eighteen troopers followed him as he galloped to head off the fugitives.

The village had been taken, but resistance was not ended. Those Cheyennes who had not won free in the first moments of panic sheltered themselves along the river bank, in ravines and hollows, and fought back feebly but valiantly until they died. Their archaic firearms, their arrows, could not avail against the hammering Spencers. Troopers on foot hunted them out and slaughtered them. Women and some children perished with their men. One squaw disemboweled a white boy, captive or foundling in the village, as the soldiers shot her down.

Slowly the war-yell and the boom of ancient muskets died away. Fewer arrows flashed through the smoke fog. The blasting carbines abolished all males of the village. There was no thought or offer of surrender. When the hour of slaughter ended they counted in one hollow the bodies of seventeen Cheyenne warriors and in a ravine, thirty-eight. One hundred and three Indian men were slain, not counting women and children. Fifty-three squaws and children were captured. Many of these had been wounded. The 7th Cavalry's loss was Captain Hamilton, killed; Captain Barnitz seriously wounded, Lieutenants Custer and March, slightly injured, eleven troopers hurt in varying degrees—and Major Elliot and nineteen men missing.

Mounted Indians appeared on the bluffs, below and overlooking the smoke-swathed village. Troopers left behind to guard the overcoats and haversacks their comrades had shed before advancing, came to the village with news that the Indians had driven them away, captured the equipment and killed the staghound Blucher. More Indians gathered on the heights. The regiment's ammunition supply was low. Then Bell, the quartermaster, drove his wagon train into the village. Troopers opened a long-range fire upon their red audience.

Lieutenant Godfrey of Troop K, returning from a round-up of the pony herd, down the valley, reported to Custer that, beyond the warrior-crowned bluffs, other villages dotted the Washita's banks; reported also that across the valley he had heard gun-fire that might be Elliot and his men in trouble.

Custer seemed to Godfrey much alarmed at tidings of the existence of further villages. He cross-questioned the Lieutenant about these but he ignored the firing Godfrey had heard. That gun-fire, Godfrey wrote long afterward, "continued long after we [his pony-hunters and himself] had reached the village; in fact, nearly all day."

Indian lodges, supplies and munitions were gathered for burning. Custer saved one lodge as a souvenir of the occasion. Continual reenforcements were arriving for the horsemen on the bluffs. The Lieutenant-Colonel sent for Godfrey again and questioned him further about the down-stream villages. Godfrey writes:

> "At the conclusion of this inquiry I told him that I had heard that Major Elliot had not returned and suggested that possibly the heavy firing I had heard on the opposite side of the valley might have been an attack upon Elliot's party. He pondered this a bit and said slowly: 'I hardly think so as Captain Myers has been fighting down there all morning and probably would have reported it.' "*

Custer then ordered Godfrey to assist in burning the village. The Indians drew closer during the destruction.

> "Two squadrons," Godfrey relates, "formed near the left bank of the stream and started on the 'Charge,' when the warriors scattered and fled. Later a few groups were seen on the hilltops but they made no hostile demonstration."

---

* Godfrey, General E. S.: "Some Reminiscences of the Battle of the Washita," *Cavalry Journal*, October, 1928.

Custer gives a more spirited version of this encounter but concludes: "The Indians were driven at every point and forced to abandon the field to us." He also says that scouting parties were sent out to look for Elliot but returned, "reporting their efforts to discover some trace of Elliot and his men fruitless."

By this time, that gun-fire heard by Godfrey "nearly all day," must have ceased.

Carbines banged briskly in the burned village where four troops completed the work of destruction by shooting the eight hundred and seventy-five ponies in the defeated Indians' herd. When the slaughter had ended, Custer assembled his command, prisoners mounted in the column and with flags flying and band blaring *Ain't I Glad to Git Out of the Wilderness* marched directly toward the hesitant warriors on the heights. These at once broke and fled. It was learned later that they abandoned the down-stream villages in headlong panic. The cavalry pursued its course until darkness concealed it. Then it faced about.

In complete silence Custer withdrew the regiment from the Washita. Custer withdrew the regiment stealthily from a field it had won with the loss of one man killed—and twenty still missing. Custer withdrew the intact regiment of seven hundred-odd men from a foe who had fled wildly at his approach. He had made no effort worth the name to find his missing Major, his Sergeant-Major and eighteen troopers.

"Custer," General Charles King wrote, "withdrew the regiment, never again to hold its undivided faith or admiration."*

---

* Graham, Colonel W. A.: *The Story of the Little Big Horn,* New York, 1926.

CHAPTER SEVEN

INQUEST

NOT the least of the incredibilities Washita's valley saw, that twenty-seventh of November, was the night-shielded flight of the victors from the field of their triumph.

Custer had stamped out the village of Black Kettle. Warriors from neighboring camps had only threatened him. They had broken at his first offensive movement. Yet now his regiment, seven hundred strong and victorious, hurried away in trepidation. It was ten o'clock when it returned from its feint toward the lower villages to the stained snow where Black Kettle's lodges had stood. The column did not pause here. Its commander urged it on as though in the darkness menace was spawning; as though disaster hovered above him on wings invisible. He had met and defeated the Cheyennes and had driven away their allies at a total cost, counting Elliot's missing, of twenty-one dead. That night, he seems to have lost momentarily his belief that the 7th Cavalry alone could whip all the Indians on the plains.

It is hard to rationalize, after sixty-six years, that swift retirement. Custer explains it was fear for his train, toiling toward him with only one troop as escort, that drove him. There is no better reason surviving.

The 7th marched till two A. M. In the valley the troops had relinquished, the Indians were fleeing even more precipitately in the opposite direction. Only a part of the regiment was permitted to halt at two. Captain West's squadron was pushed ahead to make contact with the missing train.

At daybreak the rest of the column hurried on and at ten found the wagons and West safely in camp. The briefest possible halt

was made here. Teamsters were routed out, and without even tarrying for food, haggard troops and gaunt horses pursued their
march until afternoon. In timber on the rim of the Washita Basin,
the long delayed bivouac was made. For the first time in two days,
men enjoyed a square meal, and Custer, summoning his officers,
prepared his report that California Joe and Jack Corbin were to
carry to Sheridan at Camp Supply.

Black Kettle's village of fifty-one lodges had been "conquered."
A hundred and three warriors had been slain. No mention is made
of the women and children dead. Eight hundred and seventy-five
ponies, five hundred and seventy-three buffalo robes, three hundred
and ninety lodge skins, one hundred and sixty untanned robes,
four hundred and seventy blankets, "all the winter supply of dried
buffalo meat, all the meal, flour and other provisions" had been
captured and destroyed. And then: "Two officers, Major Elliot
and Captain Hamilton were killed and nineteen enlisted men."

Custer writes this in his tent while the scouts wait to carry the
dispatch. He reports Elliot and his nineteen "killed." They are,
in fact, dead, all of them. They lie stripped and mutilated, not
more than two miles from Black Kettle's burned camp. But Custer
does not know this. There is effrontery in his calm assumption of
their death. The missing twenty men of the 7th Cavalry may be,
for all Custer knows, lost. They may be prisoners in the Indians'
hands. They may be still holding out desperately in failing hope of
rescue. He does not know. No hint of these possibilities creeps
into the report. For the sake of euphony, for the sake of propriety,
for the sake of more fundamental virtues, Elliot and his men must
be listed as dead. Custer makes them so. He executes them with
his pen in the name of Glory—the equivocal "Glory of the
Washita."

It may be that his strange spirit possessed immunity to shame,
as well as pity. The fortitude with which Custer endured the court
martial's punishment may have been only a manifestation of that
same callousness which enabled him to list, without warrant, Elliot
and his men among the killed.

Custer's book, *My Life on the Plains,* in which the Washita fight is described at length, contains no hint of compunction for his actions at the time of Elliot's death; no explanation or defense that would indicate the faintest stirring of guilt, or shame, or pity. He had felt none for the first Confederate he had killed, for the Mosby troopers he had hanged, for the deserters he had ordered slain, or for the slaughtered troopers of his command he had left for other men to find and bury. Apparently, he knew none for the twenty deserted members of the 7th Cavalry.

Unless you presume his thick indifference to agony in others; unless you see the gold-haired, brilliant devotee of Glory as an addict, ready to trample anything, all things, that may bar his way to her, Custer's desertion of his second in command and nineteen troopers collapses into the irrationality of nightmare. There is no other angle of his strange character on which to hang the facts. Attempt to rescue Elliot might risk his new-found fame. Then, let Elliot die.

Custer needed Glory greatly in that hour. Pardon contrived by Sheridan had brought him back from disgrace, but his fame still was tarnished. Complete victory over the Indians would burnish it anew. He must succeed where others, where he himself, in the past had failed. He must strike a spectacular blow for the applause of the frontier.

This he strikes at Washita. Thereafter, since he is still a semi-novice at Indian war, the presence of warriors on the heights, the report of further villages down the stream, seem perils that threaten to blight victory. If he fails on this campaign, if he does not justify his patron Sheridan's trust, his fame will be stained afresh. Elliot is missing. To find him and his men, Custer must move out from the field of his victory and risk the new-found, fragile renown. Let Elliot go.

Custer lets him go—this boyish Major who had been embarrassed by rank higher than he had hoped to gain; who had been mortified, perhaps, by his semi-failure as a commander of troops in the field, by the implicit disparagement of Custer's reorganization of the 7th when he had returned from exile. Elliot cried as he spurred after the fugitive Cheyennes: "Here goes for a brevet or

a coffin!" He, too, pursued Glory. Let him go; list him and his
men in the report as "killed"—and feel no shame.

No shame is discernible in that dispatch to Sheridan. No trace
of it can be found in Custer's narrative of Washita. And yet, the
letter the returned victor wrote to his wife from Camp Supply, as
reproduced in her *Following the Guidon,* bespeaks his compunction—or hers.

> "The sad side of the story is the killed and wounded. Major
> Elliot and six men, who charged after two Indians, and Cap-
> tain Hamilton, are gone."

The return of the column to Camp Supply was adorned with all
the trappings of triumph that Custer could contrive. A day's march
from the camp, the 7th leader sent word to Sheridan that the regiment would arrive at a certain hour on the morrow and would
pass in review for his chief's approval.

Troopers of the tardy 19th Kansas and men of the 3rd Infantry
who garrisoned the base, witnessed the display, that morning of
December second. The column marched down the slope into the
valley and passed in review before Sheridan and his staff. The
band blared *Garry Owen* through the cheers of the garrison.
Osage trackers, white scouts and the Cheyenne captives led the way
and behind them, riding at the head of his regiment that marched
in column of platoons, the conqueror, with bright hair tumbling
over his buckskin jacket's shoulders, flashed his sword in salute to
his approving General.

On the morrow, Captain Hamilton was buried. Thereafter,
preparations were begun for resuming the campaign. The government was having one of its recurrent spells of implacability toward Indians. North of the Platte, the Sioux had beaten back Carrington's soldiers. As compensation for that defeat, the army purposed to harry further the weaker tribes in the South.

On December seventh, Sheridan led a reenforced column over
the trail toward Washita. The 19th Kansas, as well as the 7th
Cavalry, rode with him to carry out his logical plan of abolishing

the Indian problem by abolishing the Indian. There were scouts
a plenty, white and red; an elderly Irishwoman to cook for Custer;
two Cheyenne women to act as interpreters, should the expedition
be perverted from battle to parley; and a long supply train. With
this last rode Daniel A. Brewster who sought his sister, Mrs.
James S. Morgan, twenty-five. She had been captured the summer
before in Kansas by Cheyennes who also held prisoner Miss Sarah
White, still alive in 1933.

The route of the column lay south of the Washita battle-field,
but a halt was made on a plateau eight miles down-stream while
Sheridan with Custer, other officers, and an escort commanded by
Captain Yates, rode to view the scene of the victory, and if possible
find trace of Elliot. De Benneville Randolph Keim, correspondent
of the *New York Herald* and author of *Sheridan's Troopers on the
Border,* accompanied them.

Frost was bright in the silent valley of the Washita. Hoarse tumult rose as the party neared the site of the destroyed village.
Screaming crows whirled up from the field like animate bits of the
embers scattered there. Wolves loped away from corpses of Cheyennes and ponies. Miserable dogs still lurked about the valley.
They were too wild for men to approach but troopers caught and
adopted some puppies.

Accompanied by Custer, Sheridan rode to a ridge where the
victor rattled through an explanation of the battle. Then, with
Keim and a small escort under Lieutenant Hale, they followed the
south bank of the stream in the direction taken by Elliot. They
seem to have had no difficulty whatever in finding where he had
died. On a ridge, they saw the torn body of a trooper. Beyond the
crest, lay the hacked corpses of the Major and fifteen more. All
were stripped. About them were scattered the spent cartridges of
their defense. Custer says that nineteen men followed Elliot. He
does not hazard what became of the missing four. The plateau of
slaughter was a scant two miles from the site of Black Kettle's
camp.

Men who rail at the inertia of Reno's beaten and half-destroyed
command, that red Sabbath on the Little Bighorn, ignore the fail-

ure of Custer and seven hundred victorious soldiers to move toward rescue on the Washita. The mystical may see, in each instance, a stark compensating pattern.

They lay, the forlorn young Elliot and his men, within two miles of the village. Most of the day of their death, Godfrey heard firing in their direction. He told Custer about it. And Custer did nothing. He is confounded here, not by the testimony of enemies, but by the narratives of two of his greatest admirers—Godfrey's and his own. Keim, the newspaperman, offers excuses too, so ponderously involved that they bear evidence of hard writing.

> "Although the fate of Elliot's party would appear as a gross abandonment by Custer, particularly for not even recovering the bodies or making some effort to learn what had become of them, when found missing after the fight, the circumstances of the event were of such a character that, while no attempt was made with that view, the conduct of Custer in ordering a withdrawal was justifiable according to the laws of war."*

Keim, who was Sheridan's guest, thereafter appends articles in defense of Sheridan's favorite. Briefly, they are:

Custer was outnumbered. This is doubtful. In any event, he took the village with a loss of one man killed and a handful more wounded. He drove off with ease the hesitant attacks of Indians from the lower villages, and when he moved out in force against them, they fled.

Custer was without supplies. Sheridan in General Field Orders No. 6, November 29, 1868, lists among the booty taken in the village, "immense quantities of dried meat and other winter provisions."

Custer's troops were without protection from the weather for the Indians had stolen their overcoats. Custer in his report of November twenty-eighth cites among his captures "five hundred seventy-three buffalo robes, four hundred seventy blankets."

Custer was worrying about the safety of his wagon train. He

---

* *Sheridan's Troopers on the Border.*

had placed it himself in whatever danger it faced. He seems not to have worried to the point of action over the fate of his Major and nineteen men.

"Custer," Keim pursues, "after the fight commenced, seeing such an extraordinary display of force, felt a natural desire to look after his wagons, for their destruction would involve the loss of the entire command and probably defeat the whole campaign. He therefore set out for the train and was hastened by experiencing greater opposition than was anticipated."*

The truth is, if Custer and Godfrey tell it, that Custer experienced no opposition whatever after he marched his command out of the burned village. "The observing warriors," says Godfrey, "followed our movements until twilight but made no hostile demonstration. Then, as if they divined our purpose"—that is, thought the lower villages were to be attacked—"there was a commotion and they departed down the valley."

From that moment, until their arrival at Camp Supply, the troopers saw no single hostile Indian.

Men of Reno's mauled and depleted battalion, beleaguered on the bluff above the Little Bighorn, think they hear firing to the north and Reno waits for the ammunition mules to arrive before starting to the relief of Custer's superior force.

Godfrey, in the captured Cheyenne village on the Washita, tells Custer of gun-fire he has heard across the valley and Custer, with a victorious regiment behind him, thinks it can't be the missing Elliot and stays where he is.

The unreality of the situation grows when it is seen how simply Sheridan's party found the place of the forsaken men's death. Custer says Myers's Battalion searched for Elliot. Benteen says no search was made. Surely any force sent to find the missing Major must have discovered him or his body. Snow was heavy on earth the morning of the battle. The trail of twenty shod horses should have been easy for even a novice to follow. In Custer's command

* *Ibid.*

there were white scouts of high reputation and Osage trackers as
well. Yet they did not find Elliot.

There is also the matter of ammunition. Apologists have said
the expedition's supply was dangerously low by the time the fight
was ended and that Custer dared not bring on another battle by
search for the missing men. If cartridges were so few, it was
scarcely provident for Custer to spend so many in shooting eight
hundred and seventy-five Indian ponies to death.

The bodies were carried to camp and, save for Major Elliot's
which was sent to Fort Arbuckle for more formal interment, were
buried by torchlight in a common grave. At dawn, the command
marched on down the Washita.

General Godfrey's "Some Reminiscences of the Battle of the
Washita" (*Cavalry Journal,* October, 1928) is the clearest and
most concise account of that foray. It limits itself entirely to facts.
It draws no conclusions, makes no judgment. Until the day of his
death, the old soldier was a staunch defender of his hero. He was
of those in whose spirits Custer had kindled that unwavering de-
votional flame. There is unconscious, blighting irony in a single
sentence of General Godfrey's narrative. He speaks of Sully's
blundering 1867 campaign and the indignation rife in the 7th,
when Sully refused to let the regiment pursue Indians who had
swept down upon its rear and had kidnaped a trooper. "We of
the cavalry," Godfrey wrote, "had been imbued with the principle
to take any risk to attempt the rescue of a comrade in peril."

It was General Charles King's belief that all subsequent dissen-
sion in the 7th Cavalry stemmed from the Elliot abandonment.
This is doubtful. Even Mrs. Custer's idealistic narratives indicate
that internal strife was present at the regiment's birth and rarely
was absent thereafter. Others have held that Benteen's enmity toward Custer began at Washita. They have adorned this theory
with so many legends that it is difficult to see the underlying fact.

By his own word, Benteen disliked his new Lieutenant-Colonel
at their first meeting. By his own word, Benteen found in Custer's
treatment of the rank and file a repellent brutality that reached a
climax in the shooting down of would-be deserters. A lifelong ab-

horrence, divinely consistent, had been well kindled in the bluff white-haired Captain before his chief left Elliot to his fate. There can be no question that this desertion increased hatred. Benteen mourned Elliot with unpremeditated candor.

Publication of his stilted prose threnody was inadvertent and anonymous. It still endures on the jaundiced pages of the *St. Louis Missouri Democrat* for February 9, 1869, and occupies the better part of a column.

Joel Elliot had been a captain in the brigade Benteen had led in the Civil War. It may have been genuine bereavement that impelled the man who had become his former subordinate's underling to celebrate the Major's death. It may have been Benteen's attempt to lessen pent indignation by composition which inspired a letter he wrote, when the column had reached Fort Cobb. He addressed this ornate and acid missive to an old Civil War comrade, William J. DeGreese of St. Louis, and DeGreese, without authorization, sent the letter to the *Missouri Democrat*. It was published anonymously as a creation of "a participant in the capture of Black Kettle's camp."

The letter's first paragraphs describe Elliot's pursuit of the escaping Cheyennes and picture floridly the probable manner of his command's extinction, hemmed in by Indians; hoping vainly for succor. Thereafter, Benteen's pen is dipped in gall.

"And now," he writes, "to learn why the anxiously looked for succor did not come, let us view the scene in the captured village, scarce two short miles away. Light skirmishing is going on all round. Savages on flying steeds with shields and feathers gay are circling everywhere, riding like devils incarnate. The troops are on all sides of the village, looking on and seizing every opportunity of picking off some of those daring riders with their carbines. But does not one think of the welfare of Major Elliot and his party? It seems not. But yet! A squadron of cavalry is in motion. They trot; they gallop. Now they charge! The cowardly redskins flee the coming shock and scatter here and there among the hills secure away. But it is the true line—will the cavalry keep it? No! No!

They turn! Ah, 'tis only to intercept the wily foe. See! A gray troop goes on in the direction again. One more short mile and they will be saved. Oh, for a mother's prayers! Will not some good angel prompt them? They charge the mound—a few scattering shots and the murderous pirates of the plains go unhurt away. There is no hope for that brave little band, the death doom is theirs for the cavalry halt and rest their panting steeds.

"And now return with me to the village. Officers and soldiers are watching, resting, eating and sleeping. In an hour or so they will be refreshed and then scour the hills and plains for their missing comrades. The commander occupies himself in taking an inventory of the captured property which he has promised the officers shall be distributed among the enlisted men of the command if they falter or halt not in the charge."

Indignation or hatred then burns ornamentation away from the narrative of Frederick W. Benteen. He pursues:

"The day is drawing to a close and but little has been done save the work of the first hour. A great deal remains to be done. That which cannot be taken away must be destroyed. Eight hundred ponies are to be put to death. Our chief exhibits his close marksmanship and terrifies the crowd of frightened, captured squaws and papooses by drooping the struggling ponies in death near them. Ah! He is a clever marksman. Not even do the poor dogs of the Indians escape his eye and aim as they drop dead or limp howling away. But are not those our men on guard on the other side of the creek? Will he not hit them?

" 'My troop is on guard, General, just over there,' says an officer.

" 'Well, bullets will not go through or around hills, and you can see there is a hill between us,' was the reply and the exhibition goes on.

"No one will come that way intentionally—certainly not. Now commences the slaughter of the ponies. Volley on volley is poured into them by too hasty men and they, jumping, get away only to meet death from a surer hand. The work progresses; the plunder, having been culled over, is hastily piled. The wigwams are pulled down and thrown on it, and soon the whole is one blazing mass. Occasionally a startling report is heard and a steamlike volume of smoke ascends as the fire reaches a powder bag, and thus the glorious deeds of valor done in the morning are celebrated by the flaming bonfire of the afternoon.

"The last pony is killed. The huge fire dies out. Our wounded and dead comrades—heroes of a bloody day—are carefully laid on ready ambulances and as the brave band of the seventh cavalry strikes up the air 'Ain't I glad to have got out of the wilderness,' we slowly pick our way across the creek over which we charged so gallantly in the early morn. Take care. Do not trample on the dead bodies of that woman and child lying there! In a short time we shall be far from the scene of our daring dash and night will have thrown her dark mantle over the scene.

"But surely some search will be made for our missing comrades. No, they are forgotten. Over them and the poor ponies, the wolves will hold high carnival, and their howlings will be their only requiem. Slowly trudging, we return to our train, some twenty miles away, and with bold exulting hearts learn from one another how many dead Indians have been seen.

"Two weeks elapse—a larger force returns that way. A search is made and the bodies are found strewn round that little circle, frozen stiff and hard. Who shall write their eulogy?

"That, my dear friend, is the *true* story of the 'battle of the Washita,' poorly told."

Weeks later, as the column was returning from that winter's campaign, Custer read Benteen's published letter. What happened thereafter is garbled. In a letter written in 1896 and now in Doctor Cole's collection, Benteen tells of returning to camp half-frozen on the day the command received long delayed mail.

"I rushed into the first tent I came to to warm myself; in a moment Tom Custer and Lt. Cook came in, Tom with a

newspaper in his hand, showing it to me, saying 'Isn't that
awful?' I looked at it, reading down a line or so and said,
'Why Tom, I wrote that myself' and so I had . . . Custer paid
me off for the letter in almost spot cash."

Benteen charges that his chief, in revenge, assigned him thereafter to Fort Dodge, though the Captain's child had died at Fort
Harker and his wife lay desperately ill there.

That is one version of the aftermath. The second is more dramatic and is vouched for by many witnesses—E. A. Brininstool,
L. M. Spaulding of Buffalo and Colonel Frederick W. Benteen,
Jr., to all of whom the elder Benteen in retirement recited the
story. Its authenticity is verified further by Colonel W. A. Graham
whose *The Story of the Little Big Horn* remains the most accurate
factual account of the battle. To him eye-witnesses, among them
General Godfrey, confirmed the more vivid tale.

Custer, this version runs, on reading the printed letter, immediately called all his officers before him. He confronted them with
the offending newspaper in one hand, and in the other a dog whip
flicked like the tail of an angry lion as he paced before his subordinates.

One of them, Custer snarled, had written this defamation. It
was evident that an officer had penned it. If he ever discovered
who had so traduced him, he intended to thrash the culprit. Benteen had arrived late in the awed semicircle before the fuming
commander. He asked to see the paper, read a few lines and
lifting his eyes from the page to his chief's suffused face, said:

"If there's to be a whipping, General, you can start in. I wrote
that letter."

Custer gulped, turned redder still and barked at last:

"Colonel Benteen, I shall see you later, sir."

Custer, so this version runs, never referred to the incident again.

It is possible that the two tales are fragments of a single story
that may not be dovetailed now, since the last eye-witness is dead.
Their apparent contradictions remain an inexplicable aftermath of
an inexplicable event.

Chapter Eight

PURSUIT

THE Sheridan-Custer column after burying Elliot's men marched through the down-stream villages that Godfrey had seen from the ridge, while rounding up the ponies of Black Kettle's band. In the wide-spread litter of headlong flight lay the bodies of two white captives, Mrs. Clara Blinn and her little son, Willie. They had been killed by the stampeding Arapahos.

These and the Cheyennes had scattered in all directions but from where a Kiowa village had stood, a broad clear trail ran down the valley. The soldiers followed it toward Fort Cobb.

At the fort, Custer's West Point preceptor, General W. B. Hazen, recovering from an Indian wound and assigned to this duty by Sherman, fed and cared for the Kiowa tribe. He had dealt fairly with his high-strung charges and had won their confidence. Chiefs of the Arapahos and Cheyennes also had come to him for counsel. Hazen had talked to Black Kettle only a few days before that leader's band had been slaughtered. The Washita fight had enormously complicated his task.

At tidings of the attack, his Kiowas had, as he phrases it, "flushed like a covey of partridges." They had run away, all of them, in blind terror. It had been difficult to lure them back again, to reassure them that this was their reservation, set aside for them by the government, and that here they were safe.

The fleeing Arapahos and Cheyennes were in more desperate state. They had no agent now to intercede for them. Colonel E. W. Wynkoop had resigned with high and bitter words. Thrice had he seen his effort to pacify panicky savages blasted by army intervention. It had been Wynkoop who had accepted the surren-

der of Black Kettle's band on Sand Creek before Chivington and
Anthony had moved in to massacre. It had been Wynkoop who
had gathered the suspicious Cheyennes about him at Fort Larned
only to have them scattered by Hancock and hunted by Custer.

And now, said Wynkoop, Black Kettle the peacemaker, Black
Kettle the forgiving, who had seen his wife shot down at Sand
Creek, had been slaughtered with his people while they had been
camped on land where they had the right to tarry and actually
had been on the way to their new reservation. Colonel Wynkoop
passes from history with this last violent protest. He feared, so
he said candidly, for his life if he attempted further to guide men
whom, it must appear, he had betrayed thrice.

The stampeding fragments of Wynkoop's tribes streamed across
the Kiowa reservation to the wilderness of the Staked Plain, and
Hazen, learning that Sheridan's punitive force actually was penetrating Kiowa land, sent a courier to the column with this message:

> "Indians have just brought in word that our troops to-day
> reached the Washita some twenty miles above here. I send
> this to say that all the camps this side of the point reported
> to have been reached are friendly and have not been on the
> war path this season."

Custer brands this dispatch in *My Life on the Plains* as the word
of a fool. Custer insists that the Kiowas whose trail the column
followed had taken part in the Washita fight. The fact was—and
Hazen proved it in a pamphlet he issued to clear his name of
Custer's defamation—that this trail had been made by the Kiowas
in their original journey to Fort Cobb. All the tribe had gathered
there by November twentieth, a week before the Washita massacre. On the eve of that slaughter, all principal chiefs of the
Kiowas had slept in Hazen's tent, one hundred and twenty miles
from Black Kettle's village.

The courier who carried the message to the advancing column
was accompanied by a number of Kiowa chiefs. Sheridan and
Custer arrested the foremost of these, Yellow Bear and Lone Wolf,

and brought them prisoners to Fort Cobb. When their chiefs were taken, the entire Kiowa nation that had reassembled about Cobb caught up its belongings and ran away again.

No account exists of the conference, held at the fort between the Kiowas' agent and the leaders of the punitive force. That is history and drama lost, for the interview must have been filled with fury. Hazen was not a scaly Indian agent whom army officers could browbeat. He was a soldier, assigned to this post by Sherman, Sheridan's and Custer's superior, yet the leaders of the invading army scoffed and, apparently, were enraged by his insistence on the Kiowas' innocence.

"I saw at once," says Hazen in the preface to his published defense, "that they held me accountable for seriously marring the success of their operations by warning them, two days previously, that the Indians between themselves and my camp were settled under my peaceful protection. . . . Their opinions that the Kiowas had fought them at the battle of the Washita were so firmly fixed that I thought it both futile and unwise to endeavor then to correct their impressions."*

Hazen had, in all probability, saved the lives of his charges; had also saved history another sullied page, but neither Sheridan nor Custer looked upon him with favor on this account. He had spoiled their campaign. Arapahos and Cheyennes already had run far beyond the column's reach. Now, the Kiowas had a defender who opposed their extermination.

Sheridan determined to hang Yellow Bear and Lone Wolf unless their tribesmen came in and surrendered within twenty-four hours. A rope was his solvent for many problems. The threatened chiefs were permitted to send a runner to their absent people. Before sunset, next day, the Kiowas marched into camp. There is splendor in this devotion of a people, returning to the source of terror for the sake of their prisoned chiefs. These were not released, for some of the Kiowas had run away too far to be recalled,

---

* Hazen, General W. B.: *Some Corrections to "My Life on the Plains,"* St. Paul, 1875.

but the rest of the tribe were admonished against further hostile acts and bidden to stay on the reservation, where they already had been when the army marched in against them.

Strife with Hazen modified Sheridan's and Custer's original sanguine intention. The reaction of the East to the "Glory of the Washita" also may have mitigated warlike aspiration. It was now late December. Echoes of denunciations of that "battle" may have spread by then even as far as Fort Cobb.

Catlin, the Indian artist, sent from Brussels an open letter to Sheridan, assailing him for the Washita slaughter, begging for the lives of people among whom the painter had ranged, unarmed and unharmed. Many closer at hand joined in the cry of outrage. There were, Custer writes, some persons "who actually went so far as to assert not only that the village we have attacked and destroyed was that of Indians who had always been friendly and peaceable toward the whites, but that many of the warriors and the chiefs were partly civilized."

A third moderating influence on Sheridan's and Custer's policy was the fact that Hazen was protecting his Kiowas and that the Arapahos and Cheyennes were too far out of range to shoot.

Wherefore, the assailants had a sudden change of spirit. They decided that the present purpose of the troops was not further to punish the tribes but only to get them all back on their reservations. Toward this end, Iron Shirt, a plains Apache, and Mahwissa, one of the Cheyenne women accompanying the column, were sent out to find the Arapahos and Cheyennes and bid them come in.

Iron Shirt returned and two Arapaho chiefs followed him to talk with Sheridan. Mahwissa did not come back. She had met a remnant of her tribe and with it she had stayed. Stone Forehead was the leader of this band, most of whom mourned for kin slain at Washita. Stone Forehead, whom the whites called Medicine Arrow, was a priest and custodian of the tribal emblem of the Cheyennes, the four Sacred Arrows that hung wrapped in a red fox pelt in his lodge.

The column had marched south from the Washita. It now was

camped on Cache Creek, near the Texas border. Here soldiers of the 7th Cavalry built a new frontier post to replace the crumbling relic that was old Fort Cobb. Men thought it should be called Fort Elliot. It was named Fort Sill.

From this camp, Custer set out with his forty sharpshooters, mule train and a few guides and scouts, including Brewster, who still sought his captured sister, to find the fugitive Cheyennes and Arapahos and persuade them to surrender. It was a daring gesture, this plunge with only a handful of followers into wilderness perilous with lurking, hostile tribesmen. Sheridan demurred when his subordinate first suggested it and then gave way to Custer's pleading.

During the two months of combined hunt and exploration that followed, the brilliance of Custer glows against the dark background of the Washita. He displayed in that long hard game of tag that dodged back and forth between Oklahoma and Texas, all those virtues for which men, to-day, remember him—bravery, determination, resource, skill that was match even for the craftiness of his quarry. He was at his best here as strategist, Indian diplomat and driver of men. He became the hound, the ardent devotee of a trail. In that long crooked hunt, he killed half his horses and wore out his troopers but he brought Arapahos and Cheyennes back to the reservations without firing a shot.

The handful he led out in mid-January rode west, skirting the southern boundary of the Wichita Mountains and crossed into the Texas Panhandle. They found the Arapahos under Little Raven, camped on Mulberry Creek. There were enough Indians to exterminate the little force. It was not Custer's guns, but his bravery and diplomacy that conquered this suspicious village. While his forty troopers remained in the background, he penetrated the Arapaho camp, talked with the chiefs and persuaded them to come in. Little Raven led his band toward Fort Sill and Custer pressed farther west to find the unslaughtered portion of the Cheyenne tribe.

Grazing was poor and forage gave out. He marched on. Mules and horses died of exhaustion while he searched along the Red River for trace of the Cheyenne village. His troopers broiled and ate the corpses and staggered forward. Neva, Blackfoot trailer, and two Arapaho guides, lent Custer by Little Raven, could find no trace of the missing tribe. The weary hunters camped at last by an unnamed creek while the three Indians, accompanied by Brewster, ascended it in hope of finding a trail. The troopers lived on horse-steaks until the scouts' return. Neva and Brewster alone came back. The Arapahos had found a two-weeks old trail and were following that.

It was hopeless to try to follow them. Men and the remaining horses were spent. With only half his mission accomplished, Custer faced about and marched back to Fort Sill. The slow pace of his exhausted column was more than he could endure. Mounted on a mule and accompanied by a half-dozen troopers, he cut loose and, guided by the compass, rode eighty miles in sixteen hours to report to Sheridan.

The Arapahos had come in. The Kiowas' chiefs, Yellow Bear and Lone Wolf, were released to their tribesmen. On the southern plains only the Cheyennes still defied the army. On February thirteenth, Sheridan turned toward civilization in company with Colonel Crawford of the 19th Kansas whose command devolved upon Colonel Horace Moore. Custer and fifteen hundred men, the 7th Cavalry mounted, the Kansas volunteers marching as infantry, were left to find the Cheyennes.

On March second, the column set out to discover an animate needle in a haystack of wilderness. They skirted the Wichita Mountains again, and left them behind. The Kansans forgot their homesickness in the toil of following the red-bearded, buckskin-clad leader, whose voice was a whiplash, who pressed on with the infatuated preoccupation of a trailing hound. Rations were limited. In the bivouacs, the 7th Cavalry's band offered music as substitute for food.

"Custer," the Kansans said later, "fed us one hardtack a day and *The Arkansas Traveller*."

They groped over endless brown miles and at length found a trail. They had marched toward smoke which had proved to be, when they had reached its source at two one morning, grass burning away from the embers of a camp-fire. At dawn, Osage trackers picked up the track of fifteen lodges. They were Cheyennes, going west, and the column followed them all that morning through rain.

At noon, when the weary soldiers halted, the Osages went on. Indian dogs, adopted by the troopers after Washita, started a noisy fight in the resting column. While it was at its height, the scouts galloped in. They had found the Cheyenne village beyond a ridge. Custer charged, but the Indians had gone. The tumult of the Washita dogs had given the alarm and since the fugitives had fled in all directions, there was no sure track now that the troops might follow.

Men expected Custer to turn back. He marched on, in the general direction the dog-alarmed band had been traveling. Day merged with day in a blurring haze of fatigue. Spent horses died until a third of the cavalry were plodding on foot. To all but the tireless man who led them, it was clear the command could not go much farther. His energy alone kept them marching. Then, one afternoon, the wilderness relented and gave them a trail.

It was only the track of a single lodge and it was many weeks old, but they followed it south. At sunset by a stream, they found the place where it had joined eleven other lodges camped there. The Indians had moved out, north-northeast. The trail was two weeks old. At daybreak, Custer followed. By mid-morning, they struck another camp-site. Twenty-five lodges had been set up here. The column made in one day three of the Indians' journeys and by nightfall found the site of a camp of one hundred lodges that had moved on only a few days before. Cook fires were kindled in hollows and kept small. After breakfast they were smothered at once by earth.

An hour after the pursuit had been resumed, it came upon a place where three hundred and fifty lodges had stood. The site had been vacated only the day before. Ashes still were warm. Custer, riding far ahead with the Osages, Cook, his adjutant, and a single orderly, looked down from a ridge upon a pony herd in a valley and the screaming boys who drove it toward a tree-shielded stream, the Sweetwater.

The column was far behind. There was a Cheyenne village among those trees. It would scatter before the troops came up. Custer sent Cook back to hurry them forward. Then, with only an orderly, he galloped after the fleeing herd, and in the valley's center, rode his horse in a circle—the plains signal for a conference.

Three mounted Indians, followed by many more, rode toward Custer who made the sign of friendship with one hand and held his revolver in the other. The Cheyennes replied in sign talk. This was Stone Forehead's, the Arrow Keeper's, village. A messenger had been sent for the priest. By the time Cook returned and the advancing troops were visible far down the valley, Stone Forehead appeared. He invited Custer to his dwelling and rode beside him and Cook into the village.

Cook was thrust into a near-by lodge. Custer stooped and entered the home of "Medicine Arrow," as he calls him. It is difficult to know which to admire more—the steel bravery of the General or the self-control of the Cheyenne warriors past whom the slayer of their kin, men, women and children moved unmolested into the place of council.

And it is hard, too, to tell exactly what took place in the lodge of the leader of a once powerful people who had been whittled down by war, reduced by white diseases, blasted by massacres at Sand Creek and Washita. It is quite certain that Stone Forehead, under pretense of holding council, laid the direst curse a priest could utter upon his self-satisfied guest. Grinnell, who made a life study of the Cheyenne people, writes:

> "The Indians say that Custer was brought into the camp and to the medicine arrow lodge, where he sat down under the medicine arrows and the keeper of the arrows lit a pipe and held it while Custer was smoking. Medicine Arrow told him in Cheyenne that he was a treacherous man and that if he came there with a bad purpose—to do harm to the people—he would be killed with all his men. Then the arrow keeper with a pipe stick, loosened the ashes in the pipe and poured them out on the toes of Custer's boots, to give him bad luck."*

---

* Grinnell, George B.: *The Fighting Cheyennes,* New Haven, 1923.

Custer's own complacent account of this same interview does no violence to the Indian story. He was sufficiently versed in lodge custom to mark the fact that neither his host nor the assembled chiefs smoked with him. He puffed alone until the pipe bowl was empty and was sorely afraid, since he was not a smoker, that the ordeal would sicken him.

He writes furthermore: "I was assigned the post of honor, being seated on the right of Medicine Arrow." Thereby, he reveals his own ignorance and confirms the Cheyenne story. In a properly raised Indian lodge, the chief guest always sat upon the host's left. The arrow keeper gave Custer the least honorable seat at the council.

That council, outwardly so gravely ceremonious, was saturated with hatred and deceit. Custer, waiting for his troops to get into position, became, as he writes, "an ardent advocate of peace measures." He also wished to be certain, before attacking, whether the Cheyennes actually had the two white women captives attributed to them. Stone Forehead, having cursed his guest as a treacherous man, also professed a wish for peace, assumed a welcoming air and when the conference ended, rode out with Custer to show him where his command might camp.

The guile with which the priest selected the site did not deceive Custer, who saw at once that the bivouac would be wholly out of sight of the Cheyenne village, and felt, furthermore, that after nightfall the Indians would flee. He posted lookouts at once to prevent this. Monasetah, the other Washita squaw carried with the column, informed him that the white women, Mrs. Morgan and Miss White, actually were prisoners in the village.

Toward evening, the sentries reported that the pony herd had been driven in and that Stone Forehead's village was filled with activity. When a party of Cheyennes visited Custer's camp, to sing and dance for him and thereby distract attention from their people's flight, their host attacked them, capturing four.

One of the prisoners was released at once with a message to Stone Forehead. This informed the priest that if he did not surrender his white prisoners and march his people to their reservation, Custer would abandon the peace he had affected to cherish, and attack the village.

There followed days of tortuous Indian diplomacy, complicated for Custer by the mutterings of the Kansas regiment who had enlisted to fight Indians and felt that it was being defrauded. The anxiety of young Brewster, most devoted of brothers, for the welfare of his sister, Mrs. Morgan—now so close at hand and in such peril—was still another problem with which the never too patient Glory-Hunter had to deal. After days of delay, his own forbearance snapped and he employed Sheridan's prescription. He told Cheyennes that unless the white prisoners were sent into camp by sunset of the next day, the captive Indians, Dull Knife, Big Head and Fat Bear, would be hanged.

An hour before the stipulated sunset, a pony bearing two figures approached the camp. Colonel Moore and two other officers of the 19th Kansas rode out toward them. Young Brewster outstripped the soldiers. He met the twin riders and embraced one of them. The camp boiled with cheering.

The rescued women were taken to Custer's tent where his Irishwoman cook supplied them with substitutes for their Indian raiment. Stone Forehead now demanded the release of the hostages. He was told these would be held until his band had returned to their reservation. They would move thither, the priest promised, as soon as there was sufficient grass to enable winter-weakened ponies to travel. Custer's command broke camp and marched back toward civilization.

It reached the Washita battle-ground, March 23, 1869, and rested there two days. Here Custer read Benteen's letter in a six-weeks-old newspaper. Thence the column moved by easy marches, for men and horses were well-nigh worn out, to Fort Hays.

The gaunt and ragged soldiers reached the post April seventh. Colonel Nelson A. Miles, commanding, sent out his band to play the victors in. They had marched many hundred miles and had fired no shot at a hostile Indian, but the man who had waded through slaughter at the Washita had brought peace to the southern plains by his skill in leading troops through wilderness and in penetrating himself the devious puzzle of the Indian mind.

Custer's winter campaign of 1868-69 exemplifies at its outset on the Washita all that was worst; in its subsequent roundup and pacification of frightened, hostile tribes, all that was best in army control of the Indian problem. The triumph, hailed by the welcoming blare of Miles's band, was not the most vivid but it was certainly among the greatest in the Glory-Hunter's career. He reviews it, without perceptible deprecation, in a letter written to his wife from his tarrying place on the Washita, March twenty-fourth.

"I have been successful in my campaign against the Cheyennes. I outmarched them, outwitted them at their own game, proved to them that they were in my power and could and would have annihilated the entire village of over two hundred lodges but for two reasons. First, I desired to obtain the release of the two white women held captive by them, which I could not have done had I attacked. Second, if I had attacked them, those who escaped, and absent portions of the tribe also, would have been on the warpath all summer, and we would have obtained no rest.

"I counselled with no one, but when we overtook the Cheyenne village, and saw it in our power to annihilate them, my command, from highest to lowest, desired bloodshed. They were eager for revenge, and could not comprehend my conduct. They disapproved and criticized it. I paid no heed, but followed the dictates of my own judgment—the judgment upon which my beloved commander said he relied for the attainment of the best results. He had authorized me to do as I pleased, fight or not. And now my most bitter enemies cannot say that I am either blood-thirsty or possessed of an unworthy ambition.

"Had I given the signal to attack, officers and men would have hailed it with a shout of gratification. I braved their opinion and acted in opposition to their wishes, but to-day no one but says I was right and any other course would have been disastrous. Many have come to me and confessed their error."*

That is Custer's opinion of Custer's own accomplishment. It is more just than the self-praise of most egotists.

---

* Custer, Elizabeth B.: *Following the Guidon,* New York, 1890.

CHAPTER NINE

PORTRAIT OF A HERO

THE footsore 19th Kansas was mustered out at Fort Hays. The 7th Cavalry camped for the summer three miles from the post on the bank of Big Creek. Elizabeth Custer joined her husband in the canvas mansion he had raised for her. A big cottonwood spread its shade above the hospital tent living-room. The three wall tents were bedroom, dining-room and guest-room; a Sibley served for kitchen and there was a Cheyenne lodge, captured at Washita, in which the negro cook dwelt. These were set, after Custer's custom in the field, further up-stream than any other tents in his command.

Voices that had cried out against the slaughter of Black Kettle's band and the abandonment of Elliot had been hushed by the subsequent skill and daring with which Custer had outwitted and pacified hostile tribes. Kiowas and Arapahos were on their reservations. Cheyennes were creeping back to theirs so that the women and children taken at Washita, the three warrior hostages kidnaped at Sweetwater, might be freed.

Custer was content for a little to bask in the warmth of his rekindled fame. A year before, he had brooded in exile over its ashes. Now men acclaimed him, once more. He had accomplished more in a single campaign against the Indians than any other officer in the service. By gun and by diplomacy he had subdued all he had encountered. He had brought about another temporary truce, secured by eternal treaties, soon to be broken.

It was a serene and happy interlude, that camp on Big Creek—a time as bright and quiet as the Kansas summer. Travelers detrained at Hays City to visit the camp of the regiment that had become an eternal part of its young leader's renown. Squadrons rode out on

220

easy bloodless patrols. The soldiers built an "opera-house" in camp and held dances and minstrel shows there. The guest tent in the Custers' dwelling was seldom without an admiring occupant. There were races and dinners and buffalo hunts.

On May sixth, A. J. Smith, Colonel of the 7th Cavalry, resigned. Colonel S. D. Sturgis took his place. He joined his command on Big Creek. Custer's fame was too bright now for him to chafe under the presence of a superior. Chief or lieutenant, all men knew and praised the most brilliant Indian fighter of his day.

A single spark of the fire that had swept the plains glowed for an instant and died. The Cheyenne prisoners were penned in a fifteen-foot stockade at Fort Hays. Rumor whispered that fellow-tribesmen would attempt a jail delivery and an officer of the garrison took a file of infantry into the stockade to thrust the three warrior hostages into a prison more secure.

None of the soldiers spoke Cheyenne; no Cheyenne spoke English. The sudden appearance of armed men sent the apprehensive spirits of Dull Knife, Fat Bear and Big Head leaping to the belief that they were to be hanged. When the soldiers grappled with them, the prisoners fought back. There was a screaming, slashing fight, beaten down at last by gun-fire. When it ended, two soldiers had been knifed, Big Head was dead, Dull Knife was dying from a bayonet thrust and Fat Bear had been knocked senseless. The women in the stockade still screeched and ran about in panic. A courier from the fort summoned Custer who flung himself on a horse, thrust his way into the stockade and by sign talk and his few words of Cheyenne speech, subdued the riot. Later, the surviving hostages were carried by army wagon to the Cheyenne reservation.

Save for this outbreak and a flood that threatened to sweep away the camp, Elizabeth Custer's summer passed without its usual companionship of terror. Her spirit unfolded in the bright presence of her beloved. They took long rides together, during which he derided his "old lady" for the slow pace she took, or else pursued her and ranging his mount alongside hers, leaned over and plucked her, screaming, from her saddle. There were picnics in which the whole Custer clan among the officers—his brother Tom, Yates,

Keogh, Weir, and a newcomer to the regiment, Algernon E. Smith (a Civil War veteran with a permanently crippled left arm) — took part. There were dinners, races and buffalo hunts for guests from the East.

During these, liquor flowed abundantly and the volatile spirits of Custer, the abstemious, were lifted by the contagion of revelry to extravagant heights. Once a guest crept away and fell asleep in a crate half full of straw. Custer, spying him, organized a funeral. The band, playing the "Dead March" from *Saul,* led the cortège. Six troopers, impressed for pall-bearers, followed with the crate containing the body of the vanquished, and behind it Custer and fellow-mourners marched.

Again, when another guest was overcome in like fashion, Custer ordered a box placed over him and pegged down to the earth on which the unfortunate had collapsed. The subsequent efforts of the prisoner to escape from his tomb sent the General into paroxysms of shrill laughter.

Whatever lapses of hospitality were visible in these jests, they were not the direct effect of liquor upon George Armstrong Custer. Throughout his life, he kept the pledge made in his youth to Lydia, his step-sister. Men who spread the libel that he was a drunkard no doubt saw him at such times when his explosive spirit had been set off by revelry about him. Red-faced, elated and noisy, he looked the drunkard he was not. Years and responsibility never changed his vehement zest for life.

His wife, intent on rearing a literary shrine to his memory, pictures Custer and his intimates as an incongruous combination of Arthurian knights and fun-loving Rover Boys. He and the satellites who were known to other officers as "Custer's Gang," bore faint resemblance to Elizabeth Custer's word portraits.

Her hero was unprofane of speech. Colonel Varnum remembers only two occasions when he used so strong an expletive as "damn." Custer touched neither alcohol nor tobacco but he and his chosen companions were a hard-riding, a gambling and, save for himself, a hard-drinking set. The feats of the Custer brothers at the poker table are army legends. The General owned race-horses and matched them, not always to his profit. It was the belief of General Hugh L. Scott, who joined the 7th Cavalry just after the Little Bighorn disaster, that Custer's cronies were not the most reliable and responsible officers in his regiment.

In October, 1869, the placid interlude, brightened by Glory's presence, ended and was replaced by the monotony of a winter in garrison. The camp on Big Creek broke up and the 7th Cavalry marched back to Fort Leavenworth. Here the restless energy of Custer, which had been fed by praise all summer, stirred and fretted and at last found outlet in an attempt at authorship.

Custer began to write the story of his life. He struggled through an account of his earlier years, insisting that his wife sit beside him during the agony of composition and then, despairing, laid the unfinished manuscript of his autobiography aside. He was then thirty years old. He looked much older.

His spirit was eternally adolescent, or else it possessed the unconquerable insurgency of the bucking horse, the "wild one" of the rodeos. It may have been permanent youth that inspired his defiances and rebellions. If this be so, no hint of that juvenility can be found in portraits of the man.

There is precocious ruthlessness in that face. It might be the visage of one ten years his senior. The narrow planes and harsh angles of cheek-bones, forehead, nose and chin have the bleak, expedient sharpness of the hawk's profile. No softness, no hint of contemplation is here. The deep-laired eyes are challenging. The brows are thick above a rapaciously curved nose. A big mustache hides a mouth that must have been thin-lipped and quick-tempered, and the shallow chin has more of intemperance than strength. The forehead is high and a hint of imminent baldness makes it appear more lofty still.

Custer's hair and mustache were a bright gold. He wore the former long or short as it suited his whim. His wife writes that his head was always close cropped in garrison yet photographs taken of him there show curls falling about his shoulders. The eyes were a bright and sparkling blue and his skin was fair, so tender that it burned scarlet on campaign. This permanent flush, plus the still brighter hue of his sun-skinned nose, plus his wild whoopings when amused, were warrants for the still existent rumor that he was a drunkard.

He was just under six feet in height. His erect and raw-boned body looked taller. He was broad of shoulder, slim of hip and had enormous, big-knuckled hands. In movement, he was nervously abrupt. His high-pitched temperament colored his speech. His voice was shrill and piercing and in moments of excitement rattled forth words at a tremendous rate, sometimes catching and hanging on a phrase in endless repetition. "All right-all right-all right-all right" was his familiar expletive. He was a fine shot with rifle or pistol and a magnificent horseman.

The struggles of the strenuous spirit pent in that superb body may have aged his face. Emotion drove him to demonstrative excesses and equally incomprehensible reticences. To some, he seemed the most engaging and informal of comrades; to others a snobbish martinet. The impartiality of love with which his wife had listed his whims, his eccentricities, makes it easier to comprehend why men in the lifetime of George Armstrong Custer were so at variance in their estimate of him; why men in the years since then have quarreled so bitterly over his character.

Elizabeth Custer mitigated her bereavement by including in her monument to him, all that she could recall of her beloved—even the little, insignificant, invaluable things—the dancing, whooping and juba-patting of his merriment; his afternoon "romps" during which he pursued her throughout their dwelling with howls of laughter and uproariously barking dogs; his habit of picking her up, carrying her about and setting her down wherever it pleased him; his ready tears; his insistence, when rare illness smote him, that she also take the medicine prescribed for him, so that she might know how vilely it tasted; his passion for music; his interest in natural history; his love for soup and apple dumplings and raw onions; his insistence that no meal was complete unless beef were included; his habit of lying flat on earth or floor. Her love saw his eccentricities as enduring charm. What her lord had touched forever was sanctified for her.

GENERAL AND MRS. CUSTER IN HIS STUDY AT FORT LINCOLN, 1873

From the collection of E. A. Brininstool

She saw not selfishness, or excessive egotism, in the way he would run off and hide when most visitors appeared, leaving her to bear the brunt of entertainment. She discerned nothing odd in his withdrawal from the life of the garrison. She tells, with worship, how he would lurk in his study when she was giving a party and disrupt it by sending her frequent notes during the evening, summoning her to his side. If there were dancing, he would command her presence and, in his own chamber, waltz with her to music in the adjoining room. This exclusiveness scarcely could have endeared him to the garrison.

Once, when she tarried too long on a neighborly call, Custer sent his orderly with a package which proved to be her nightgown. When alone at a meal they sat, not at the table's opposite ends, but side by side.

For all his devotion to and need of her, there were limits beyond which she dared not pass. He had the egotist's dread of wife-management. Problems of his command were forbidden ground on which she might not trespass with counsel or even discussion. She never knew of a contemplated change of post or the plan for a new campaign, until the news was common property. He insisted that she treat his enemies among his officers with a cordiality that she found it hard to feign. He had all of her. There were precincts within him where she might not venture.

His study was a miniature natural history museum. Trophy heads glared down from the walls—buffalo, antelope, deer and bear. A grizzly's skin was spread before the fireplace. Stuffed jack-rabbits, an eagle, a fox, a sandhill crane and a snowy owl perched on bookcases and mantel. A photograph of his wife in her wedding-gown shared the honor of a place on Custer's walls with pictures of McClellan, Sheridan and Barrett and himself. The General's dearest art treasures were two Rogers groups, endlessly battered by moving—*Wounded to the Rear* and *Letter Day*. After arrival at each new post, he spent long hours repairing with glue and plaster damages of the most recent journey.

He was harsh with members of his command and ruthlessly cruel to foemen. He was tender to his wife. He would break down and weep while reading aloud to her of the death of no one more intimate than Daniel Webster and could order the pursuers of deserters to bring in none alive. He could cripple a buffalo and wait for an audience to gather before he killed it, yet he would turn a marching column aside to spare a meadow-lark's nest. He was a strict disciplinarian to underlings and a most insurgent subordinate.

Men found him pompous, overbearing, inflated with pride. Intimates denied all these defects. Visitors who had endured his churlish withdrawals formed one radical impression of his character. Those who shared his hours of unbridled hilarity and practical joking held diametrically opposite opinions. He was indifferent or magnanimous toward his many actual enemies. Men said he was incapable of hatred, yet his virulent detestation of one man, Secretary of War Belknap, was to cause his downfall and death.

To the woman who loved him, none of the eccentricities of a singular spirit was apparent. He was her hero, her golden paragon, half child, half deity, who enveloped her in the sunlight of his presence and left all the world in shadow when he departed. "With all the vicissitudes of those twelve eventful years," she wrote afterward, "I never have known him to have a minute's depression."*

One of her books is dedicated to him, who "made those who followed him forget in his sunshiny presence half the hardship and the danger."

Late in the winter of 1869-70, Elizabeth Custer and her husband got away for a brief visit to New York. There they reveled in the luxury for which she had starved. They wept together at plays. She remembered at concerts that her husband had begged her not to speak to him till the program's end, lest she mar the emotions music quickened. So she kept silent.

The following summer was spent peacefully at Fort Hays where Custer commanded the garrison. The Indian question still seemed to have been settled. Only in the North, a slow ferment was at

---

* *Boots and Saddles.*

work among the Sioux that was to father the last great battle of a desperate people. The winter of 1870-71 was spent in Monroe and New York.

The 7th Cavalry's term of frontier duty was over. Prospect of separation from his beloved plains was so painful to Custer that he applied for a transfer or any other possible arrangement that might leave him on the frontier. This was denied.

The 7th Cavalry's Lieutenant-Colonel, was assigned to a two-company post at Elizabethtown, Kentucky, forty miles south of Louisville. The rest of the regiment in small detachments hunted moonshiners and Ku Klux Klansmen elsewhere in Kentucky and in Tennessee and South Carolina. There were no such distractions in sleepy Elizabethtown. Glory was far away. Custer strove to woo her by a second attack upon his memoirs. Articles written during his two-year sojourn here appeared in *The Galaxy,* a magazine long since defunct, and in 1875 were embodied in a book *My Life on the Plains.*

He was better with the sword than with the pen. His literary style adhered to the Victorian convention whereby adjectives and nouns were wedded for life. For Custer, "rifle" never appeared in public without its consort, "trusty." "Comrades" forever was linked with "gallant." "Steed" and "noble" were eternally joined. His writing had vigor but scant skill. He hewed to his task, letting infinitives split where they might.

In appearance and by nature, he complied so little with the popular picture of an author that when his first article appeared in print many were skeptical. Rumor whispered that his wife really had written it and color was lent that fable by Custer's insistence that she sit beside him while he worked. The allegation galled him. He referred to it often in his later letters to her.

He must have believed that he had cause for grievance against many men. It is certain that many disliked him and, recalling old quarrels, were worried when they heard that Custer was writing his plains experiences.

In those reminiscences there are bitter diatribes against the Indian Bureau but no single instance in which the author employs the ammunition of print to blast a personal enemy. Even Benteen escapes. Such omissions may have been due to a magnanimous spirit. It is more likely that they were merely a fiery temper's inability to hold a grudge.

Indirectly, these repressions had their reward. In the years that elapsed between his death and their own, almost none of his enemies smirched his reputation with printers' ink, though their reticence may have been more a tribute to Custer's widow than to him.

The Custers dwelt in Elizabethtown in a small tenant dwelling beside what was then the Hill residence and is now the Community House. Few still living in the town remember him but what they recall is typical. This was the horse-raising district of Kentucky and Custer invested lavishly in its chief product. His stable and the racers he entered at Louisville—Frogtown, Bluegrass, Vic and others—cost him ten thousand dollars during his Kentucky sojourn. He also added here to his pack of hounds and inherited thereby much woe. His animals murdered other dogs and slaughtered farmers' pigs. The Lieutenant-Colonel at length bestowed the rank of dogtender-in-chief upon his orderly, John Burkman, who exercised the hounds, chained in pairs.

It is doubtful whether any sleepy provincial hamlet could have pleased Custer, yet his sojourn in Elizabethtown for the most part must have been serene, since so little legend remains concerning it. Men still recall a brawl in which he took part, but that was at Louisville. In the heat of a political debate, Custer is said to have slapped the face of Colonel Blanton Duncan. Friends intervened and hushed up the matter.

In October, 1871, Custer was called to Chicago briefly to aid Sheridan in military police work following the great fire. In January of the following year, he was summoned to the plains again. The Grand Duke Alexis of Russia had journeyed half-way around the world to hunt buffalo and Custer and Buffalo Bill Cody were among those assigned by the government to accompany him.

Least conspicuous of the plainsmen who were to make sure that royalty slaughtered buffalo was a stocky, wistful man with sad gray eyes and a drooping mild mustache. Among the garish and

raucous scouts and guides, Charley Reynolds was drably inconspic-
uous, but even Cody regarded him with respect. Illinois-born and
well-educated, Reynolds had turned to the plains for respite from
no man knows what sorrow. He was soft-voiced and shy. He never
trumpeted his prowess after the fashion of the frontier but he was
a great scout, an expert guide, a mighty hunter and he understood
Indians better perhaps than any white man of his era. Plainsmen
called him "Lonesome Charley." The Sioux in whose lodges he
was welcome had named him "Lucky Hunter." It is probable that
Custer met Reynolds here for the first time. They were to die in the
same battle four years later.

The grand ducal party mobilized at Omaha and set out for the
plains, by rail as far as North Platte and thereafter by wagon under
cavalry escort. Sheridan, who superintended the hunt, saw that
nothing was omitted. Even Indians were supplied in the person of
Spotted Tail, meekest and perhaps wisest of Sioux chiefs, with a
number of his reservation tribesmen. The Grand Duke enjoyed
himself. He shot eight buffalo—or thought he did, thanks to the
unapparent cooperation of Bill Cody. He cast amorous eyes on
Spotted Tail's pretty daughter and he took an instant liking to
George Armstrong Custer. When the hunt ended, the Glory-
Hunter accompanied Alexis east. At Louisville, Mrs. Custer joined
the party. They went south with the Grand Duke to New Orleans.

In March, 1873, the 7th Cavalry received orders sending it back
to the plains. The regiment was to rendezvous at Memphis and
journey by steamer, rail and horse to Dakota territory. Events were
marshaling, men were moving to their places for the last act in the
tragedy of a defrauded and desperate people.

PART THREE

HERO

PART THREE: HERO

CHAPTER ONE

PROLOGUE

FORCES that molded the three remaining years of George Armstrong Custer's life had the fatality of Greek tragedy. Above their basic motive rose overtones of human greed, mendacity, robbery.

The latest eternal treaty with the Sioux had endured nearly five years. Elements beyond any man's control were rising to crush it.

Dabbling in these forces and striving vainly to guide their onrush into devious channels were bewildered red leaders and unreliable white. While an elated man in his early thirties hurried with his wife, his two troops of cavalry, his great pack of hounds, his caged mocking-birds and canaries and his saddle string of thoroughbreds toward Memphis, the stage already had been set for the final impact of a westward-moving civilization and a desperate neolithic people.

The treaty that the great Sioux chief, Red Cloud, imposed on the white men in 1868 is the only admission of defeat the United States ever signed. Until the forts on the Bozeman Road had been abandoned, until the garrisons had withdrawn from Indian country, Red Cloud would not even consent to talk with the peace commissioners. By the treaty, finally established, the Sioux and their allies, the Northern Cheyennes, won everything for which they had fought.

The Bozeman Road was closed. All of what is now the state of South Dakota, west of the Missouri, was set aside as a permanent reservation for the Sioux. The Indians were granted, for as long as there were buffalo on the plains, "the right to hunt on any land

233

north of the Platte." It was agreed, furthermore, that no subsequent treaty should be considered valid "unless executed and signed by at least three-fourths of all the adult male Indians occupying and interested in the same." Hereafter, a few bribed or bullied chiefs could not sell their people's land.

Article 16 of the treaty was worded loosely and was to cause infinite trouble. It set forth: "The country north of the North Platte and east of the summits of the Big Horn Mountains shall be held and considered unceded Indian territory."

On this indefinitely limited land "no white person or persons shall be permitted to settle or occupy any portion of the same or, without the consent of the Indians first had and obtained, to pass through the same."

Through some odd oversight, no northern boundary was named for this unceded tract. The Sioux claimed, by right of conquest from the Crows forty years earlier, that their land extended to the Yellowstone.

While Red Cloud had fought, the Sioux Nation had followed him. All men who loved their land and hated the whites had served with him. There was Sitting Bull, already great in fame as priest and orator; Gall, the widow's son, a dour and bitter fighter, and Crazy Horse, probably a greater cavalry leader than Custer, Sheridan or Stuart. These and lesser chiefs had led the Sioux and the northern branch of the Cheyenne people in their war for independence.

Sitting Bull, Gall, Crazy Horse were sublimely valiant, or ignorant, or both. They had fought and beaten the soldiers. They believed that they could halt and drive back all white armies. When Red Cloud listened to the wheedlings of peace commissioners at Fort Laramie, they jeered. When he went in at last and signed the treaty, they refused to go with him. When he returned later to urge them to take up farms on the newly made reservation, they paid him no heed. They remained hostile, in that they intended to keep inviolable the land they ranged and since that country was said by the treaty to be "unceded Indian territory" they were within their rights in occupying it.

The men who thrilled to the clangorous voice of Sitting Bull and followed the grim Gall and the laughing Crazy Horse were the nucleus of the great host of Sioux and Cheyennes who later rose to defeat Crook twice and half abolish the 7th Cavalry. They were unreconstructed patriots, but by dwelling in the wild far country drained by the Powder, the Bighorn and other rivers flowing northward into the Yellowstone, they broke no stipulation of the new treaty Red Cloud had signed. Once again it was the white man who shattered it and the army was his mallet.

Four months after the Laramie treaty had been proclaimed by the President, Sherman issued an order that all Indians, not actually on their stated reservations, were to be under the jurisdiction of the army and "as a rule will be considered hostile."

He had no authority for this ruling but the army was again embroiled in another of its endless squabbles with the Indian Bureau. His order broke the solemnly established treaty which he himself had signed. The "wild Indians" as Sitting Bull's parish was called, were outlawed thereby. From this time on, the story of the Laramie treaty is the tale of those that preceded it—increasing white pressure, heat bred by friction, outrage and indiscriminate revenge therefor upon the innocent and guilty.

In 1871, the calamity-booming Sitting Bull was justified in his predictions of imminent white perfidy. The Sioux learned that a railroad was to be driven clear through the heart of their land. No such formality as the approving vote of three-fourths of the Sioux Nation was requested by the sponsors of the Northern Pacific. Instead the government built protecting forts, Abraham Lincoln, near Bismarck, North Dakota, and Ellis in Montana. General Stanley conducted a preliminary survey in 1872. The 7th Cavalry was recalled to the plains in 1873 to aid the surveyors at their treaty-violation.

Three steamers bore the reunited regiment from Memphis to Cairo. Colonel Sturgis was in command and Custer had time to devote to his wife, his horses and his dogs. One of the hounds broke away from the distracted Burkman and leaped aboard a St. Louis packet just as it pulled out from Memphis. Custer telegraphed friends in that city to meet the boat, get the stowaway and ship it back to him again.

From Cairo, the regiment traveled by rail to Yankton. There, Sturgis received orders to report to headquarters at St. Paul for staff duty and one squadron of the regiment was detached under a new major, Marcus A. Reno, to escort the surveyors who were establishing the western United States-Canadian boundary.

He was not, in the estimate of officers who served under him, a particularly pleasant person, this Major Reno. He was sleek but with a thin mustache, a thin-lipped mouth and tired sunken eyes. If his nature were not lovable he had at least an excellent war record and had won the brevet of brigadier-general. He had served during the Shenandoah campaign as the cavalry's chief of staff. He had known Custer then and had formed no high opinion of his soldierly qualities. Reno was older than the 7th's Lieutenant-Colonel and a West Pointer. Throughout his service in the regiment his contact with Custer necessarily was brief for he did not return from the boundary survey until late in 1874. Much has been written of enmity between the men. There is no evidence that this existed, save for Reno's own admission that he had small regard for Custer's military ability.

At Yankton, the 7th Cavalry—less the squadron detached with Reno—made ready to march again under its old leader into land already simmering with red resentment. Charley Reynolds, the mild and wistful, was to serve as guide. It was new country to Custer's command and, thanks to the guns and arrows of Red Cloud's warriors and the mounting truculence of the "wild Indians," still largely virgin to white penetration. The immobile sea of dim prairie, the fir-darkened Black Hills beyond and, north and west of this holy place, the valleys of many small rivers where game abounded, were Sioux land. Those whom Sherman arbitrarily had classed as "hostiles" intended to keep it so by aloofness from white persuasion if possible or else by battle.

From now on, in the few years remaining to Custer, the vivid threads of his personality are caught up and woven into the lurid fabric of that period's history. All of him, the praise- and blameworthy alike, colored and hastened events, as though his brilliant spirit, its daring, its wilfulness, its pride and hunger for glory were a reagent which, added to those murky and troubled times, precipitated tragedy.

To many, he is the arch hero of that era's terrific climax. To others, he is a super-scoundrel. Actually he was neither. No single man, no group of men, directed the forces that grumbled and muttered and burst at last into a crescendo of strident cavalry trumpets and flatly thumping Sioux drums; of hammering guns and rolling hoofs and a wild, manifold shouting.

One more superstitious than Custer, or less completely armored in self-confidence, might have read an omen in the welcome the West accorded her returning lover that spring.

The troops, the horses and the clamorous pack of dogs detrained amid the welcoming cheers of Yankton's citizenry. The soldiers began the erection of Camp Sturgis on a level space about a mile from the town. Many of the officers, since the weather was raw and chill, sought shelter in Yankton's hotels. Custer elected to stay with his men and a tent was raised for him. This his wife shared.

The sky grew gray. The wind became keener. So bitter was the increasing cold that it numbed even Custer, the usually immune. He, his wife and their cook deserted the tent for a near-by cabin. Troopers and their horses were ordered to find quarters in Yankton, for the first whistling gray streamers of a blizzard lashed the camp.

In this hour, Custer was smitten by one of his rare fits of illness. This, of itself, must have been profoundly terrifying to a wife who regarded her lord as above mortal weakness. A surgeon fought his way through the snow to the cabin, prescribed, and departed promising to return shortly. The blizzard closed in. For thirty-six hours thereafter, the stricken man, his wife and cook and castaways who groped to the equivocal refuge of the cabin were immured in the whirling pallor of the storm.

No one could reach them from town. Fuel gave out and Elizabeth Custer lay in bed beside her suffering man for their mutual warmth, rising at intervals to share with him the medicine her husband would not take otherwise. They were cut off from the outside world, yet they did not lack for company. Mules and horses, huddled in the lee of the shanty, brayed and whinnied through the blizzard's screeching. Lost soldiers stumbled to the door of the cabin and reeled in, some of them with feet and hands frozen. Mrs. Custer revived them with raw alcohol from her spirit lamp. They lay on the floor and groaned beneath the rugs she spread. After two nights and a day, the storm abated and Custer improved. He was able to drink coffee and eat bits of steak that had been cooked over candle flame. Eventually a rescue party from Yankton got through to the cabin. Some men, a number of horses and eleven of Custer's precious hounds perished in this storm.

Thereafter, the unseasonable snow vanished in the warmth of spring and the regiment prepared for the five hundred miles overland march to Fort Rice, where the military escort of the Northern Pacific surveyors was to assemble. There was gaiety in Yankton, then capital of the territory. There was a ball for officers of the 7th Cavalry and a reciprocal review for the Territorial Governor.

Three Missouri River captains, half steamboat men, half scouts, moored their craft at the Yankton pier. Abner Shaw's *Peninah* and Mart Coulson's *Far West* were laden with the regiment's supplies. Grant Marsh took aboard his *Key West* the regiment's women and children and the officers' personal baggage. While the cavalry marched, these shallow-draft, stern-wheel craft were to move upriver, keeping contact with the column.

Elizabeth Custer rode with her husband when the 7th moved out from Yankton. She and the General's sister were the only women to accompany the troops throughout that long journey. Margaret Custer had been married the year before to Lieutenant James Calhoun, golden-haired and handsome, who had risen from the ranks in the Civil War and had joined the 7th Cavalry January 1, 1871. Another newcomer to the command was Lieutenant Charles Varnum, a youngster fresh from West Point, and still alive as this is written, last of all the gay and valiant company who led their men north that spring.

Elizabeth Custer, in after-years, wrote lyrically of that march. She remembered with keenest delight the nightly bivouac—the troopers thrashing the undergrowth to scare out snakes before they raised their tents; the tender blue of woodsmoke drifting through the company streets; accordions wheezing in the dusk and the merry talk of her husband's satellites seated on the buffalo robes spread before his dwelling.

She recalled, too, the blitheness of Custer's spirits, emancipated at last from the routine of garrison life and foot-loose again in his beloved West—his jests, his shrill merriment, the hours he spent in the evening extracting cactus thorns from the feet of his hounds, the comic speeches he would insist his dogs had made, particularly one venerable bitch whom he had christened Lucy Stone.

She remembered how he teased her when she took all the shirts she had made him the winter before and presented them to John Burkman, the orderly with the permanent appetite whom Custer had nicknamed "Old Nutriment." These shirts were the brave scarlet that was the Glory-Hunter's favorite color but they blazed so conspicuously here in the drab wilderness that she feared to let him keep them. The big white hat he wore on this and all later marches was obvious enough.

There was some warrant for her timidity. The old reckless Custer was unleashed once more. With an independent command, far from the supervision of a superior, he was behaving less like a leader of troops in the field than one of his hounds just freed from kennel. He was careless, he was headstrong. He ranged far in advance of the column, despite the ever present danger of Indians, for no better reason than to savor once more the provocative flavor of peril.

Once he outstripped his wife and his adjutant, Lieutenant Cook, and they, following in haste, ran square into a group of Sioux warriors squatting in a thicket about a fire. These sprang up, bows and guns in hand. Cook faced them calmly and bade Mrs. Custer ride on. She obeyed and presently the Lieutenant too withdrew in safety, but Elizabeth Custer fainted in her saddle when at last she reached her husband's side.

Blizzards and privations and terrors, sudden and stark as these, seemed to her small price to pay for the bliss of his companionship.

The column arrived on the Missouri's bank, opposite Fort Rice on June tenth, and even before he had reported to Brevet Major-General D. S. Stanley, Colonel of the 22nd Infantry and commander of the forming expedition, Custer was embroiled in a quarrel.

Stanley had sent Captain Joseph Labarge, an old river man, and his steamer, the *DeSmet,* to ferry the 7th Cavalry across. Custer attempted to take charge of the craft. Labarge objected and there was a violent dispute which ended when Labarge took his steamer back across the river, leaving the column stranded on the bank. Stanley had to intervene and pacify both parties before the crossing could be accomplished.

There was no room at the crowded fort for women. Mrs. Custer went up-river to Bismarck and thence east by train. She spent that summer in the familiar company of the dread which squired her whenever she and her husband were apart. There was reason for her fear. The Yellowstone expedition was more purposeful, yet no less provocative than Hancock's earlier foray.

The government had held a club behind its back and had offered a persuasive other hand to the Sioux. In March, when preparation for the invasion already was well under way, the Reverend John P. Williamson and Dr. J. Daniels had been sent out to talk to the "hostile Indians" and persuade them to permit the railroad to run through their territory and, incidentally, through the Laramie treaty. On May ninth chiefs of the recalcitrants met with the commissioners. The Sioux were unanimous. They did not want a railroad built across their land. They did not want any white men in their country.

Legally, that ended the matter. The Commissioners notified the Indian Bureau that permission for the road had been refused but they added that, in their opinion, there would be "no combined resistance to the construction" because the Sioux had "neither ammunition or subsistence to undertake a general war."

CHAPTER TWO

YELLOWSTONE

THE escort for the Northern Pacific's surveyors left Fort Rice, June 20, 1873. The government had chosen no light instrument to smash the treaty with the Sioux. The force led by Colonel Stanley, former commander of the Army of the Cumberland, consisted of ten companies of the 8th and 9th Infantry, three companies of the 17th, one of the 6th, five companies of the 22nd, two field pieces manned by squads of the 22nd, and ten troops of the 7th Cavalry. Lieutenant Frederick Dent Grant, the President's son, had a place on Stanley's staff. Charley Reynolds was chief of scouts. In all, there were 1540 soldiers, 275 wagons and ambulances, a herd of beef cattle, 353 civilian employees and 27 Arikaras, blood enemies of the Sioux.

Among these last was Bloody Knife, a temperamental warrior with a resolution and energy past that of most of his fellows who regarded this and similar expeditions as magnified picnics. He formed an abiding friendship with Custer, became his favorite Indian scout and died at the Little Bighorn. The virtues of the leader of the 7th Cavalry were those that lay close to Indian hearts. They were not so apparent to Stanley.

The Fort Rice column was to meet at Muddy River the Northern Pacific engineers, who were led by General T. L. Rosser, Custer's old classmate and Civil War opponent. Twenty-five men of the 7th Cavalry had been sent to the railhead at Bismarck to escort the surveyors and their wagons.

It seemed at the outset that the heavens reiterated the protests of the Sioux. On fourteen out of the first seventeen days' march it rained, turning the earth to slime, bogging the train. In the first

241

six days, the column was able to crawl only forty-five miles. On June twenty-fourth, a terrific hailstorm battered the engineers with stones so heavy that they broke wagon tops.

Foul weather did not depress Custer. He does not even mention the downpour in letters to his wife. He had become again, at the touch of the wilderness, the exuberant, impatient leader, tireless, intolerant of authority. By the time the march was well under way, he was indulging his old zest for superior-baiting and was more than willing to show Stanley, an old Indian fighter himself, how the expedition should be run. The column's commander was patient but less dull than he may have seemed. On June twenty-eighth, Stanley wrote his wife:

"I have had no trouble with Custer and will try to avoid having any, but I have seen enough of him to convince me that he is a coldblooded, untruthful and unprincipled man. He is universally despised by all the officers of his regiment, excepting his relatives and one or two sycophants. He brought a trader in the field without permission, carries an old negro woman and a cast-iron cooking stove and delays the march often by his extensive packing up in the morning. As I said, I will try but am not sure I can avoid trouble with him."*

Three days later, Custer, still testing how much he might impose upon his superior, carried his experiment too far. In his July first letter to his wife, Stanley recounts:

"I had a little flurry with Custer as I told you I probably would. We were separated four miles and I intended him to assist in getting the train over the Muddy River. Without consulting me, he marched off 15 miles, coolly sending me a note to send him forage and rations. I sent after him, ordered him to halt where he was, to unload his wagons and send for his own rations and forage and never presume to make another movement without orders.

---

* Stanley, General D. S.: *Personal Memoirs,* Cambridge, 1917.

"I knew from the start it would have to be done and I am glad to have had so good a chance when there could be no doubt who was right. He was just gradually assuming command and now he knows he has a commanding officer who will not tolerate his arrogance."

This sharp yank at the curb, this corrective jabbing of the spurs tamed the deliberate insurgent. Thereafter, as always when reproof had been swift, severe and certain, Custer was contrite and placating. He recognized the dominating hand and apparently he bore no grudge. Throughout the rest of the expedition's long march, he was Stanley's eager and respectful subordinate. The column's commander writes on August fifteenth that Custer "behaves very well since he agreed to do so." Stanley named a newly discovered creek for the 7th leader and accorded him a measure of trust and sympathy.

It was Custer who directed construction of the ingenious pontoon bridge of wagon bodies and empty water kegs whereby the expedition crossed the swollen Muddy River, July first. On this day, the hail-bruised engineers joined the column. The arrival of Rosser, who gracefully praised Custer's tactics in Rosser's own defeat at Woodstock, may have been compensation for Stanley's sternness.

In any event, Custer was not long abased. His letters to his wife are filled with the wild enthusiasm of a youngster on vacation. The weather improved. As the expedition marched more deeply into Indian country, game became incredibly plentiful—animate evidence why the Sioux cherished this land—and the column moved forward, fringed by slaughter in which Custer took a leading part. Naturalists in the expedition taught him the principles of taxidermy and he, whom no march could tire, spent hours in the evening skinning and curing heads and hides. When darkness suspended these tasks, he gossiped with Rosser on the buffalo robe spread before his own tent and when his classmate had retired, sat late at his camp-table, writing prodigious letters to his Elizabeth. One, composed on this expedition, is eighty pages in length. Many of them soothe her constant fear that he might venture too far ahead of the rest of the column and be killed.

Rosser accused him in jest of being more interested in return to his wife than in what the expedition might accomplish.

"I did not tell him I was already counting the days."

On this, as in all such gropings through uncharted wilderness, Custer was a superb pioneer and guide, resourceful, daring and with an uncanny sense of direction. Now that the quarrel between them had subsided, Stanley found it advisable to send him ahead with a squadron to find a road for the column through the jumble of buttes and coulées that blocked its way beyond the Little Missouri. Somewhere ahead lay the Yellowstone and somewhere along its shore was tied Grant Marsh's *Key West,* supply laden. It was Custer who worked his way through the insane confusion of badlands, reached the river and discovered the steamer.

Eight miles above the mouth of Glendive Creek, the expedition built a base camp on the south bank of the Yellowstone and named it Stanley's Stockade. Two troops of the 7th Cavalry and a company of the 17th Infantry were left here as garrison. The *Key West* ferried the rest of the column across to the river's north bank. From here on, the engineers were to survey a route for the railroad that was to shackle the unceded Indian country with steel.

Thus far, the expedition's ponderous armament had been only a galling and delaying weight. No single hostile had been seen. Tracks found by the scouts had been only those of small hunting parties, though once some Indian or Indians had fired at long range into the camp at night. The terrain north of the Yellowstone was difficult. Paw-shaped badlands, brown and gray, splotched with the black of stunted fir and the dull green of sage, reached almost to the water's edge. Custer and a squadron continued to lead the way and work out a trail for the toiling column. On August fourth, he met the Sioux.

The advance-guard, Moylan's and Tom Custer's troops, had halted that noon in a grove of cottonwoods on the Yellowstone's bank, almost opposite the mouth of the Tongue River. Many mounts had been unsaddled when six Sioux rode down, screeching, in an attempt to stampede the horses. The carbines of the videttes rattled. The warriors swung wide and withdrew with provocative deliberation, toward a heavier growth of timber up-stream. Troopers whose horses had remained saddled formed under Tom Custer and pounded out in pursuit. The 7th's commander ordered Moylan to follow with the rest of the men and spurred into the lead.

The brown horsemen loped away before the cavalry's heavy advance but the slowness of their flight woke suspicion in Custer. He halted the pursuit and then rode forward with two orderlies, following the fugitives but narrowly watching the timber toward which they retreated. He sprung the trap laid there.

Out of the trees' concealment burst three hundred warriors—on Custer's estimate—lashing their ponies. Guns boomed through screaming, bright and fierce as the arched flight of the arrows. Custer and his orderlies wheeled their horses and fled toward the line where Tom was dismounting his men. They reached it safely. A carbine volley split the charge. The racing ponies whirled away. The troopers on the firing line and those approaching under Moylan fell back to the timber's shelter.

Dismounted men lay at the edge of the grove and shot, extremely badly, at warriors, ablaze with paint and splendid in war bonnets, who ran their ponies up and down the line. The Sioux fired the grass, but it was too green to burn briskly. For three hours troopers spent ammunition lavishly and ineffectively, and Bloody Knife won Custer's praise by shooting one warrior from his horse. When Custer tired of this aimless battle, mounted his men and charged, the Indians broke and fled. The cavalry chased them three miles but troop horses could not overtake the fleet ponies. Two Indians and five of their mounts were killed. One trooper and two horses were wounded.

Two other white men, riding ahead of the main body to join the advance-guard, were caught and slain by the Sioux. These were John Honsinger, veterinary surgeon of the 7th Cavalry, and one Baliran, the trader whom Custer had brought along without Stanley's permission and who, Stanley said, had caused much trouble by selling liquor to the troops. Apparently, the 7th Cavalry had been immune to his depredations for its leader wrote to his wife on July nineteenth: "I am prouder and prouder of the 7th, Libbie. Not an officer or man of my command has been seen intoxicated since the expedition left Fort Rice."

The determination of the Sioux to defend their land, had been made plain. Four days later, when the column struck the trail of a large village moving ahead of it up the Yellowstone, Custer and the 7th Cavalry were sent in pursuit. All scouts and guides were assigned to the command. Wagons and tents were left behind. At ten on the night of August eighth, Custer led out his punitive force by the light of a lopsided moon.

Here, and in his earlier and later pursuit of Indians, one can see the foreshadow of doom. With a trail to follow, Custer always was smitten by the obsession of the hound. Nothing, once the scent was hot in his nostrils, could distract him from his infatuated pursuit. Only the most absolute of barriers could check him. With a quarry running ahead, Custer threw aside all but the stark intention to overtake the fugitive.

He marched his command until daybreak of August ninth. The regiment rested in a ravine until eight A. M. Pursuit was resumed and continued until noon. Then, since the Indians seemed only a little away ahead, Custer hid his command in timber until nightfall, intending, after the Washita formula, to strike their camp early next day. If he had continued his advance he might have overtaken the fleeing Indians for when the march was resumed at six-thirty P. M., scouts found, six miles up the Yellowstone, the place where the Sioux, a few hours earlier, had crossed to the south bank of the river.

At dawn of August tenth Custer attempted to follow. The cavalry splashed through shoals to an island in midstream, but beyond that the brown flood ran so swift and deep that cavalry horses could not breast it. All that day men attempted to cross that brief stretch of tormented water and failed. A log raft that they constructed was snatched away. Lieutenant Weston managed to swim to the far shore, bearing a line, but when he crawled out on the bank there was nothing available to secure it.

There was no particular purpose, beyond that of slaughter, in following the Sioux farther. Voluntarily, the Indians had removed themselves from the route of the column. Custer refused to abandon his attempt to reach them. His efforts toward that end became fantastic. He ordered beef cattle killed and tried to construct from their green hides coracles or "bullboats" such as Indians sometimes employed. At sunset, a few Sioux rode down the river's far bank to water their ponies and discovered the regiment. They whirled about and fled. On the morning of August eleventh, Indians on the Yellowstone's south shore opened fire on the cavalry.

Thereafter, a long-range aimless flight developed and endured most of the day. Above and below the banging carbines of the 7th, warriors swam their ponies across and appeared on the bluffs in its rear. Caught between two fires, Custer dismounted a detachment and drove the Indians from the bluff but not before Lieutenant Charles Braden had been wounded, Private Tuttle, Custer's orderly, had been shot through the head, and several cavalry horses, including Custer's own, had been killed.

There were a thousand warriors, according to soldiers' estimates, in this fight. The south bank of the Yellowstone was crowned by women and children whose shrill encouragement pierced the din of war yells and guns. Outnumbered and heavily pressed, Custer adopted the tactics that had served him so well on the Washita and in the skirmish a few days before. He ordered a charge.

The band blared *Garry Owen*. The yelling troopers swarmed up the steep north bank, young Charley Varnum and a detachment of A Troop clearing out a nest of Indian sharpshooters on the way. The Sioux fled before the rush, scampered out of range of the cavalry pounding in pursuit, and crossed again to the river's south shore. Stanley's column arrived and threw a few shells across the river. The Indians vanished. They had killed four troopers and wounded four more. Custer believed that in this and the earlier fight, his command slew forty Sioux. He had, at least, swept the course of the expedition clear of "hostiles" for no mass attempt was made thereafter to check its march. He also had acquired a dangerous scorn for the Sioux as fighters.

The column continued up-stream until, on August fifteenth, it reached that rough squat column of rock on the Yellowstone's north bank, called Pompey's Pillar. That was the limit of the river survey assigned to the engineers. From August seventeenth to nineteenth the column marched over the divide between the Yellowstone and the Musselshell and worked its exploratory way thereafter sixty-five miles down-stream toward the Missouri. This normally was fertile country but the grass had been cropped short by a vast herd of buffalo that recently had grazed along the valley. Forage was scant and Stanley turned back toward the Yellowstone with his infantry and guns.

Custer begged permission to strike directly cross-country with his command to Stanley's Stockade far down-river, and his decorous conduct had rehabilitated him so thoroughly that the expedition's leader granted him permission to try. The engineers accompanied the cavalry. It was wholly unknown country, unmapped, uncrossed before by troops, into which the 7th plunged. Custer's singular sense of direction, his instinctive skill as explorer and guide, brought his regiment through with ease. From the stockade, which he reached September sixth, he wrote a gloating letter to his wife.

"At headquarters it was not believed that I would get through. So strong was the impression that in the official order issued for my movement there was a clause authorizing me to burn all my wagons or other public property if, in my opinion, such steps were necessary to preserve life. I could not help but smile to myself as I read that portion of the order."*

Pride in his own prowess was extended in a later letter to include the regiment he led. He exults:

"What a history and a reputation this 7th Cavalry has achieved for itself! Although a new and young regiment it has left all the older fellows in the lurch until today it is the best and most widely known of any in the service."†

---

* *Boots and Saddles.*
† *Ibid.*

The *Josephine,* with Grant Marsh in command and laden with supplies for Stanley, steamed up to the stockade on September ninth. Marsh invited the 7th's commander to dinner aboard.

"For the first time this season, I tasted new potatoes and cucumbers but these were not the greatest. What do you imagine was a greater luxury? RAW ONIONS!!!! Even at this great distance I almost tremble when I inform you that I not only had onions for dinner but the captain of the boat gave me a whole bushel of fine, large ones."*

The *Josephine* ferried the cavalry across to the stockade. For two days the regiment rested there before starting back to Fort Lincoln. The man who had led it throughout the expedition, who had guided it over one hundred and fourteen miles of unexplored territory in five days, felt no need for recuperation. He spent the two days' respite in composing long letters to his wife and writing another article for *The Galaxy.*

"Not only did I do that instead of resting because of the appeals of magazine editors but it behooved me to get off my contributions with some regularity for if I stop now, those who attribute them to you would say all the more it was because you were not along to do the work for me."†

The 7th Cavalry reached Fort Lincoln on September twenty-third. Immediately thereafter, Custer turned his face toward Monroe where his wife waited for him. With Sheridan he tarried briefly at a reunion of the Army of the Tennessee in Toledo and then went on to Michigan.

Unaware of his coming, Elizabeth Custer was walking along Monroe's main street when a voice whooped behind her and strong arms plucked her up and whirled her around, to the amazement of the spectators. It is doubtful whether she was aware of them. She only knew that her husband had come to take her from the peace and luxury of her home back to the terrors of the frontier, and her cup of bliss was overflowing.

* *Ibid.*
† *Ibid.*

CHAPTER THREE

THE LEASHED LION

LESS than three years of life remained to him now. George Armstrong Custer was almost thirty-four but the precocious virtues of his youth had been kept intact—ambition, restless brilliance, vitality. His past was adorned by fame. His future, once again, was bright with promise of further renown, yet it was actually a dying man who returned, hard, tanned, insatiably vigorous, from the long march beside the Yellowstone. The trail he now followed was tragically short, but Glory waited at its end.

More normal mortals were tossed about in the chaos of a people's overthrow and survived. Men no less valiant than he, endured the flood, unscathed. It was not accident that extinguished Custer.

He was not the fury-hounded hapless man of Greek drama, unless it be that the Eumenides nest in a man's own heart. The tragedy in which he went down had grandeur. The part he played therein was less exalted. He was not the austerely innocent, the God-destroyed. Fate whirled him along, with many others, white and red. He was less the doom-overwhelmed hero than the puppet, whose movements were directed, whose death was devised, by the guiding strings of conduct a wilful life had spun.

Men whispered, for long after his naked body had been found on the brown slope above the Little Bighorn, that Custer had killed himself. Indian bullets stopped his hungry heart, yet in a broader sense the fable had its truth. It was the fiery essence of the Glory-Hunter that consumed him and many whom he led.

There was a pause, this fall of 1873, between the first and second acts of the culminating tragedy. The thunders of the final upheaval still were far away. The first provocation had been offered the Sioux. The westward path of an unsanctioned railway had been established. Soldiers and Indians had clashed, but even among the hostiles who listened to the clangorous voice of Sitting Bull, and followed Crazy Horse, Gall and Two Moons of the Cheyennes in battle, there was no move toward war.

On their reservations, many of the Sioux remained meekly. In their cherished haunts along the Powder, the Rosebud, the Tongue and the Bighorn, the "wild Indians" dwelt with almost equal patience. Among the whites themselves, there was bitter strife. The War Department struggled to wrest control of the Indian problem from the Department of the Interior. The astigmatic Sheridan, who could see only red outrage and was blind to white, arbitrarily blamed all frontier thievery and shooting upon the hostiles and demanded that the troops be given authority to "search out, capture and punish all whom it can be shown have been absent from their agencies and off the reservations."

Few seemed to consider this a presumptuous request, even though the treaty signed at Laramie expressly granted the Sioux and Northern Cheyennes the right to hunt on all unceded land. Provisions were sent by the government to its wards with the understanding that Indians would supply a large part of their own subsistence by the chase. If the Indian could not seek game in land beyond the reservation, the Indian would starve—as many did starve in the years now imminent.

Sheridan's further recommendation aimed at an absolute smashing of the treaty. He urged the establishment of "a large military post near the base of the Black Hills."

The Black Hills were a mystically precious portion of the Sioux domain—a land of quick streams and dark firs and sky-reaching mountains where the Wisdom dwelt. Thither men repaired to worship Him.

So the plot trembled on the verge of precipitation when the winter of 1873-74 closed down and established truce.

At Bismarck, when Custer, his wife and a woman friend who had accompanied her reached the end of the railroad, the Missouri already was frozen to its channel. Troopers rowed them across the open water and on the farther shore, Tom Custer welcomed his kin. In the dusk, one house on the officers' line blazed with light. This was the new home that Elizabeth Custer had not seen. As she entered, the 7th's band played *Garry Owen* and *Home Sweet Home* and friends in the garrison thronged about her. There were fires blazing on the hearths, dinner was ready, and the dwelling was completely furnished and in order. All these matters Custer had ordered, before he had gone east for his wife.

Six troops of the 7th were quartered at Fort Abraham Lincoln which stood on a flat stretch of the Missouri Valley, some miles southwest of Bismarck. A square of buildings, enclosed the parade-ground and outside their rectangle stood the stables, huts for the Arikara scouts, the sutlers' store and billiard-room, and a scattering of other buildings. All water had to be drawn from the Missouri. Bluffs to the west cut off a portion of the winter's gales, but the cold was bitter. This was the largest and best appointed post that Custer had commanded. His wife recalled their sojourn there with reminiscent affection that was purblind to all ills, climatic and human.

While weather permitted, Custer hunted with his pack of forty hounds. When winter closed its immobilizing hand and robbed him of this respite, the monotony of the frontier post filed at his taut nerves. Sedentary routine forever galled him. He can not have been the ideal commandant, nor is it probable that snow-bound Fort Abraham Lincoln was the harmonious haven his wife's fond memory pictured. Glory ignored the fort that winter and Custer displayed the irritability of the addict denied his drug. Matters at which he might have laughed in more active days became mountainously important. He railed at the Department of the Interior, still wrestling with the War Department for control of the Indians, and his wife who heard him and cherished his every word later portrayed the Indian agent as Iscariot and the army officer as Galahad.

Custer did little during his stay at the fort to endear his memory to the population of Bismarck. He withheld himself from association with citizens, though his brother occasionally slipped into town to buck the gambling games that flourished there. One of the commandant's bursts of rage still is remembered in the capital of North Dakota.

C. H. McCarthy of Bismarck, a reputable citizen and a former member of the territorial legislature, had received the contract to furnish cord wood to the post quartermaster during this winter. He was chopping trees on Sibley Island which lay within the government reservation when Custer had him arrested. McCarthy was clapped into the guard-house where he remained for three days before he was able to get word to friends in Bismarck.

E. A. Williams and John A. Stoyell, lawyers, visited the post on behalf of their client. Custer absolutely refused to release him and, after a quarrel, the attorneys left the fort threatening to refer the matter at once to the Quartermaster-General. By the time they had returned to Bismarck, McCarthy had reached the town, too. Immediately after the lawyers' departure from Lincoln, he had been freed, marched to the edge of the reservation and warned never to enter it again.

Later, on Custer's complaint, McCarthy was rearrested by the civil authority and arraigned before a United States commissioner. The case against him was dismissed but his associates were unwilling to let the matter rest there. The Burleigh County Pioneers Association, of which McCarthy was a vice-president, adopted a long resolution of grievances against Custer, sent copies to General Alfred H. Terry, commanding the Department of Dakota; to Sheridan and Sherman and printed the complaint in the *Bismarck Tribune* and the St. Paul *Pioneer Press*.

Shortly thereafter, McCarthy was elected sheriff of Burleigh County.

In the cold and the quiet and the circular routine of a frontier fort, the spirit of the Glory-Hunter went back and forth with the malaise of the caged lion, whose lean and tawny counterpart he was. His quarrelsome eyes fell upon the post sutler and straightway one of the self-spun cords of conduct that guided George Armstrong Custer tightened and drew him toward his death.

Robert C. Seip, the post trader, by his very presence at the fort, represented an abolished privilege. Until 1870, all sutlers—a blend of saloon keeper, general store proprietor and club steward—had been chosen by the commandant of each post, with the advice of subordinates. Since that year, the appointment of sutlers had been the prerogative of the Secretary of War. Seip had been selected by General William C. Belknap, the then Secretary, who was a close friend of President Grant. With Seip, Custer became entangled in a trivial, fateful dispute.

The Commandant insisted that the prices charged by the sutler were too high. When Seip refused to lower them, Custer permitted his troop commanders to buy supplies for their men in Bismarck and resell them at cost to their soldiers. Seip protested and when the Post Commander laughed at him, went over his head to the Secretary of War. Belknap issued an order, supporting the sutler and overruling Custer. A bored and irascible spirit magnified this rebuff into profound affront.

If the issue had been larger and more dignified, or if Belknap's reproof had been more blasting, it might have rankled less. The man who had endured a court martial's heavy punishment without resentment; who had grown contrite and obedient when Stanley had reprimanded him, girded against this minor check. It was only a scratch upon his pride but in the long winter it festered and would not heal. Custer, the magnanimous, who normally could bear no grudge, grew to hate Belknap. There was fuel for that hatred on the frontier. Rumors floated about of corruption in which the Secretary of War was steeped, and the man who reproved his wife for heeding gossip accorded any tale that blackened Belknap's name an eager unscrupulous belief.

There was one break in the winter's numb routine. On a bitter night the Custers' quarters caught fire and burned to the ground. Directed by the Commandant in boots, a red nightshirt and a vest containing his watch and money, soldiers saved what furniture they could.

Custer chose as substitute dwelling half of a double house, in the other portion of which his brother Tom lived. He settled his remaining effects in the two days following and had fires blazing, lamps lighted and the band playing *Home Sweet Home* before he would permit his beloved to enter.

The explosiveness of his pent spirit was exemplified in the spring of 1874. Indians swept down one morning upon the mule herd beyond the fort, and with flapping buffalo robes and manifold screeching ran off with the animals. The dust of their retreat was still high in the sky when bugles in Lincoln stuttered "boots and saddles."

The pursuit that Custer led that day was a headlong scramble. Officers and troopers plunged for the nearest horses, saddled or bareback, and streamed out after a hunter who in the thrill of the moment had almost forgotten that he was post commandant. He did fling to one officer the order to command in his absence, but when the disheveled expedition had rushed out of sight, it was discovered that only a handful of men remained, the band and a few more—far too slight a force to defend the fort. Almost all the garrison had gone tearing off after Custer.

Long after, the mind of Elizabeth Custer bore scars inflicted by the terror of that day. She and other women saw the dust of the chase fade on the horizon. They marked the concern in the faces of the few men remaining. If the raid on the mules were part of larger Indian strategy, designed to weaken the garrison before attack, it had succeeded perfectly. Men and women waited all day for the assault to come. Every male capable of bearing arms was placed on duty. The women huddled together. A few of the more valiant carried pistols. Others watched the westward bluffs through field-glasses and saw in each irregularity on the summits the crouching form of an Indian scout. Late in the afternoon an approaching dust-cloud revealed anti-climax. It had hid neither a war-party nor the returning cavalry. A few troopers drove in the rescued mules and reported that Custer and his command were still chasing Indians. Darkness added its dread to the anguish of those who waited in the almost unprotected fort.

The fearful stillness was blown away at last by rollicking cadences of *Garry Owen*. The troops had returned. They had caught no Indians. If the headlong, unscrupulous pursuit had been typical of Custer, the fact that he had called out the band to celebrate his return was equally characteristic. Apart from the temporary crippling of the men who had ridden forty miles bareback that day, the Post Commandant's reckless gesture had no evil consequences. Custer's luck still held. It was not to serve him always.

In the summer of 1874, however, fortune still smiled. To the joy of its leader, to the familiar, recurrent terror of his wife, the 7th Cavalry was to take the field. The army, by force if not by law, was to assume disastrous control of the Indian problem. Sheridan's demand for a fort in the Black Hills had been heeded. An expedition was to penetrate and explore the Sioux Olympus.

The march of troops into this country would smash the Laramie treaty to bits. This was no question, as men pretended there had been on the Yellowstone expedition, of unceded land which the Sioux and Northern Cheyennes might or might not legally possess. The treaty had said that the Black Hills and what is now the rest of trans-Missouri South Dakota were "set apart for the absolute and undisturbed use and occupation of the Indians."

The treaty also had promised that the land would be kept absolutely free of all white intrusion save for "such officers, agents and employees of the government as may be authorized to enter upon Indian reservations in discharge of duties enjoined by law." No statute had existed then, none existed now, providing for the construction of a fort in the heart of the Indian country, or even for the exploration thereof, yet an army was mobilizing for these purposes.

The expedition assembled at Fort Lincoln. It consisted of ten troops of the 7th Cavalry, one company of the 17th and one of the 20th Infantry, a three-inch field piece and three Gatling guns, about a hundred Indian scouts, mostly Arikaras, one hundred and ten wagons and three hundred beef cattle. Charley Reynolds served as guide for the expedition and Custer had on his personal staff Lieutenant-Colonel George A. Forsyth, old comrade in Sheridan's cavalry, and Lieutenant Frederick Dent Grant, son of the President.

Boston Custer, next to the youngest of the clan, had come from the East this summer, seeking health. He was a gaunt young man with thin side-whiskers. He hoped the plains' pure air and outdoor life would cure his troublesome cough wherefore he surrendered himself to his brothers' care. Placing an invalid in the hands of these twain was like mounting a paralytic on a bucking broncho. Custer's letters often mention how he and Tom bedeviled the young man.

The truculent aspect and intention of the command was modified by the inclusion of a scientific staff. Captain William Ludlow was chief of the engineers who would map the Black Hills. Geologists, a photographer, two practical miners and a zoologist were included. This last was George Bird Grinnell, later student of the Cheyennes and other plains tribes.

With the band blaring *The Girl I Left Behind Me,* the column moved out from Fort Lincoln, July second. The train rolled in four parallel columns. Ahead of these jolted the Gatlings and the field piece. On either side of the moving oblong of white-topped wagons, marched the infantry. Beyond their lines, and in the van and rear, the cavalry jangled while a screen of mounted Indians flung far out on either flank and in front, watched for sign of their enemies, the Sioux into whose land the government was sending an army to determine where an illegal fort should be built. The curtain had risen on the second act of the tragedy and George Armstrong Custer, with the zest for adventure brightening his face, rode at his army's head.

CHAPTER FOUR

EXPLORATION

THE wagon sails beat southwest over an immobile, uncharted ocean. The ponderous column settled into the routine of the trail. Days were bright and grazing was good. Small bands of Sioux flitted before the advance or followed the rear-guard from afar. Smoke signals smudged the horizon.

The monotony of the journey that wearied other men, elated Custer. Those who had never seen him foot loose in the wilderness, marveled at his stamina. On his favorite charger, Dandy, or his alternate, Vic, he was as brilliantly active as a winging swallow—dashing off to pursue antelope with his hounds; galloping up a height to survey the land ahead; storming down the column's length, hair flying, body chiming with his horse; plaguing his brother Boston, writing long letters to his wife while weaker men slumbered.

"It is now a quarter to one. Breakfast is at four and 'Boots and Saddles' will sound at five."*

The wind blew upon his smoldering spirit. He was loose again on Glory's trail. This time there was no churlish superior to check his glee, or tarnish bright imaginings of the battle, the adventure, the mystery toward which the creaking wagons, the foot and horse and guns of his army moved.

They followed the Little Missouri into the southeast corner of Montana. They turned up the valley of the Belle Fourche, march-

* *Boots and Saddles.*

258

ing in from the northwest upon the legend-adorned, the holy, the enigmatic hills whose great peak, Inyan Kara, already notched the summer sky.

For more than a hundred years, white men had known vaguely of these mountains that lifted themselves in beauty from the surrounding monotony of the plains. French trappers had seen them before the republic was born. Jedediah Smith, General Harney and other explorers had observed their broken, tremendous battlements of pale rock and dark fir. A geologist, Dr. F. V. Hayden, had penetrated them twice before the Civil War. Since then, few had ventured thither. These austere peaks and rich valleys were sacred to the Sioux and about them extravagant yarns of the frontier had woven romance, incredible and provocative.

The strategic value of the Black Hills had small share in such tales. They had a single theme—gold.

There was, so the reiterant whisper ran, incredible gold in this most cherished part of the Sioux domain. Indians had come to traders' posts with small amounts of dust found there. The march of Custer toward the Black Hills magnified the legends. The frontier waited to hear, not whether he had found a favorable site for the treaty-forbidden fort that Sheridan planned, but if the streams of the region actually were graveled with gold. It was for gold that the whites had torn Colorado from the Cheyennes and Arapahos. If there were pay dirt in the Black Hills, they would take these from the Sioux. With a golden lever, the army could topple the Indians into a war that would mean their extinction.

At the foot of Inyan Kara, northwest bastion of the hills, the column halted on July twenty-second. Custer and a handful of civilians and soldiers climbed the peak but the view it had promised was curtailed by smoke to the west and north where Indians, fearing farther advance by the troops, were burning the grass.

A valley ran from Inyan Kara's base toward the heart of the hills. The column turned from the glare and dazzle of the plains into a still place of deep shadow and narrow, peak-severed breadths of sunlight. The valley blazed with flowers and the cavalry rode with wreaths of blossoms about their chargers' necks and on their own hats so that the command seemed more a moving festival than an army.

Day by day, they rode through beauty deeper into what men had said was the great fortress of the Sioux. If this had been Custer's belief, if he had hoped for martial glory here, he was to be sorely disappointed. A hundred warriors might have defended these mountains and forests against ten times their number but the Black Hills were not the citadel but the cathedral of the Indians. Hither they came for respite and the mystical communion with Deity which no white mind ever has fathomed.

Custer looked for hostiles. The miners searched the streams for gold. Traces of the bright metal gleamed in pans, and the expedition on July twenty-fourth encountered five lodges of Sioux, camping where they had every possible right to be, and promptly surrounded the band.

Custer went among the stiff still captives, assured them that his intention was peace and invited the handful of warriors present to visit his camp. Five of them came in and received gifts of food. When they wished to return to their own camp, Custer for no clear reason, insisted that an escort of troopers accompany them. The Indians took fright and fled. One of them was shot and another, One Stab, was held as prisoner-guide. Whatever doubt the Sioux might have had concerning the purpose of the expedition must have been abolished now. Yet they attempted no reprisals.

The column camped in the valley of French Creek at a place Custer named Custer Park. He, Captain Ludlow of the engineers, Colonel Forsyth and several civilians rode out with an escort under Varnum to scale Harney Peak. From this height twin elevations to the northwest were named Terry Peak and Custer Peak. It was after dark when the climbers rejoined the escort, and Custer, the trail finder, was for once hopelessly lost. Varnum had taken compass bearings and guided the party back to camp. A year later in St. Paul, Ludlow introduced the youngster to General Terry as "the only man Custer ever let lead him."

The point at which gold in paying amounts was first found still is in dispute, but during the column's sojourn in Custer Park, it was

OFFICERS OF THE BLACK HILLS EXPEDITION, 1874.

1. Capt. of Engineers, Wm. Ludlow; 2. Capt. Geo. Yates; 3. 1st Lieut. Donald McIntosh; 4. Capt. Tom Custer; 5. 2nd Lieut. Geo. D. Wallace; 6. 2nd Lieut. J. M. Harrington; 7. 1st Lieut. Jim Calhoun; 8. Lt. Col. G. A. Forsyth; 9. Lt. Col. G. A. Custer; 10. A Professor; 11. 1st Lieut. T. M. McDougall; 12. Major J. G. Tilford; 13. Bloody Knife; 14. Capt. Miles Moylan; 15. Fred Grant; 16. Lt. C. H. Varnum; 17. 1st Lieut. A. E. Smith; 18. Lt. B. H. Hodgson; 19. Capt. Owen Hale; 20. Capt. F. W. Benteen; 21. Lt. E. S. Godfrey; 22. Capt. F. M. Gibson.

discovered, probably by the miner, Horatio Nelson Ross. Custer
wrote dispatches extravagantly proclaiming the discovery, and sent
Reynolds on the difficult and dangerous journey to Fort Laramie
with the tidings. The scout got through by riding at night and hiding by day. The flamboyant tidings were telegraphed east to be
blazoned on every newspaper front page.

Gold, Custer wrote, with more drama than accuracy, was plentiful in the Black Hills. There were veins of auriferous quartz "on
almost every hillside." Furthermore, "The miners report that they
found gold among the roots of the grass."

Geologists on the expedition later objected violently to the rap-
tures of Custer's dispatch. It was exaggerated, yet no deliberate
plan for breaking the power of the stubborn Sioux could have been
more effective.

Left to itself, national conscience might never have sanctioned
more than piecemeal theft of the Indian country. Voices might
have been raised in protest if Sheridan had built the fort he
planned in the Black Hills. News of gold swept away compunction. Americans cared little for the army's frontier troubles with
hostile Indians and less about who should occupy harsh dry land
in Dakota and beyond. But gold!

It fired the minds and hearts of men who had been dazed by the
panic of 1873. There were agrarian troubles. The East was pov-
erty-stricken. There was gold in the Black Hills at the root of the
grass, in veins on almost every slope. At once, invasion of the
Sioux land began.

Before Custer's column had returned to Fort Lincoln August
thirtieth, after an uneventful march, the first prospectors had penetrated the Black Hills. The Sioux complained and troops were detailed to oust the trespassers, most of whom, when marched from
the reservation and released, turned around and went back again.
Some of the hardiest spent the winter of 1874-75 in the hills. The
following summer, the flood of the gold-hungry broke all barriers.

Meanwhile the fame of George Armstrong Custer had blazed
anew. It still soared, rocket-like, on the impetus of his dispatch,
when, with band pumping *Garry Owen,* he returned to Fort Abra-

ham Lincoln. Elizabeth Custer, hearing the 7th Cavalry's hymn of triumph and the cheering of the infantry who composed the temporary garrison, resolved that no eyes save their own should witness her reunion with her husband. She remained indoors until her idol, sunburned, long-haired, rode his horse onto the parade-ground. Then her resolution failed and she found herself in Custer's arms with the whole fort as audience.

"From the clouds and glooms of those summer days, I walked again into the broad blaze of sunshine which my husband's blithe spirit made."*

Lashed to the axle of an ambulance was a keg of spring water, borne all the way from the Black Hills as Custer's gift to her who loathed the murky, alum-flavored Missouri fluid. The couple spent a brief leave in New York and returned to the winter-bound obscurity and galling monotony of Fort Abraham Lincoln where the sinful sutler continued to spread himself and other annoyances plucked at the nerves of a man who longed for action and was doomed to routine.

The spectacular good fortune that heretofore had followed Custer seemed to have turned from him at last. He had led an army out to challenge the Sioux. They had not stood against him. Save for the brief fame his report had won him—and this was overshadowed now by tales of more lucrative strikes—two months of marching had added scant luster to his name.

George Armstrong Custer's luck was ebbing as it eventually withdraws from even the most incredibly lucky. Fortune, the polyandrous and whimsical, had tired of him. His purposes, his actions no longer were blessed by her. All he did now had the disastrous bruskness of an increasingly exasperated man. Heretofore his most reckless and careless actions frequently had been transformed into triumph. Hereafter none of his movements was to gain him completely the thing for which he reached, and often they were to be only a stumbling toward calamity.

---

* *Boots and Saddles.*

It is doubtful whether, during this winter, Custer knew that luck had left him. He was too great an egotist quickly to lose faith in himself. At length he must have felt the desertion, for he was to grow gloomy, nervous, placating. He was none of these during the winter of 1874-75.

Lonesome Charley Reynolds drifted into the fort and told Custer what he had heard a young warrior relate that fall at a medicine dance, the great religious rite of the Sioux. Rain-in-the-Face had boasted that more than a year earlier, he had overcome and slain two white soldiers. By his description, Reynolds knew that the Indian meant Honsinger, the veterinary, and Baliran, the trader, killed August 4, 1873, while Custer was fighting the Sioux on the Yellowstone.

The legal and ethical aspects of that deed were scrambled. On an expedition into Indian country there were technically no noncombatants. Baliran and Honsinger were of the soldier force and therefore, to Indian minds, soldiers. Furthermore, they had been slain while Custer actually was in battle with the slayer's people. No retribution would have been visited upon the white who had killed Indians under such circumstances, but Custer decided at once that Rain-in-the-Face must be arrested.

The young man belonged to that part of his tribe which dwelt about the Standing Rock agency. On December twenty-first, Captain Yates and Tom Custer marched Troop F of the 7th Cavalry under sealed orders from Fort Lincoln. These orders, when opened directed the troop to go to the Standing Rock store where Indians had gathered to draw their rations and there capture the murderer, Rain-in-the-Face.

Tom Custer and a half-dozen soldiers lounged about the store until, among the press of bartering Sioux, they recognized their man. They fell upon him and hustled him out, and the kin of the warrior, who followed them wrathfully, found themselves facing the carbines of Yates's command. Rain-in-the-Face was brought to Lincoln, was manacled and lodged in the guard-house.

Custer had his prisoner. He seems to have been uncertain thereafter what to do with him. Chiefs of the Sioux and kinsmen of

Rain-in-the-Face came to the fort and begged for his release. Custer refused, and the man remained in jail for many weeks until subsequent events solved an embarrassing problem.

Custer's attention turned to another, more immediate irritation. The granaries of the fort were being systematically plundered and the Post Commandant assumed the rôle of detective. In time, he found a culprit trooper who confessed that he had been the accomplice of certain residents in Bismarck, where the stolen grain still was stored.

Immediately, Custer marched his regiment upon Bismarck. The dubious legal aspects of the maneuver do not seem to have troubled him. With no other warrant than force of arms, he and his men entered barns and warehouses in the town and recovered the purloined grain. He took back to the fort not only this but a number of the plunderers as well, who were lodged in the guard-house. The ringleaders eventually were turned over to the civil authority. They were tried and convicted. Before that, one of the more energetic miscreants managed to escape by hacking a hole in the guard-house rear wall and when he departed, that embarrassing prisoner, Rain-in-the-Face, vanished also.

Some of the innumerable lies that cloud the Little Bighorn battle deal with the subsequent career of Rain-in-the-Face. Mrs. Custer in her *Boots and Saddles* writes that the vengeful warrior cut out Tom Custer's heart. Longfellow proclaims rhythmically that the young Sioux excised George Armstrong Custer's heart. Those who recovered the bodies attest that neither man was so mutilated.

Spring came at last to Dakota and in its train the advance-guard of a fresh host of gold-seekers rolled in upon the Black Hills. The government in general and the army in particular now was to suffer the consequences of the expedition it had so blithely authorized.

War with the plundered Indians would have been a grateful mask for white thievery, but war, which many expected and not a few hoped for, did not come. The Sioux, who had swarmed like hornets under Red Cloud to fight against the Bozeman Road, remained inexplicably patient in the face of greater robbery. The summer of 1875 was the most peaceful that the plains had seen in many years. The wild Indians on the unceded land carried on their century-old war with the neighboring Crows and Shoshones but few whites were molested.

The army, which had caused the government's present plight, went through idiotically comic motions of driving trespassers from Indian land. Troops under Dodge and Crook were sent to clear the Black Hills of interlopers. Even Custer, for a short time that summer, took the field. Miners on French Creek had laid out a town-site and had christened it Custer City. On August fifteenth, Custer marched them solemnly out of Indian territory. Where-upon, most of them turned about and went back. Similar tactics were employed by prospectors whom Dodge and Crook had evicted. By the spring of 1876, there were eleven thousand whites in Custer City alone. And still the Sioux, reservation and "wild" bands kept the peace.

There was to be no war that year, no opportunity for the Glory-Hunter to exchange old laurels for new and the spirit of Custer fretted and fumed. The sutler, Seip, enflamed an idle and queru-lous mind into hatred of the whole system whereby he was ap-pointed and of General Belknap, Secretary of War. Rumor fed Custer's resentment, which grew so reckless that, when Belknap on a tour of inspection visited Fort Lincoln, the Commandant de-liberately slighted the Secretary. Military courtesy prescribed that Custer should receive the distinguished visitor at the reservation's boundary. Instead, he waited in his office for Belknap to call and when Seip sent in a basket of champagne for the entertainment of the guest, Custer ordered him to take it back.

So the summer passed while men made feeble efforts to avert the rising torrent. The peace had collapsed under larcenous pres-sure. Nothing could restore it, now. The government attempted to buy from the Sioux the Black Hills country that its citizens al-ready had stolen, and found itself thwarted by a clause of the Laramie treaty.

This provided that no sale of Sioux land could be legal unless three-fourths of the tribe's adult males voted thereon. Not one-eighth the required number gathered for the council the white commissioners held.

The summer waned and the fateful winter of 1875-76 drew in. The climacteric act of the tragedy had opened when Custer was granted two months' leave and fled with his wife and brother, Tom, from the dreary frontier to the gaiety of New York.

CHAPTER FIVE

COURSE OF EMPIRE

THERE are three main themes in the tragedy that reached catharsis that Sunday of slaughter on the Little Bighorn. They move toward their end even while Custer, elated and relieved, rides with his wife and brother, Tom, away from frontier boredom toward New York. Men and that remoteness called circumstance, or doom, or destiny, guided the triple themes. It is doubtful whether far greater men could have checked their inevitable march. The mortals involved therein had little of greatness.

First in the trinity of motives is the dangerous mental state of white authority, civil and military. The Black Hills have been stolen and those who now tacitly sanction the theft find themselves compelled to justify perfidy by further crime. White men have taken the Black Hills. They must sin further to secure their current loot. Wherefore, army and Indian Bureau alike prepare to break the power of the increasingly indignant Sioux and abolish forever the troublesome frontier.

Second, there is the rekindling desperation of a brutally defrauded people who have distrusted white treaties, with warrant; who had been wheedled, cajoled, bullied into making one more; who now see their last protection, barring their own feeble weapons, more callously violated than all its predecessors. The Sioux did not make this last great war of their race. It was thrust into their faces by men and circumstance.

Circumstance, or doom, is responsible for the third precipitating motive. White men cheat and neglect the reservation Sioux. Impersonal forces are leagued as savagely against the sufferers. An element no more human than the weather hurries on the tragedy.

267

The forces move, irresistible as triple floods. They meet and blend and wreak immense destruction. They grip the brightest of the trivial figures in their path. They sweep up George Armstrong Custer and whirl him about and suck him under.

He and his wife reached New York early in the fall of 1875. The town offered manifold reliefs to hungers of the body and the spirit—theaters, restaurants, music and the admiring hospitality of town-bred folk for one who had fought the blood-thirsty savages and had hunted buffalo in a land of romance. The editors of *The Galaxy* praised Custer and wanted more articles. Barrett, Custer's intimate, was appearing as Cassius in *Julius Cæsar*. Save when some dinner or other social affair interfered, the Glory-Hunter spent each evening in his friend's dressing-room.

Custer was financially embarrassed and it is probable that he confided to Barrett his need of money. His wife relates how her hero laughed when they were compelled to use horse cars instead of cabs or when he had to appear at the houses of the wealthy in a shabby overcoat. Barrett learned also of the manifold sins of Belknap, the Secretary of War. "For some unexplained reason," the actor wrote artlessly later, "General Custer believed the secretary to be his enemy."*

There were luncheons and dinners and receptions. There were visits to the theater where Custer and his wife wept together. There were the praise and the adulation of lion hunters. Two months went by. Tom Custer returned at the end of his leave to bleak Fort Lincoln. His brother applied for a three months' extension to Sheridan, who granted it, and Lachesis measured the thread and Clotho raised her shears.

Sheridan indulged his favorite, though on the frontier the flood was rising. It was weather, not men, who struck first against the Sioux. Winter came early and the snows were tremendous. Indian agents reported that hunting would be hampered and that the reservation dwellers would need additional rations before the new year. Congress rose to the emergency by passing the deficiency

---

* Whittaker's *Life.*

measure the following spring. Meanwhile, well-disposed Indians starved.

Beyond the reservations, on the unceded land where the parishioners of Sitting Bull still ranged, game was plentiful. Many Indians, with their agents' permission, left the reservations to stave off hunger by hunting there.

On December 6, 1875, the Indian Bureau issued drastic orders to all agents with the Sioux and Northern Cheyennes. The army was already planning to consolidate white occupation of the Black Hills by abolishing the troublesome "wild" Indians living on unceded land. The army had been worried by the exodus of starving Sioux and Cheyennes from the reservations. The Indian Bureau, for once, agreed with the military arm. The order of December sixth informed the agents that all Sioux and Northern Cheyennes who were off their reservations after January 31, 1876, were to be regarded as hostiles.

The order did not reach the agents on their drift-smothered reservations until December twentieth. The more conscientious immediately sent out runners to find and summons their charges and the "wild" Indians as well. In summer, it was no small task to track down villages scattered over so vast a territory. In a heavy winter, it was almost impossible. The messengers found a few bands of hunters, reservation and wild, in tepees huddled under protecting bluffs by frozen streams. There is no record that even the "hostiles" reached were defiant. There is no record that Sitting Bull, Gall or Crazy Horse ever received the warning at all.

Most of the Indians notified sent word by the runners that they would report in spring, when impassable drifts had vanished and winter-starved ponies could march. The few who were able to plow back to the reservations were disarmed at once, for on January seventeenth, orders commanding this and prohibiting further sale of guns or ammunition had been received. This apparent preliminary to massacre alarmed red hearts further.

Many of the runners themselves could not get back to the reservations until mid-February. On February first, the Indian Commissioner, John Q. Smith, surrendered control of all Sioux and Cheyennes, not then with their agents, to the War Department. On February seventh, Sheridan received authority to proceed against the hostiles.

Disarmed and starving on their reservations, with all promise of succor as vain and mendacious as the now thoroughly pulverized Laramie treaty, the monumental patience of the Indians snapped. Those who were able, fled at once to the far villages of the hostiles. Many more, when spring came, followed them, for by then the purpose of the army had been made plain.

In New York, Custer dined at the Century Association and addressed the members thereafter. The subsequent congratulations of men of literary eminence kindled novel ambition. He talked a new project over with Barrett, who approved. Thereafter the Glory-Hunter scouted along an unfamiliar path toward fame and more negotiable reward. He signed a contract with Redpath's Literary Bureau to deliver a series of lectures the following winter. Barrett volunteered to coach his intimate in delivery and stage presence and Custer, already five months absent from his command and with war brewing on the frontier, asked a further extension of his leave.

His application was refused by General Belknap, and the denial blew upon a long-cherished resentment. The Secretary of War, whom Custer had hated long for no more personal cause than a single slight, now had dealt his subordinate an actual injury. When opportunity for reprisal appeared, Custer took it with the headlong, inconsequent fury of his cavalry charges.

There may have been no intention of affront in Belknap's denial of a subordinate's request. Custer was needed on the frontier, where Sheridan, into whose hands the fate of the Sioux had been placed, was trying to organize one of his favorite winter campaigns. He purposed, with Washita's successful butchery in mind, to strike a winter-bound foe, who, like Black Kettle's doomed band, had no knowledge of his intentions.

General Terry was preparing to march against Sitting Bull. He had sent out Arikara scouts and Lonesome Charley Reynolds to find the site of his village. When it was discovered at last, it was too far away for cavalry to plow thither through the heavy snows. Terry's expedition was delayed, but Crook marched in sub-zero weather from Fort Fetterman. Not far from the post, which was west, northwest from Fort Laramie, Sioux and Cheyenne followers of the war chief Crazy Horse, had made their winter camp on the Powder River. Toward this, Crook moved with ten troops of the 3rd Cavalry to accomplish what the 7th had wrought years before on the Washita. But Crazy Horse was not Black Kettle.

Crook's column halted a night's march from the village and six troops, upward of three hundred men, were sent forward in darkness under Colonel J. J. Reynolds. Until, in the wintry dawn, a wakeful boy yelled and the clap of a carbine answered him, it is probable that Crazy Horse's band had no knowledge of the impending war.

The chief's followers numbered not more than two hundred and fifty warriors. As the yelling, shooting troopers closed in, they fled, half clad and with only what weapons were at hand, into the timber about the village. Reynolds captured the pony herd, all the winter supplies, all reserve ammunition and burned the village, leaving its survivors afoot and shelterless in an arctic world. Reynolds marched back toward Crook. Crazy Horse and his men followed. They bedeviled the column all that bitter day. They swept in and recovered the captured ponies and, when Crook joined Reynolds, the Indians ran off with the beef herd and chased the thwarted expedition back to Fort Fetterman. Crook paid no tribute to the man who with a handful of homeless warriors had beaten him. Crook talked of a court martial for Reynolds.

Tidings of the impending campaign came to the aggrieved and fuming man who prepared, late in February, to leave New York for the frontier. The certainty of new Indian war might or might not cheer Custer. Another event which he was to mistake for fortune's favor but which, actually, was to be a clause in his self-prepared death-warrant, fired him with malicious exultation. General Belknap suddenly was involved in malodorous scandal.

A congressional committee headed by Heister Clymer, Belknap's former roommate at Princeton College, was investigating War Department expenditures. Early in March while the Custers were packing, a vindictive real-estate agent appeared before the body, told a damaging story of Belknap's share in the profits of army sutlers and furnished a list of witnesses who supplied absolute confirmation. On March second, Belknap handed Grant his resignation. Rumor said the discredited man planned to flee the country. On March fifth, he was arrested.

The downfall of Custer's enemy was complete, yet even so thorough an abasement did not satisfy the man who, thanks to Belknap, had hurried away from New York with bags, baggage and three new hounds. Custer had no compunction about striking a prostrate foe. He hated Belknap, but he must have known that he himself possessed little or no competent evidence against his enemy. Yet he wrote to Clymer, offering to appear as a witness before the committee.

Another terrific series of blizzards had thwarted General Terry's intention of an early march against the Sioux. At St. Paul, Custer reported to his superior and received from officials of the Northern Pacific the loan of a private car on which to complete the journey to Bismarck. The coach was attached to a train consisting of four passenger cars, another filled with merchandise and eight more, fuel laden. An engine pushed a plow before the train's two locomotives.

Forty miles from Bismarck, at Crystal Springs, the snow-drifts broke the plow and the train stuck. The telegraph wires were intact, and Lincoln's garrison was informed of its Commandant's plight. A mule-drawn sleigh, accompanied by Tom Custer, went to his relief. After six days' imprisonment in their private car which they had shared with Colonel C. A. Lounsberry and old Colonel Thompson, a former officer of the 7th Cavalry, the Custers were rescued. The precious hounds were passengers in the sleigh. The human castaways, a woman among them, had to wait another ten days for relief.

General Terry, a gallant and patient gentleman, had felt relief when his subordinate had reported. The Department Commander had confided in Custer his plans for the coming campaign. These must have lifted high a heart already cheered by the long-cherished blow its owner had dealt Belknap.

An expedition consisting of the entire 7th Cavalry, some infantry and guns was to march to the Yellowstone from Fort Lincoln as soon as possible after the snows withdrew. This was not to be either an escort or an exploring column. It was to fight the Sioux until all wild Indians on unceded land were abolished or driven to reservations. There was promise of Glory, past that which a lecture tour could afford, in command of this little army.

Terry had had a brilliant record in the Civil War but he was not an Indian fighter. With Sheridan's approval, he had chosen Custer to head the expedition. There would be much to do before the snows were gone. Terry counted on Custer to do it. One week after he reached Fort Lincoln, the noose the 7th's leader had looped for Belknap's own undoing pulled tight about the contriver. Custer received a summons from the Sergeant at Arms of the House, commanding his presence before the Clymer committee, there to reveal what he knew of the iniquity of General Belknap.

Terry had hoped to launch his campaign not later than April first. The return of its leader to Washington would throw all plans askew. At his suggestion, the volunteer witness wired Clymer, March sixteenth:

"While I hold myself in readiness to obey the summons of your committee, I telegraph to state that I am engaged upon an important expedition, intended to operate against the hostile Indians and I expect to take the field early in April. My presence here is deemed very necessary. In view of this, would it not be satisfactory for you to forward me such questions as may be necessary, allowing me to return my replies by mail?"

This artless solution of a self-imposed problem found no favor in the eyes of the committee. On March twenty-fourth, Custer passed through St. Paul again, en route to Washington. Terry forbore, out of faith in and kindliness toward the distressed man, to appoint a new leader for the column.

Custer hastened to Washington, expecting in his vast ignorance of Congressional procedure, to return immediately. He did not get back to St. Paul until the first week in May and then he was under technical arrest. Grant, Sherman and Sheridan all had denounced him and Terry was his only defender.

CHAPTER SIX

WHOM GODS DESTROY

GENERAL GEORGE A. FORSYTH was Sheridan's inspector-general
and Custer's friend. Forsyth had served as aide to his chief through
the Shenandoah and Appomattox campaigns. He had fought the
Cheyennes at Beechers Island. He had accompanied the Glory-
Hunter on the Black Hills expedition. Forsyth knew the background of Custer's needless assault upon the already prostrate Belknap. Years thereafter, he summarized it thus:

> "When General Belknap was imprisoned and undergoing
> trial, Custer wrote that he knew of certain things regarding
> the appointment of post traders on the upper Missouri River,
> which things the prosecution thought they needed to insure
> conviction. . . .
> "Custer was summoned to Washington of course. When he
> was questioned by the House Committee of Prosecution, it
> was apparent that he did not know anything. His evidence
> was all hearsay and not worth a tinker's dam."*

This is the estimate of an admiring friend. The farrago of opinion and second- and third-hand gossip which the volunteer witness
presented to Clymer and his associates, affords no reason to tinker
with Forsyth's verdict.

By incompetent and scandalous testimony Custer tangled the net
he had designed for Belknap about august personages whose indignant reaction only served more deeply to involve him. The
anti-climax furnished by the man's testimony is not comic. It masks

---

* Brady, Cyrus T.: *Indian Fights and Fighters,* New York, 1902.

tragedy's approach. Reckless, headlong action had served Custer all his days. Now it was to hurry his end. Luck had been his high speed organism's balance wheel. Without it, the machine raced and destroyed itself.

Lieutenant-Colonel and Brevet Major-General George Armstrong Custer appeared March 29, 1876, before the committee that was framing the case for Belknap's impeachment. He opened assault upon his enemy with a diatribe against sutlers, the high prices they charged, their sinful influence on young officers and then proceeded to denounce the Fort Lincoln trader. He described in detail his quarrel with Seip and Belknap's intervention in the sutler's behalf. He then accused Belknap of sharing in Seip's profits.

How did he know this? Well, after Belknap's downfall Custer had questioned Seip and Seip had confessed that a portion of his income from the sutler's store "was paid to a man named General Rice who was supposed to be an intimate friend of the Secretary of War here in Washington. Seip was always under the impression that a portion of it went to the Secretary of War."

Incompetent, irrelevant and immaterial. The lean witness is discomfited by the indifference of legally trained men to these tidings. Prodded by questions, he hurries on. He has further defamation to offer and he places it recklessly. He smears the name of Orville Grant with the soot of rumor. Orville is the younger brother of the President of the United States. What has he done?

Custer has heard that when one Raymond was appointed sutler at Fort Berthold, "this man Raymond showed the telegram to several persons in Bismarck and claimed that he paid Grant $1000. for getting the appointment for him."

Incompetent, irrelevant and immaterial. The committee shies away from this recital of unverified rumor and guides the witness's testimony back to the matter at hand. If Custer has found irregularities in the conduct of Seip, why has he not reported them to the Secretary of War? Custer pulls at his heavy golden mustache and blurts: "Because I was just as suspicious of the Secretary as I was of the sutler."

Why? Does he know—actually know of a case in which a sutler

has paid Belknap for his appointment? The witness squirms. He does not, "but we always regarded the Secretary of War as silent partner in these transactions."

Incompetent, irrelevant and immaterial. The committee members frown and yawn. Where is the ammunition for impeachment promised by this witness? Custer, spurred by growing skepticism, plunges ahead.

He has heard from an artist—one Huntington, whose first name he has forgotten—that Belknap has been ordering oil portraits wholesale. Custer believes these are being paid for by fraudulently used government funds. What ground has he for this belief? Just his belief.

The witness is floundering, irked, perhaps, by the covert smiles of the committee. Insanely, Custer raises his sights and aims at a higher, more dangerous target.

He speaks of President Grant's order, extending the boundary of the Sioux reservation to the east bank of the Missouri River. Ostensibly, this has been done to keep rum pedlers away from the Indians. Custer does not think this was the real reason, but, when asked to give it, tardy caution checks him. He "would rather not answer that question."

He hesitates, then lurches on, admitting that it "was the general impression along the river that the order was for the benefit of the traders." He casts slur, born of rumor, in the face of the President of the United States himself.

Thereafter he returns with a doomed persistence to further besmirching of Orville Grant. He has heard that when the post trader at Fort Peck was about to be removed, the trader, in defense of his job, obtained affidavits of some sort against Leighton Brothers and Orville Grant "and he showed them the affidavits and they allowed him to continue his trade."

Incompetent, irrelevant and immaterial. Yet the committee permits the witness to continue and Custer embarks upon a general denunciation of the crookedness of Indian agents. Speech rattles from him as he describes how agents frequently sign receipts for materials which never are delivered at the reservations but are sold elsewhere to the profit of agent, shipper and carrier. And then the Glory-Hunter produces the sole competent bit of testimony in his entire gossipy recital. The bored committeemen sit straighter.

At Custer's own post, eight thousand bushels of corn have been delivered in sacks bearing the Indian Bureau brand.

> "I declined to receive it and it was reported to Department Headquarters and the matter was carried clear to Washington and an order came back from the Secretary of War that the forage must be received."

Here at last is direct accusation. At once Custer becomes target for excited questions. He is disturbingly, incredibly vague.

It is his belief that the corn was paid for twice, once by the Indian Bureau, once by the army. That is his conviction. He has nothing to support it. He does not even know the name of the contractor who furnished the corn. He is sure that it was the Secretary of War who gave him orders to receive it but he has no clear memory of the date. He thinks it was the previous September. He does not know the name of the agent accomplice in this alleged plot.

This shrill and red-faced man in the witness chair is a professional soldier, acting commander of a regiment. He who has ordered court martials, who must have sat on them himself, who even has faced one as defendant, seems entirely ignorant of the rules of evidence. He has launched innuendo, offered gossip, repeated scandal and this affair of the corn in Indian Bureau sacks is the sole fact he has produced. Even about this, a happening in his own command, he is not positive. He thinks; he believes; it is his recollection. . . .

Further cross-questioning brings out nothing more definite. Again, Custer adorns the name of his fallen enemy, Belknap, with fantastic hearsay.

A man named John Smith has told the witness that Belknap's trip to Canada has been for the purpose of expediting rum-running across the border so as to furnish "better facilities for the traders."

As for other frauds among agents and sutlers, Custer believes they have been multitudinous and that the Secretary of War has shared in them all. Why is he so sure of this? He discharges his last fusillade of words:

"They could not possibly have been carried on to anything like the extent they were without his connivance and approval and when you ask me how the morale and character of the army is affected, I, although belonging to the army, think that it is one of the highest commendations that could be made of the service to say that it has not been demoralized when the head has shown himself to be so unworthy."

Custer's testimony ends. He steps down with relief that appears general. He has struck with the rash fury of his onslaughts in war. Luck was with him then. It has left him now, though of this he seems still unaware. He is purblind to what he has done. He is not conscious of the net about him or of the imminent wrath of one he has tangled therein.

George Armstrong Custer has plastered the already discredited name of the late Secretary of War with innuendo and gossip, in which there is only a single valuable accusation—the affair of the corn sacks. He has appeared before the committee to tell about Belknap's iniquity, but he has not limited himself to besmearing the erstwhile friend of President Grant. He has tarred the President's younger brother, Orville, with the same unscrupulously wielded stick. He has hinted that the President of the United States, his own commander-in-chief, has been guilty of expediting frontier graft. No man determined on self-ruination could have gone further. Grant will not bear such defamation meekly.

It is over now. He can return to Fort Lincoln and lead the punitive column into the field. Glory that he will win by whipping the feeble Sioux will blunt whatever reprisals outraged officialdom may wish to launch. But is it over? Clymer is speaking. General Custer will be pleased to remain in Washington. The committee preparing the impeachment of General Belknap may have further need of him. The net he has woven closes about Custer.

From Fort Ellis in Montana, General Gibbon is preparing to march a column eastward to the Yellowstone, there to meet the force that Custer is to lead westward. General Crook, from Fort Fetterman, is to invade the southern portion of the Sioux domain. Spring is here; the plains are drying; Custer's command-to-be is mobilizing at Fort Lincoln, and its leader must tarry in Washington.

Custer wires explanations to Terry and promises imminent return. His chief does not remove him from command and substitute another. Terry waits, impatiently but sympathetically.

The days dragged on into weeks. The self-trapped man fretted and fumed in Washington and presently the drizzle of rumor, in which the capital forever lies, rusted and began to leak through his armor of self-confidence. It was whispered that the President was furious with Custer. Disturbed by these rumors, the offender called at the White House to explain matters to Grant—how he would have accomplished this is a mystery—and was refused audience. Later, he called again, and once more the President declined to see him.

The increasing pressure of the net about Custer disturbed but did not yet frighten him. If he had erred in Washington he could erase memory of that mistake by a brilliant campaign against the Sioux. The entire 7th Cavalry, completed by the return of three troops that had been serving in the Gulf States, waited at Lincoln for the chief under whom it would make brief and glorious work of the Indians. Though other certainties gradually left him, Custer never questioned his ability to whip all the hostiles in America with his command alone. He smiled with tolerance on those who thought that the impending campaign would be the most bitter and bloody of all Indian wars.

While he waited for Congress to release him, he made several brief trips to New York During one of these, Charles Osborn, associate of Jay Gould, gave a lunch in the soldier's honor. Among the guests was General Grenville Mellen Dodge, Civil War veteran and chief engineer of the Union Pacific Railroad. Dodge recalled later:

"Custer, in his conversation and in his assertion of what his regiment would do, said that his regiment could whip and defeat all the Indians on the plains and was very rash in his statements. The lunch was a long one and the champagne flowed freely. I paid very little attention to them because I knew they were all talking big."*

Dodge was wrong. This was not big talk. It was Custer's solemn conviction and a direct cause of his death. On the following day, when the soldier called at his office, Dodge told him "that if he was going to fight the Indians with any idea that they were to be easily whipped, he was greatly mistaken." This was probably first of the many warnings men gave the Glory-Hunter. He accorded it no more heed than he did subsequent counsel. "Custer," Dodge relates, "still seemed to carry the idea that the reason the Indians had not been thoroughly punished was because the right kind of troops had not gotten after them."†

The column waited at Fort Lincoln, and Terry worried; and Custer, idling in Washington, fumed at the deliberate procedure of Congress and was increasingly disturbed by reports of the President's displeasure.

At last, he reappeared before the committee. His testimony was brief, possibly through belated caution, but questions prodded him into further assault on Belknap. He discussed the gag rule that the Secretary of War had imposed on army officers. His evidence set on foot odd coincidence. As instance of Belknap's arrogance, Custer cited the case of General Hazen, one time agent for the Kiowas at old Fort Cobb. Hazen, the witness charged, had violated the stifling rule of the Secretary of War and had been, in consequence, exiled to desolate Fort Buford, a thousand miles up the Missouri.

When Custer's downfall came, Terry sought a substitute leader of the expedition. Hazen was his choice but Hazen, as a result of Custer's testimony, had been summonsed by the committee and already was on his way to Washington.

---

* Perkins, J. R.: *Trails, Rails and War,* Indianapolis, 1927.
† *Ibid.*

Though his downfall now was imminent, its victim seemed still unaware of the gravity of his plight. On April twentieth, he wired Terry that the ordeal was over and that he was about to leave Washington. Before he could depart, Congress caught him again. He was ordered to remain at the capital as a prospective witness in the impending impeachment of Belknap—to testify to the delivery at Lincoln of those misbranded sacks of corn.

Here began the wild struggle of a man, indignant, then frightened, then thoroughly abased, to escape from the trap into which he had thrust himself. He appealed to all available authority for release. He implored Sherman to intercede with Clymer on his behalf. The General of the army refused but promised to speak of Custer's wish for release to Alfonso Taft, Belknap's successor and father of a later president.

Taft took Custer's plea to Grant, who saw the exposed weakness of his self-elected enemy and struck against it with the violence of wrath long pent. The President ordered the Fort Lincoln column to move under some other leader, since it seemed so essential that Lieutenant-Colonel Custer remain in Washington.

Sherman wired these instructions to Sheridan in Chicago. On the morrow, when Custer called again, the General showed him a copy of that dispatch. Grant's vindictive blow drove an already distracted man to the verge of frenzy. To his panicky request for aid, Sherman had only one answer: "See the President."

Twice heretofore, Custer had tried and failed. One so involved could not shrink from the nauseous taste of further humiliation. He, the original assailant, must sue for pardon, or his dream of glorious victory over the Sioux, if not the dreamer himself, was ruined. Before he called on Grant, Custer went to Clymer and managed to wring from the impeachment manager, since his actual importance as a witness against Belknap was slight, dismissal of the subpœna that held him in Washington. Thereafter, he called at the White House and sent in his card to Grant.

The President ignored him entirely. He did not decline to see Custer. He did not grant him an interview. He let his defamer wait long hours in an anteroom and review, while he sat and rose and paced the floor and sat again, the possible fate of one who, without warrant, slanders his commander-in-chief and his commander's kin.

Grant at this time was a sorely tried man, pestered by the press, bitterly assailed by the opposition. Custer was one person at least against whom he properly could strike back. The President let him stew in ignominy.

At three that afternoon (May second), Acting Quartermaster-General Ingalls, arriving to see the President, found Custer still waiting and learned from him of his plight. Ingalls spoke of it to Grant who replied that he did not want to see him. When Ingalls carried this message to the victim, Custer wrote a letter to Grant. Since Whittaker, his eulogist, reproduces it, the culprit must have tarried to make a copy. It read:

> "To His Excellency, the President: Today for the third time, I have sought an interview with the President—not to solicit a favor except to be granted a brief hearing—but to remove from his mind certain unjust impressions concerning myself, which I have reason to believe are entertained against me. I desire this opportunity as a matter of justice and I regret that the President has declined to give me an opportunity to submit to him a brief statement which justice to him as well as me demanded.
>
> "Respectfully submitted,
> > "G. A. Custer, Lt. Col. 7th Cavalry,
> > "Bvt. Maj. Gen., U. S. A."

The pious reproach and the priggish forbearance of this document could have done little to soothe Grant's resentment. After sending in his letter, its author left the White House and tried to call on Sherman. The General was in New York. Whom else Custer conferred with before taking train for Chicago that night, is a mystery to which circumstantial evidence alone offers solution.

That unreliable witness indicates he talked at length with the Washington correspondent of the *New York World*. This paper launched, May fourth, a virulent attack on Grant for his treatment of Custer. It assailed him by editorial and in a news story headed "GRANT'S REVENGE." The latter termed the President's removal of Custer from command of the Fort Lincoln column "the most high-handed abuse of his official power which he has perpetrated yet." It continued:

"When the news came to General Sherman and Secretary Taft, both went to the President and protested that it would not do. General Sherman went further and said that Custer was not only the best man, but the only man fit to lead the expedition now fitting out against the Indians. To all their entreaties, Grant turned a deaf ear, and said that if they could not find a man to lead the expedition, he would find one: that this man Custer had come on here both as a witness and as a prosecutor in the Belknap matter to besmirch his Administration, and he proposed to put a stop to it.

"By advice of General Sherman and Secretary Taft, General Custer went to the White House to call on the President, although he said he did not believe it would be of any use, for he had done nothing but his duty, nothing that he had any apologies to make for doing and nothing that he would not do again under the same circumstances.

"He had come on here in obedience to law. Nevertheless, in deference to their judgment, he went to the White House and sat in the waiting room unsent for until the President's calling hour was over, although he repeatedly sent in his card. Finally he wrote a letter to the President and left it, in which he stated that he called for the purpose of disabusing the President's mind, if he had heard any statements that he (Custer) had said or done anything against the President personally.

"It is understood that the President will publicly assign as his reason for relieving Custer that he is here and will not go back to his command in time to take charge of the expedition now getting ready to start against the Indians; but it is also understood that General Custer will be back in time, for the managers have relieved him from their subpoena and General Grant will have to make some other excuse to the people."

Editorially the *World* branded Grant's act thus:

"There has never been a President of the United States before who was capable of braving the decent opinion of the country so openly and shamefully as this, for the sake of wreaking such a miserable vengeance."

One of the President's many disqualifications for office was his vulnerability to criticism. This attack in an anti-administration paper stirred him sufficiently to order his son and secretary, U. S. Grant, Jr., to demand an accounting from Sherman. The General of the army at once disavowed all responsibility whatever. His long disclaimer ends:

"I say most emphatically that General Custer, though relieved as a witness by the Committee, was not justified in leaving Washington under the circumstances of the case and that the enclosed newspaper paragraph gives a wrong statement of the whole case.

"I surely never protested to the President or to anybody, nor did I ever intimate that General Custer 'was not only the best man but the only man fit to lead the expedition, etc.' I believe the Army possesses hundreds who are competent for such an expedition and I knew that General Terry, who is perfectly qualified for the highest military duty, had already been chosen to conduct the same expedition.

"I will show this letter and its enclosures to the Secretary of War, and most respectfully report that General Custer is now subject to any measure of discipline which the President may require. Whether he is responsible or not for the enclosed newspaper paragraph I have not the means of knowing and I surely cannot believe that he could so report the case."

The biographer of almost sixty years later can find no evidence whether or not the belief of the General of the army was justified.

Custer reached Chicago on May fourth, the day of the publication of the *World's* attack on Grant. An aide of Sheridan met him on the platform with a copy of a telegram from Sherman:

"I am at this moment advised that Gen. Custer started last night for St. Paul and Fort Abraham Lincoln. He was not justified in leaving without seeing the President or myself. Please intercept him at Chicago or St. Paul and order him to halt and wait further orders. Meanwhile, let the expedition from Fort Lincoln proceed without him."

The Lieutenant-Colonel's gratuitous assault upon the fallen Belknap had concluded with his own downfall.

CHAPTER SEVEN

STRUGGLE

CUSTER had leaped upon his prostrate enemy, Belknap, and had gone down almost as disastrously. He had attacked without scruple, certain that whatever official irritation his testimony might arouse could be nullified by his prowess in the impending campaign. The order that met him on the Chicago station platform was more than mere demotion. The hand was Sherman's but the voice was Grant's. The old soldier had outmaneuvered the younger. Custer had attacked recklessly. Grant had struck in behind him, destroying his line of retreat and base.

This was ruin or its shadow. The President's reprisal upon the hothead who had assailed Grant's friend, Grant's brother, and had aspersed Grant himself, ethically may have been dubious. It was a humanly angry counter-attack, not without provocation, though the Chief Executive used official channels to avenge personal affront. He was not a scrupulous warrior, but neither was Custer, who must have known, as he read the dispatch a second time, the chill loneliness of the forsaken by fortune.

The Glory-Hunter had incurred the wrath of the Chief Executive and the compliant disapproval of the General of the army. Grant had abolished Custer's hope of redeeming himself in a triumphant campaign against the Sioux. The 7th Cavalry, the splendid regiment that could whip by itself all Indians on the plains, would ride to battle under some other leader. That man would win fame on which Custer had depended while the Glory-Hunter suffered whatever further punishment Grant contemplated.

The struggle of the man entangled in the self-woven net progressed from indignation, through frenzy, to abject pleading. Bit

287

by bit, Grant's implacability stripped from the Glory-Hunter pride, self-confidence, self-respect, and left him at last, as severe reproof always left him, placating, wheedling, contrite.

Custer went at once to Sheridan's headquarters. In 1867-68, the General had consoled his favorite in another similar crisis. He was less sympathetic now. Sheridan was impatient with the recklessness that had wrought avoidable disaster and the words of Sheridan, when roused, could be brutal as a musket butt. After verbal scathing, the Division Commander permitted Custer to appeal by telegraph from Sherman's order. During that May fourth, the unhappy man sent three wires eastward to the General of the army, each less self-sure than the last.

The first was long and recited the circumstances of the culprit's last call at the White House and its result. It detailed his attempt to report to Sherman. There are vestiges of defiance in its conclusion:

> "While at the War Department that day, I also reported the fact of my proposed departure to the Adjutant General and to the Inspector General of the Army and obtained from them written and verbal authority to proceed to my command without visiting Detroit as previously ordered to do. At my last interview with you, I informed you that I would leave Washington on Monday night to join my command, and you, in conversation, replied that 'that was the best thing I could do.' Besides you frequently during my stay in Washington called my attention to the necessity for my leaving as soon as possible."

There seems to have been no answer to this redundant defense. The silence drove Custer from reproach to appeal. His second wire read:

> "I desire to call your attention to your statement to me in your office that I should go in command of my regiment. Also to your reply when I inquired if the President or other parties had any charges to make against me. In leaving Wash-

ington I had every reason to believe I was acting in strict accordance with your suggestions and wishes. I ask you, as General of the Army, to do me justice in this matter."

Still, the implacable silence. In the face of this, Custer telegraphed a third time with new meekness:

"After you read my dispatch of today, I would be glad if my detention could be authorized at Fort Lincoln where my family is instead of at this point."

Sherman did not answer. Grant kept silent. Other telegrams bearing indirectly upon Custer's plight had come to Sheridan's headquarters and the distraught man may have seen them. Terry had submitted to Sheridan the names of several officers as possible commanders of the Fort Lincoln column. Sheridan had cared for none of the selections and had ordered Terry himself to lead the expedition.

There remained only one chance for inclusion in the column. This lay not with the brusk Sheridan but with Terry, the kindly, the tolerant. Custer went to St. Paul.

The vainglorious, swaggering cavalry leader who had stopped at Terry's headquarters, en route to Washington on March twenty-fourth, had been a far different man from him who entered now. Custer was disheveled. There was tragedy in his eyes and a break in his voice as he laid his plight before his superior. Terry listened with sympathy on his bearded face and was moved by tears that ran down Custer's cheeks.

There was further humiliation in store for the frantic man. A telegram to him from Sherman had been forwarded to St. Paul. It read:

"Before receipt of yours, I had sent orders to General Sheridan to permit you to go to Abe Lincoln on duty but the President adheres to his conclusion that you are not to go on the expedition."

Another and further blow impended. Before he could comfort, Terry was obliged to chide, and his words completed Custer's abasement.

Terry took up the matter of the Indian Bureau corn, sole competent testimony in Custer's Washington recital. The General told the frantic man that the corn had been transferred legitimately from the Indian Bureau to the War Department and that it had been his order, not Belknap's, which had bidden Custer to accept it. The only worth-while evidence the witness had offered had been absolutely wrong.

It is well to remember this in the light of events to come, for the incident is a peephole through which one may look upon the chaotic mental state of him who stood then at the threshold of his death. Custer had journeyed to Washington and had testified before the committee, without taking the inconsiderable trouble to ascertain whether it had been Terry, or Belknap who had issued the order. Orders as a rule have names attached. Orders, at a military post, are filed. So certain had been George Armstrong Custer of the innate rightness of his beliefs that he had not felt it necessary to match them with fact.

He recanted now. He telegraphed Clymer, withdrawing the only worth-while evidence he had uttered, explaining that he had talked to Terry and that it "was he and not the late Secretary of War who sent the order to Fort Lincoln that under certain instructions intended to protect the government, the corn in question should be received. . . . The receipt of this order," he adds, "was reported to me and at the time I derived the impression that the order emanated from the War Department."

If the bread of recantation and humility was bitter in his mouth, there was more to be eaten. Terry, a former attorney, now became Custer's actual counsel. Terry was sure from the attitude of Sheridan, Sherman and Grant, that the disgraced man would never be reinstated as commander of the expedition. There was a chance, however, that tact and a carefully phrased final appeal to the President might enable Custer to accompany the column as commander of the 7th Cavalry, under Terry. They talked the matter over and it was Terry who on May sixth, inspired the canny dispatch that Custer signed:

"To his Excellency the President of the United States through Military Channels:

"I have seen your order, transmitted through the General of the Army directing that I be not permitted to accompany the expedition about to move against the hostile Indians. As my entire regiment forms a part of the proposed expedition and as I am the senior officer of the regiment on duty in this department, I respectfully but most earnestly request that while not allowed to go in command of the expedition, I may be permitted to serve with my regiment in the field.

"I appeal to you as a soldier to spare me the humiliation of seeing my regiment march to meet the enemy and I not to share its dangers."

This appeal, framed by a kindly gentleman to aid a brother officer in distress, acquired endorsements during its eastward passage through military channels. Terry himself appended:

"In forwarding the above I wish to say, expressly, that I have no desire whatever to question the orders of the President or of my military superiors. Whether Lieutenant-Colonel Custer shall be permitted to accompany the column or not, I shall go in command of it. I do not know the reasons upon which the orders given rest; but if these reasons do not forbid it, Lieutenant Colonel Custer's services would be very valuable with his regiment."

This has none of the indignation or shrill appeal of Custer's own dispatches. It is intercession by one who knows men and the insidious forces that may break obstinacy. Sheridan's endorsement of his erstwhile favorite's appeal was far less suave and outwardly non-partizan. He wrote:

"The following dispatch from General Terry is respectfully forwarded. I am sorry Lieutenant-Colonel Custer did not

manifest as much interest in staying at his post to organize
and get ready his regiment and the expedition as he now does
to accompany it.

"On a previous occasion, in 1868, I asked executive clem-
ency for Colonel Custer to enable him to accompany his regiment against the Indians and I sincerely hope that if granted
this time, it may have sufficient effect to prevent him from
again attempting to throw discredit upon his profession and
his brother officers."

It was not Sheridan's but Custer's Terry-inspired appeal that
abated Grant's stubborn vindictiveness. On May eighth, Sherman
wired to Terry:

"General Sheridan's enclosing yours of yesterday touching
General Custer's urgent request to go under your command
with his regiment has been submitted to the President, who
sent me word that if you want General Custer along, he withdraws his objections."

Then followed counsel from Sherman which was made more
ironic by the fact that Mark Kellogg, a newspaperman, died with
the 7th Cavalry's leader on the Little Bighorn hills:

"Advise Custer to be prudent, not to take along any newspapermen, who always make mischief, and to abstain from
personalities in the future. . . ."

Custer learned of his reinstatement when he appeared at headquarters of the Department of Dakota, Wabasha and Fourth
Streets, St. Paul, early on the morning of May eighth. It is not
known how he received tidings that lifted him out of the slough of
despair. Though he was not to command the expedition, at least
he was to accompany it at the head of his regiment. There was
still chance that he might obscure his recent abasement by new and
more brilliant glory—thanks to Terry.

He must have been grateful to Terry, yet his conduct immediately after that interview is scarcely more logical than his headlong

accusation of Belknap in connection with the sacks of Indian Bureau corn.

Custer, the proud, had endured protracted spiritual lashing from Sheridan, Sherman, Grant. He had seen his hope of resurgence through a victorious campaign snuffed out. He had eaten of humiliation until his spiritual stomach had cried out against the unendurable ration. Custer, the famous Indian fighter; Custer, leader of the 7th Cavalry that, alone, could purge the plains of every hostile; Custer, the former chief of the expedition that had waited at Lincoln had been saved from a fate that he himself might have visited on an insubordinate private, largely by the intervention of Terry, who knew nothing of Indian campaigning yet now was to command Custer himself in the field.

It may have been ungrateful resentment; it may have been jest; it may have been only the sudden freedom of an ego long tortured that inspired Custer's alleged boast, the very morning of his restoration to command of the 7th. Whatever fathered that bragging, there can be small doubt that he uttered it.

From headquarters, Custer went to the Metropolitan Hotel where he lodged. There he met Captain William Ludlow, his comrade on the Yellowstone and the Black Hills expeditions, and now en route to duty in Philadelphia. To Ludlow, he babbled his tidings with the vivacity of a mind released from pressure. Ludlow said that Custer crowed that he intended to "cut loose" from Terry at the first opportunity and run the campaign to suit himself, adding that he had got away from Stanley and would be able "to swing clear of Terry."*

This was not a tale that Ludlow kept until after the event. The following morning, when Terry and Custer had left by special train for Fort Lincoln, the Captain repeated the conversation to Colonel Farquahar of the engineers, Assistant Adjutant-General Ruggles and General Card, Terry's Chief Quartermaster. All these officers later had clear recollection of the story. There is no doubt that it was factual. Even Colonel Varnum, last survivor of Custer's

---

* Hughes, Colonel R. D.: "The Campaign Against the Sioux in 1876," *Journal of the Military Service Instruction of the United States*, January, 1896.

officers and an idolizer of his chief, believes in Ludlow's absolute integrity.

Terry must have occupied much time during the journey from St. Paul to Bismarck in discussing with his subordinate problems of the campaign, about which Custer, due to his sojourn in Washington and his subsequent agitation, knew little.

The commander of the invincible 7th Cavalry may have smiled inwardly at his chief's belief in hard fighting ahead. There was warrant for Terry's conviction. From Arikara scouts and, more impressively, from Charley Reynolds himself, who had gone his lonely way about the hostile camp, Terry had learned this numbered from fifteen hundred to two thousand lodges which would shelter from three thousand to four thousand warriors. Reynolds had muttered in his soft apologetic voice that the Sioux were truculent, well-armed and willing to fight. It was the army's intention to carry the battle to them.

The Yellowstone goes northeast across the southeast corner of Montana. The triangle cut off by the river from the rest of the state was the heart of the wild Indians' domain. Flowing north to the Yellowstone through the unceded land were many streams and creeks, joining the greater river like crooked, wide-spaced teeth in a comb. The Little Missouri lay farthest east. Beyond this, ran turgid O'Fallon's Creek, the larger and even muddier Powder and then the clearer flows of Tongue, Rosebud and Bighorn.

These drained a land, abrupt and strange as Indian music; a region of misshapen buttes and hills with sharply angled peaks; a country cursed by the eroded nightmares of badlands and blessed with rich valleys where grazing was lush and game abounded; a place of diamond-bright air and stinging sun and hard winds that drove in their season thunder-storm and blizzard; an untamed land, savage and brilliant as the defiant folk who held it. Toward this, the army moved to break the power of the Sioux, of Crazy Horse and Gall and Two Moons of the Northern Cheyennes; of Sitting Bull, the priest and statesman whose voice sang of victory to thousands of dark believers.

The most powerful force the plains ever had seen was to be

launched against these chieftains and their clansmen. The plans of the army had the usual virtue of looking well on paper.

From the south at Fort Fetterman, General Crook, whom the Crazy Horse had whipped once already this year, was to march with ten companies of the 3rd Cavalry, five of the 2nd Cavalry, and six companies of the 4th and 9th Infantry. His force of over a thousand was to move to the head of the Tongue River and work north, driving the hostiles before it. Crook would soon be under way.

In Montana, General Gibbon already had marched with six companies of the 7th Infantry from Fort Shaw and four troops of the 2nd Cavalry under Major James E. Brisbin from Fort Ellis. The expedition, which numbered with its Crow allies more than four hundred men, was to move down the north bank of the Yellowstone taking care lest fugitive Sioux cross the flood.

Meanwhile at Fort Lincoln, the long delayed eastern column was preparing at last to get under way. The entire 7th Cavalry, twelve troops, under Custer; four companies of the 6th Infantry under Major O. H. Moore, a company of the 17th Infantry and a battery of four Gatling guns, served by a platoon of the 20th Infantry under Lieutenants Low and Kinzie, made this the most powerful of the three commands although in men it was no stronger than Crook's.

Terry and Custer from the east, Gibbon from the north, Crook from the south, were to close in upon the enemy with the smooth facility authors of military plans expect and field commanders sweat blood vainly to attain. Custer, Gibbon and Crook, waking old echoes of Appomattox by joint assault on another foe, were to surround and crush the Sioux whose hereditary enemies, the Crows and Shoshones, would block the hostiles' escape to the west. Gibbon and Terry were to join hands on the Yellowstone—if the Sioux had not been abolished before they met—and carry out the work of extermination under Terry's command. Crook was to operate independently but in concert. It was an elaborate plan. On May tenth, the commander of the expedition and the leader of the 7th Cavalry alighted at Fort Lincoln to put into action the portion allotted to them.

Chapter Eight

SOLDIERS' FAREWELL

On a level space, three miles below Fort Abraham Lincoln, tents stood in ranks and one hundred and fifty wagons were parked. Here, under the quickening sun of spring, the expedition waited. The clamor of cavalry trumpets, the lighter voices of infantry bugles, decreed the routine of each identical day, and rumors, profuse and fantastic, blew along company streets with dust and smoke and the reek from the horse-lines.

The rumors concerned Custer, the column's still absent leader. Officers muttered them to one another and as the calamitous flavor of fatherless tales increased, the sleek and hollow-eyed Major Marcus A. Reno may have dreamed of leading into battle the regiment he temporarily commanded, and Benteen, white-haired, ruddy, vindictive, may have grinned.

Veterans of the 7th Cavalry's reunited twelve troops hammered the rudiments of soldiering into a heavy increment of recruits and, between times, swapped new rumors with the doughboys of the 6th and 17th Infantry or the men of the 20th who served as crews for the four brass-bound Gatling guns. Scouts, teamsters and packers exchanged the latest fraudulent tidings and all day long a sullen, quarrelsome sound ran through a camp fermenting in idleness.

On May tenth, the brawling swelled into sharper, more purposeful racket. Boredom vanished in a rising tide of excitement. Men spoke and moved more quickly and there was a new lilt even to the accordion-like braying of mules. Officers bawled to hurrying orderlies, or dodged about clasping sheaves of papers. Terry had arrived. Terry and his staff were at Fort Lincoln and with him was Custer, not arrested, not jailed, not disgraced, but authorized to lead his own regiment into the field.

This was no rumor. The bearded General and Custer, paler for his long absence from western sunlight, appeared in camp. The voice of the Glory-Hunter had its old crackle and bite as he conferred with his officers. Despite long delay, the column was not ready to move and the fact that his own absence was in part responsible did not temper his criticism.

His speech snapped about his subordinates' ears. Here were youngsters, like Lieutenant James G. Sturgis, the absent Colonel's son, fresh from West Point. Here were veterans whose lives already were part of the regiment's history, whose deaths were to be its glory.

Keogh, the swaggering, bibulous soldier of fortune; Smith of the crippled left arm; Yates, martinet commander of the gray-horsed "bandbox troop"; Tom Custer, the jaunty, with the twin bars of a captain on his new shoulder-straps; "Queen's Own" Cook of the baldhead and the long black side-whiskers, and Calhoun, the handsome husband of Margaret Custer, endured with the rest of the officers the Lieutenant-Colonel's criticism and exhortation. No intimation of imminent immortality shadowed them. When their chief ended and the others tramped out, his favorites pressed about their idol to wring his hand.

The regiment that Custer believed invincible was far from the peak of its fighting strength. Its ranks contained from thirty to forty per cent. recruits. It was grievously under-officered. The commissioned men on detached duty included the colonel, two majors, four captains and seven lieutenants. Several troops had only one officer. So great was the lack that Lieutenant John J. Crittenden, 20th Infantry, was detailed at his own request to duty with the 7th Cavalry and died with its leader.

The 7th may have been the smartest regiment in the service. It was not the most harmonious, and rumor, on which it had fed in the weeks past, had widened fissures in its structure.

In the days to come, those who rationalized and romanticized the tragedy created, among other fictions, the myth of a feud between Reno and Custer. There is no evidence that this existed.

It is probable that, later, Reno grew to loathe Custer's memory as a man will detest another whose death has brought him obloquy. There is scant warrant for the tale of earlier animosity. Generals Scott and Garlington, who joined the 7th Cavalry immediately after the campaign, never in those early days heard the story of this alleged hatred. Colonel Varnum, sole surviving officer who rode with Custer, also denies it. So does Theodore Goldin, veteran of the Little Bighorn. Benteen hated his superior with divine consistency. Other officers in his regiment disliked Custer. The only warrant for the legend of a Reno-Custer feud is the Major's later admission that, through long acquaintance, he had come to have small regard for his Lieutenant-Colonel's military ability.

One spirit found the unprepared state of the expedition unmitigated blessing. Elizabeth Custer had a last brief and golden interval between loneliness and loneliness. For almost two months she had waited at the fort for her husband's return. She had steeled herself for the immediate severing of their reunion. Now, days of respite had been granted her. To these, her beloved added one more.

Boston Custer had returned from the East to seek health on another of his brother's campaigns. Boston was accompanied by young Reed, son of Lydia Reed and namesake of the Glory-Hunter. The lad was seventeen and was called "Autie," the family nickname for his uncle. If a child were to ride with the column, surely Elizabeth Custer might go too.

Her husband tempered his refusal. When the column marched, his wife and his sister, Mrs. Calhoun, could accompany it and share its first night in camp. On the morrow, they must return to the fort but as soon thereafter as possible, Elizabeth Custer should rejoin her lord on the Yellowstone.

The steamer *Far West* was tied at the pier even now. Men loaded the flat-bottomed, twin-stacked, stern-wheel craft with supplies and piled wood for fuel on her lower deck. She would steam up the Missouri and Yellowstone with three companies of the 6th Infantry under Major Moore aboard to meet the column at Stan-

"THE CUSTER CLAN"

Eight of the members of this hunting party in 1875, died, the following year, at the Little Bighorn

1. Lt. James Calhoun, 7th Cavalry; 2. A Mr. Swett of Chicago; 3. Capt. Stephen Baker, 6th Infantry; 4. Boston Custer; 5. Lt. W. S. Edgerly, 7th Cavalry; 6. A Miss Watson; 7. Capt. Myles W. Keogh, 7th Cavalry; 8. Mrs. James Calhoun (Maggie Custer); 9. Mrs. G. A. Custer; 10. Lt. Col. G. A. Custer, 7th Cavalry; 11. Dr. H. O. Paulding, Medical Corps; 12. Mrs. A. E. Smith; 13. Dr. G. E. Lord, 7th Cavalry; 14. Capt. Thomas B. Weir, 7th Cavalry; 15. Lt. W. W. Cook, 7th Cavalry; 16. Lt. R. E. Thompson, 6th Infantry; 17 and 18. The Misses Wadsworth of Chicago; 19. Capt. Thomas W. Custer, 7th Cavalry; 20. Lt. A. E. Smith, 7th Cavalry.

ley's Stockade. Captain Grant Marsh, whose leathery face looked with equal competence over his pilot-house window-sill or the rim of a poker hand, had promised Mrs. Custer that she should be passenger on his next up-stream trip.

The tempo of the camp did not slacken again. Anvils chimed. Whips popped and teamsters swore as the one hundred and fifty wagons of the expeditions rolled to the fort and returned, laden with stores.

The wagons, great six-mule vehicles of the army and lighter two-horse carts supplied by contractors, would go only as far as the Yellowstone. Thereafter, the column's supplies would be carried by mule trains. None of the troops was familiar with this type of transportation though there were packers to teach them. Terry and Custer had too much to do in this final week of frenzied preparation to drill them now.

There might be small need for mules. Scouts of no great reliability but a deal of insistence reported the hostiles were camped on the Little Missouri, far to the east of the Powder, the Rosebud and the Bighorn. If this were true, the campaign would be brief— a march, a battle and then peace, or at worst, a summer's pursuit of the beaten fragments of the Sioux Nation.

So gossip of the camp ran. Charley Reynolds, a drab and wistful figure among the vociferous scouts, confided to Terry and Custer that the Sioux would not run. This, Reynolds offered shyly, would not be like the feeble skirmishes Custer had fought on the Yellowstone in 1873. The Sioux were itching for war. They would take a deal of licking. Reynolds, while he talked, fondled a bandaged right hand on which a felon had developed. He smiled gently at suggestions that he stay behind. He would not miss this campaign. It meant the biggest battle the West had ever seen. No one paid much heed to the soft-voiced, deprecating Jeremiah. How could any one believe him here in the glitter of arms and the cadenced movements of a thousand soldiers and the loading of mountains of munitions into wagons? Terry and Custer were too busy, or too indifferent, to take his words to heart.

Together, with the General as brain and Custer as vigorous executive arm, they organized the column. Terry did all in his power to help the other forget his subordinate position. The General consulted with Custer and permitted the Lieutenant-Colonel to carry out their decisions. He even ignored Sherman's advice and allowed Mark Kellogg to join the column.

Kellogg, then a resident of Bismarck, was studying law and at the same time serving as local editor of the *Bismarck Tribune* and correspondent for St. Paul newspapers. He had been a telegrapher during the Civil War. He went with the expedition as representative not only of the *Tribune* but of the *New York Herald*.

In his last dispatch before the column marched, Kellogg extols Terry's gentility and Custer's energy. He finds that the General's "courteous manner and kindly tones win the fast affection of the men in his command.

"General George A. Custer," Kellogg pursues, "dressed in a dashing suit of buckskin, is prominent everywhere. Here, there, flitting to and fro in his quick, eager way, taking in everything connected with his command as well as generally, with the keen, incisive manner for which he is so well known. The General is full of perfect readiness for the fray with the hostile red devils and woe to the body of scalp hunters that comes within reach of himself and brave companions in arms."*

Far beyond the bluffs to the west of Fort Lincoln, the flood that has lifted all winter now runs high. No one heeds Reynolds who warns of its strength. No one pays even momentary attention to the mutterings of the Arikara scouts who are to accompany the column, and who voice variations of Lonesome Charley's belief.

Least of all, can the utterers of ill omen impress the dashing Glory-Hunter, brave in new buckskins; secure in his belief that his regiment alone can sweep the continent clear of hostiles; hungry for the new fame he must have to erase the stain of recent humiliation. Custer is deaf, obstinate, feverishly ardent. When the col-

---

* *Bismarck Weekly Tribune,* May 17. 1876.

umn marches from Fort Lincoln he and the destiny that decrees the flood have prepared the scaffold for his execution.

By Sunday, May fourteenth, the column was ready. Orders were issued for its start on Monday. Late on Sunday, rain poured, swamping the plains, bogging laden wagons where they stood, drenching the camp and the sullen men who snarled at mention of Custer's name.

The paymaster had arrived, bearing two months' cash due each man of the regiment. There were privation and peril ahead, and across the river at Bismarck waited the hearty flesh-pots of the frontier where troopers might forget imminent ordeal.

Terry postponed the march until Wednesday, May seventeenth, but the 7th's leader, intolerant of the frailties of lesser men, refused to have his soldiers paid until they were safely away from temptations of the town. The paymaster would ride out with the column. He would distribute his treasure the first night in camp. Thereafter, troopers could not waste their pay carnally. Later, the Sioux who stripped the slain scattered the unspent, useless bits of paper over the battle-field of the Little Bighorn.

The bugles abolished the camp on the hot and foggy morning of May seventeenth. At six, the wagon train groaned out toward the westward bluffs that seemed to shake and twitch in the heating air. The infantry and the Gatlings, each drawn by four condemned cavalry horses, led the way, and behind followed the mule teams, ears flopping, coyote tails swinging from headstalls, and then the horse-drawn contractors' wagons. The 7th, the scouts and twenty-five Arikara warriors lingered on the tramped and rutted earth where tents had stood. At seven, trumpets stuttered "to horse."

Six hundred troopers swung into the saddle as they spoke again. Despite their grievance, his men cheered Custer as he rode along their line, a golden figure in his new buckskins. Above the wide collar of his blue flannel shirt and his scarlet cravat, his face was fiercely elated. His wide-brimmed hat was in his hand and his close-cropped head shone yellowish pink. He and Varnum had run horse clippers over their skulls the night before.

With his wife and sister, his civilian brother and nephew, Custer

took his place at the head of the column of fours. The 7th moved
out through the mist, not on the trail of the wagon train, but
toward the fort.

Rumor, or foreboding, had been at work there. The families of
those who rode to war were so fearful that Terry had ordered the
cavalry to march to Lincoln that disconsolate women might be
cheered by sight of the regiment's splendor and might. The band
struck up the 7th's battle song. The wood-winds squealed, the
brasses pumped and brayed its rollicking measures. The column
followed the red and blue personal flag of the Glory-Hunter past
the log huts of the Arikaras, where women keened; past the married soldiers' quarters, where women wept, and onto the parade-
ground of the fort.

> "Where'er we go they'll dread the name
> Of Garry Owen in glo-o-ory."

The regiment halted. Married men dismounted and left the
ranks to bid their wives farewell. Some women fled thereafter with
tight and stricken faces to the shelter of their homes. Others waved
valiantly as the band struck up *The Girl I Left Behind Me*. With
Custer's brown gelding, Dandy, dancing in the lead, the 7th Cavalry rode away. Through the thinning fog, the sun's disk appeared
and grew brighter.

The last four clattered out of the fort. The proud regiment
slowly dwindled into insignificance on the broad plain. The last
brave echo of the band's music came through the stifling air to
those who watched. Sunlight streamed down. One watcher cried
and pointed and all looked upon what they later believed had been
omen.

A mirage lifted half the distant regiment from earth. Those at
the fort saw part of the 7th Cavalry, each distant horse distinct,
each tiny rider clearly outlined, riding across a heat-blanched sky.
For a space they marched miraculously between earth and heaven.
Then the mirage vanished. Only the deliberately crawling, earth-
bound horsemen remained.

The column camped that night beside the Little Heart River. Incautiously kindled fires set dry grass ablaze and there was much excitement and some danger before it was extinguished. The paymaster distributed his cash among the grumbling soldiers. On the morrow, he escorted Custer's wife and sister to the fort. Elizabeth Custer, looking back, saw her husband ride away, bright, blithe and valiant, at the head of his men. This was the memory she cherished all her days.

Thereafter, rains swept down and swamped the toiling column. Earth became a morass and each new camp fresh misery to all save Custer, who seemed immune to wet and chill and mud. He had divided his regiment into two wings, placing one under Reno's command, the other under Benteen, the senior Captain. While the rest of the expedition floundered and grumbled, the 7th's leader rode ahead on Dandy or his bright sorrel, Vic, exalted once more by the spell of the trail—that path to Glory he would recapture for the confusion of his enemies. In four days the column made forty-six miles.

The rains ended. The plain steamed under ardent sun that gave it the bright brief green of spring. Meadowlarks sang with the trumpets each morning. The pace of the column and the spirits of its members mounted. The expedition was following the trail taken by Stanley in 1873, familiar ground to veterans of the 7th. Terry placed more and more responsibility on Custer. Terry did not guard his rank jealously. He was not like Stanley who on this very trail had berated the junior who had tried to run the expedition to suit himself.

The indulgence of Terry, the sun and the wind and the verdant wilderness were release to a long kenneled hound. Custer's horse trod on the heels of scouts who searched vainly for Indian signs through an empty land that glittered brown and green as a snake's new skin. He rode twice the distance other men accomplished in a day; galloping up and down the expedition's toiling length, whirling away across the plains with his dogs, Tuck, Swift, Lady and Kaiser, and yet he came into camp each night fresher, more vigorous than all others. He contrived, with his brother Tom, fresh practical jokes upon Boston Custer. He talked with Terry, of evenings, until the General grew weary. He wrote long letters to his wife, filled with assurances that he took no needless risks, sprinkled with self-admiration.

"General Terry just left my tent a few moments since and when I asked him not to be in a hurry, he said, 'Oh, I'll leave you, for you must be tired and I want to go to bed.' I did not tell him that I was going to write to you before I slept. . . .

"Bloody Knife [his favorite Arikara] looks on in wonder at me because I never get tired and says no other man could ride all night and never sleep. I know I shall sleep soundly when I do lie down; but, actually, I feel no more fatigued now than I did before mounting my horse this morning."*

They saw no Indians. The column crawled across contemptuous wilderness that changed like dull opal beneath the marching clouds. From the trail, to the circular horizon where heat spun violet haze, no men save they moved in this reticent land; no man, the scouts reported day by day, had moved since the snows except for six lodges, whose trail they found but did not follow, for the Sioux—so the rumor ran—were camped in force upon the Little Missouri.

Gibbon was on his way, marching his squadron of cavalry, his battalion of infantry and his Crow allies down the Yellowstone's north bank. On May twenty-ninth, Crook and his thousand started north from Fort Fetterman toward that same river. That day, Terry's command reached the Little Missouri. The three columns that were to destroy the hostiles all were moving. They needed only to find the enemy.

Along the murky Little Missouri that angled through badlands, there was no sign whatever of Indians. On May thirtieth, Custer took four troops of the 7th Cavalry and half the scouts and rode twenty miles up the crooked river. He found no single hostile nor even trace of one.

---

* *Boots and Saddles.*

The campaign would be longer than the optimistic had believed. The hostiles lurked somewhere along the twisting valleys of the rivers ahead, the Powder, the Tongue, the Rosebud, the Bighorn. Men must flounder through the geological delirium of the badlands to reach their watershed. On May thirty-first, the column crossed the Little Missouri and George Armstrong Custer led the way.

CHAPTER NINE

HIDE-AND-SEEK

THE strange depression that later was to envelop Custer, to the wonder of all who knew him, had not yet blunted his swordlike spirit. He still strained at the easy tether by which Terry held him and found delight in displaying his uncanny ability as a guide for the column.

Custer led the way across the Little Missouri and through the badlands, a place of grotesquely rounded gray and brown buttresses, and insanely crooked gullies. He considered himself, and probably he was, a better guide than any of the professionals with the expedition. Only twice, so he wrote his wife, had he been absent from his cherished place at the column's head and each time the command had got lost.

His self-esteem still burned with a hungry adolescent flame. His delight in jests which demanded suffering victims endured. On May thirty-first, George and Tom Custer inflicted on the ailing Boston what the Glory-Hunter rated among the most priceless of his jokes. The three had ridden ahead, beyond the toiling column's sight, to work out a route through the badlands and Boston had dismounted to pry a pebble from his pony's hoof. While he was preoccupied, his brothers rode away, hid their horses and scaled a butte to peer down upon their kinsman who looked about and found himself apparently deserted in perilous country. Custer wrote his wife:

"I fired my rifle so that the bullet whizzed over his head. I popped out of sight for a moment, and when I looked again, 'Bos' was heading his pony towards the command, miles away.

306

I fired another shot in his direction and so did Tom and away
'Bos' flew across the plains, thinking no doubt the Sioux were
after him."

"I do not know," the man confides in a later letter, "what
we would do without 'Bos' to tease."*

So far there had not been that cessation of Custer's high spirits,
wherein men were to read omen, yet on the morning of June first,
the whole expedition was prisoned and the Arikaras were frightened by a heavy snowfall.

The storm was a blizzard, lifted out of January into the end of
spring. No Indian, no white man in the expedition could recall
its like in June. For two days, the whirling flakes held the camp
blindfolded and inert beside Sentinel Buttes. Not until June third,
when the heaped drifts shrank miraculously under a hot sun, could
the march be resumed and by then rations were low.

That day, scouts from the Yellowstone met the column. Two
white men and an Indian guide brought dispatches from Major
Moore whose companies of the 6th Infantry had been borne by the
Far West to Stanley's Stockade, and from General Gibbon who was
marching his command down the north bank of the Yellowstone.
Terry camped that night on Beaver Creek, a tributary of the Little
Missouri, and sent orders back by the scouts, halting Gibbon's
march and instructing Moore to have a boatload of supplies
brought to the mouth of the Powder River. There had been, the
scouts had reported, no sign of Indians along the Yellowstone east
of the Powder.

The column marched southward up the Beaver and then turned
sharply west, hurrying over sage-studded dry plains, groping
through the petrified convulsion of badlands, to O'Fallon's Creek.
Beyond, earth had shrugged and corrugated itself into so terrific a
jumble that Reynolds, in trying to guide the command through,
got hopelessly lost on June seventh. It was Custer to whom Terry
turned. It was he, with his eerie sixth sense, who guided the col-

* *Boots and Saddles.*

umn into camp on the muddy Powder—"too thick to drink; too thin to plough"—twenty-five miles from its mouth. West of the Powder ran the other rivers of the wild Sioux country—the Tongue, then the Rosebud, then the Bighorn.

Here ended the reiterant monotony of the march—reveille, breakfast, the toil of matching pace all day to the lumbering deliberation of the wagons, camp and the smell of smoke and the 7th's band blaring and snorting merrily in the dusk. The calm opening of the tragedy's final act slipped imperceptibly into swifter tempo. The column was deep in Indian land. Each empty mile behind increased the promise of battle in every mile ahead, and Crook was coming up from the south and Gibbon held the Yellowstone's north bank while Terry and Custer closed in from the east. Day by day, the force that was to abolish the Sioux drew nearer its still hidden goal.

Terry's column remained in camp on June eighth, save for the troops of Moylan and Keogh which escorted the General and his staff to the mouth of the Powder. Here Terry found the *Far West* and also a rowboat that had come down-stream from Gibbon. It bore Major James S. Brisbin, commanding the cavalry squadron of the Montana column, and Captain J. C. Clifford. The report they gave Terry quickened the beat of subsequent events.

Since April, Gibbon had been patrolling the northern bank of the Yellowstone lest the Sioux break free of the closing net and stampede across the river into the north. Gibbon's command had lost some horses and a few men in minor brushes with the hostiles. In mid-May, from a distance, Lieutenant J. H. Bradley, Gibbon's chief of scouts, had seen smoke blanketing the valley of the Tongue and had believed a large village there. On May twenty-seventh, Bradley had crossed the Yellowstone with his most daring Crows. Not all of them had been willing to go. Gibbon's red allies were in a state of perpetual fear. The Sioux, they kept reiterating, were too many, too strong. They would gobble up Gibbon and Terry or whatever force the whites might send against them.

Bradley and his scouts, with cavalry under Captain Clifford, had worked their way up through the pinnacle-spined backbone of gray

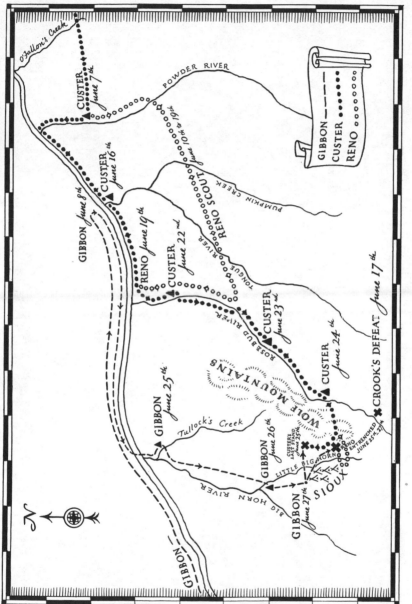

THE 1876 CAMPAIGN AGAINST THE SIOUX

(After L. C. Rennick)

rock and stunted fir that separated the Rosebud and Bighorn Valleys. From a height they had looked down upon the distant smoke and the movement and the grazing pony herd of a big Sioux village and, when sudden turmoil in the camp made them fear they had been discovered, had retired and crossed in safety to Gibbon on the Yellowstone's far shore.

There had been no tidings from Crook, but for the Gibbon and Terry columns, the marching and searching was almost over now. To west were Indians—many Indians, who seemed indifferent to the imminence of the soldiers. Terry sent a white scout and an Arikara with a message to Gibbon and on June ninth went upstream on the *Far West* to meet his subordinate.

The stern-wheeler groaned as she bucked the muscular brown current, and in his pilot-house Grant Marsh muttered that he had never seen the Yellowstone so high at this time of year. The rains of spring, the unseasonable snow, had set all streams bank full. Gibbon, riding down-stream with a troop of the 2nd Cavalry as escort, met his chief at a place known thereafter as Steamboat Point. Here was held the first of the councils of war that in the next fortnight were to bring about the tragedy's climax. A year thereafter, Gibbon, who limped all his days from a Civil War wound, wrote of his first consultation with Terry:

"He informed me that he had heard nothing from General Crook and intended on his return to Powder River to send a cavalry command on a scout up that river and across it west to the Tongue and Rosebud. If no Indians should be discovered then the only remaining chance would be further up the Yellowstone where from my observation there must be some Indians, and if General Crook should strike them from the south, it would be all the more necessary for us to guard the line of the river and prevent any escape to the northward."*

To guide Terry's scouting column, Gibbon lent him Minton ("Mitch") Bouyer, a famous half-breed Sioux scout and the man most familiar with the country in either command.

---

* Byrne, P. E.: *Soldiers of the Plains*, New York, 1927.

Terry ordered Gibbon to countermarch his command to a point on the Yellowstone's north bank opposite the Rosebud's mouth. Terry returned, June tenth, to his own column's camp on the Powder River. Here while his men had struggled with mules, drafted for pack work from the government teams, Custer had wrestled with still another article for *The Galaxy.*

"Day before yesterday I rode nearly fifty miles, arose yesterday morning and went to work at my article, determined to finish it before night, which I did amidst constant interruptions. It is now nearly midnight and I must go to bed, for reveille comes at 3."*

Apparently he paid small heed to the difficulties of insurgent mules and men unskilled in packing, but there was squealing and plunging and much bitter swearing in the dust of an improvised corral where clumsy troopers strove to bind loads on humped unwilling backs. "Custer's train," said General Scott, "was a disgrace."† It was more than that. It was one of the elements that wrought his destruction.

He had spent his life's last day of comparative leisure at his desk. Terry's return abolished chance of further relaxation for any one. The General wasted no time when battle lay beyond the horizon. On the afternoon of June tenth, Major Reno with the right wing of the 7th Cavalry, a Gatling and a mule train, set out, guided by Bouyer, to rake the unknown land for trace of hostiles. Reno's orders bade him go up-stream to the forks of the Powder, scout Mizpah Creek and then, crossing the divide, come down the valley of the next stream westward, the Tongue.

On June eleventh, the rest of the column marched for the mouth of the Powder. Terry, who had ridden along that valley, was certain that the wagon train could not get through in less than two days. Custer, to whom the General entrusted guidance of the expedition, brought horse, foot, guns and train to the Powder's mouth

---

* *Boots and Saddles.*
† Scott, General Hugh L.: *Some Memories of a Soldier,* New York, 1928.

in a single day. The column had no rations left when it reached the Yellowstone.

Meanwhile, on Terry's order, the *Far West* had steamed downstream to the mouth of Glendive Creek where Major Moore's infantry guarded the supplies put ashore at Stanley's Stockade. With garrison and all munitions aboard, the stern-wheeler kicked herself back up-river to the Powder's mouth. Here Terry had decided to establish the base for the impending campaign. All wagons were to be left, even the 7th's doughty band was to remain.

There was haste in the movements and thoughts of men, in the march of Gibbon back to the Rosebud's mouth, in the preparations of the 7th's remaining troops to move up-stream to the Tongue, there to await Reno's return. No tidings had come from Crook and the spur of rivalry pricked the soldiers lest he abolish the Sioux before the Dakota and Montana columns could strike.

A second river-boat, the *Josephine,* arrived and dumped fresh supplies in the base camp at the Powder's mouth. Custer had hoped that his wife might be on board. He and the remaining half of his command at last were ready to march with a Gatling and the still unreliable mules. Gloom shadowed the troops' departure from the Powder. The day before they left, a boat which was to carry their last letters and Custer's *Galaxy* article down-stream to Fort Buford overset with Sergeant Fox and two soldiers of the 6th Infantry on board, and Fox was drowned. Captain Marsh and Kellogg, the correspondent, fished in the river for the sunken mail sacks, recovered them and spent the night drying out the letters.

On June fifteenth Custer marched for the Tongue, skirting lines of buttes behind which rose bare dun hills. On June sixteenth he camped by the Tongue and his men pulled down and plundered Indian burial scaffolds that had been raised beside the river's mouth. On June seventeenth Crook, far up toward the headwaters of the Rosebud River, met the Sioux.

Crazy Horse led them. Crazy Horse, darling of warriors, outmaneuvered a thousand soldiers and two hundred and fifty Crow and Shoshone allies. Crazy Horse sent Crook, staggering on his heels, back to his base camp, with nine men dead and twenty-seven wounded. The General, who most nearly rivaled Custer as an Indian fighter, waited for reenforcements before he dared venture northward again.

Thereafter, events dropped swiftly into place to form the tragic pattern set by circumstance and the minds of wilful men.

On June nineteenth, Reno's six troops returned from scout, to the mouth of the Rosebud instead of the Tongue, as he had been ordered. Across the Yellowstone, Reno talked with Gibbon by signal flag and later, when a Crow from Gibbon's command had swum the stream, sent him back with a letter.

There were, so Reno reported, no Indians on the Powder, none on the upper reaches of the Tongue, none in the Rosebud's valley; but from this last a wide trail, stamped by the hoofs of a myriad ponies and scored by thousands of lodge poles, led up-stream and turned to the right as though to cross into the valley beyond the piled gray rubble of the Wolf Mountains. The Sioux called that further valley the Greasy Grass. White men were to know it as the Little Bighorn.

To Custer and Terry, waiting with the other half of the 7th at the mouth of the Tongue, came on the evening of June nineteenth, a courier from Reno, bearing his news. The Major, the dispatch read, already was marching toward the Tongue. Terry sent orders for Reno to halt and wait the arrival of Custer's command that would ride up-stream while Terry himself went up to the Rosebud's mouth on the *Far West*.

Custer's six troops marched over sage-sprinkled, level land, backed by low brown hills. The cliffs that bordered the Yellowstone's north bank were ocher and maroon where the early sun smote them and deep blue shadow filled their ravines. Midway between Tongue and Rosebud, Custer's men met Reno's trail-worn troopers and weary mules and horses.

There were formalists among the officers of the 7th who grumbled at Reno's disobedience to Terry's orders and muttered that he should be court-martialed for having come down the Rosebud Valley when Terry had commanded him to return by the Tongue. More significant is Custer's opinion of his Major's action. The

Glory-Hunter, with the scent of Indian quarry already twitching his nostrils, disparaged Reno, not for his neglect of orders but because he had not carried disobedience further.

It is probable that when the severed halves of the 7th reunited on June twentieth, somewhere between the Rosebud and the Tongue, Custer, a red and truculent figure with his sunburned face and sprouting auburn whiskers, informed the Major of his displeasure. He did not conceal it from his wife, and later he spoke of it to Varnum. To Elizabeth Custer, her husband wrote on June twenty-first from the camp the reunited regiment had made—a short distance below the Rosebud's mouth:

> "The scouts reported that they could have overtaken the village in one day and a half. I am now going to take up the trail where the scouting party [Reno's] turned back. I fear their failure to follow up the Indians has imperilled our plans by giving the village an intimation of our presence. Think of the valuable time lost! But I feel hopeful of accomplishing great results."*

At noon of June twenty-first, the *Far West* with Terry aboard came churning past the 7th Cavalry's bivouac and slanted in to the north shore opposite the Rosebud's mouth where Gibbon's much-marched command waited. Terry ordered Gibbon's column to move up-stream as soon as possible to a point across from the mouth of the Bighorn. Before nightfall, the command was under way.

Gibbon, himself, came aboard the *Far West* which then dropped down and tied up beside Custer's bivouac on the south bank. The commander of the 7th Cavalry immediately boarded the craft and retired into her cabin with his superiors. While they talked there, a thunder-storm followed by a shower of hailstones pelted the camps on either shore, broke the sultry heat and set a cool wind blowing.

They sat at a table with a map spread thereon and evolved their

* *Boots and Saddles.*

battle plan—Gibbon, with the lines of imminent illness upon his face; Terry whose kindly tired eyes looked with sympathy on the eager figure of the younger man with the red stubble fogging his jaw line. Triumph in the campaign meant much to Custer, and Terry felt toward his subordinate the fondness benefactors more often experience than beneficiaries.

Together, the trio evolved strategy to bring about annihilation of the hostile Sioux. The three seem to have been in accord. In all the welter of lies and distortions that has covered the facts of the subsequent week, none charges disagreement or even demurral in the cabin of the *Far West* that afternoon. Yet something strange happened there. Some spiritual blow was dealt Custer, who entered expectant and emerged profoundly depressed.

This was the military problem Terry, Gibbon and Custer sought to solve: Reno had found the trail of a big village, four hundred lodges at least, in the valley of the Rosebud. He had found that it turned west toward the divide and believed that it crossed over the Wolf Mountains into the valley of the Little Bighorn. This is a shorter branch of the Bighorn River that joins it from the southeast, thirty-odd miles from the main stream's mouth.

Some of Gibbon's Crow scouts believed the Sioux had concentrated on Tullock's Creek. On June eighth, they had seen thick smoke above the valley of this stream which rises in the Wolf Mountains and flows into the Bighorn close to its mouth. On Tullock's or the Little Bighorn, Terry, Gibbon and Custer intended to catch the enemy between two fires, roll them up, destroy them. This was the plan they evolved:

Custer on the morrow, June twenty-second, would ride up the Rosebud with the entire 7th Cavalry. Gibbon's command and Terry with his infantry and Gatlings would march for the mouth of the Bighorn where the *Far West* would ferry it across. Custer would come down the Little Bighorn Valley from the south. Gibbon would march into it from the north, and what was caught between the advancing columns would be crushed. The two commands would meet in the valley on Monday, June twenty-sixth.

Terry asked Custer how far he would march each day and the

other replied about thirty miles at the start. Then, the General pointed out, if Custer followed the trail found by Reno, he would get to the Little Bighorn Valley ahead of the slower moving infantry of Gibbon. It would be better for Custer to go farther up the valley of the Rosebud—Terry measured the map with dividers as he spoke—perhaps even to the headwaters of the Tongue which curl like a westward-reaching hook beyond the source of the Rosebud, before moving over into the Little Bighorn Valley. That extra marching would give Terry and Gibbon time to get into position before the 7th Cavalry came storming down from the south.

It was a clumsy and precariously balanced plan. Custer's later military error of dividing his force in the presence of a superior enemy has its precedent here. The maneuver reflects small credit on the combined efforts of three veteran generals, yet so it was framed, apparently, without dissent among its framers.

So it was set forth in the much contested, much dissected, much analyzed instructions issued by Terry for Custer just before he marched, June twenty-second. That indefinitely phrased document has had its every word tested, its each comma and period examined, all its sentences twisted and stretched in a fifty-odd-year-old controversy that promises to be immortal.

CHAPTER TEN

LAST PARADE

THE conference in the *Far West's* cabin ended. Chair legs scraped as the three men rose and the light speech and laughter which succeeds the settlement of heavy problems followed. Then a lithe red man in buckskins clapped his wide hat upon his close-cropped golden head and walked down the gangplank of the stern-wheeler toward his death.

Under the subsequent magnification of tragedy, each trivial event has become a portent. Each inconsequence of the succeeding four days has furnished fuel for controversy's fires. Perhaps no hours in American history have been inspected more closely than the last in the life of George Armstrong Custer.

Each recorded instant therein has been turned inside out by those who search for a secret where, actually, there is none. Insignificances have been inflated by prejudice and partizanship. Happenings have been rooted up wholesale and reassembled with unscrupulous inaccuracy to serve the purposes of Custerphobe and Custerphile. Wherever reticence has left the record empty, lies have sprouted and still flourish, to exalt or to defame that buckskin-clad figure who went down the gangplank of the *Far West* the afternoon of June 21, 1876, with the long light of sunset upon him and Terry's plan of campaign or some more cryptic weight burdening his spirit.

Custer had boarded the boat, elated and excited. He went ashore irritable and contagiously apprehensive. No man can say what wrought the change which his officers remarked. If the self-confidence that had buoyed his wild spirit all his days had gone now,

316

it does not seem to have been either Terry or Gibbon who had kidnaped it. They went far beyond judicial fairness to insure the success of the expedition up the Rosebud.

Gibbon, despite the march that was ahead of his own command, turned over to Custer the best guides he had. Mitch Bouyer, the only man completely familiar with the wild country south of the Yellowstone, was to go with the 7th Cavalry. Six of Gibbon's Crow scouts would accompany him as supplementary guides. Since Terry wished Custer to search the headwaters of Tullock's Creek for Indian signs, Gibbon also surrendered another man who knew that part of the land well—George B. Herendeen, a civilian. When Custer had complied with his superior's order, Herendeen was to ride down Tullock's Creek with dispatches and meet Terry at the tributary's mouth.

All favor was shown the man for whom heretofore the prospect of pursuit and battle had been strong liquor, yet when the trumpet blew officers' call in the bivouac of the 7th Cavalry, those who responded were astonished by the transformation in their chief.

They gathered about his tent beside the Yellowstone on whose swift currents lay sunset light. Some who listened to the nervous voice rattle through orders for the morrow were clad in buckskin like their chief. Others wore blue, bleached by the sun, dulled by the dust of the long march. None of Custer's men had ever heard him speak so dismally on the eve of campaign.

First of all, he abolished the division of the regiment into two six-troop "wings" heretofore commanded by Reno and Benteen. Hereafter all troop commanders were to report directly to Custer. This order left Reno wholly without command.

The twelve mules assigned to each troop were to carry a fifteen-day ration of hardtack, coffee and sugar, a twelve-day ration of bacon. The twelve strongest pack animals in the command were to transport twenty-four thousand rounds of reserve ammunition. Each trooper was to carry one hundred carbine, eighteen pistol cartridges and twelve pounds of oats. Extra forage must also be borne on the pack-mules.

A dubious murmur ran through the group who listened with

attention and the beginnings of wonder in the twilight. Some troop commanders demurred. Reno's mules already were spent from their recent scout. If the animals were too heavily laden, they would break down. Custer snarled at the objectors almost as though he were washing his hands of the whole matter:

"Well, gentlemen, you may carry what supplies you please. You will be held responsible for your companies. The extra forage was only a suggestion, but this fact bear in mind: We will follow the trail for fifteen days unless we catch them before that time expires, no matter how far it takes us from our base of supplies. We may not see the supply steamer again."*

He wheeled about, still singularly agitated, and flung over his shoulder as he entered his tent:

"You had better carry along an extra supply of salt. We may have to live on horsemeat before we get through."

The group before the tent dispersed, bewildered, downcast, muttering. Where was the familiar glee of Custer on the eve of battle? What had happened to him? Godfrey, who was of that conference, wrote later:

> "Some of the officers made their wills; others gave verbal instructions as to the disposition of personal property and distribution of mementoes. They seemed to have a presentiment of their fate."†

Others, less affected by the strange gloom in the bivouac, or else determined to shake it off, foregathered that night on the *Far West*, Tom Custer, Calhoun and Keogh among them, and played poker with Grant Marsh and Lieutenant Crowell of the 6th Infantry until dawn. In his tent, the Glory-Hunter wrote to his wife.

About the 7th's camp-fires and on the *Far West*, men discussed the plan of campaign and some, like Major Brisbin of the 2nd Cavalry, who deemed Custer "an insufferable ass" and "a wild man," predicted disaster.

---

* Godfrey, General E. S.: "Custer's Last Battle," *Century Magazine*, January, 1892.
† *Ibid.*

There was grumbling too in Gibbon's column at the favoritism displayed to the 7th Cavalry, and Lieutenant Bradley recorded in his diary that the assignment of Bouyer to Custer "leaves us wholly without a guide while Custer has one of the very best in the country. Surely he is being afforded every facility to make a successful pursuit."

That night, conversations heavily weighted with doom took place on the *Far West* where Brisbin, the officious and truculent, sought Terry in his cabin and urged that the four troops of the 2nd Cavalry be joined to the 7th and that Terry go in command of the combined column.

The General shook his head.

"Custer," he said, "is smarting under a rebuke of the President and wants an independent command and I wish to give him a chance to do something."

Brisbin persisted and Terry said at length, sharply: "You do not seem to have confidence in Custer."

"None in the world," Brisbin replied. "I have no use for him."

Terry hesitated and said at last: "Well, speak to him anyway about going with him if you like and see what he says."

"And if," Brisbin persisted, "he thinks well of it and the columns are united, you will go in command of both?"

"Yes," Terry nodded. "I will."

Brisbin found Custer on the foredeck of the *Far West* that evening and made his offer to which Custer replied briskly, shaking his head: "The 7th can handle anything it meets."

Similar refusal met Lieutenant Low's eager plea that part or all of his Gatling battery be permitted to accompany Custer's command.

That night a northwest wind blew clouds over the stars and ranged through the bivouac so that men shivered in their sleep. It was still blowing at dawn when the trumpets sang and Tom Custer, Calhoun and Keogh, red-eyed and impoverished, stumbled down the *Far West's* gangplank, leaving in Crowell's hands sundry I. O. U.'s.

Gray clouds hid the sun that morning of June twenty-second.

The 7th Cavalry made ready for the march. It was to travel light. No tents were to be taken. The tumult by the river bank, shouting of men, trampling of horses and braying of mules, the clash and dull glitter of weapons, fired Boston Custer and his cousin, Armstrong Reed, who were to be left on the *Far West* until their warrior brothers returned.

Thought of returning from the frontier without having been actual eye-witnesses to the destruction of the Sioux suddenly became unendurable. They stole ashore and sought the 7th's commander. He was pleased by their spirit and took them along. Ignoring Sherman's admonition, he also included Mark Kellogg in the column. It would be well to have a newspaper bard to sing the glory of the impending victory. Kellogg could play for the public those brighter fanfares that the exigencies of military dispatches prohibited.

Terry's orderly dodged through the tumult of the 7th's bivouac and delivered to Custer written instructions for the maneuver. This was the famous, eternally debated document. To any one not too wholly committed to hair-splitting, its purpose is plain. It may have been Brisbin's candidly expressed dislike and distrust of Custer that inspired Terry to record at the expedition's outset its scope and purpose. The General's loyalty to and sympathy for his subordinate may have influenced the form of the missive, which is more like the letter of a placating and admiring intimate than a military document. It read:

> "Colonel:
> "The brigadier general commanding directs that as soon as your regiment can be made ready for the march, you proceed up the Rosebud in pursuit of the Indians, whose trail was discovered by Major Reno a few days hence."

Then, as though to apologize for opening bruskness or to soothe and extol the man who owed his inclusion in the expedition to Terry, the General pursued:

"It is, of course, impossible to give you any definite instructions in regard to this movement; and were it not impossible to do so, the department commander places too much confidence in your zeal, energy and ability to wish to impose upon you precise orders which might hamper your action when nearly in contact with the enemy. He will, however, indicate to you his own views of what your action should be, and he desires that you should conform to them unless you shall see sufficient reason for departing from them."

Terry remembers that, but for the fiasco in Washington, Custer himself might be writing such instructions to a subordinate. Terry has ridden the high-strung creature with a loose-reined indulgence that Stanley never would have approved. So he still guides him now, and even the most important part of the letter is cast in the tentative tone of one addressing an equal.

"He thinks that you should proceed up the Rosebud until you ascertain definitely the direction in which the trail above spoken of leads. Should it be found (as it appears almost certain that it will be found) to turn toward the Little Horn, he thinks that you should still proceed southward, perhaps as far as the headwaters of the Tongue and then turn towards the Little Horn, feeling constantly, however, to your left, so as to preclude the possibility of the escape of the Indians to the south or southeast by passing around your left flank. The column of Colonel Gibbon is now in motion for the mouth of the Big Horn. As soon as it reaches that point, it will cross the Yellowstone and move up at least as far as the forks of the Big and Little Horns. Of course its future movements must be controlled by circumstances as they arise, but it is hoped that the Indians, if upon the Little Horn, may be so nearly inclosed by the two columns that their escape will be impossible."

Hereafter, the instructions become more peremptory as though at last the soldier supplanted the friend. The final paragraph of the courteous and tactful instructions reads briskly:

"The Department Commander desires that on your way up the Rosebud you should thoroughly examine the upper part of Tullock's Creek, and that you should endeavor to send a scout through to Colonel Gibbon's column with information of the result of your examination. The lower part of the creek will be examined by a detachment from Colonel Gibbon's command. The supply steamer will be pushed up the Big Horn as far as the forks if the river is found to be navigable for that distance and the Department Commander, who will accompany the column of Colonel Gibbon, desires you to report to him there not later than the expiration of the time for which your troops are rationed, unless in the meantime you receive further orders."

It is certain that Custer read his instructions at once, for at eleven o'clock, an hour before his regiment marched, he wrote to his wife a final letter in which he transcribed the General's tribute to his "zeal, energy and ability." Self-praise is the last surviving work of Custer's indefatigable pen. At twelve o'clock, the 7th Cavalry moved out.

Whatever military pomp the wilderness could muster attended the command's departure. Terry and his staff, Gibbon and Brisbin disembarked from the *Far West* and rode up-stream to a little eminence beyond the bivouac. The raw northwest wind still blew across a gray sky. It whistled in the sage about the reviewing party and sent dark droves of ripples hurrying over the Yellowstone. The waiting horsemen could not see the camp but beyond the concealing fold of the land they heard the gust-broken voices of trumpets sounding "boots and saddles," and presently up from the hollow Custer came galloping.

Cook, the gigantic side-whiskered adjutant, accompanied him and close behind pounded an orderly bearing a wind-tormented flag, the swallow-tailed banner, red and blue, with crossed silver sabers that had been Custer's personal emblem since first he had led the Michigan Brigade.

The Glory-Hunter, buckskin clad, his red-bearded face elated, reined in beside his superiors. His plunging horse had thrown care

"Now, Custer!" calls Gibbon in jest or out of his knowledge of the man. "Don't be greedy! Wait for us!" "No," the buckskin-clad horseman calls back cryptically, "I won't."

off the cantle. Custer hailed his associates and matched jests with them for a moment before a rising chorus of trumpets checked speech and made all men turn.

The 7th Cavalry was coming up the valley with massed trumpeters in advance. Forked star-and-stripe guidons were uneasy specks of color above the dark river of horsemen, and low dust blew away beneath trampling hoofs. The head of the column vanished in a hollow, emerged magnified, and behind it, marching fours flowed interminably down the farther slope.

Custer's men were on the move once more, riding from the glamour of the past into legend. Their chief smiled proudly as the splendid regiment drew near. The red-faced trumpeters swung out of line, and, still sounding their hosannahs, halted beside the reviewing party to play the regiment through.

Young Charley Varnum, chief of scouts, leads his followers past—the swarthy Bouyer in half-Indian garb; Reynolds with his felon-infected right hand in a sling; Herendeen, the courier who is there to carry back Custer's tidings to Terry; the bearded Fred Girard, the grinning black Isaiah Boardman, interpreters; Mark Kellogg, the correspondent, astride a mule; Bloody Knife and the twenty-four Arikara scouts, sullen men with loose black hair blowing beneath bandeaus of cloth or buckskin; the tall merry Crows lent by Gibbon—Goes Ahead, White Man Runs Him, Curly, Half Yellow Face, White Swan, Hairy Moccasin. These pass above the low blowing dust and behind them like the clangor of the bugles made flesh, with jangling arms and squeaking leather, moves the rippling blue and yellow mass of the regiment.

Dry brown men who remember Washita, sunburned recruits whose saddle soreness is still an acute memory, faces that grin, faces that frown in the shadows of the slouch hats' brims—these, and the chargers' tossing heads that sweep past, four by four; these and the flickering guidons and the beat of carbines against the burdened saddles; these, and the mincing mules whose packs even now are slipping askew, all are to be part of their leader's fame. Past him and Terry and Gibbon they ride to become eternal satellites to the glory, heart-stirring as the shouting trumpets, of George Armstrong Custer. Terry takes the salutes of officers riding at the head of their troops and calls to each a kindly word of farewell.

The last fours swing past. The last rebellious mule is shepherded along. The trumpeters hush their clamor and fall in behind as the column moves up the ridge whose farther slope leads into the Rosebud Valley. Custer smiles at the compliments of Terry and Gibbon, clasps hands with them and wheels to follow the regiment whose boasted power is enough to abolish all Indians on the plains. Gibbon, in jest or out of his knowledge of the man, calls after him:

"Now, Custer! Don't be greedy! Wait for us!"

The buckskin clad horseman raises a hand in acknowledgment.

"No," he calls back cryptically, "I won't," and gallops off. Under the gray sky, the cold wind sings through the sage as Terry, Gibbon and the rest ride back to the *Far West.*

CHAPTER ELEVEN

PRELUDE TO SLAUGHTER

HE WAS committed to the flood. George Armstrong Custer rode over the ridge his regiment had crossed and down to the rising tide of ordained calamity, which was to be the agent, but not the author, of his death.

The twelve troops, with their lagging mules, splashed through a ford near the mouth of the Rosebud, a clear, pebbly-bottomed, slightly alkaline stream, and marched up its far bank. Above, the clouds split and showed blue sky. Sunlight, blazing through, turned the dust of the march to gold. Men, who repacked the burdens that slipped from mules or prodded the lagging creatures onward, sweated while they swore.

For eight miles, the valley was broad. Thereafter, for the additional four they marched that day, bluffs shouldered in on either hand. They bivouacked in timber at the foot of a rocky height. Grass was plentiful and there were many fish in the stream. Men found, when camp had been made, that the strange mood which had oppressed their leader the day before, the gloom which the excitement of departure had banished, now had returned and again possessed him.

The valley was roofed by sunset when a trumpet stuttered officers' call. The regiment's sole major, its captains and lieutenants, assembled about their leader's camp-bed and those who in the past had been fired by, and those who had mocked at, Custer's flaring elation when a trail led toward battle, were depressed by his dismal air even before he spoke officially.

"It was not," Godfrey recalls, "a cheerful assemblage."

Nor was it the headlong, sublimely self-confident Custer of old who talked to his subordinates in a singularly placating tone. Custer spoke of his reliance on his officers—he who heretofore had felt the need of dependence on no one. The sad voice professed trust in their judgment, discretion and loyalty.

It recited instructions for the marches ahead—no further trumpet calls, "boots and saddles" at five A. M., each troop commander to be responsible for the welfare of his command in all things except the start and the camping place on each day's journey. These were to be ordered by Custer himself. The pack-mules attached to each troop hereafter were to be herded together in the column's rear under command of Lieutenant E. C. Mathey.

Thereafter, with a puzzling air of self-justification, Custer explained to his astounded officers, who never had been informed of reasons for his acts, why he had refused the offer of Brisbin's Squadron of the 2nd Cavalry. Godfrey's report of that confidence reveals his chief's blindness to logic.

Custer told the uneasy circle about him that he expected to meet not more than fifteen hundred Indians. He believed that the 7th Cavalry alone could defeat these. If they could not, there was no regiment in the service that could. Wherefore, the addition of a squadron under Brisbin—equal in strength to at least a third of Custer's present force—could not affect the issue. Furthermore, the inclusion of four troops of the 2nd would be certain to mar the harmony of the 7th and cause jealousy. It was for the same shaky reason that he had refused the offer of Low's Gatlings.

After this strange baring of a normally reticent spirit, the plaintive voice revealed a startling purpose. Godfrey reports it thus:

"Troop officers were cautioned to husband their rations and the strength of their mules and horses, as we might be out for a great deal longer time than that for which we were rationed, as he intended to follow the trail until we could get the Indians, even if it took us to the Indian agencies on the Missouri River or in Nebraska."*

---

* Godfrey, General E. S.: "Custer's Last Battle," *Century Magazine*, January, 1892.

The council ended on the identical note of appeal that had launched it. Custer begged his officers to bring him either then or later, whatever suggestions they might have for expediting the march. Dazedly, the men rose and walked away. Lieutenant Wallace strode beside Godfrey and at length broke the silence.

"Godfrey," said Wallace, "I believe General Custer is going to be killed. I have never heard him talk in that way before."*

Stars appeared in the crooked strip of sky above the valley. The voice of the river grew as sleep settled over the bivouac and darkness intensified the mental gloom of those still awake. Red men, as well as white, were subject to the oppressive dread. About their camp-fire, Bouyer, the half-breed Sioux, Half Yellow Face, the Crow, and Bloody Knife conversed in sign talk. As Godfrey passed, Bouyer checked him with apprehensive questions. The guide heard without conviction the soldier's boast that the 7th Cavalry could whip the Sioux.

"Well," he shrugged. "I can tell you we're going to have a God-damned big fight."

Stars swung above the sleeping regiment; above the *Far West,* tied for the night a few hours' run up-stream from the Rosebud's mouth; above the bivouac of Gibbon's column, en route for the Bighorn. Reveille did not sound in the 7th Cavalry's camp on the morning of June twenty-third. At three o'clock, the horse guards shook the troopers from their slumbers.

Sunlight slanted through smoke of spent camp-fires when the column moved at five A. M. Already a screen of scouts—Arikaras, Crows and whites—had gone forward under Varnum. Custer led the regiment out. The reorganized pack-train was massed at the column's tail and Benteen's H Troop brought up the rear. Mules strayed and straggled and lost their packs.

Encroaching bluffs blocked the regiment's advance. In the first three miles, the column forded the Rosebud five times. Then, on the right, the valley widened. Five miles farther along the timber-dotted level bank Custer found the trail he sought.

---

* *Ibid.*

There were many circles of packed earth where lodges had stood. Bent brush showed where wickiups—temporary shelters—had been fashioned. Grazing ponies had "clipped the grass, almost like a lawn mower" and beyond the litter of the camp, a broad trail ran up-stream churned by hoofs, raked by dragging lodge poles.

Scouts gathered about Custer. He shook his head and turning to Lieutenant Varnum, said:

"Here's where Reno made the mistake of his life. He had six troops of cavalry and rations enough for a number of days. He'd have made a name for himself if he'd pushed on after them."*

The hunt was up. The buckskin-clad horseman pushed forward and behind him the mounting metallic roar told of the cavalry's quickened pace. Five miles they hurried and then were forced to halt and wait for the pack-train to catch up. When the mules at last rejoined the column, it pushed on, forded the Rosebud, rode fifteen miles up the left bank, crossed the stream again and camped in the old wreckage of Indian travel on the right shore. On either side the stream, hills rolled back, lightly timbered, scored by deep ravines. There was scant grazing that night for horses that had done thirty-three miles.

Fires were extinguished after supper. Men slept soddenly beneath the sparkling sky. This arched above the Gibbon column, in bivouac on the Yellowstone's north bank opposite the Bighorn's mouth; above the *Far West,* tied up farther down-stream. The stern-wheeler came abreast of Gibbon's command on the morning of June twenty-fourth shortly after the 7th Cavalry had resumed its march.

At daybreak, Crow scouts had reported to Custer that the trail ahead was broader and fresher. In the face of these tidings he could not bear to match his pace to the deliberation of the mule-hampered column. He took two troops and rode far in advance. Almost every loop of the river now was stamped with the circles of vanished lodges. Broken branches and pony droppings and the ashes of fires told him how swiftly he was overhauling the quarry.

---

* Coughlan, Colonel T. M.: *The Life of Colonel Charles A. Varnum.* MSS.

Custer and his escort passed the lashed sapling framework of a dance lodge and a brown withered object swung therefrom in the wind. Crows identified it as a white man's scalp, probably of a 2nd Cavalry trooper killed in a brush with the Sioux during Gibbon's march down the Yellowstone. Crows also reported that over the ridge to the right lay the headwaters of Tullock's Creek and that they had seen what looked like smoke signals down its valley.

At noon, Custer halted and when his regiment rejoined him, ordered coffee made. Varnum and the scouts had ridden on ahead. While the column rested on the Rosebud's right bank, Custer summoned his officers. They gathered where his headquarters flag, staff thrust in the earth, whipped in the steady blast of a south wind, and again at this conference something was wrong. It may have been the nervousness of their leader; it may have been prescience of impending disaster. Whatever its source, many of the officers were in the jumpy state of mind that is receptive to ill omen.

They heard their commander's tidings. The trail was freshening hourly. Custer believed the smoke reported from the Tullock's Valley to be only mist. When scouts in the advance sent back word, the regiment would move on, but with increased caution. Each troop would take a separate course so as to diminish the dust of the march.

The officers were dismissed. As Godfrey started to leave, the wind blew over Custer's headquarters flag. It fell toward the rear. Godfrey recovered and replanted it. It fell toward the rear. He picked it up and dug its staff into the earth, supporting it against a sage-brush. It stood now but some of those who had marked its double fall saw an augury of defeat.

At four, scouts returned and reported to Custer. He led his regiment forward and again they forded the Rosebud. The stream's left bank was ridged by the passage of unnumbered lodge poles. Hourly, the wide trail of the Sioux grew heavier and fresher. The regiment camped at seven-forty-five below a bluff. It had marched twenty-six miles. Fires were small and soon extinguished. Horses

were not unsaddled. Mules retained their packs. The whisper ran
through the bivouac that scouts still were following the trail, which
had left the river's edge and now inclined westward. If it crossed
the divide into the valley of the Little Bighorn, so rumor muttered,
the regiment would march that night. Meanwhile, weary men
rolled up in their blankets and caught what sleep they could. At
the mouth of Tullock's Creek, forty-five miles distant in a bee line,
Terry camped with the men of Gibbon's column.

Gibbon himself lay on the *Far West* while the boat worked her
way up the Bighorn. He had been stricken with intestinal colic
and did not rejoin his command until June twenty-sixth.

A company of infantry and a Gatling had been left on the Yellowstone's north bank to guard the command's surplus stores. The
rest of the infantry, Brisbin's Squadron of the 2nd Cavalry and two
Gatlings had been ferried across the stream and had marched up
the Bighorn to the Tullock's mouth.

Earlier in the day, twelve of the bravest of Gibbon's Crows had
been sent to scout up Tullock's Creek. They had gone ten miles,
seen a wounded buffalo and had stampeded back. They were afraid
of the Sioux.

In Custer's camp men slept and horses and mules had grazed.
Beyond the wide scar of the Indian trail, grass was abundant, for
the Sioux had not tarried here. At nine that night the scouts returned. Reno's earlier report had been correct. The trail ran over
the divide into the valley of the Little Bighorn.

Circumstance deals Custer one more thrust. It had small subsequent part in the development of the tragedy. His own hands, his
own headstrong, headlong spirit contrived it. Yet fate intervenes
here, as accessory.

The trail he has followed has been made, so his scouts have told
him, by four hundred lodges. There have been wickiups too. In
all, perhaps fifteen hundred warriors have crossed the Wolf Mountains into the Little Bighorn Valley. This is the estimate Custer
has given his officers. It is probably accurate. But these fifteen
hundred warriors are only a fraction of the host assembled on the
Little Bighorn. A portion, and only a portion, of the greatest

mobilization of Indian might this continent ever saw had met Crook on the upper reaches of the Rosebud June seventeenth and had beaten him back. The Indians whom Custer followed had taken no part in that fight. They were additional reenforcements to the hostiles, but the man who followed them had no knowledge of this.

Circumstance or the luck whose darling Custer had been, turns against him now as his scouts report and he sends his orderlies to wake and summon his officers. He does not know that Crook has been defeated. He is rashly certain that the Sioux he follows are all his regiment will have to face. This is fate's part in his destruction.

Officers, roused by the questing orderlies, stumbled through windrows of slumbering men and toward the bright speck in the gloom that was a candle on Custer's table. The conference was brief.

Custer told his blinking and disheveled subordinates the course of the trail and his intention of getting as close to the top of the divide as possible before daybreak, there to hide and attack on the twenty-sixth. He ordered them to be ready to march at eleven-thirty. Varnum with Reynolds, Bouyer, the Crows and some Arikaras had been sent to a peak overlooking the farther valley. Lieutenant Hare of Troop K was detailed to command the remaining scouts.

The officers returned to their troops. Gradually, as the hour for the march approached, the valley filled with clamor. Soldiers, freshly wakened, found their mounts and sought their places in the column by a universal and noisy game of blind man's buff. Mules brayed and horses whinnied. Officers bawled for strayed members of their troops and these shouted back. The clatter of arms and equipment, the tumult of voices filled the black valley with confused and doleful sound.

They were to march at eleven-thirty. They did not get under way till after midnight. The reassembling of the regiment took time. There was renewed difficulty with the mules and it was an interminable job for Mathey and Keogh, who had the rear-guard, to collect the beasts and start them forward. At last Custer, with Fred Girard, interpreter, and Half Yellow Face, the Crow, moved out at the head of his command.

Girard was of the many who warned his chief of the Indian might. While they waited for the column to get under way, Custer asked the interpreter how many hostiles they were likely to meet. Girard told him at least twenty-five hundred but the estimate was offered to a man apparently deaf.

Once the regiment marched, the clamor and the confusion multiplied. The column's actual course is not certain, but the best evidence indicates that it strove to follow the valley of Davis Creek, a tributary of the Rosebud, up to the divide. The sky was clouded and darkness was curdled further by the mounting dust. No man could see the rider ahead of him. The blind column proceeded chiefly by scent and hearing. Men who no longer breathed dust knew that they had strayed from the line of march. Some troopers beat their tin cups against their saddles to aid those who followed. There was shouting and much heartfelt swearing and now and then an explosive rattle and thumping as a horse fell. Any Indian in a range of several miles and not stone deaf must have heard that uproarious advance.

At length, even Custer perceived the vanity of further tumultuous groping. Scouts assured him he could not possibly reach the ridge before daybreak and word was passed back, halting the disrupted column which had marched ten miles. Dawn found its scattered elements in the valley of the dwindling stream. Its water was so bitter with alkali that horses and mules would not drink it. Coffee made therefrom scored men's throats.

Dawn also found Varnum and his men asleep at the foot of a rocky pinnacle on the ridge's crest that red men called the Crow's Nest. As the dim mass took form against the paling sky, Hairy Moccasin, the smallest and most alert of the Crows, left his slumbering companions and climbed to its top. Varnum was wakened by his voice and saw the Indian stamped against gray heaven.

The Lieutenant and the others swarmed up the peak. On either hand, earth fell away in fir-dappled slopes of gray rock. Far down

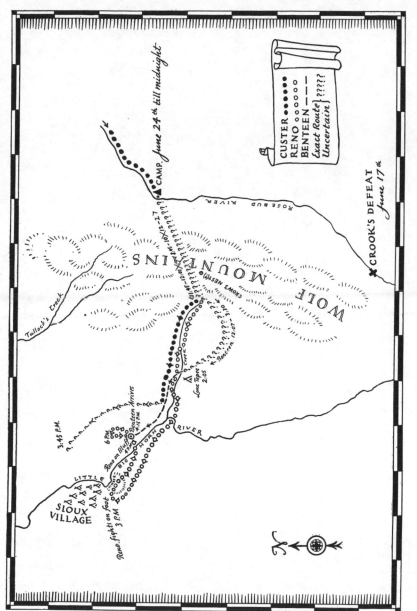

The Little Bighorn Battlefield

(After Col. W. A. Graham)

the eastern slant, the smoke of the 7th Cavalry's fires crept up across a watery daybreak and the Crows snarled. Did Custer think, they asked, that the Sioux were blind?

To the west, the land went down in broken steps to a wide valley where night still dwelt. They watched one another's faces grow sharper in the quickening light. They saw the timber-shielded Little Bighorn snaking its way across the plain. Then, one by one, the Indians exclaimed and stared to the north.

The morning mist seemed thicker and darker there and beneath it was the sense rather than the sight of movement, a confused wide-spread stirring. The Crows jabbered in awed voices and Reynolds said mildly: "That's the biggest pony herd any man ever saw."

"Biggest village," Bouyer amended. "A heap too big."

Light grew stronger. The sun was coming up behind gray clouds. Varnum's strained eyes were bleared by seventy hours' scouting with scant sleep.

"Look for worms," Bouyer advised him, for the movement of the vast and distant pony herd was like the pulsating and twitching of tangled angleworms. Still Varnum saw nothing, but the excitement of those about him left no room for doubt. He scribbled a hasty note to Custer and sent it down-hill by an Arikara.

The regiment, when the messenger reached it shortly before eight A. M., still rested in the valley where it had made its fires. Custer, on receiving Varnum's note, leaped bareback on his horse and rode through his command shouting to his officers to be ready to march at eight o'clock. When he returned to the column's head, Bloody Knife approached him, face glowering with earnestness.

There were too many Sioux yonder, Custer's favorite scout told his chief. It would take days to kill them all. The Glory-Hunter laughed. The imminence of an enemy had restored his pre-battle elation.

"Oh," he retorted tolerantly, "I guess we'll get through them in one day," and swinging into the saddle, gave the order for the advance.

For two hours and a half, the regiment crawled up the hostile slope, gray rock below, gray sky above. Clouds still hid the sun's brilliance but not its heat. The air grew sultry so that the upward scrambling men and horses sweltered under an ash white sky. The regiment marched ten miles and then, a mile or so from the ridge's summit, hid in a ravine at Custer's order while he himself rode ahead to the Crow's Nest.

Varnum and his scouts still kept vigil there. Custer listened skeptically to their report of a colossal village to northward and with scarcely more credulity to the tale of Sioux who had been seen, scouting along ridges above the cavalry's advance. He stared into distance that swam in plum-colored haze and shook his head; clapped field-glasses to his eyes and looked long again. Despite the insistence of the Indians, despite the efforts of Reynolds and Bouyer to help him see, Custer rasped at last:

"I've been on the plains a good many years. My eyesight is as good as yours. I can't see anything that looks like Indian ponies."

Bouyer blurted: "If you don't find more Indians in that valley than you ever saw before, you can hang me."

"All right, all right, all right," Custer rattled with a short laugh. "It would do a damned lot of good to hang you, wouldn't it?"*

In the distance hung the blue haze of lodge smoke. Dim beneath its veil crawled the enormous pony herd. Custer left the lookout, still insisting that he saw no sign of Indians; that he believed none were there. The waiting regiment had gained meanwhile more definite evidence of the presence of the Sioux.

Sergeant Curtis of Troop F had lost clothing from his saddle roll on the march up-hill. While the regiment sweated in the ravine, waiting its chief's return, Curtis obtained permission from Captain Yates to ride back in search of the missing raiment. Presently, he came galloping to report to Yates that he had found, not what he sought, but a breadbox, dropped from one of the mules. About the box had been Indians, Sioux, who had fled at his approach.

Yates told Keogh who informed Cook, the adjutant, who, when Custer returned to the hiding regiment, informed his chief.

---

* Coughlan manuscript.

That morning of June twenty-fifth, Terry lingered on Tullock's Creek, expecting Custer's courier. He marched three and a third miles up the valley in hope of meeting him and sent Lieutenant Bradley and fifteen mounted infantry still farther. The Crows would not go. They feared the Sioux.

Chapter Twelve

CRESCENDO

FROM the concealing ravine on the eastern slope of the Wolf Mountains, where weary men drowsed and thirsty horses stood with drooping heads, a trumpet spoke. That brazen voice, silent for sixty hours past, tore through the sultry air, bounced echoing from the gray cliffs. It shouted officers' call, and those who had not already gathered about Custer scrambled up the ravine's side and joined him.

It was then about eleven-thirty on the morning of June twenty-fifth.

Men who had marched all the day before and most of the night were too weary for many questions; too spent perhaps to see the paradox in their leader's orders. Despite the insistence and the warnings of his scouts, Custer did not believe there were Indians in the Valley of the Little Bighorn. Since scouts and Sergeant Curtis had seen the Sioux, it would be useless to hide here any longer. The regiment would move at once toward a foe in whose existence its commander disbelieved. Each troop would march as it made ready. Benteen's men were the first to lurch up out of the ravine.

The others followed. Behind them, Mathey with seven soldiers from each troop and five or six civilian packers herded along the one hundred and sixty mules of the train. McDougall's B Troop, forty-five strong, brought up the rear.

The cloudy sky burned white before the vertical sun. Heat soaked into dusty men and sweating horses as the reformed column toiled up to the divide and went over its ridge. Five hundred and ninety-odd soldiers, plus scouts, interpreters and packers, rode down beneath a pillar of dust to the Little Bighorn.

They caught, as they crossed the summit, glimpses of an olive green valley, fifteen miles away. They marked where, to the north, heat haze was tinged with blue and wondered dully at Custer's skepticism. That surely was smoke. It was now seven minutes past twelve P. M. and the trail they followed went down-hill.

There was ground for further wonder immediately thereafter. Custer spoke to Benteen whose troop was foremost in the column. The white-haired Captain turned in his saddle, bawled an order and swung left oblique out of the line of march, moving toward a line of bluffs four miles away with Troops H, D and K—his own, Weir's and Godfrey's.

Reno, still without command, unconsulted by Custer and aggrieved, flung a question at Benteen as he passed.

"Going to those hills to drive everything before me," the Captain replied dryly and led his squadron onward. The Major had scant time to brood over this new evidence of neglect, for Cook, Custer's adjutant, rode up to him and announced:

"The General directs that you take specific command of Companies M, A and G."

"Is that all?" Reno asked as the Adjutant turned and Cook flung assent over his shoulder.

The Chief Trumpeter galloped away on the course Benteen had taken and, overhauling him, delivered additional directions from Custer. If no Indians were found on the first line of bluffs, the Captain should proceed to another farther line.

The column, meanwhile, scraped and slithered down the irregular folds of the mountainside. It followed still the Indian trail that bordered the course of a little stream, called Sundance then and later renamed Reno Creek. The Major had assumed command of Moylan's, McIntosh's and French's troops. He led them along the left bank of the watercourse. Custer, with his brother's Troop C, Smith's E, Yates's F, Keogh's I and Calhoun's L, went down along the right bank. Apprehensive Arikaras and Crows under Varnum and Hare moved before the twin columns. With Custer rode his brother Boston, his young nephew and namesake, Armstrong Reed, and Mark Kellogg, the correspondent.

Benteen was out of sight now, but Custer turned and spoke to Sergeant-Major W. W. Sharrow who trotted off, to bear to the senior Captain further elaboration of the original orders. If neither line of bluffs yielded Indians, Benteen was to move into the valley beyond and if this proved barren into the valley beyond that.

Meanwhile, in columns of twos, Custer's five troops and Reno's three rode toward the Little Bighorn. The sunless heat weighed down the men. Dust plastered the flanks and barrels of reeking horses. Ridges on either hand had closed in upon the command so that, as they descended, they caught no further sight of the valley. Stunted firs were aromatic in lifeless air that shook to the dull sound of hoofs, the quarreling voices of leather and steel, the mumbling speech of tired soldiers. Already the pack-train with all supplies and reserve ammunition had lagged behind.

So they rode for eight or ten miles, dazed by fatigue, wilted by heat—Reno's one hundred and twelve, Custer's two hundred and twenty-five men—while the stream that parted them deepened and grew vocal and the sharp pitches of the ridges flattened. Rocks and dwarfed firs crept past and vanished. Bare rolling foot-hills succeeded them, curved earthen surges, olive with the browning grass of spring. Through these the stream twisted and the trail still followed it.

When they had marched ten or twelve miles, the Indian trail ran wholly along the creek's right bank. Custer signaled with his white hat for Reno to cross. The Major obeyed. His three troops followed. The two commands moved down the stream's right side, parallel and fifty yards apart. Lieutenant Wallace, who kept the column's itinerary, looked at his watch. It was two P. M.

They had seen no Indians. The nervous scouts who preceded the column on a trail now alarmingly fresh had caught no glimpse of the Sioux. Then, in the valley before them, they saw the brown lonely cone of a single lodge. Its smoke vent was empty. No dogs, no children moved about its latched door-flaps.

Arikaras approached it with increasing boldness, at last tore open its entrance. A dead warrior lay with his gear beside him, a brother of Circling Bear, Sioux chief. He had died in the fight with

Crook eight days before. As a spiteful blow against their enemies, the Arikaras set fire to the lodge.

The columns had halted. Girard, scout and interpreter, rode to a knoll. The lodge burned reluctantly with pallid flames and a towering smoke. Girard from his lookout yelled to Custer.

"Thar go yore Injuns, runnin' like devils."

Custer joined him and saw beyond the knoll some forty Sioux warriors cantering their ponies toward the river and yelping derision. He shouted for the Arikaras to follow them. They glowered and refused, nor could his scornful suggestion that they turn in their weapons and go home shake them free from terror.

There were at least some Indians in this valley despite the scoffing of Custer. He had seen them. His eager voice stiffened aching spines and tightened faces that had sagged with weariness. The twin column lunged forward at a trot, at a gallop. Side by side they roared down the valley, and Cook, veering from Custer's side, ranged his horse alongside Reno's. Orders jolted from him:

"The Indians," Cook shouted, long black whiskers streaming, "are about two and a half miles ahead and on the jump. Follow them as fast as you can and charge them and we will support you."

Reno galloped on with the Adjutant and Keogh who had followed on his charger, Comanche. Custer slackened pace so that the distance between the Major's column and his increased. It was then two-fifteen P. M.

The Indian trail the 7th had followed for days crossed to the left bank of the creek. Reno's three troops pursued it. A hill thrust in between them and Custer's command, blocking further views of the laggards. Ahead were trees and the glitter of moving water. Above foliage, a great dust-cloud rose in the northwest.

Cook and Keogh accompanied Reno's command to the river. Girard rode to another knoll that gave him clear view downstream. There was delay at the ford. The horses waded into the Little Bighorn's flow and thrust parched muzzles deep. They would not cross until they had drunk. The Arikara scouts were unwilling to cross at all. They listened sullenly to Varnum's exhortations and some of them vanished.

Gradually Reno got his command to the farther bank. Cook and Keogh shouted, "Good luck," and turned to rejoin Custer. Girard rode down from the knoll. He had seen the source of the great dust. Beneath it were Indians, many Indians, rushing upstream along the river's left bank. The scout hailed Cook and told of his discovery.

Cook replied: "All right. I'll go and report."

The Adjutant rode back to Custer. On the stream's far bank, Reno was forming. Varnum, half frantic, shouted to Girard that the Arikaras refused to go farther. In their own tongue, Girard lashed them and a dozen crossed the river with him, Varnum and Hare, Reynolds, Boardman, the negro, and other scouts.

Bellowing officers subdued confusion on the Little Bighorn's left bank. Troopers guided their dripping mounts into place. The command solidified. Reno took his place at its head and gathered in his charger's rein. Nervous horses reared. The Major called:

"Take your time. There are enough ahead for all of us."

Before him rolled a plain, bordered on the left by shelving higher ground, on the right by timber-shielded loops of the river. Farther to the right, across the stream, were brown cliffs, ravine scored, and above their broken perpendiculars, treeless hills went back toward the gray, fir stippled ridges of the Wolf Mountains.

Ahead of the Major for two miles, the plain ran drab, undulant and empty. Then a peninsula of timber, thrust out to the left from the river bank, cut off more distant view and above the leafy barrier, the dust-cloud towered. Reno looked at the ranked column behind him. Beyond it, the ford was empty. No brilliant figure in buckskin led five troops into support. The Major turned to Trooper McIlargy, his striker, and bade him ride to Custer with news that the Indians were coming in force. Then, rising in his stirrups, he shouted his orders:

"Left into line. Guide center. Gallop."

The column woke. Fours shifted and wove. The line spread out across the valley and moved forward. Presently when through dust behind him, the Major still could see no sign of support, he sent

Trooper Mitchell, a cook, back with further, more urgent message to Custer.

Neither McIlargy nor Mitchell ever was seen again. They were killed in passage or else they died on the heights with Custer.

The Glory-Hunter had not followed Reno to the ford. He had led his men at a trot on the Major's trail. Then, for reasons no man may ever know, Custer had swung sharply to the right and had ridden up into the brown hills to the north. The men of Keogh and Smith, Yates, Calhoun and Tom Custer had followed him down-stream above the bluffs that walled the Little Bighorn's right bank; down-stream behind the flutter of the familiar blue and red pennant; down-stream, away from Reno and into a nation's Valhalla.

Across the river in the valley below, Girard thought he glimpsed Yates's gray horse troop, riding hard along the ridges, and Lieutenant De Rudio insisted that later Custer had appeared on a height above the plain and had waved his hat.

Meanwhile, Reno went down the valley before his line and looked often over his shoulder for the promised support. Behind him galloped Moylan's Troop A and French's M, strung out across the plain with Varnum's scouts and reluctant Indians on the left against the higher ground. In the rear McIntosh's Troop G rode in reserve.

The squadron swung around the peninsula of timber that obscured the lower valley. Before them, as though earth were ablaze, the dust-cloud smoked to heaven. Above the roar of the advance, men could hear from that bilious murk high voices—Sioux voices—screeching like souls in torment, and where the dust thinned, momentarily, horsemen moved and feathers were slivers of light in the haze.

Out of that prototype of later smoke-screens, Indians darted, screaming, to fire and vanish. Up from before the charging line, sprang a Cadmean crop of warriors. Ahead of the troopers, a ravine split the plain. It was full of Sioux. And the valley behind Reno was empty of support.

Facing the half-hidden host before him, one hundred and twelve troopers seemed dauntingly few to Reno. He had not even the dubious aid of his Indian allies now. At the first whoop of the Sioux, all these save Bloody Knife and one or two more had vanished, leaving Varnum and Hare to hold the left flank with a handful of scouts. G Troop was thrown into line to fill that gap.

Reno marked the ravine ahead. Military training, or more human caution, told him the Sioux who advanced only to retreat were not afraid. They were luring him into ambuscade. He flung up his hand and dragged on his charger's rein.

"Halt," Reno shouted before his charge had struck a single enemy, or his troopers had fired a shot. "Halt! Prepare to fight on foot."

There was a moment of plunging confusion. At least one unhappy recruit was carried on by his bolting mount into the shrill obscurity ahead, to return no more. The horse-holders, veterans all, each galloped four steeds back into the shelter of the timber. The thin line of footmen wavered and shrank from the crackle of bullets overhead, the sibilant flight of arrows. Then it steadied and began earnestly to bang away at yelping horsemen who swooped and wheeled like swallows in the yellow gloom.

The line plodded forward a hundred yards. A breath of air lifted the dust-screen an instant and men saw a host of horsemen and beyond them unnumbered lodges. The line advanced no farther. It knelt or lay and shot as rapidly as it might into the cloud ahead that hid no man knew what enormity. Sergeant Hynes of Troop A was dead. One or two more had been hit. The Sioux wheeled and came closer, blazing away at the troopers who replied quickly and blindly. The accuracy of both reds and whites was deplorable. The rapid fire heated the troopers' Springfields and cartridges jammed in the breeches. Men had to cut out the empty shells before they could shoot again.

Word came from the timber that Sioux were massing on the stream's far bank, that Sioux were crossing to get at the horses. Reno withdrew G Troop from the firing line and sent it back to protect the animals. Still, there was no sign of Custer and through the Major's mind may have crept the recollection of the scandalous regimental legend concerning another Major of the 7th Cavalry, Elliot by name.

Others were conscious of Custer's betrayal of his promise. Wallace, who had heard Cook's orders to Reno and who had remained on the firing line when McIntosh, his commander, had withdrawn his troop to the timber, bawled to Captain Moylan that some one ought to be sent to hurry up support. Both officers pled with Billy Jackson, a half-breed scout. He shook his head and waved to the rear.

"No one," he shouted, "could get through that."

There were Sioux behind as well as before the line now and more were sweeping around the weak left flank or pouring down from the heights on the left. The troopers were being surrounded on the open plain. There still was equivocal safety in the timber. The line went back to the shelter of brush and the few large trees.

Here was confusion. Officers lost their commands in the thickets. Horses plunged. Sioux bullets slashed through foliage or smacked against solid wood. Mounted Indians swarmed about the timbered peninsula, firing and screaming in high fierce voices. Others on foot worked up from the river and set the wood on fire.

Reno's ammunition was growing low, thanks to recruits who fired more for the comfort of the sound than for marksmanship. The Sioux were filtering through a line too thin to defend the entire grove. The defense bent backward from the river side of the wood. The Indians crawled forward. Dust billowed in from the plain, where screeching Sioux circled. The tangle of brush and cottonwoods filled with a brawling, fearful sound—panicky banging of guns, white shouting and savage screeching, screams of horses and the harsh rip of bullets through foliage. One hundred-odd men were surrounded by thrice their number and more Indians continually were arriving from the village. It was now about three-thirty P. M. Where was the promised support? Where was Custer?

History can not see him. Glory, for whom he rode northward through the hills, is mute. Even the route over which he led two hundred and twenty-five men to death is in dispute. All men ever will know surely of that last red hour is contained in the brief recitals of two who saw only its dawn—Daniel A. Kanipe, of Carolina, sergeant in Tom Custer's Troop C, and Trumpeter John Martin, born Giovanni Martini and a Garibaldi veteran, who had been detailed from Benteen's Troop H, to serve as orderly to the Regiment's commander.

When Custer turned toward the hills, two ways were open to him. Beyond the first ridge that crowned the bluffs above the Little Bighorn, a shallow valley runs northward. Beyond a second ridge to the east of this valley, is another ravine, and many hold it was along this that the five troops rode. Since men with Reno believed they saw Custer and portions of his command on the heights and since, furthermore, he twice rode to a promontory to survey the valley below, it is probable that he led his men along the westerly ravine. They rode at a gallop. The pace was so hard that some of the weary horses gave out. The riders of two of these later joined Reno.

Somewhere, early in that rush northward, the troopers caught a glimpse of the dust-enveloped Little Bighorn. Kanipe says they cheered at the sight and Custer cried: "Hold your horses, boys. There's plenty down there for all of us."

The rounded hills cut off their view. They galloped farther. In a breathing space, Tom Custer called Kanipe, who, long after, remembered his instructions thus:

"Go to Captain McDougall. Tell him to bring the pack train straight across country. If any packs come loose, cut them and come on quick. A big Indian village. If you see Captain Benteen, tell him to come quick. A big Indian village."*

Kanipe swung his horse out of line and spurred it back. The column launched into a gallop again. At its head, the Glory-Hunter rode. Behind his bright sorrel, Vic, pounded the horse of his orderly, Trumpeter Martin. Here is the testimony of the last white survivor to see George Armstrong Custer alive:

"There was a big bend on the hill; he turned these hills

---

* Kanipe, Daniel A.: *A New Story of Custer's Last Battle*, Contributions of the Historical Society of Montana.

and went on top of the ridge. All at once, we looked on the bottom and saw the Indian village. At the same time we could only see children and dogs and ponies—no Indians at all. General Custer appeared to be glad and supposed the Indians were asleep in their tepees. We could not see the timber because it was under the hill—nor anything of Reno's column. I rode about two yards from General Custer.

"After he saw the village he pulled off his hat and gave a cheer and said: 'Courage, boys, we will get them and as soon as we get them, then we will go back to our station.'

"We went more to the right from the ridge and down to a ravine that led to the river. At the time General Custer passed the high place on the ridge, or a little below it, he told his adjutant to send an order back to Captain Benteen. I don't know what it was. Then the Adjutant called me—I was right at the rear of the General—and said, 'Orderly, I want you to take this dispatch to Captain Benteen and go as fast as you can.'"

Martin, the second messenger, rides back along the trail Kanipe already has taken. Behind him Custer and the five troops vanish, with pounding hoofs and the roar of equipment, in a dust-cloud that is the forerunner of eternal glory.

From the ridge Custer has looked down upon a myriad brown cones of lodges, stippling for more than three miles the Little Bighorn's western bank. He has seen the earlier warnings of his scouts made manifest. He who had scoffed at these discovers they had been underestimates. This is the village whose existence he has doubted and it is incredibly vast.

A year later, General Hugh L. Scott, then a lieutenant in the 7th Cavalry, came to the Little Bighorn Valley on the expedition sent to rebury the dead. Scott counted along the stream the sites of eighteen hundred lodges and never completed his tally. There were many wickiups as well. Men have estimated the strength of the host that broke the 7th Cavalry at all the way from twelve hundred and fifty to eight thousand warriors. Scott's count proves that there must have been at least four thousand and against them

Custer rode with a total force of less than six hundred troopers.

At first sight of that village, he should have read omen in its sinister quiet. He knew Indians too well to believe that at midday they were sleeping, as Martin reports. The trumpeter's English was faulty. Custer probably said that he had "caught the enemy napping." Elation rather than alarm seems to have possessed him, yet he sent at once to recall Benteen and the note Cook scribbled and Martin bore has the disjointed haste of panic. It read:

> "Benteen, come on—big village—be quick—bring packs.
> W. W. Cook.
> "P. S. Bring pacs."

With that frantic message, the history of George Armstrong Custer ends. In the blank that intervenes before men found his stripped body, unnumbered theories flourish.

In the river bottom, Reno with three troops strives to hold back a rising red tide.

Miles away to the southeast, Benteen with three troops. is growing weary of a "wild-goose chase" that reveals only more and more broken land and no Indians.

Miles up the trail from the divide, Mathey and eighty men struggle with the lagging pack-train.

Behind this, McDougall and his troop fume.

Martin sees the dust smoke up as Custer leads his two hundred and twenty-five down toward the Valley of the Little Bighorn. The rest of his last pursuit of Glory is hidden from men.

Chapter Thirteen

DIES IRAE

One more adherent rides hard to join George Armstrong Custer in death. A mile or so back along the trail, Martin, his last messenger, encounters Boston Custer. Earlier in the day the young man's horse had failed him and he had returned to the pack-train for another. He flings a question at Martin who grins and points the way. Boston spurs his mount along the endless road his brothers and cousin, Reed, and brother-in-law, Calhoun, already have taken.

Benteen had grown tired of "valley hunting." His choleric mouth grew ever tighter about the stem of his pipe. Lieutenant Gibson of his troop and six skirmishers preceded his column. Part of the time, the Captain rode ahead even of them. There had been no Indians beyond the first line of bluffs, or the second, and continually the country grew rougher, pushing him out of his original line of march toward the down-hill trail Reno and Custer had followed.

Benteen at last gave up the hunt, technically disobeying his commander's orders, and definitely turned back to rejoin Custer. The column came out of the badlands where Sundance Creek spread a marshy pool beside the trail Custer and Reno had traveled about two hours earlier. It halted there to water suffering horses. These had marched some thirty miles in fifteen hours without a drink. It was now three-thirty P. M.

As Benteen's command moved off from the pool, the first mules of the pack-train came charging down-hill, attendant troopers cursing horribly, and plunged into the water. Benteen moved on, passing the smoldering tepee that Custer's scouts had fired. Kanipe came riding. He grinned as the troopers cheered, shouted that the

347

Indians were "on the run" and after reporting to Benteen, went on to the pack-train.

Two miles from the ford where Reno crossed, Trumpeter Martin approached, spurring a weary horse. Indians had fired on him and a bullet had wounded his mount. He had not known this till Benteen pointed it out. The Captain read Cook's message. Martin smiled confidently in response to his questions:

"Eenjuns," he reported, "eesa skedaddling."

Benteen scribbled a note to McDougall and sent Martin on up the trail, showed Cook's message to Captain Weir whose troop was in advance, and then went down toward the river at a smart trot. The valley was filled with smoke and dust and the squadron heard the far popping of gun-fire. An Indian came up from the ford, driving captured ponies ahead of him. It was Half Yellow Face, the Crow, who, when Benteen bawled a question about the soldiers, pointed toward a bluff on the column's right.

Meanwhile dust and smoke had darkened the grove where Reno's three troops were besieged. The banging of Springfields had a panicky sound. There was the lilt of imminent triumph in the Indians' yells. No responsive, reassuring cheer echoed the shouts of beleaguered officers and men. No trumpet split the tumult to signal approach of Custer's promised support. No trumpet proclaimed to the scattered troops Reno's determination to leave the timber. The Major gave the order which some heard and some did not.

Those who obeyed led their horses into a clear space in the grove's center and mounted there. As the column was forming Sioux fired pointblank from a thicket. A trooper of M screamed, "O God, I've got it!" and pitched from his horse. Bloody Knife, the valiant Arikara, was at Reno's side. The Major heard the thwack of the bullet that split his skull. Reno launched his "charge" from the timber.

He left his dead and wounded. A dozen troopers and Lieutenant De Rudio of Troop A, Herendeen, Reynolds and other scouts were deserted in the grove. At the head of Troop A in column of fours, with part of G following and M in the rear, Reno rode out and made for the ford by which he had crossed.

The plain swarmed with Indians, "thick as trees in an orchard," who gave way, wolf fashion, before the column's head, and, wolf-like, ranged along its right flank to pull down the weak and laggard. Painted bodies burned dimly in the dust. The haze shook with shrill yelling and the uneven roar of gun-fire. Sioux laid their rifles across their ponies' withers and pumped lead into the fleeing column. Sioux watched until men had emptied their revolvers, then closing in, shot or stabbed them. Lieutenant Donald McIntosh of Troop G, the half-breed Indian, was killed close to the timber. Lonesome Charley Reynolds died therein and those who later found his headless body counted sixty empty cartridges about it. Isaiah Boardman, the negro interpreter, was slain there too.

More and more Sioux ranged along the column's right flank as though the desperate troopers were buffalo. The catlike ponies leaped in toward soldiers whose guns were empty, the screaming riders slipped from sight behind their mounts when cavalrymen aimed at them.

Varnum, aghast at the mounting panic of the retreat, ran his horse to the head of Troop A, shouting:

"For God's sake, boys, don't run. Don't let them whip us."

A voice replied sharply: "I am in command here, sir!"*

It was Reno's. He rode in the forefront of the retreat.

The head of the column kept fair order, but the rear frayed and was increasingly lashed by terror. The pressure of the Sioux forced the command away from the ford by which it had entered the valley. The war yell soared higher, Indian guns blazed as Troop A swung to the left and led by the Major, who had lost his hat, went over a five-foot bank into the belly-deep water of the Little Bighorn.

The stream at this point was some twenty-five feet wide, and running full. The farther bank was eight feet high with a fissure therein whereby active horsemen might scramble up. Above, the bluff rose steeply, with narrow ravines scoring its high brown wall. There were Indians on the heights firing down at the troopers.

---

* Coughlan manuscript.

There were ever more Indians on the west bank, shooting into their backs.

No effort was made to guard the ford, or to control the order in which terrified troopers plunged their mounts into the river. The breadth of water became a stew of thrashing horses, screaming men, foam and the small brief fountains struck by bullets. The fugitives could ascend the far bank only one by one. The stream was jammed with fear-roweled cavalry fighting for that single passage, while from the rear the Sioux poured in their fire. Many died here.

Doctor De Wolf, assistant surgeon, reached the far bank and there was killed. Lieutenant Benny Hodgson, Reno's adjutant and a favorite in the regiment, was wounded as he reached the west shore. He caught the stirrup of a trooper and was towed across, only to be shot through the head as he reached the east bank.

Spurring and lashing their horses, the survivors rode them up the ravine with ungainly rabbit-like jumps. On the plateau above, the breathless, hatless Major strove to reorganize the remaining half of his command. Men saw Benteen's three troops come riding toward them through the hills. It was now about four-thirty.

Reno, a handkerchief bound about his head, was firing his revolver at Indians far out of range when Benteen's column joined the remnants of his own. Varnum, wild with grief at the death of his friend Hodgson, was blazing away, equally vainly, with a carbine.

If the Sioux had followed, they might have rolled up over the Major and Benteen as well, but the gun-fire from the valley slackened and died, save for occasional snipers' shots. The horsemen began a quick movement down the valley.

Benteen, the grimly efficient, shared his troops' cartridges with Reno's survivors and organized the defense. A semicircle of higher peaks blocked view of the village and whatever down-stream event summoned the victorious Sioux. On the hill, nerve-shattered men cursed the name of Custer. Lieutenant Hare on Godfrey's horse rode back to the pack-train to hurry it in and to bring back with him ammunition mules.

CUSTER'S LAST STAND
June 25, 1876; 4 P.M.
Photo of a group by Dwight Franklin

Down-stream, to the north, men heard the brawl of guns. Not all those on the hill heard volleys, though to De Rudio and others, still trapped in the timber and saved later by the withdrawal of the Indians, the concerted blasts were plain. The firing rolled away to the north, and Captain Weir of Troop D muttered to his lieutenant, Edgerly, that Reno ought to move to the support of Custer.

Edgerly assented and Weir asked whether, if Reno permitted, the Lieutenant would follow his Captain toward Custer with Troop D. Edgerly agreed and when Weir, without authorization, rode out alone over the hills toward the north, Edgerly, presuming permission had been granted, led Troop D after its commander.

They reached a height from which they could look down the valley and saw the lodges standing along the stream and the unbelievably wide and slowly shifting carpet of the pony herd. On a hill three miles away, Indians swarmed like disturbed ants. There was no sign of Custer. It was now close to five P. M.

Hare had brought in two ammunition mules, with a trooper guiding each by the bridle and another behind, lashing the stubborn brute along. McDougall's troop, Mathey and the rest of the train, arrived about five o'clock. So few Indians remained that Herendeen and eleven troopers abandoned in the timber were able to rejoin the command.

The reorganized column moved out in the direction Weir had taken, slowly and with difficulty for there were wounded and each of these had to be borne in a horse blanket by four men. At about six P. M. when the command reached the promontory where D Troop lingered, the Indians had completed the mission that had called them down-stream and were returning.

The column fell back toward its original position with French's A and Weir's D covering the retreat. The impatient Weir here learned the power of the Sioux. These came on so fast and in such numbers that the covering force turned into fugitives. Troops A and D went back like hunted rabbits. Godfrey's Troop K, dismounted, checked the pursuit and then retired. What remained of the 7th Cavalry stood at bay.

Benteen took charge of the defense, routing out skulkers, thrusting the troopers into line, barking orders with magnificent self-possession.

"Wallace," he shouted. "Form your troop here."

"Troop?" Wallace panted, grinning shakily, "I've got just three men."

"Very good. Form your three men here."

From higher ridges and peaks, that ringed the plateau where the soldiers lay, guns began to talk. The reports quickened, then blurred into a steady daunting roar. Bullets blew sand about the troopers and killed or wounded men and horses. The storm of lead continued while the sun went down, a red lacquer disk slipping through a rift in the cloud. The firing ebbed with dusk and ceased with darkness.

All night long, while the besieged fortified their position, a witches' sabbath endured in the valley. Great fires blazed and there rose wild yelling, the wailing minors of Indian song and the flat rhythm of many drums. There were trumpet calls, too, sounded in derision by some gifted Sioux, on an instrument taken from Custer's command. Troopers believed that their leader was returning or that Crook was riding to their rescue. It was a night of dread and of blasted hope, worse than terror. No one seems to have thought of going down to the river for the water they were to need so sorely on the morrow.

Some of the beleaguered were so utterly weary that they slumbered. Edgerly, waking, encountered Major Reno in the darkness and remembered how the unhappy man exclaimed: "Great God, I don't see how you can sleep!"

Up through the Bighorn Valley, Terry was marching that night of June twenty-fifth. The *Far West* was moving up-stream with Gibbon, still ill, on board. Terry had led the column across country from the valley of Tullock's Creek. His attempt at a short-cut had been disastrous. The command had become entangled in terrific badlands. Terry's Crows were frightened and more useless with every mile. There were no white guides with the column. Herendeen was with Reno's besieged command and Bouyer, who knew this country like the palm of his hand, lay dead with Custer.

The infantry halted at length, completely spent. Terry pressed on with his cavalry. He had promised Custer, Terry told his staff, that he would be at the foot of the Little Bighorn Valley on June twenty-sixth.

They rode through blackness, intensified by rain. In the crooked country, Low's Gatlings got lost and were found again and the cavalry at last was stalled on a bluff above the Bighorn, from which they were guided to camp on the shore by Little Face, one of the less timorous Crows. Terry's men barely had gone to sleep when the day began for Reno's.

The seven remaining troops of the 7th Cavalry had had scant slumber. Through the hours of darkness, they had entrenched desperately, digging rifle-pits with the three spades in the command, with knives and tin cups; piling dead animals and the packs into redoubts. The horses and mules had been taken with the wounded into a hollow on the plateau. The line the troops established was horseshoe shape, with the open end toward the bluff. The ridges commanded it. When those to eastward grew sharp against a faintly paling sky, the first Indian rifle heralded dawn.

All that morning, while showers came and went, a lead storm beat upon the position. The troopers saw few Indians but a horde waited in the valley for place on the firing-line, and within carbine range hundreds invisible screeched and yelped and wreathed the peaks with the smoke of a steady fusillade that battered against barricades and frail earthworks; that killed mules and horses and hit not a few men crouched behind inadequate protections. Reno lost sixteen killed and forty-odd wounded on that hill.

Throughout the deadly blizzard, it was Benteen who best kept head and heart. It was he who by direct action and by prompting his Major, controlled the defense. The Indians crept close to his side of the horseshoe. Benteen insisted that Reno lend him French's troop from the other side of the defense and led H and M in a charge that drove back the Sioux. White-haired, erect, imperturbable, he was immune to bullets and fear.

"Captain, sorr," Sergeant Mike Madden objected, "ye tell us to keep down. It's yourself should keep down. They'll git ye."

"Oh, pshaw," Benteen grinned. "They can't hit me."

Madden later was wounded and lost a leg. It was Benteen who gave the order for a charge that Reno led to clear the other side of the horseshoe of an inward creeping enemy.

At ten that morning, the firing abated, dwindling into occasional sniping through which hardy souls stole down to the river, dived under fire across a little beach and obtained precious water for the wounded. Thereafter, the gusts of bullets came fitfully like a failing storm. There was another heavy outburst at two, with many flights of arrows, but this faded, and after three there was no firing at all. Grimed and haggard men, who long had looked at death, now stared without belief at life's incredible fairness.

Below them the valley filled with smoke. The Indians had fired the grass. At seven that evening, the handful on the hill beheld the awesome passage of the military might of the Sioux. Through the shifting smoke-screen, the Indian host moved up-stream in an enormous compact column, three miles in length, almost a mile in breadth. They marched with the deliberation of the retreating grizzly. The massed dark horsemen passed and vanished, followed by thin cheering from the survivors of the regiment that, alone, could whip all hostiles on the plains.

That noon, June twenty-sixth, Terry, the convalescent Gibbon, the cavalry and guns, reached the Valley of the Little Bighorn and waited impatiently for the infantry to catch up. Bradley and the scouts had talked that morning to three Crows, Hairy Moccasin, Goes Ahead and White Man Runs Him, who had called across the bank-full Bighorn to the disbelieving troops that Custer and all his men were dead. Thereafter all Indians still remaining with the Terry-Gibbon column had deserted.

When the infantry joined him, Terry moved ahead. It was Bradley, scouting in advance, who marked how the Sioux gathered in the distance to contest farther passage. Toward dark, the column bivouacked in hollow square. Two white scouts, Bostwick and Muggins Taylor, who had been sent to establish contact with Custer, returned angrily swearing that the country was "stiff with

Sioux." In Terry's camp, the General and some others felt dread at which the rest of the officers scoffed. Nothing, the skeptical insisted, could happen to Custer, the eternally fortunate.

On the morrow, the Sioux were gone. Toward noon, Bradley and his scouts found on a hill, east of the Little Bighorn and opposite the northern end of the vanished village, the stripped bodies of many men.

Custer lay toward the northern end of a ridge whose slope went down to the river. He had fallen, not at the summit but a little way below it, and down the slope and along the ridge to the south were scattered the fragments of the command that had been burst apart and abolished by the power of the Sioux.

Some thirty men, including his brother, his nephew and most of his officers, had died close to Custer. Many of them were stripped. A few were mutilated. He himself had been shot in the left side and temple. With his dead about him he lay as, eight years earlier, the young and eager Major Elliot had lain, center of a ring of slain, on the frosty grass above the Washita.

The wounds that had killed George Armstrong Custer, Lieutenant-Colonel, 7th Cavalry, Brevet Major-General, United States of America, were not apparent. Among the blasted bodies that still bore impress of the fury which had passed over them, his was unmarred by agony or terror. He who found it wrote:

"His expression was rather that of a man who had fallen asleep and enjoyed peaceful dreams."

George Armstrong Custer well may have lain content. Glory, sought all his stormy life, was his at last and forever.

CHAPTER FOURTEEN

POST MORTEM

THE battle of the Little Bighorn was at once the most intimate and enigmatic of conflicts. Its leader won by defeat and death a legend-hallowed immortality, far more radiant than the fame complete victory could have gained. Its tragedy and its mystery still hold the minds of men.

Half the battle is clear and half is dark; half is vocal and half mute. The reports of Reno and Benteen; the testimony offered at the Major's 1879 court martial, which the unhappy man demanded to clear his name; the published and unpublished recollections of those who survived the fight in the river bottom and on the hill speak with informative, if sometimes contradictory, garrulity. There was no white eye-witness to the destruction of Custer and his five troops.

Indians who exterminated them have told their stories, fantastic or factual, through the mouths of usually illiterate interpreters to frequently unscrupulous writers. Little that is sure can be rescued from that confusion, yet two things on which red witnesses agree destroy some of the pinchbeck drama that has been built about George Armstrong Custer's death.

It was over quickly. In one furious hour at most, all his command was abolished. The Indians did not know it was Custer whom they fought. Most of them believed the soldiers were Crook's, returning from earlier defeat.

The rest is only the voiceless testimony of naked bodies, strewn on that hillside above the Little Bighorn, and the subsequent clamor of theorists and partizans.

Reno sent Wallace to meet Terry's advancing column. From the

General the Lieutenant learned of Custer's destruction. Soiled scarecrows on the stinking, lead-sown hill cheered hoarsely as Wallace led Terry toward them. Some of them wept and the General himself was crying as he dismounted. When the wounded had been borne down into the fire-blackened valley, men turned to the wreckage cast along a brown slope by the fury of the Sioux.

The haste that followed furnished additional fuel for later contention. Those who gathered up Custer's dead were hurried and apprehensive soldiers. The Sioux had withdrawn, but they might return. Already, they had defeated a heavier force than Terry's and had half destroyed "the best cavalry regiment in the service." Dread made men deaf to the demands of history. Much that then might have been established definitely has been lost forever.

No one now knows the exact course taken by Custer in his march across from the Rosebud. No one can be sure which of the Wolf Mountains' peaks was called the Crow's Nest. The floods of more than a half-century have shifted the course of the Little Bighorn itself. Soldiers who retrieved Custer's dead failed to determine, that hot June twenty-seventh, the exact route whereby five troops rode to their death.

Some historians say that Custer led his command northward behind the first ridge east of the river; others believe he followed the ravine to the east of the second ridge. Some hold that he rode thereafter down a valley to a shallows in the river known as the Middle Ford. Others deny this. No one knows.

Sole survivor of the slaughter whom the soldiers recovered was Comanche, charger of Captain Keogh. He had been left on the field, too grievously wounded for the Sioux to take. He recovered and for the rest of his days appeared, saddled but unridden, with the regiment on parade.

Officers who viewed the hill where Custer fell, read the story stripped and battered corpses told and sought no further. These, by their positions, testified to ambuscade and headlong rout. Custer, who knew so well the military virtue of the surprise attack was destroyed by his own favorite strategy.

From the positions of his dead, soldiers believed the Sioux had leaped upon him suddenly and in terrific force. The first charge apparently had come from the southwest. It had whirled the troopers northeastward up the slope toward its L-shaped ridge. Many died before they reached the height and only Keogh and Calhoun were able to form their commands for defense. They perished with their men on the ridge's southern end. The dead of these two troops lay in fairly regular order along the foot of the L. From there to its top, where Custer and the rest of his officers died—save Lieutenants Sturgis, Harrington and Porter whose bodies never were identified—there was no sign of organization. The red charge caught and killed men as they ran or stamped them out when they turned at bay.

"There was no line on the battle-field," Benteen told the Reno court martial. "You can take a handful of corn and scatter it over a floor and make just such lines."

The testimony of Lieutenant Wallace and others confirms this.

The brilliant and daring leader of cavalry, the Murat of the American Army, was caught off balance and abolished by dash and skill and power greater than his. It is probable that when Trumpeter Martin saw Custer look down upon the village and heard him exclaim at its apparent emptiness, the trap already had been laid. It is strange that one who knew Indians saw nothing sinister in the spectacle of those quiet and manless lodges.

Knowledge ends here and surmise succeeds it to rationalize, if possible, how came it that Custer who had promised to support Reno's attack on the village's up-stream end, died on a hill some five miles down-stream from where the Major crossed to attack.

Custer, while he still followed Reno's course, may have heard from Girard via Adjutant Cook that the Indians were pouring out to meet the Major. The Lieutenant-Colonel may have determined to strike the Sioux on their left flank while Reno assailed them from the front. It may have been for this purpose that he rode away to the north. He had no detailed map. One finds, as one follows to-day the general route of the five troops down-stream, that bluffs on the Little Bighorn's right bar horsemen from the river. On June 25, 1876, this discovery may have come belatedly

MAJOR MARCUS A. RENO
From the collection of E. A. Brininstool

to Custer, forcing him to hurry farther and farther north, seeking a crossing and finding extinction.

The positions of the dead preclude any possibility of long or stubborn resistance. Custer's half of the battle must have begun while Reno was at bay in the timber or earlier. It must have ended before the pack-train joined the Major on the hill.

The public demanded a living scapegoat and Reno was chosen for the rôle. Persistent slander in which Custer's first biographer, Frederick Whittaker, led the way, impelled the miserable man at last to demand a court martial. This sat in Chicago and its verdict cleared Reno. It did not halt the vilification. The Major drank himself out of the army in 1880 and died six years later in hospital at Washington, D. C. To this day, men quarrel over whether he was hero or scoundrel.

If he were coward, the court did not think so, nor did the troopers he led in battle. A week after Terry found them, still holding their hill, every enlisted man surviving in the 7th Cavalry, two hundred and thirty-six of them, signed a petition to the President and Congress, imploring that Reno be advanced to Custer's rank and that Benteen be promoted to Major. Noncoms and privates are not usually so devoted to men they have found craven.

Reno had none of Custer's flair and brilliance. He was a careful, a perhaps unduly excitable officer. These qualities caused him to check his charge down the valley before he had had a man slain. His subsequent orders breathe none of the hot gallantry of the forlorn hope, but they saved a portion of his regiment from extinction. Perhaps Lieutenant De Rudio's two-edged epigram is a shabbily tragic figure's most accurate epitaph:

"If we had not been commanded by a coward, we would all have been killed."

In the days immediately following the battle, Reno and Benteen were deemed the heroes of the defense. Sherman, General of the army, wrote on August 5, 1876, of "The judicious and skillful conduct of Major Reno and Captain Benteen." The petition signed by the 7th Cavalry's survivors emphasizes this. The findings of the court martial confirm it.

Reno's herohood endured while the dead hastily were buried and the wounded were carried down-stream and placed aboard Grant Marsh's *Far West*. It began to crumble when published tidings of the battle shook the nation.

Circumstance, which has rarely more wholly controlled battle or its aftermath, twisted and thwarted even the news of the tragedy. On June twenty-seventh, Terry wrote a dispatch for publication and sent it by Muggins Taylor, the scout, to Fort Ellis. When Taylor reached the fort, the wires were down. Meanwhile Marsh, with his cargo of wounded, had set the blunt bows of the *Far West* down-stream. He bore a confidential report from Terry to Sheridan which was to be filed at Bismarck.

The rivers were high and Marsh, straining the *Far West's* boilers, got to Bismarck before the dispatch Taylor bore reached a telegraph station. Sheridan and Sherman, who were in Philadelphia, read Terry's confidential message. Sherman gave it to a man whom he believed to be a telegraph messenger and bade him relay it to the War Department. This individual was a masquerading reporter and Terry's report which was designed only for his superiors' eyes, was made public before the message he had framed for popular consumption reached the East. His apparently contradictory versions of the tragedy laid the foundation for controversy. The anguish of the bereaved, ripening into wrath, intensified it.

The widows and orphans at Fort Abraham Lincoln were first of the outside world to learn of the disaster. A black-swathed steamer brought the tidings. Marsh, in conformity with the sentimentality of his day, had draped the upper works of his craft in crape obtained at Fort Buford. White-faced women flocked to the sable boat and met a blow that darkened their lives. She who was to devote the rest of hers to adornment of her husband's memory wrote:

"This battle wrecked the lives of twenty-six women at Fort Lincoln and orphaned children of officers and soldiers joined their cry to that of their bereaved mothers. From that time,

life went out of the hearts of the 'women who weep' and God
asked them to walk on alone and in shadow.''*

In June of 1877, the new Troop I, 7th Cavalry, whose forerunner
had perished entire with Keogh, returned to the Little Bighorn
battle-field as escort to Colonel Michael V. Sheridan, the General's
brother. To him was assigned the task of reburying the hurriedly
interred dead and bearing the slain officers East for reburial.

All these were exhumed save the body of Lieutenant Crittenden
whose parents wished it to rest where their son had fallen. The
other subordinates now lie in Fort Leavenworth's cemetery, far
from the field of their death, far from the man who led them
thither. The body of George Armstrong Custer was buried, October, 1877, at West Point.

Elizabeth Bacon Custer's fifty-odd years of glorification have en-
shrined her husband in the folk-lore of America. She proclaimed
him hero and, since she was his widow, men who thought otherwise
held their peace. She outlived them all.

Custer became a hero and because the fiction-craving American
mind demanded a villain for the drama, Major Reno arbitrarily
was cast for this part. Neither man was wholly fitted for his rôle.

Those who acknowledge destiny may discover in the career of
George Armstrong Custer a spiritual force that, meeting the obstacle of circumstance, made his end inevitable. Placed as he was
and molded as he had been, the tragedy he wrought was unavoid-
able. The deeply worn conduct grooves in which his fiery spirit ran
led inevitably to his doom. Toward it, he had taken his first steps
as a child. He died when and as he did, because, being George
Armstrong Custer, he could not do otherwise.

He was a man to whom abasement was intolerable; to whom renown was essential. In pursuit of Glory, he had lynched enemy
soldiers and inspired mutinies. The spring of 1876 had found him
in deep disgrace. He had appeared ridiculously before the Clymer

---
* *Boots and Saddles.*

Committee. He had incurred the animus of Grant, of Sherman. Even Sheridan had lost patience with his favorite, and Custer, the peerless Indian fighter, had been forced to weep before Terry for inclusion in the expedition he himself had planned to lead.

He had won permission to accompany the column but this was no evidence that the ire of his superiors had been assuaged. He had besmirched Grant's family with hearsay scandal. The President's wrath had been increased further by newspaper attacks that some one, perhaps Custer himself, had inspired. The man's normal yearning for Glory was intensified by need. He must have her to reburnish his fame. She must envelop him in such splendor that popular applause would still the hostility of superiors, even as Washita's triumph had wiped out memory of earlier disgrace.

That was Custer's problem when in the cabin of the *Far West* on June twenty-first, he received the orders that Terry later embodied in the much-dissected letter of instructions.

Others have examined each penstroke of this document. Defenders have insisted that it was not an order, but merely a list of suggestions. Despite such hair-splitting, there can be no doubt that Custer's superiors in that council of war regarded the plan they framed and the instructions Terry set down, as explicit, and in some aspects mandatory.

On the very day of that council, Terry wrote to Sheridan:

"Custer will go up the Rosebud tomorrow with his whole regiment and thence to the headwaters of the Little Horn, thence down the Little Horn."

Gibbon wrote to Terry later in the same year:

"Except so far as to draw profit from past experience, it is perhaps useless to speculate as to what would have been the result if your plan had been carried out."

Both superiors expected Custer to be governed by the letter. Others in Gibbon's column offer testimony confirming that expectation.

Devotees have pictured George Armstrong Custer as innocent victim of a plot in which every one from the President of the United States to his own pack-train was implicated. There is little warrant for this theory.

You must admit the existence of a wide-spread and foul conspiracy to defame a dead man, with reputable officers as conspirators, or else concede that Terry and Gibbon did not lie and that Custer disobeyed his orders, instructions, directions.

On this matter, the victim's record appears as witness against him. All his life, he had been insubordinate. His career at the Academy; his blind recklessness in the war; his dispute with Sully; his disobedience in 1867 that led to his court martial and suspension; his squabble with Stanley, his scorn of Reno for not disobeying his orders and bringing the Sioux to battle—these trace the groove in which his nature ran. It is probable that Custer marched on June twenty-second, already determined to ignore for his own ends his instructions from Terry. It is more than probable. One of his most stalwart defenders by implication asserts it.

The last sentence in Terry's letter reads peremptorily:

"The supply steamer will be pushed up the Big Horn as far as the forks, if the river is found to be navigable for that distance; and the department commander (who will accompany the column of Colonel Gibbon) desires you to report to him there not later than the expiration of the time for which your troops are rationed, unless in the meantime you received further orders."

Twenty-four hours after the conference that evolved the plan of campaign, Custer, according to General Godfrey, informed his assembled officers in their first camp on the Rosebud of his determination to defy Terry's definite order. Godfrey writes:

"Troop officers were cautioned to husband their rations and the strength of their mules and horses as we might be out for a great deal longer time than that for which we were rationed, as he intended to follow the trail until we could get the Indians, even if it took us to the Indian agencies on the Missouri River or in Nebraska."

Here is positively expressed intention of flat disobedience. Custer caps this with further insubordination. Terry has directed:

"The Department Commander desires that on your way up the Rosebud you should thoroughly examine the upper part of Tullock's Creek and that you should endeavor to send a scout through to Colonel Gibbon's column with information of the result of your examination."

George B. Herendeen was assigned to Custer's column for this specific purpose. Crow scouts reported to Custer that they saw smoke in the valley of Tullock's Creek. He made no attempt to examine that ravine but held Herendeen with the column. Colonel Varnum, chief of scouts in that campaign, says that his commander never even mentioned Tullock's Creek to him and kept the scouts on the left of the advance instead of to the right where the watercourse lay. By this act Custer flatly disobeyed, and also broke the precariously arranged time schedule of the campaign.

Terry tarried at the mouth of Tullock's Creek, June twenty-fourth and June twenty-fifth, awaiting word from Custer. He marched more than three miles up the valley and sent Lieutenant Bradley six farther in search of Herendeen. If Custer had obeyed, Terry would have reached the Little Bighorn earlier, for after his vain delay he strove to make up time by going cross country without competent guides and became tangled in badlands that held up his march. Herendeen knew that country. If Custer had sent the scout back, he could have guided Terry through.

The man who had deserted his advancing brigade at Brandy Station to chase personally after a railway train; who had deserted his regiment at Fort Wallace to go and see his wife; who had striven to throw off Stanley's command during the Yellowstone expedition, was deeply habituated to insubordination. Duty, when weighed against Glory, was—had always been—a little thing. If

Custer could reach the enemy before Terry arrived, he could win a mighty victory. He never questioned his own and his regiment's ability to whip all the Indians in creation.

When he had triumphed, Mark Kellogg, the newspaperman, would magnify his achievement. The hero in shining new journalistic armor would then be immune to the wrath of Grant. Custer needed Glory too much to share her favor with Terry and Gibbon. He was a hard-pressed egotist and a gambler. He planned to whip the Sioux alone.

That, if Ludlow is to be believed, was his intention before he joined the expedition. If Ludlow misunderstood Custer's alleged threat to cut loose from Terry and run the campaign to suit himself, it was a prophetic misunderstanding.

Doubtless, the Glory-Hunter recognized the risk of his chosen course. If he met with failure, his career as a soldier was ended. He was in disgrace already and about to betray Terry, his sole remaining benefactor. If he did not win a great victory, his insubordination might lead to another, more final court martial. He played a long shot to win, with the unscrupulous rashness of his cavalry assaults.

Once he had committed himself, the weight of his self-assumed responsibility must have borne down his spirit. Custer's officers were astonished and downcast by their leader's gloom. He, whose wife had never seen him depressed for a single hour, was steeped in strange melancholia.

There was further abnormality. The leader who was wont to keep his plans to himself explained them now in detail to his officers. He who heretofore had been vaingloriously confident of his own prowess appealed plaintively to his subordinates for loyalty and support. Part of his self-confidence had been shorne. What remained killed him.

Custer could ask his officers for their aid but he would not defer to other men's beliefs. He was infatuatedly certain that his estimate of the hostiles' strength was correct. He believed that at most he would meet fifteen hundred Indians, and held to that conviction with a doomed obstinacy.

There was no ground for that conviction. Terry did not share it.
On March twenty-fourth he had telegraphed Sheridan: "The most
trustworthy scout on the Missouri"—probably Reynolds—"recently
in the hostile camp reports not less than two thousand lodges and
that the Indians are loaded down with ammunition."

On the eve of the departure of the expedition from Fort Lincoln,
Terry wired his chief again: "It is represented they have fifteen
hundred lodges, are confident and intend making a stand." Normally there were two or three warriors to each lodge.

After the column marched, Kellogg sent similar tidings back to
the *New York Herald*. Bouyer and the Crow scouts insisted from
the outset that the Indians were too many for the 7th Cavalry to
handle. Frank Girard warned Custer, Bloody Knife warned him,
Reynolds warned him. He paid them no more heed than he had
accorded the predictions of the scouts and Osages before Washita
and continued to insist that the Indians whose trail he followed
were all he would have to meet. He never appreciated until he
looked down from the Little Bighorn bluffs on that vast, silent
village that the quarry he had pursued had been only a fraction of
the immense host gathered there.

Earlier knowledge of the Sioux strength might have made small
difference to him. The man who had charged with a single troop
at Gettysburg against Stuart's command, who had swept down on
Appomattox Station without ever determining what force was
laired in the woods behind the railroad, who had attacked at
Washita with no knowledge of Indian strength, had never respected the number of the enemy.

Custer marched up the Rosebud with a waxing preoccupation in
the trail he pursued. On the night of June twenty-fourth, he followed it out of the Rosebud Valley and up the hills toward the
Little Bighorn. Terry's letter of instruction had read: "Should
it"—the trail—"be found (as it appears almost certain that it will
be found) to turn toward the Little Horn, he"—Terry—"thinks
that you should still proceed southward, perhaps as far as the
headwaters of the Tongue, and then turn toward the Little
Horn. . . ."

On the night of the twenty-fourth, Custer deliberately disobeyed these instructions. Partizans have pled that Terry's letter in no sense was an order though the General, in that missive, spoke of it as such. They have based their contention on the phrase whereby Terry disclaims any intention to hamper his subordinate's conduct "when nearly in contact with the enemy."

Custer on the night of June twenty-fourth was at least thirty miles from the enemy, yet he turned sharply off the route Terry had prescribed.

From here on, his conduct becomes more difficult to understand. The threads of his purpose are too obscurely tangled, completely to unravel them.

One can not, by admonition, pull the hound from the quickening scent. Custer was chasing the Sioux as he had pursued the Cheyennes to Washita and in the subsequent campaign, as he had followed the Sioux on the Yellowstone. He would not, or could not, relinquish that warm and promising track. His expressed intention was to reach the summit of the divide before dawn and there hide twenty-four hours until sunrise of the twenty-sixth, the day appointed by Terry. Perhaps he himself believed that this was his purpose. It was the strategy that had served him at Washita. He also had employed it in his Yellowstone brush with the Sioux.

Something more than preoccupation on a trail may have impelled Custer to depart from his instructions. By obeying them, by marching on up the valley of the Rosebud, he ran the risk of meeting Crook. If Crazy Horse had not driven Crook back on June seventeenth, the two columns might have joined. Custer had no knowledge of this defeat. He only knew that a force under a superior officer was supposed to be in the region of the upper Rosebud. He had no wish to relinquish his independent command to the guidance of higher authority. The glory he needed could not be shared. Fear of encountering Crook may have combined with the infatuation of the chase to turn him aside.

When Custer's blindfolded march toward the divide begins, all subsequent attempt at justification of his conduct crumbles under the impact of incredible fact. His advance becomes the wild rush

of the high-strung man who, with his goal at last in sight, casts
away all save the desire to attain it. Custer throws off in that last
dash what education and training should have made instinctive.
Even his knowledge of Indian warfare is discarded.

No skilled Indian fighter would have attempted that clangorous,
turbulent, blundering advance through darkness toward an imminent savage foe whose exact position he did not know. If the band
he followed had scouts within earshot, they must have had ample
warning of his approach.

Subsequent events achieve a crescendo of fantasy. Custer rides
to the Crow's Nest. He can not see the Indian village. He dis-
believes the scouts who say it is there. Meanwhile he has neglected
the most elementary precautions to shield his advance.

He has scouts and Arikaras but he makes no attempt to screen
his force. Indians on his front peer down upon his column and
retire. Indians in the rear are discovered trying to open a breadbox dropped from a pack-mule and get away. Custer, on word of
this, decides to march to attack a village that he does not believe
is there. He makes no reconnaissance to determine the position or
strength of the enemy.

There are further incredibilities. Colonel T. M. Coughlan in his
fine tactical study, *The Battle of the Little Bighorn*, lists their as-
tounding number. Custer with less than six hundred men moves
forward against an enemy which he himself believes outnumbers
him almost three to one; which his scouts insist is far more numerous than that. Almost his first act violates a cardinal military
principal. He divides his inferior command into four fractions.

He leaves McDougall's troop and eighty-four men, detailed as
pack escort, to bring along the mule train. He sends Benteen and
three troops southwest to find Indians. He later orders Reno and
three more to attack the village. With the remaining five troops,
he rides away. Custer confides no complete plan of battle to his officers. He makes no arrangement for communication between the
scattered subdivisions. When committed to conflict, he, the commander, has less than half his outnumbered force under his control
and only a vague idea where the remaining seven troops are.

Thus he made his last effort, the frantic clutching of a desperate man to lay hands once more on Glory. Fate, the requiting, ordained that an earlier, equally rash attempt which had won him fame should be precedent for this that wrought his death.

In the dust and confusion and mystery of the Little Bighorn, there are echoes of the Washita and half discernible similarities to that earlier rehabilitating victory. In each fight Custer followed a trail and found a village whose strength he did not pause to determine before attack. Before each, Indians and scouts warned him of peril. In each, he divided his force and sent the fractions beyond his control.

At Washita, Custer's luck was at its zenith. At the Little Bighorn, at its nadir. Bad generalship won his first Indian fight and lost him his last.

Even in the battle rapture that filled him, the Glory-Hunter, when he first looked down upon that ominously still village, must have experienced the chill recognition of fortune's desertion. By then, he had doomed himself past all possible reprieve.

It was too late then to move in any direction but forward. The momentum of earlier rashness carried him on. He could not withdraw. His precipitance had shattered Terry's plan and disgrace must follow retreat now. Furthermore, his force was scattered.

He had wagered his future and was too deeply involved to quit the game. He could only bet the scant amount remaining, sending couriers for Benteen and McDougall, pressing on for the last rash stroke of a constitutionally reckless man. Such a blind attack had won at Appomattox and at Washita. But fortune then still was his.

There is further parallel. Godfrey heard far-away guns that must have been those of Major Elliot's trapped men, calling across the snow of Washita's valley. Godfrey and others on the bluff above that Little Bighorn heard firing to the north before Reno rode out on a mission that Custer at Washita apparently never attempted. Circumstance displays at times an odd retribution.

No such impersonal force laid the Glory-Hunter, defeated, yet invested with enduring fame, on the slope above the mild, tree-shielded river. He found in death the object of his lifelong quest. His fall was not star-ordained. It was in himself.

The compass needle of his spirit ever swung toward his end. Intimation of his immortality runs, reiterant, through all his life. One hears it first as a little boy whispers through bloody lips to his father: "You and me can whip all the Whigs in Ohio." One sees it, not only in the clamorous avalanches of his cavalry charges, not only in the wilfulness of his insubordinations, but, most clearly, in the leap of a humiliated yellow-haired stripling from his place in the spelling-bee's line and the blow that sends a window-pane into fragments about the face of his defamer.

Awed schoolmates stare at the Custer boy. The tinkle of shattered glass is loud in the silence. It will be borne and magnified by the years into the screaming and gun-fire that lapped a height above the Little Bighorn.

THE END

BIBLIOGRAPHY

BIBLIOGRAPHY

ALEXANDER, JOHN H.: *Mosby's Men*. New York, 1907.
BATES, CHARLES F.: *Lost and Won*. New York, 1926.
Battles and Leaders of the Civil War. New York, 1887-88.
BEYER, W. F. and KEYDEL, O. F.: *Deeds of Valor*. Detroit, 1903.
Billings Gazette. June 21, 1931.
Bismarck Weekly Tribune. May 17, 1876.
BOURKE, JOHN G.: *On the Border with Crook*. New York, 1891.
BOWERS, CLAUDE G.: *The Tragic Era*. Boston, 1929.
BRACKETT, WILLIAM S.: "Custer's Last Battle." Contributions of the Historical Society of Montana. Volume 4.
BRADY, CYRUS TOWNSEND: *Indian Fights and Fighters*. New York, 1902.
BRANCH, F. DOUGLAS: *Westward*. New York, 1930.
BRININSTOOL, E. A.: *The Custer Fight*. Hollywood, 1933.
BRININSTOOL, E. A.: *Fighting Red Cloud's Warriors*. Columbus, 1926.
BRININSTOOL, E. A.: *A Trooper with Custer*. Columbus, 1925.
BROWN, JESSE and WILLARD, A. M.: *The Black Hills Trails*. Rapid City, S. D., 1929.
BURDICK, USHER L.: *The Last Battle of the Sioux Nation*. Fargo, 1929.
BYRNE, P. E.: "The Custer Myth." *North Dakota Historical Quarterly*. 1932.
BYRNE, P. E.: *Soldiers of the Plains*. New York, 1927.
CARRINGTON, FRANCES C.: *Army Life on the Plains*. Philadelphia, 1910.
CARRINGTON, MARGARET IRVIN: *Ab-sa-ra-ka*. Philadelphia, 1878.
CATLIN, GEORGE: *An Open Letter to General Sheridan*. Brussels, 1868.
CHITTENDEN, HIRAM M.: *History of Early Steamboat Navigation on the Missouri River*. New York, 1903.
Chronological List of Actions, Etc., with Indians from January 1, 1866, to January, 1880. Adjutant-General's Office, 1888.
Compilation of All the Treaties between the United States and Indian Tribes, A. Washington, 1873.
COUGHLAN, COLONEL T. M.: "The Battle of the Little Bighorn." *Cavalry Journal*, January, 1934.
CULLUM, G. W.: *Biographical Register of the Officers and Graduates of the U. S. Military Academy at West Point, New York*. New York, 1891.

CUSTER, ELIZABETH BACON: *Boots and Saddles.* New York, 1885.

CUSTER, ELIZABETH BACON: *The Boy General.* New York, 1901.

CUSTER, ELIZABETH BACON: *Following the Guidon.* New York, 1890.

CUSTER, ELIZABETH BACON: *Tenting on the Plains.* New York, 1887.

CUSTER, GEORGE ARMSTRONG: *My Life on the Plains.* New York, 1874.

DELAND, CHARLES E.: *The Sioux Wars.* South Dakota Department of Historical Collections. Pierre, 1930.

DELLENBAUGH, FREDERICK S.: *George Armstrong Custer.* New York, 1917.

DIXON, JOSEPH K.: *The Vanishing Race.* New York, 1913.

DODGE, RICHARD J.: *Our Wild Indians.* Hartford, 1882.

EARLY, JUBAL A.: *Autobiography of.* Philadelphia, 1912.

Fargo Forum. March 20, 1927.

FINERTY, JOHN F.: *Warpath and Bivouac.* Chicago, 1890.

FORSYTH, GEORGE A.: *Thrilling Days in Army Life.* New York, 1900.

GODFREY, GENERAL E. S.: "Custer's Last Battle." *Century Magazine,* January, 1892.

GODFREY, GENERAL E. S.: "Some Reminiscences of the Battle of the Washita." *Cavalry Journal,* October, 1928.

GORDON, GENERAL JOHN B.: *Reminiscences of the Civil War.* New York, 1903.

GRAHAM, COLONEL W. A.: *The Story of the Little Big Horn.* New York, 1926.

GRINNELL, GEORGE BIRD: *The Cheyenne Indians.* New Haven, 1923.

GRINNELL, GEORGE BIRD: *The Fighting Cheyennes.* New York, 1915.

Hammersley's Army and Navy Register. New York, 1888.

HANSON, JOSEPH MILLS: *The Conquest of the Missouri.* Chicago, 1909.

HAZEN, GENERAL W. B.: *Some Corrections to "My Life on the Plains."* St. Paul, 1875.

HUGHES, COLONEL R. P.: "The Campaign against the Sioux in 1876." *Journal of the Military Service Instruction of the United States,* January, 1896.

KANIPE, DANIEL A.: "A New Story of Custer's Last Battle." Contributions of the Historical Society of Montana.

KEIM, DE B. RANDOLPH: *Sheridan's Troopers on the Border.* New York, 1870.

KIDD, A. J.: *Personal Recollections of a Cavalryman.* Chicago, 1893.

KING, CHARLES: *Campaigning with Crook.* New York, 1890.

LIBBY, O. G.: "The Arikara Narrative." North Dakota Historical Collections. Volume 4.

LONGSTREET, GENERAL JAMES: *From Manassas to Appomattox.* Philadelphia, 1895.

McCLELLAN, GENERAL GEORGE B.: *McClellan's Own Story.* New York, 1886.

McClernand, General Edward J.: *Diary of.* New York, 1927.

McClernand, General Edward J.: "With the Indians and Buffalo in Montana." *Cavalry Journal,* 1927.

McLaughlin, James: *My Friend the Indian.* New York, 1926.

Marquis, Thomas B.: *A Warrior Who Fought Custer.* Minneapolis, 1931.

Moore, Colonel Horace: *The 19th Kansas Cavalry in the Washita Campaign.* Oklahoma City, 1923.

Mosby, Colonel John S.: *Memoirs of.* Boston, 1917.

Nesbitt, Paul: "The Battle of the Washita." Oklahoma Historical Chronicles. Volume 3.

Newhall, F. C.: *With Sheridan's Cavalry in Lee's Last Campaign.* Philadelphia, 1866.

New York Herald. December, 1868-January, 1869.

New York Herald. 1876.

New York World. 1876.

O'Harra, C. C.: *Custer's Black Hills Expedition of 1874.* Rapid City, S. D.

Paxson, Frederick L.: *A History of the American Frontier.* New York, 1924.

Perkins, J. R.: *Trails, Rails and War.* Indianapolis, 1927.

Price, George F.: *Across the Continent with the 5th Cavalry.* New York, 1883.

Record of Engagements with Hostile Indians within the Military Division of the Missouri. Washington, 1882.

Remsburg, John F. and George J.: *Charley Reynolds.* Kansas City, 1931.

Report of the Joint Committee on the Conduct of the War, 38th Congress, January 10, 1865.

Report of the Secretary of War, 1876.

Review of the Trial of General George Armstrong Custer. Bureau of Military Justice. Washington, D. C.

Rodenbough, General T. F.: *The Army of the United States.* Washington, 1895.

Roe, Charles F.: *Custer's Last Battle.* New York, 1927.

Ronsheim, Milton: *The Life of General Custer.* Cadiz, O., 1929.

Sheridan, Philip H.: *Memoirs of.* New York, 1888.

Spotts, David L.: *Campaigning with Custer.* Los Angeles, 1928.

St. Louis Missouri-Democrat. February 9, 1869.

Stanley, General D. S.: *Personal Memoirs.* Cambridge, 1917.

Testimony of General Custer before the Committee on Expenditures of the War Department. Washington, 1876.

Thomason, Captain J. W.: *Jeb Stuart.* New York, 1930.

Tremain, H. E.: *Last Hours of Sheridan's Cavalry.* New York, 1904.

Vestal, Stanley: *Sitting Bull.* Boston, 1932.

Wallace, G. D.: *Custer's Last March.* New York, 1927.

WALSH, RICHARD J.: *The Making of Buffalo Bill.* Indianapolis, 1928.

WHEELER, COLONEL HOMER W.: *Buffalo Days.* Indianapolis, 1925.

WHITTAKER, FREDERICK: *A Complete Life of General George A. Custer.* New York, 1877.

WILLIAMSON, J. J.: *Mosby's Rangers.* New York, 1895.

WINGET, DAN: *Anecdotes of Buffalo Bill.* Chicago, 1927.

WISSLER, CLARK: *Indians of the Plains.* New York, 1927.

INDEX

INDEX

Adams, Judge, 180
Ain't I Glad to Get Out of the Wilderness, 196, 207
Aldie, 49, 51
Alexandria, 122, 128, 129, 152
Alexis, Grand Duke, 228-229
Algeria, 37
Allegheny County, 20
Amosville, 57
Anderson, General, 73, 76, 77, 94, 105
Anderson, Thomas F., 81
Antelope Hills, 188
Anthony, Maj. Scott, 149, 210
Anthony, Susan B., 149
Apaches, 185, 212
Appomattox, 107, 116, 145, 275, 295, 369
Appomattox Court House, 104, 108, 110
Appomattox-Lynchburg Road, 108, 111
Appomattox River, 100, 101, 108
Appomattox Station, 108-109, 121, 366
Arapahos, 149, 150, 157, 165, 179, 181, 182, 185, 189, 193, 209, 211-214, 220, 259
Arikaras, 241, 252, 256, 270, 294, 300-302, 304, 307, 309, 323, 327, 331, 333, 337-340, 348, 368
Arkansas, 48
Arkansas River, 172, 189
Arkansas Traveller, The, 214
Arlington, 37
Army of Northern Virginia, 68, 100, 101, 110, 114, 115
Army of the Cumberland, 241
Army of the James, 89, 96, 102, 108
Army of the Potomac, 39, 40, 45-47, 52, 58, 61, 63-65, 69, 89, 91, 96, 101-103, 126
Army of the Shenandoah, 74-76, 87
Army of the Tennessee, 249
Army of Virginia, 92
Augur, General, 179
Austin, 128, 135
"Autie"
    see Custer, George A,

Averill, Colonel (later General), 42, 47
Ayres' Brigade, 97

Bacon, Judge Daniel S., 24, 45-47, 49, 59-61, 141, 179
Bacon, Elizabeth
    see Custer, Elizabeth
Baliran, 245, 263
Ball, Cadet, 30
Ball, Sara Martha, 20
Banks, 73
Barnard, General, 40, 41
Barnitz, Captain, 172, 194
Barrett, Lawrence, 41, 145-146, 225, 268, 270
Barringer, Brigadier-General, 102
Barton, General, 106
"Battle of the Little Bighorn, The," 368
Beaver Creek, 187, 188, 307
Beaver Dam Station, 67, 68
Beech Point School, 24
Beechers Island, 275
Belknap, Sec. William C., 226, 254, 265, 268, 270-273, 275-279, 281-282, 284, 286, 287, 290, 293
Bell, Capt. James M., 191, 195
Belle Fourche, 258
Benet, Lieut. Stephen Vincent, 31
Benet, Poet Stephen Vincent, 31
Benet, William Rose, 31
Benteen, Brig.-Gen. Frederick W., 142, 204, 228, 296, 303, 317, 327, 356
    description of, 153-154
    dislike of, for Custer, 18, 155, 204-205, 298
    letter written by, 205-208, 218
    on the Little Bighorn, 336-338, 344-348, 350-354, 359, 368, 369
    quoted, 155, 203, 358
Benteen, Col. Fred. W., Jr., 208
Bentonville, 90
Berryville, 82
Big Creek, 165, 220, 221, 223
Big Head, 218, 221

379

Big Horn Mountains, 234
Bighorn River, 235, 251, 294, 299, 305, 308, 313, 314, 321, 322, 327, 328, 330, 353, 354, 363
Bighorn Valley, 309, 352
Bingham, John A., 26-28, 30
Bismarck, 235, 240, 241, 251-254, 264, 272, 276, 294, 300, 360
Bismarck Weekly Tribune, 253
    quoted, 300
Black Hills, 134, 168, 236, 251, 256, 257, 259-262, 264, 265, 267, 269
Black Hills expedition, 256-261, 275, 293
Black Kettle, 149, 150, 193, 197, 198, 201, 205, 209, 210, 220, 270
Blackfoot, 214
Bladensburg, 123
Blair, Governor, 46, 47, 49, 51
Blinn, Mrs. Clara, 209
Blinn, Willie, 209
Blodgett, Private, 109
Bloody Knife, 241, 245, 304, 323, 327, 333, 342, 348, 366
"Blucher," 183, 194
Blue Ridge, 49, 72, 84, 90
"Bluegrass," 228
Bluff Creek, 184
Boardman, Isaiah, 323, 340, 349
Boots and Saddles
    quoted, 143, 226, 248, 249, 258, 262, 264, 304, 306-307, 310, 313, 360-361
Bostwick, 354
Bouyer, Minton ("Mitch"), 309, 310, 317, 319, 323, 327, 331, 333, 334, 352, 366
Bowen, Lieut. Nicholas (later Captain), 40, 42
Boyd's Seminary, 24
Boydton Plank Road, 93, 94
Bozeman, 149
Bozeman Road, 157, 159, 186, 233, 264
Braden, Lieut. Chas., 247
Bradley, Lieut. J. H., 308, 319, 335, 354, 355, 364
Brady, Cyrus T.
    Indian Fights and Fighters
    quoted, 275
Brandy Station, 60, 67, 121, 364
Breckenridge, 71
Brewster, Daniel A., 201, 213, 214, 218
Brininstool, E. A., 208

Brisbin, Major James S., 295, 308, 318-320, 322, 326, 330
Brussels, 212
Bryant, John W., 40
Buck, Colonel, 38
Buckland, 60, 120
"Buckland Races," 61, 86
Buffalo, 141, 142, 208
Buford, 52, 56, 65
Buford's Division, 56
Bull Run, 34, 36-37
Bureau of Military Justice, 171, 175
Burkesville, 92
Burkman, John, 228, 235, 239
Burleigh County Pioneers Ass'n., 253
Burnside, 45
Butler, 68, 69
Byrne, P. E., 181
    Soldiers of the Plains
    quoted, 309
"Byron," 145

Cache Creek, 213
Cadiz, 27
Cairo, 140, 235, 236
Calhoun, Lieut. James, 238, 297, 318, 319, 337, 341, 347, 358
Calhoun, Mrs.
    see Custer, Margaret
California, 144, 148
California Joe, 184-185, 190, 191, 193, 198
Camp Sturgis, 237
Camp Supply, 187-189, 198, 200, 203
"Campaign Against the Sioux in 1876, The"
    quoted, 293
Campaigning with Crook
    quoted, 187
Campbells Are Coming, The, 151
Canada, 278
Capehart's Brigade, 94, 95, 110
Capitol Hill, 124
Card, General, 293
Carpenter, Captain, 174
Carr, 162
Carrington, 157, 159, 200
Carter, 81
Carvajal, 139
Cashtown, 52
Catlin, 212
Cavalry Corps, 50, 51, 63, 64, 66-68, 75, 116, 118, 120, 124, 125, 142, 185

Cedar Creek, 86
Cedarville, 76, 120
Centerville, 33, 35, 37, 38
Century Ass'n., 270
Chamberlayne's Run, 93
Chambersburg, 52, 72, 73
Chancellorsville, 49
Chapman, Capt. Samuel, 80-81
Charles City-Richmond Road, 89
Charles O'Malley, 23, 35
Charlottesville, 69
Chesterfield Station, 69
Cheyennes, 149, 150, 157, 159, 162-165,
   168, 169, 179-181, 185, 189, 193,
   194, 197, 199-201, 203, 205, 209-
   217, 219-221, 234, 235, 251, 256,
   257, 259, 269-271, 275, 294, 367
Chicago, 228, 282, 283, 285, 286, 287,
   359
Chickahominy, 40-42, 68
Chivington, Col. John, 149, 164, 210
Cholera, 172-173
Churchill, Trooper, 54
Cimarron, 182
"Cincinnati," 114
Circling Bear, 338
Cisco, Johnny, 57-58, 127
City Point, 90, 91
Civil War, 33-115, 119, 122, 151, 153,
   155, 158, 205, 222, 238, 241, 259,
   273, 280, 300, 309
Clarke, Major, 61
Clifford, Capt. J. C., 308
Clymer, Heister, 271-273, 275, 279, 282,
   290, 361
Coates, Doctor, 170
Cody, "Buffalo Bill," 228-229
Cold Harbor, 69
Cole, Dr. Philip G., 155, 207
Colorado, 144, 149, 259
Colorado Rockies, 143
"Comanche," 339, 357
Comanches, 159
Complete Life of General George A.
   Custer
   quoted, 38, 43, 48, 50, 59, 60, 141,
      268, 283
Comstock, Will, 166
Congress
   see United States Congress
Conotton, 24
Cook, Lieut. William W., 152, 166, 171,
   173, 174, 180, 185, 193, 207, 239,

Cook, Lieut. William W.—*Continued*
   297, 322, 334, 337, 339-340, 343,
   346, 348, 358
Cooper, Wickliffe, 151
Corbin, Jack, 172, 190, 191, 198
Corps
   I, 61
   II, 65, 100, 102, 103
   V, 65, 96, 97, 100-102, 108
   VI, 65, 69, 72, 73, 87, 100, 102-104,
      106, 107, 110-111, 118
   IX, 65, 125
   XVI, 151
   XXIV, 102, 108, 110-111
Corse, General, 98, 106
Coughlan, Col. T. M.
   "The Battle of the Little Bighorn,"
      368
   The Life of Col. Charles A. Varnum
      quoted, 328, 334, 349
Coulson, Mart, 238
Council Bluffs Bugle, The
   quoted, 189
Crawford, Col. S. J., 184, 214
Crazy Horse, 234, 235, 251, 269, 271,
   294, 311, 367
Creal, A. B., 23
Crittenden, Lieut. John J., 297, 361
Crook, General
   as an Indian fighter, 235, 265, 271,
      280, 295, 308, 309, 311-312, 331,
      339, 352, 356, 367
   in the Civil War, 18, 87, 91-95, 102-
      106, 109, 111, 118, 120
Crook's Second Cavalry Division, 91, 93,
   94, 102, 103, 111, 118
Crowell, Lieutenant, 318, 319
Crows, 234, 265, 295, 304, 308, 311, 312,
   314, 317, 323, 327, 328, 330-333,
   335, 337, 348, 352-354, 364, 366
Crow's Nest, 332, 334, 357, 368
Cryssoptown, 21
Crystal Springs, 272
Cub Run, 37
Culpeper, 118
Culpeper Court House, 58
Culps Hill, 54
Curly, 323
Curtis, Sergeant, 334, 336
Custer, Boston, 21, 257, 258, 298, 301,
   304, 306-307, 320, 337, 347, 355
Custer City, 265
Custer Creek, 243

Custer, Elizabeth, 42, 44-46, 51, 62, 122-123, 126, 140, 144-145, 165-167, 181, 204, 220, 238, 240, 249, 251-252, 298-299, 301, 303, 361
at Fort Lincoln, 252-256, 262
at Fort Riley, 152, 156-158, 160, 166, 172, 173, 176-177
at the War Department, 87-88
at Winchester, 88
Boots and Saddles
quoted, 143, 226, 248, 249, 258, 262, 264, 304, 306-307, 310, 313, 360-361
courted by Custer, 45-49, 58-61
first meeting with Custer, 24
Following the Guidon
quoted, 200, 219
gift from Sheridan, 115
in Big Creek camp, 220-222
in Kentucky, 227-229
in New York, 226, 227, 262, 266-268, 272
in Texas, 133-134, 139
in Washington, 61, 62, 63, 87-88, 99
letter from Sheridan, 115
letters from her husband, 61, 91, 99, 160-162, 164-166, 189, 200, 219, 227, 242-244, 246, 248-249, 257-258, 304, 306-307, 313, 318, 322
letters to her husband, 173
marriage of, 61
nurses her husband, 237-238
on presidential tour, 142
presents flags, 122
quoted, 130, 141, 154, 159, 223-226, 239
second meeting with Custer, 39
Tenting on the Plains
quoted, 127, 145, 146, 161, 162, 173, 176-177
trip to Alexandria, 127-129
Custer, Emmanuel, 20-22, 134, 139-140, 370
Custer, "Fanny"
see Custer, Geo. A.
Custer, Gen. George Armstrong
adopts runaway slave, 57
aide of Kearny, 37-38
ambitions of, to be lecturer, 270
ancestors of, 20-21
and Grant, 141, 176, 178, 274, 276-277, 279-292, 362, 365
and Johnny Cisco, 57-58, 127

Custer, Gen. G. A.—*Continued*
and Mosby's men, 80-84
and Sheridan
see Sheridan, Gen. P. H.
appointment to West Point, 26
arrests of, 31, 175, 180, 182, 274
as guide, 306, 307-308, 310
as rear-guard, 92-93
as witness for Clymer Committee, 272, 273, 275-279, 281, 290, 361-362
at Appomattox Station, 109-110, 366, 369
at Fort Leavenworth, 175-176, 178-180
at Fort Lincoln, 252-257, 262-266
at Fort Riley, 150, 152, 155, 156-157, 160
at Gettysburg, 54-56
at U. S. Military Academy, 27-34, 121, 182, 209, 363
at Waynesboro, 90
autobiography of, 223
see My Life on the Plains
Benteen's dislike of, 18, 155, 204-205, 208, 298
bids farewell to Third Division, 127
birth of, 20
brigadier-general, 51
burial of, at West Point, 17, 361
captures supply trains, 109-110
character of, 19-20, 161, 225-226, 361-362, 368-370
charges against, 175
congratulatory order of, 116-117
contemporaries' opinion of, 18
court martial of, 162, 171, 175-176, 178-180, 363
death of, 18, 21, 26, 59, 250, 292, 325, 346, 354-356, 358
depression of, 306, 314, 316-318, 325-326, 329, 365
descriptions of, 27, 74, 108, 112, 119, 133-134, 143, 223-226, 300, 301
dogs of, 133-134, 145, 152, 160, 161, 162, 164, 183, 190, 194, 224, 228, 233, 235-239, 252, 258, 272, 303
early life of, 21-25, 370
first lieutenant, 5th Cavalry, 42, 47
first meeting with future wife, 24
flag presentation, 87-88, 121-122, 173
friendship for Lawrence Barrett, 41, 145-146, 225, 268, 270
hatred of Belknap, 226, 254, 265,

Custer, Gen. G. A.—*Continued*
268, 270-273, 275-279, 281-282,
284, 286, 287, 293
his courtship, 45-47, 48-49, 58-61
his Mexican scheme, 139-141
horses of, 34, 106, 108-109, 124-126,
135, 145, 160, 165, 222-223, 228,
233, 235, 247, 258, 302, 303, 344
house of, is burned, 254
hunts, 134-135, 143, 160, 161, 164-
165, 190, 221, 222, 228-229, 243,
252, 258
illness of, 237-238
in Big Creek camp, 220-223
in closing Civil War engagements,
101-106
in Kentucky, 227-229
in New York, 140, 226, 227, 262,
266-268, 270-272, 280
in Texas, 123, 133-135, 139, 140
in the Shenandoah, 74-79
in Washington, 32-34, 61, 62, 87-88,
122-126, 155-156, 276-280, 281-
283, 294
insubordination of, 98, 162, 171-175,
242-243, 363-365, 370
interest in taxidermy, 243
kills his first foe, 42-43
leaves of absence, 39, 59, 140-142,
226-227, 262, 266, 268, 270
letters from his wife, 173
letters to his wife, 61, 91, 99, 160-
162, 164-166, 189, 200, 219, 227,
242-244, 246, 248-249, 257-258,
304, 306-307, 313, 318, 322
lieutenant of G Troop, 36-37
lieutenant-colonel, 142
major-general of volunteers, 84, 98,
118
marriage of, 61
mutiny under, 130-132, 152, 162, 166-
167, 170-172, 176
My Life on the Plains, 198, 210, 227
quoted, 157, 163, 176, 192
on Black Hills expedition, 256-261
on Hancock expedition, 158-167, 168-
172
on McClellan's staff, 40-45
on Pleasonton's staff, 47-48, 49-51
on presidential tour, 142
on runaway horse, 126
on the Little Bighorn, 336-347, 351,
357-358, 368-369, 370

Custer, Gen. G. A.—*Continued*
on Washita campaign, 188-207, 209-
219, 366, 367, 369
on Yellowstone expedition, 241-249,
367
opposes Rosser, 85-88
parents of, 20, 134, 139-140, 145, 370
peaceful pursuit of Indians, 213-219
pledge of abstinence, 39, 222
practical jokes of, 134, 139-140, 222,
257, 258, 303-304, 306-307
preliminaries to Little Bighorn, 301-
335
prepares regiment for final expedition,
296-300
quoted, 172, 182, 212, 273, 278, 279,
283, 288-289, 291, 318, 324, 328,
333, 334, 344
reinstated in service, 183-184
Reno's dislike of, 236, 298
reorganizes 7th Cavalry, 184-185
reproved by Longstreet, 113
restored to command of 7th Cavalry,
292, 297
résumé of Civil War career, 119-122
second lieutenant, 32
statue of, 142
style of writing, 227
suspension of, from service, 175-176,
363
Terry's orders to, 320-322, 362-364,
366
trip to Alexandria, 127-129
trouble with McCarthy, 253
trouble with Seip, 254, 262, 265, 276
uniform of, 57, 74, 84
with grand ducal party, 228-229
wounded, 58-59
writes for *The Galaxy,* 227, 249, 268,
310, 311
Custer, Jacob, 21
Custer, John, 21
Custer, Margaret Emma, 21, 238, 297,
298, 301, 303
Custer, Maria, 20, 21, 23, 145
Custer, Matilda, 21
Custer, Nevin J., 21
Custer Park, 142
on French Creek, 260
Custer, Paul, 20
Custer Peak, 260
Custer, Thomas W., 173, 221, 252, 254,
272

Custer, Thomas W.—*Continued*
  birth of, 21
  boyhood of, 23-24
  captures flags, 101, 105-106
  captures Rain-in-the-face, 263
  death of, 24, 264, 355
  gets commission, 88, 140
  goes hunting, 134
  in New York, 266-268
  is made captain, 297
  is transferred to brother's regiment, 152
  is wounded, 194
  on the Little Bighorn, 337, 341, 344, 347
  on Yellowstone expedition, 244-245
  plays poker, 222, 253, 318-319
  practical jokes of, 134, 140, 257, 303-304, 306-307
  quoted, 344
  reads Benteen's letter, 207-208
  wins medals of honor, 106
Custer's Brigade, 54, 57, 58, 60, 61, 69, 80
  see Michigan Brigade
"Custer's Last Battle"
  quoted, 318, 326, 327
"Custis Lee," 106, 145, 165

Dabney Mills, 99
Dakota, 158, 229, 261, 264, 311
Dan River, 118
"Dandy," 258, 302, 303
Daniels, Dr. J., 240
Danville, 103, 118
Danville Highway, 108
Davidson, Major John W., 150
Davies, 94, 124, 126
Davies' Brigade, 93, 111
Davis Creek, 332
Davis, Jefferson, 27, 100
Deatonville Road, 103, 104, 105
Deep Creek, 102
Defoe, General, 106
De Greese, Wm. J., 205
Delafield, Col. Richard L., 27, 30
Delawares, 166, 169
Denver, 144
Department of Dakota, 253, 292
Department of the Interior, 251, 252
Department of the Missouri, 146, 179
Department of the Upper Arkansas, 166
De Rudio, Lieutenant, 341, 348, 351, 359

Desertion, 171-172
  see Mutiny
DeSmet, 240
Detroit, 140, 288
Devin, Gen. Thomas C., 18, 65, 89-92, 94, 97, 98, 102-106, 109, 111, 112, 117, 118, 124, 126, 142
Devin's Brigade, 65
Devin's First Division, 93, 110
De Wolf, Doctor, 350
Diaz, 139
Dickerson, Joe, 24
Dinwiddie Court House, 93, 94, 96, 97, 120, 122
Dodge, Gen. Grenville Mellen, 265, 280-281
Dogs, 150, 162, 180, 182
"Don Juan," 109, 124-126
Doughty, Col. Calvin S., 50
Downer's Station, 174
Drummond, Lieutenant, 36
Dull Knife, 218, 221
Duncan, Col. Blanton, 228

Early, 71-73, 76-79, 84, 86-90, 117, 120
Ebbit House, 33
Edgerly, Lieutenant, 351, 352
Eichelberger, Major R. L., 32
Elder, 54
Eliza, 57, 70, 123, 128, 145
Elizabethtown, 227
  Community House of, 228
  Hill residence of, 228
Elliot, Major Joel H., 19, 151-152, 170-171, 182, 184, 190-191, 193-205, 209, 213, 220, 343, 355, 369
England, 181
Ewell, General, 56, 104, 106
Ewell's Corps, 103, 104
Examining Board, 151, 156

Falling Waters, 57
Far West, 238, 298, 307-309, 311-314, 316, 318-320, 322, 324, 327-328, 330, 352, 360, 362
Farmville, 102, 103, 107
Farnsworth, Capt. E. J., 51
Farnsworth's Brigade, 53-54
Farquahar, Colonel, 293
Fat Bear, 218, 221
Fetterman, Capt. William, 157
Fifth Military District, 179

Fighting Cheyennes, The
    quoted, 216
Finnegan, 152
First Division, 65, 89, 93, 103, 124, 128, 151
Fisher's Hill, 79, 87
Fitzhugh, Lieut. Charles, 68
Fitzpatrick, Israel, 21
Fitzpatrick, Lydia, 21
    see Reed, Lydia
Fitzpatrick, Maria Ward
    see Custer, Maria
Five Forks, 93, 97-99, 120, 122
Following the Guidon
    quoted, 200, 219
Forsyth, Lieut.-Col. Geo. A. (later General), 256, 260, 275
Fort Abraham Lincoln, 235, 249, 252, 253, 255-257, 261-263, 265, 268, 272, 273, 276, 279-282, 284, 286, 289, 290, 293, 295, 296, 300, 302, 360, 366
Fort Arbuckle, 204
Fort Berthold, 276
Fort Buford, 281, 311, 360
Fort Cobb, 182, 192, 205, 209-213, 281
Fort Dodge, 165, 182, 184, 185, 187, 188, 208
Fort Ellis, 235, 280, 295, 360
Fort Fetterman, 271, 280, 295, 304
Fort Garland, 143
Fort Harker, 162, 173, 174, 208
Fort Hays, 165, 166, 169, 172-174, 183, 184, 218, 220, 221, 226
Fort Laramie, 149, 234, 261, 271
Fort Larned, 150, 159, 161, 162, 180, 181, 210
Fort Leavenworth, 151, 159, 175, 178, 180, 223, 361
Fort McPherson, 166
Fort Peck, 277
Fort Phil Kearny, 157
Fort Rice, 238, 240, 241, 246
Fort Riley, 58, 144, 146, 150, 156, 160, 166, 172-175
Fort Sedgwick, 170
Fort Shaw, 295
Fort Sill, 213
Fort Snelling, 149
Fort Wallace, 166, 167, 170-174, 184, 364
Fort Wise, 149
France, 128

Fredericksburg, 49, 66
Fremont, 27, 73
French, Captain, 337, 341, 351, 353
French Creek, 260, 265
"Frogtown," 228
From Manassas to Appomattox
    quoted, 113
Front Royal, 80-83

Galaxy, The, 227, 249, 268, 310, 311
Gall, 234, 235, 251, 269, 294
Galveston, 139
Gansevoort, Colonel, 80
Garlington, General, 154, 298
    quoted, 153
Garry Owen, 151, 193, 200, 247, 252, 255, 261, 302
Geary, General, 114
Getty's Division, 87
Gettysburg, 30, 52-56, 120, 366
Gibbon, General, 103, 280, 295, 304, 307-313, 315, 317, 319, 321-324, 327-330, 352, 354, 362-365
Gibbs, Major Alfred, 151
Gibson, Lieutenant, 347
Girard, Fred, 323, 332, 339-341, 353, 366
Girl I Left Behind Me, The, 190, 257, 302
Glendive Creek, 244, 311
Godfrey, Gen. E. S., 18, 122, 182, 202, 208, 209, 329, 337, 350, 351, 369
    "Custer's Last Battle"
        quoted, 318, 326-327
    quoted, 203, 325, 363-364
    "Some Reminiscences of the Battle of the Washita"
        quoted, 195, 196, 204
Goes Ahead, 323, 354
Gold, in Black Hills, 259-261, 264-265
Goldin, Theodore, 298
    quoted, 154
Goldsboro, 90
Gordon, 111
    quoted, 113-114
Gordonsville, 71
Gordonsville Road, 70, 71
Gould, Jay, 280
Graham, Col. W. A.
    The Story of the Little Big Horn
        quoted, 196, 208
Grant, Lieut. Frederick Dent, 241, 256
Grant, Orville, 276, 277, 279, 287
Grant, Gen. U. S., 124, 141
    as president, 157, 176, 178, 179, 235,

Grant, Gen. U. S.—*Continued*
    241, 254, 272, 274, 276-277, 279,
    280-292, 319, 359, 362, 363, 365
    in Civil War, 64, 66, 69, 72, 73, 76,
    77, 88-92, 96, 99, 101, 107, 110,
    113-115
Grant, U. S., Jr., 285
Greasy Grass, 312
    see Little Bighorn Valley
Great American Desert, 148
Greathouse, Captain, 129
Gregg, General, 47, 49, 54, 55, 65, 69, 70,
    76, 94-96, 120
Gregg's Brigade, 55, 94, 95, 105
Gregg's Second Division, 49, 54, 66, 69,
    76
Griffin, 97, 100, 101
Grinnell, George Bird, 181, 257
    The Fighting Cheyennes
    quoted, 216
Guerrier, Edmond, 163
Guerrillas, 73, 80, 82
    see Rangers

Hail Columbia, 94
Hail to the Chief, 94
Hairy Moccasin, 323, 332, 354
Hale, Lieutenant, 201
Half Yellow Face, 323, 327, 332, 348
Halltown, 77
Hamilton, Alexander, 153
Hamilton, Capt. Louis McLane, 152-153,
    167, 173, 174, 191, 193-194, 200
Hampton, Wade, 54, 70
Hampton's Division, 54
Hancock, General, 146, 156-165, 172-175,
    179, 210, 240
Hancock's Brigade, 40
Hanover, 52, 54
Hard Robe, 190, 192
Hardee, Lieut.-Col. Wm. J., 27-28, 30
Hare, Lieutenant, 331, 337, 340, 342,
    350
Harney, General, 259
Harney Peak, 260
Harper's Ferry, 72
Harrington, Lieutenant, 358
Harrison County, 20, 24
Hawes' Shop, 69
Hayden, Dr. F. V., 259
Hays City, 220
Hazen, Gen. William B., 31, 182, 192,
    209, 210, 212, 281

Hazen, Gen. William B.—*Continued*
    *Some Corrections to "My Life on the
    Plains"*
    quoted, 211
Heintzelman, Col. Samuel P., 36, 37
Hempstead, 133-135
Henry House, 36
Herendeen, George B., 317, 323, 348,
    351, 352, 364
Hickok, Wild Bill, 164
Hodgson, Lieut. Benny, 350
Home Sweet Home, 252, 255
Honsinger, John, 245, 263
Hood, General, 128
Hooker, 47-49, 52, 64
Hopedale, 24
House Committee of Prosecution, 275-
    279, 281, 290, 361-362
House of Representatives
    Sergeant at Arms of, 273
Hughes, Col. R. D.
    "The Campaign Against the Sioux in
    1876"
    quoted, 293
Humphreys, 103, 104, 107
Hunter, General, 69, 71-73
Hynes, Sergeant, 342

Illinois, 144, 148
Indian Bureau, 146, 147, 159, 179, 181,
    185, 227, 235, 240, 267, 269, 278,
    290, 293
Indian Fights and Fighters
    quoted, 275
Indian Treaties
    see Treaties, Indian
Indian Wars, 147-150, 151, 162-170, 172,
    174, 181, 182, 184-207, 244-247,
    251, 255, 260, 265, 271, 280, 308,
    311-312, 329, 341-355
Indiana, 129
Indians, 143, 144, 146, 160, 170, 179,
    183, 184, 186, 255, 284, 291, 292,
    321, 326
    see Indian wars *and* tribe names
Ingalls, Quartermaster-General, 283
Inyan Kara, 259
Iron Shirt, 212

"Jack Rucker," 135, 145
Jackson, Andrew, 148
Jackson, Billy, 343
Jackson, Lieutenant, 171

Jackson, Stonewall, 43, 73
Jacksonian Democrats, 22
James Canal, 89, 90
James City, 60
Jeff Davis Legion, 55
Jefferson, Joe, 127
Jetersville Station, 102-103
Johnny Fill Up the Bowl, 94
Johnson, Charles, 171
Johnson, General, 85, 86, 97
Johnson, President, 141, 142
Johnson, Trooper, 175
Johnston, Joseph, 39, 40, 90-92, 101, 118
Johnston's Division, 94
Jones, David L., 81
Josephine, 249, 311
Juarez, 139, 140
Julius Cæsar, 268

"Kaiser," 303
Kanipe, Daniel A., 345, 347
  "A New Story of Custer's Last Battle"
    quoted, 344
Kansas, 144, 149, 150, 158, 177, 182, 201, 220
Kansas Pacific, 144, 146, 180
Kearney, Brig.-Gen. Philip, 37-38, 52
Keim, De B. Randolph
  Sheridan's Troopers on the Border, 201
    quoted, 188, 202, 203
Kelley, Cadet, 30
Kellogg, Mark, 292, 300, 311, 320, 323, 337, 365, 366
Kennedy, Sergeant-Major, 194
Kentucky, 227, 228
Keogh, Capt. Myles W., 152, 222, 297, 308, 318, 319, 331, 334, 337, 339-341, 357, 358, 361
Kernstown, 88
Kershaw, General, 106
Key West, 238, 244
Kidder, Lieutenant, 170, 172, 174
Kilpatrick, Gen. Judson, 18, 49-50, 51, 56, 58, 60-63, 65, 68, 178
Kilpatrick's Brigade, 49
Kilpatrick's Division, 54, 56, 60, 120
King, Gen. Charles, 196, 204
  Campaigning with Crook
    quoted, 187
Kingsbury, Lieutenant, 36
Kinzie, Lieutenant, 295

Kiowas, 159, 165, 179, 185, 189, 193, 209-212, 214, 220, 281
Ku Klux Klansmen, 227

Labarge, Capt. Joseph, 240
Lacy's Springs, 88, 120
"Lady," 303
Lake Michigan, 23
Laramie treaty, 233-235, 240, 251, 256, 265, 270
Last Hours of Sheridan's Cavalry
  quoted, 96, 98
Leavenworth, 179, 180
  see Fort Leavenworth
Lee, Gen. Custis, 106
Lee, Fitzhugh, 55, 60, 70, 93, 98, 111, 120
Lee, Lieut. John W., 44
Lee, Gen. Robert E., 49, 52, 56, 57, 65-69, 72, 73, 75, 77, 82, 90-94, 96, 99-103, 107-111, 113-117, 121
Leighton Brothers, 277
Letter Day, 225
Life of Col. Charles A. Varnum, The
  quoted, 328, 334, 349
Life of General Custer, The
  quoted, 115
Lighthouse Point, 71
Lincoln, Abraham, 30, 64, 90
Lincoln monument, 142
Lincoln, Tad, 90
Little Arkansas River, 150, 159, 179
Little Arkansas treaty, 150, 159, 179
Little Beaver, 190, 192
Little Bighorn, battle of, 51, 152, 153, 168, 181, 187, 223, 241, 264, 298, 341-354, 356-358, 369
Little Bighorn battle-field, 160, 301, 361
Little Bighorn River, 17, 21, 74, 193, 201, 203, 250, 267, 292, 314, 333, 336, 338-341, 344, 345, 349, 355-358, 364, 366, 369, 370
Little Bighorn Valley, 154, 312, 314, 315, 330, 336-345, 353, 354, 366
Little Face, 353
Little Heart River, 303
Little Horn, 321, 322, 366
  see Little Bighorn
Little Missouri River, 244, 258, 294, 299, 304-307
Little Raven, 213, 214
Lomax, 78, 85, 86
Lone Wolf, 210, 211, 214

Lonesome Charley
    see Reynolds, Charley
Longstreet, Gen. James, 40, 111, 112, 114
    From Manassas to Appomattox
        quoted, 113
Louis Napoleon
    see Napoleon III
Louisa Court House—Gordonsville Road,
    70
Louisiana, 123, 128, 179
Louisville, 127, 128, 227-229
Lounsberry, Col. C. A., 272
Love, Lucien, 81
Low, Lieutenant, 295, 319, 353
"Lucky Hunter"
    see Reynolds, Charley
"Lucy Stone," 239
Ludlow, Capt. William, 257, 260, 293,
    365
Lynchburg, 80, 108-110
Lynchburg Road, 111
Lyon, Captain, 134

MacKenzie, 18, 96, 97
MacMahon, Quartermaster-Sergeant, 171
Madden, Serg. Mike, 353-354
Mahwissa, 212
"Maida," 183
Malvern Hill, 42
Marsh, Capt. Grant, 238, 244, 249, 299,
    309, 311, 318, 360
Martin, John, 344-345, 346-348, 358
Maryland, 20, 49, 56
Maryland Avenue, 124
Massachusetts, 150
Mathey, Lieut. E. C., 191, 326, 331, 336,
    346, 351
Maximilian, 123, 128, 129, 135, 139
McCarthy, C. H., 253
McClellan, Gen. George B., 38, 41-42,
    44-47, 64, 121, 225
    McClellan's Own Story
        quoted, 41
McDougall, 336, 346, 348, 351, 368, 369
McDowell, 33-37
McIlargy, Trooper, 340, 341
McIntosh, Lieut. Donald, 152, 337, 341,
    343, 349
McIntosh, Col. John B., 55
McLean, Wilmer, 114-115
McMaster, 81
McNeely Normal School, 24

Meade, 52, 56, 57, 64, 66, 103, 108, 111,
    124
Mechanicsville, 68
Medicine Arrow, 212, 216-217
Medicine Lodge Creek, 179, 183
Medicine Lodge treaty, 179, 182, 188,
    193
Meigs, Lieut. John R., 84
Memoirs
    by Sheridan, quoted, 75, 98
Memphis, 229, 233, 235
Merritt, Wesley, 18, 51, 65, 68, 77, 78,
    84-91, 95, 98, 100-102, 109, 110,
    114, 120, 121, 123, 124, 126, 128,
    142
Merritt's Brigade, 65
Merritt's Cavalry Corps, 97, 112
Merritt's Division, 79
Metropolitan Hotel, 293
Mexican Army of Liberation, 139, 140
Mexico, 22, 134, 135, 139
Mexico City, 37
Michigan, 23, 39, 42, 46, 145, 249
Michigan Brigade, 20, 51, 53, 54, 56, 58,
    61, 63, 67, 69-71, 74, 129, 130,
    322
    see Custer's Brigade
Middle Ford, 357
Middleburg, 82
Miles, Col. Nelson A., 101, 218, 219
Miles's Division, 100
Miller, 104
Miller's Battery, 103
Milner, Moses
    see California Joe
Minnesota, 148, 149
Mississippi River, 139
Missouri, 28, 33, 148
Missouri Democrat, 205
Missouri River, 144, 233, 238, 240, 248,
    252, 256, 262, 275, 277, 281, 298,
    326, 364, 366
Missouri Valley, 252
Mitchell, Trooper, 341
Mizpah Creek, 310
Monasetah, 217
Monocacy Junction, 72
Monroe, 23-24, 39, 42, 44-46, 58, 59, 140,
    141, 181-183, 187, 227, 249
    Presbyterian Church of, 61
Monroe Doctrine, 123
Montana, 152, 158, 235, 258, 280, 294,
    295, 308, 311

Monterey Gap, 56
Moore, Col. Horace, 214, 218
Moore, Major O. H., 295, 298, 307, 311
Morgan, Mrs. James S., 201, 217-218
Mosby, Col. John, 75-77, 80, 82-83, 102, 166, 169, 199
Mosby's men, 75-77, 80-83
Mosby's Men
    quoted, 82, 83
Mount Jackson, 79
Moylan, Lieut. Myles, (later Captain), 155, 170, 244, 245, 308, 337, 341, 343
Muddy River, 241-243
Mulberry Creek, 213
Musselshell River, 248
Mutiny
    see Custer, G. A., mutiny under
My Life on the Plains, 176, 198, 210, 227
    quoted, 157, 163, 192
Myers, Captain, 193, 195
Myers's Battalion, 203

Namozine Church, 101, 106
Namozine Creek, 100
Napoleon III, 37, 128, 129, 139
Nebraska, 149, 326, 364
Neva, 214
New Athens, 24
New Jersey Brigade, 37
New Market, 87, 142
New Orleans, 123, 128, 139, 229
New Rumley, 20-23, 26, 142
"New Rumley Invincibles, The," 22
"New Story of Custer's Last Battle, A"
    quoted, 344
New York, 140, 262, 267, 270, 271, 280, 283
New York Herald, 201, 300, 366
New York World, 283
    quoted, 284-285
Newhall, Col. F. C., 99
    With Sheridan's Cavalry in Lee's Last Campaign
    quoted, 102, 109, 112
North Anna River, 69
North Carolina, 90-92, 101, 118
North Dakota, 235, 253
North Platte, 229, 234
Northern Cheyennes, 251, 256, 269, 294
    see Cheyennes
Northern Pacific, 28, 235, 238, 241, 244, 272

O'Fallon's Creek, 294, 307
Ohio, 20, 22, 24, 151, 370
Oklahoma, 150, 180, 188, 189, 213
"Old Nutriment"
    see Burkman, John
Omaha, 229
One Stab, 260
Opequan River, 77, 78
Orangeburg and Alexandria Railway, 39
Ord, 89, 102, 103, 107
Oregon, 144, 148
Osages, 190, 192, 193, 200, 215, 366
Osborn, Charles, 280
Overby, William Thomas, 81

Palmer, Major I. N., 36
Parker, James P., 28, 33
Pawnee Fork, 162-165
Pawnee Killer, 163, 166
Peach Orchard, The, 54
Peninah, 238
Peninsula, the, 43, 68, 69, 121
Pennington, 54, 70
Pennington's Brigade, 90, 95, 108, 110
Pennsylvania, 49, 52, 53
Pennsylvania Avenue, 33, 124-125
Pequods, 150
Perkins, J. R.
    Trails, Rails and War, quoted, 281
Petersburg, 72, 73, 77, 88-93, 99-101, 116, 118
Petersburg-Lynchburg Railway, 108
Pettigrew's Brigade, 52
Peyton, Colonel, 113
"Phil Sheridan," 145, 160
Pickett, 54, 97
Pickett's Division, 94
Pioneer Press, 253
Platte River, 149, 150, 157, 165-172, 174, 200, 234
Platte Valley, 144
Pleasonton, General, 47, 49, 51, 58, 64, 65, 119
Pompey's Pillar, 248
Port Republic, 79
Porter, Lieutenant, 358
Potomac River, 47, 48, 72, 77, 120
Powder River, 235, 251, 271, 294, 299, 305, 307-312
Powell, Brig.-Gen. Wm. H., 82, 83
Prince Edward-Danville Pike, 101, 108
Princeton College, 271
Prospect Station, 107

Rain-in-the-Face, 263-264
Raleigh, 90
Rangers, 77
    see Mosby's men
Rappahannock, 39, 47, 49, 57, 58, 82, 83
Raymond, 276
Reams Station, 92
Rectortown, 82
Red Bead, 170, 172
Red Cloud, 149, 157, 186, 233-236, 264
Red River, 129, 213
Redpath's Literary Bureau, 270
Reed, Armstrong, 298, 301, 320, 337,
    347, 355
Reed, David, 23
Reed, Lydia, 23-24, 39, 50, 59, 222, 298
Regiments
    1st Dragoons, 39
    1st Massachusetts Cavalry, 124
    1st Michigan Cavalry, 51, 60, 78
    1st Mounted Rifles, 39
    1st New Jersey, 55
    1st North Carolina Cavalry, 55
    1st Ohio, 56
    1st U. S. Cavalry, 39
    1st Virginia, 55
    1st West Virginia, 56
    2nd Dragoons, 39
    2nd New York, 109, 110
    2nd Rhode Island Infantry, 75
    2nd U. S. Cavalry, 33, 36, 37, 39, 81,
        150, 170, 295, 309, 318, 319, 326,
        329, 330
    3rd Infantry, 182, 200
    3rd Michigan Cavalry, 130-132
    3rd New Jersey, 109
    3rd Pennsylvania, 55
    3rd U. S. Cavalry, 39, 271, 295
    4th Artillery, 68
    4th Infantry, 295
    4th Kentucky Cavalry, 151
    4th Massachusetts Cavalry, 155
    5th Michigan Cavalry, 51, 55, 56, 60,
        61, 76
    5th U. S. Cavalry, 39, 42, 47, 52, 135,
        187
    5th Wisconsin, 40
    6th Infantry, 241, 295, 296, 298, 307,
        311, 318
    6th Maine, 40
    6th Michigan Cavalry, 51, 54, 77
    7th Michigan Cavalry, 46, 51, 55, 77,
        78

Regiments—Continued
    7th U. S. Cavalry, 17, 129, 142, 144,
        182-184, 236, 238, 272, 283,
        287, 290, 293-295, 359, 361
        at Fort Lincoln, 252, 273, 280
        band of, 151, 185, 188, 190, 193,
            196, 200, 207, 214, 247, 252,
            255-257, 261, 297, 302, 308,
            311
        final expedition
            departure on, 301-302
            preparation for, 296-300
        in camp on Big Creek, 220-223
        in Kentucky, 227-229
        leader of
            see Custer, Geo. A.
        mutiny in
            see Custer, Geo. A., mutiny
                under
        officers of, 151-155, 297
        on Black Hills expedition, 168,
            256-261
        on Hancock expedition, 156-172
        on Little Bighorn, 168, 235, 292,
            336-359, 366
        on Washita campaign, 188-207,
            209-219, 271
        on Yellowstone expedition, 168,
            240-249
        organization of, 150-151, 155,
            168, 184-185, 187
        preliminaries to Little Bighorn,
            303-335
        troops of
            A, 160, 193, 247, 337, 341,
                342, 348, 349, 351
            B, 193, 336
            C, 193, 337, 344
            D, 160, 193, 337, 351
            E, 162, 171, 193, 337
            F, 162, 165, 193, 263, 334,
                337
            G, 162, 165, 190, 193, 337,
                341, 342, 348, 349
            H, 160, 190, 193, 327, 337,
                344, 353
            I, 193, 337, 361
            K, 162, 193, 331, 337, 351
            L, 337
            M, 160, 190, 193, 337, 341,
                348, 353
    8th Illinois Cavalry, 51
    8th Infantry, 241

Regiments—*Continued*
9th Infantry, 241, 295
9th U. S. Cavalry, 142
10th Missouri Cavalry, 153
13th New York Cavalry, 80
17th Infantry, 241, 244, 256, 295, 296
19th Kansas Volunteer Cavalry, 183-184, 188, 200, 214, 218, 220
20th Infantry, 256, 295-297
22nd Infantry, 240, 241
25th New York Cavalry, 75, 77, 78
37th Infantry, 174
Reno Creek, 337
Reno, Major Marcus A., 296, 303, 317, 318, 330, 361
court martial of, 356, 358
description of, 236
dislike of, for Custer, 236, 298
on the Little Bighorn, 201, 203, 337-354, 359-360, 368-369
Powder River expedition, 310-315, 320, 328, 363
quoted, 337
Republican party, 26, 27
Republican River, 146, 166, 167, 169, 170, 180
Reynolds, Charley, 229, 236, 241, 256, 261, 263, 270, 294, 299, 300, 307, 323, 331, 333, 334, 340, 348, 349, 366
Reynolds, Col. J. J., 271
Reynolds, Lieut.-Col. John F., 30, 31
Rhodes, Henry C., 81
Rice, General, 276
Richmond, 47, 61, 65-69, 83, 86, 89, 91, 92, 100, 101
Richmond and Danville Railroad, 92, 101, 102
"Rienzi," 114
Ringgold, 56
Rio Grande, 123, 129, 139, 140
Rip Van Winkle, 127
Rogers, 225
Romero, Ambassador, 141
Ronsheim, Milton
The Life of General Custer
quoted, 115
Rosebud River, 160, 168, 173, 251, 294, 299, 305, 308-313, 320-322, 325, 327-329, 331, 332, 357, 362-364, 366
Rosebud Valley, 309, 312, 314, 324, 367
Rosedale, 145

Ross, Horatio Nelson, 261
Rosser, Gen. Thomas Lafayette, 28, 85-88, 93, 120, 121, 241, 243
Round Top, 54
Ruggles, Ass't. Adj.-Gen., 294
Russia, 228
Ruth, 128

Sailor's Creek, 104, 106, 120
St. Louis, 145, 182, 235
St. Paul, 236, 253, 260, 272-274, 286, 289, 294, 300
Fourth St., 292
Wabasha St., 292
San Antonio, 128
Sand Creek, 149, 150, 157, 159, 162, 164, 193, 210, 216
Saul, 222
Scofield, Secretary, 182
Scott, Gen. Hugh L., 153, 223, 298, 345
Some Memories of a Soldier
quoted, 310
Scott, Gen. Winfield, 33, 129
Second Division, 65, 124
Seddon, J. A., 82
Seip, Robert C., 254, 262, 265, 276
Senate, 150
Sentinel Buttes, 307
Seventh (7th) U. S. Cavalry
see Regiments
Seward, 139
Seymour's Division, 104, 106
Sharrow, Serg.-Maj. W. W., 338
Shaw, Abner, 238
Shenandoah River, 72, 82
Shenandoah Valley, 69, 72-79, 84, 85, 87, 89, 103, 120-122, 125, 169, 173, 236, 275
Shepherdstown, 120
Sheridan, Col. Michael V., 361
Sheridan, Gen. P. H., 42, 121, 124, 182, 213, 214, 225, 234, 249, 253, 256, 261, 275, 282, 285, 360, 366
and grand ducal party, 229
as head of Fifth Military District, 179
at Chicago fire, 228
attitude toward Custer, 64-65, 69, 73, 84, 87, 88, 122, 133, 141, 142, 178, 179, 183, 188, 190, 199, 213, 268, 273, 274, 288-293, 362
cavalry of, 20, 64-65, 75, 84, 86, 89, 91, 92, 100, 101, 103, 106-108, 151, 185, 256

Sheridan, Gen. P. H.—*Continued*
  cavalry of—*Continued*
    see Cavalry Corps and Sheridan's
      Robbers
  command of Cavalry Corps, 64, 66
  description of, 64, 108
  division commander, 288
  fighting the Indians, 186, 189, 200-
    201, 203, 209-212, 270
  headquarters of, 88
  in the Civil War, 64-70, 75-77, 79, 87,
    90, 91, 93-95, 97-104, 109, 110,
    113, 114, 118, 120
  letter to Mrs. Custer, 115
  Memoirs, 64
    quoted, 75, 98
  Mosby's letter to, 83
  on the border, 134, 139, 140
  ordered to New Orleans, 123, 128
  quoted, 84, 85, 95, 111, 130-131, 150,
    183, 188, 202, 251, 291-292
  transferred to Department of Mis-
    souri, 179
Sheridan's Robbers, 85, 88, 103, 115, 118,
    123, 124
  see Cavalry Corps
Sheridan's Troopers on the Border, 201
  quoted, 188, 202, 203
Sherman, General, 90-92, 118, 146, 209,
    235, 236, 253, 274, 282-286, 288-
    290, 292, 293, 300, 320, 360, 362
  quoted, 157, 182, 183, 359
Shields, 73
Shoshones, 265, 295, 311
Shreveport, 128
Sibley Island, 253
Sigel, 72, 73
Simms, Captain, 112-113
Sioux, 18, 59, 148-149, 157, 163, 165-
    170, 172, 180, 181, 200, 227, 229,
    233-237, 239-241, 243-247, 251,
    256-265, 267-273, 277, 279, 280,
    282, 287, 294, 295, 299, 301, 304,
    307-309, 311-312, 314, 320, 327,
    329-357, 363, 365-368
Sitting Bull, 234, 235, 251, 269, 270, 294
Smith, Algernon E., 222, 297, 337, 341
Smith, Col. Andrew J., 151, 156, 166,
    172, 174-175, 221
Smith, Jedediah, 259
Smith, John, 278
Smith, John Q., 269
Smith, Kirby, 36

Smith, Gen. W. F. "Baldy," 40, 95, 96
Smith's Brigade, 94, 95
Smoky Hill River, 146, 166, 168, 180
Smoky Hill Road, 164, 165
Soldiers of the Plains
  quoted, 309
Solferino, 37
Solomon River, 182
*Some Corrections to "My Life on the
    Plains"*
  quoted, 211
Some Memories of a Soldier
  quoted, 310
"Some Reminiscences of the Battle of the
    Washita"
  quoted, 195, 196, 204
South Carolina, 30, 227
South Dakota, 233, 256
Southside Railroad, 92, 93, 99-101
Spaulding, L. M., 208
Spotted Tail, 229
Stagg's Brigade, 103, 104
Staked Plain, 210
Standing Rock, 263
Stanley, Gen. D. S., 178, 235, 240, 241,
    244, 245, 247, 248, 303, 321, 363,
    364
  Personal Memoirs
    quoted, 242-243
Stanley's Stockade, 244, 248, 249, 298-
    299, 307, 311
Stanton, Secretary, 87-88
Staunton, 89
Steamboat Point, 309
Stebbins Academy, 23
Stone Forehead, 212, 216, 218
Stoneman, Gen. George, 39, 47
Story of the Little Big Horn, The, 208
  quoted, 196
Stoyell, John A., 253
Stuart, J. E. B., 49-50, 54-56, 60-62, 66-
    68, 75, 84-86, 101, 120, 234, 366
Stuart's Corps, 54
Sturgis, Lieut. James G., 297, 358
Sturgis, Col. S. D., 221, 235, 236
Sully, Brig.-Gen. Alfred, **182-184, 187,**
    188, 204, 363
Summit Springs, 162
Sundance Creek, 337, 347
Sutherland Station, 100
Sweetwater, 215, 220
"Swift," 303

Tabernacle Church, 102
Taft, Alfonso, 282, 284
Tall Bull, 162
Taylor, Muggins, 354, 360
Telegraph Road, 66
Tennessee, 227
Tenting on the Plains
  quoted, 127, 145, 146, 161, 162, 173, 176-177
Terry, Gen. Alfred H., 98, 178, 179, 253, 260, 270-274, 280-282, 285, 289-297, 299-304, 306-317, 319, 323-324, 330, 335, 352-357, 360, 362, 365, 369
  quoted, 291, 320-322, 362-367
Terry Peak, 260
Texas, 28, 123, 128, 131, 133, 135, 140, 145, 179, 213
Texas Panhandle, 213
Third Division, 51, 61, 63, 65, 66, 84, 86-90, 92, 93, 98, 103, 105, 108, 109, 116-117, 124, 127, 128, 155, 165
Thompson, Captain, 54, 193, 194
Thompson, Colonel, 272
Tod's Tavern, 66
Toledo, 151, 249
Tongue River, 244, 251, 294, 295, 305, 308-313, 321, 366
Topeka, 188
Torbert, Gen. A. T. A., 65, 69-71, 73, 84, 85, 88, 89, 120, 121
Torbert's Division, 66, 69, 73
Trails, Rails and War
  quoted, 281
"Traveller," 114-115
Treaties, Indian, 148-150, 157, 159, 179-180, 188-189, 192, 193, 233-235, 240, 251, 256, 265, 267, 270
Tremain, Maj. H. E., 95
  Last Hours of Sheridan's Cavalry 96, 98, 126
Trevilian Court House, 121
Trevilian Station, 69-71, 118, 120
Troops
  A, 6th Michigan, 54
  G, 5th Cavalry, 36, 37, 39
  M, 5th Cavalry, 47
  see Regiments
  7th Cavalry, troops of
"Tuck," 303
Tullock's Creek, 314, 317, 322, 329, 330, 335, 352, 364
Tullock's Valley, 329

"Turk," 145
Tuttle, Private, 247
Two Moons, 251, 294

Union Pacific Railroad, 144, 280
U. S. Congress, 82, 140, 141, 142, 148, 152, 268, 274, 280, 281, 359
U. S. Military Academy, 17, 26-36, 52, 85, 121, 151, 182, 209, 236, 238, 297, 361
United States Volunteers, 151
Urbana, 47, 48

Varnum, Col. Charles A., 18, 122, 153, 222, 238, 247, 260, 293-294, 298, 301, 323, 327-329, 331-334, 337, 339-342, 349, 350, 364
"Vic," 228, 258, 303, 344
Viers, Matilda, 21
Virginia, 33, 57, 82, 90, 92, 108
Virginia Central Railroad, 67, 69, 84, 88-90

Wadsworth, Major, 36
Wallace, Lew, 72
Wallace, Lieutenant, 327, 338, 343, 352, 356-358
Walnut Creek, 182
War Department, 33, 45, 87-88, 122, 152, 159, 251, 252, 270-272, 288, 290, 360
Warren, General, 97-98
Warren's Division, 97
Washington, D. C., 32-34, 37, 43-44, 47, 59, 61-63, 72, 73, 87, 118, 122, 124-126, 141, 155, 273-276, 279-283, 285, 288-290, 294, 321, 359
  Capitol Hill, 124
  Maryland Avenue, 124
  Pennsylvania Avenue, 124-125
Washington, George, 20
Washita Basin, 198
Washita, battle of, 74, 164, 186, 192-196, 204, 212, 213, 215-217, 220, 246, 270, 323, 366, 367, 369
Washita battle-ground, 218, 219
Washita campaign, 188-207, 209-219
Washita River, 188, 192, 193, 196, 197, 201-203, 210, 271, 355
Waynesboro, 84, 89, 117
Webster, Daniel, 226
Weir, Captain, 222, 337, 348, 351
Weitzel, General, 101

"Wellington," 34
Wells-Fargo Express, 58
Wells's Brigade, 95, 110
West, Captain, 193, 197
West Point, 71
   see U. S. Military Academy
Weston, Lieutenant, 246
Whigs, 22, 370
White Antelope, 140
White Horse, 163
White House, 124, 125, 280, 282-284, 288
White House Landing, 90, 91
White Man Runs Him, 323, 354
White-Oak Road, 93, 97
White Oak Swamp, 42
White, Sarah, 201, 217-218
White Swan, 323
Whittaker, Frederick, 46, 113, 120
   A Complete Life of General George A. Custer
      quoted, 38, 43, 48, 50, 59, 60, 141, 268, 283
Wichita Mountains, 183, 213, 214
Wilderness, The, 65
Willard's Hotel, 123
Williams, E. A., 253
Williamsburg, 40, 44
Williamson, J. J.
   Mosby's Men
      quoted, 82, 83
Williamson, Rev. John P., 240
Wilson, J. H., 65, 84
Wilson's Third Division, 68, 76
Winchester, 76-79, 82, 85, 87-89, 120

Wisconsin, 148
Wise's Brigade, 94
With Sheridan's Cavalry in Lee's Last Campaign
   quoted, 102, 112
Wolf Creek, 188, 190
Wolf Mountains, 312, 314, 330, 336, 340, 357
Woodstock, 85, 86, 120, 243
"Woodstock Races," 86
Wounded to the Rear, 225
Wright, 103
Wynkoop, Col. E. W., 150, 159, 162-164, 180, 181, 209-210

Yankee Doodle, 94
Yankton, 236-238
Yates, Lieut. George W. (later Captain), 51, 201, 221, 263, 297, 334, 337, 341
Yellow Bear, 210, 211, 214
Yellow Tavern, 67, 68, 118, 120
Yellowstone expedition, 178, 240-249, 256, 293, 364
Yellowstone River, 28, 168, 173, 234, 235, 244, 246-248, 250, 263, 273, 280, 294, 295, 298, 299, 304, 307-310, 312, 317, 321, 322, 328-330, 367
Yocomico River, 47
York River, 71
Yorktown, 40
Young, Major H. K., 75
Young's Scouts, 102